80
Readings

80 READINGS compiled by David Munger

Copyright © 1992 by HarperCollins Publishers Inc.

ISBN: 0-673-52233-4
          94 95 9 8 7 6 5 4 3

80 Readings

Compiled by the
HarperCollins Editors

David Munger,
General Editor

HarperCollins*College**Publishers*

CONTENTS

RHETORICAL CONTENTS

Cause and Effect

Definition

Description

Narration

Argument

Preface

When we set out to prepare *80 Readings*, we wanted to do several things. We wanted to create a truly interesting and diverse collection of readings to accompany our best-selling handbooks. We wanted a reader that could stand on its own. We wanted a reader that could be used in different ways by many different types of instructors and students. But most of all, we wanted a reader that was affordable.

As publishers, we are always looking for ways to cut costs, but only recently has the technology become available to bypass many of the traditional (and expensive) modes of production. Instead of hiring a compositor, we used OCR (optical character recognition) software to scan in text, and desktop-published the book using personal computers. Producing the manuscript in-house also saved money. The result is a reader which costs substantially less than any currently available.

We also knew that instructors wouldn't be willing to sacrifice quality. That's why we sent this manuscript to reviewers (and revised to their requests) who knew the rigors of using readers in class. The result, we feel, is a reader which compares favorably to many costing three times as much.

We chose a thematic organization for this reader, both because it is the organization most instructors prefer and because it helps keep student interest up by providing prolonged exposure to a single issue. However, for instructors who prefer keeping to the rhetorical modes, or for students who want to use it as a guide, we do include a rhetorical table of contents.

The chapters can, of course, be followed in any order. Further, many of the selections have links to more than one unit: *If Shakespeare Had Had a Sister*, for example, could be covered as part of the *Writers and Literature* chapter, where it is currently found, or it could be covered in *Changing Perspectives on Women*. Some of the links between the chapters are pointed out in the introductions to selections; some, students and instructors will find on their own.

Each selection's introduction includes a short biography of the author and a brief summary of the selection. Most also give suggestions for pre-reading thought and activity.

The readings themselves are a mix of some of the most popular selections of all time (*Once More to the Lake, On Keeping a Notebook, A Modest Proposal*); some which are familiar, but aren't usually found in composition readers (*Pericles' Funeral Oration, The Communist Manifesto, War Message to Congress*); and some which have never, to our knowledge, been reprinted (*An American Childhood, My Speech to Graduates*, and many of the student essays).

The twenty student essays are spread out evenly through the book. Some are research papers; some respond to the readings; some are simply about the issues of the chapter they are contained in.

Instructors' Materials. Instructors using this book have the advantage of access to the HarperCollins *Resources for Writers* program. Among the many resources, they may find *Teaching Writing: Strategies and Practice* by Josephine Koster Tarvers particularly useful. This book (now in its third edition) includes the winning ideas of the 1991 HarperCollins Fellowship competition, and is available from a HarperCollins representative or regional office. If *80 Readings* is being used in conjunction with *The Little, Brown Handbook*, the Instructor's Annotated Edition of that text includes a wealth of teaching ideas and additional hints at using the HarperCollins *Resources for Writers* package. For more information, contact your representative or regional office.

This book could not have been produced without the help of some very important contributors. The reviewers, Roger M. Haley of New Mexico State University-Alamogordo, Richard Peake of Clinch Valley College, and Elizabeth Rankin of the University of North Dakota, gave us terrific insider advice. Constance Rajala came up with some great readings. Anne Smith provided early insight and support. Mark Gerrard and Pearl Klein always had good ideas, and contributed essays they wrote as freshmen. Finally, Margaret Munger gave unstinting support while working on several publications of her own.

David Munger
Patricia Rossi
Jane Kinney
Laurie Likoff

Chapter 1:
Writers and Literature

Joan Didion

ON KEEPING A NOTEBOOK

Joan Didion (1934-   ) has become one of our nation's most acclaimed essayists and novelists. She continues to produce novels, essays, magazine articles, and recollections, most notably *Salvador*, a novel published in 1983. In "On Keeping A Notebook," Didion explores the desires and feelings of guilt that make it necessary for her to keep a notebook. As you read the essay, try to remember specific details about a period in your own life that you have fond recollections about.

"'That woman Estelle,'" the note reads, "'is partly the reason why George Sharp and I are separated today.' *Dirty crepe-de-Chine wrapper, hotel bar, Wilmington RR, 9:45 a.m. August Monday morning.*" Since the note is in my notebook, it presumably has some meaning to me. I study it for a long while. At first I have only the most general notion of what I was doing on an August Monday morning in the bar of the hotel across from the Pennsylvania Railroad station in Wilmington, Delaware (waiting for a train? missing one? 1960? 1961? why Wilmington?), but I do remember being there. The woman in the dirty crepe-de-Chine

1

wrapper had come down from her room for a beer, and the bar-
tender had heard before the reason why George Sharp and she
were separated today. "Sure," he said, and went on mopping the
floor. "You told me." At the other end of the bar is a girl. She is
talking, pointedly, not to the man beside her but to a cat lying in
the triangle of sunlight cast through the open door. She is wearing
a plaid silk dress from Peck & Peck, and the hem is coming down.

Here is what it is: the girl has been on the Eastern Shore, and
now she is going back to the city, leaving the man beside her, and
all she can see ahead are the viscous summer sidewalks and the 3
a.m. long-distance calls that will make her lie awake and then
sleep drugged through all the steaming mornings left in August
(1960? 1961?). Because she must go directly from the train to
lunch in New York, she wishes that she had a safety pin for the
hem of the plaid silk dress, and she also wishes that she could forget about the hem and the lunch and stay in the cool bar that
smells of disinfectant and malt and make friends with the woman
in the crepe-de-Chine wrapper. She is afflicted by a little self-pity,
and she wants to compare Estelles. That is what that was all
about.

Why did I write it down? In order to remember, of course, but
exactly what was it I wanted to remember? How much of it actually happened? Did any of it? Why do I keep a notebook at all? It
is easy to deceive oneself on all those scores. The impulse to write
things down is a peculiarly compulsive one, inexplicable to those
who do not share it, useful only accidentally, only secondarily, in
the way that any compulsion tries to justify itself. I suppose that it
begins or does not begin in the cradle. Although I have felt compelled to write things down since I was five years old, I doubt that
my daughter ever will, for she is a singularly blessed and accept-
ing child, delighted with life exactly as life presents itself to her,
unafraid to go to sleep and unafraid to wake up. Keepers of private notebooks are a different breed altogether, lonely and resis-
tant rearrangers of things, anxious malcontents, children afflicted apparently at birth with some presentiment of loss.

My first notebook was a Big Five tablet, given to me by my
mother with the sensible suggestion that I stop whining and learn
to amuse myself by writing down my thoughts. She returned the
tablet to me a few years ago; the first entry is an account of a
woman who believed herself to be freezing to death in the Arctic
night, only to find, when day broke, that she had stumbled onto the
Sahara Desert, where she would die of the heat before lunch. I

have no idea what turn of a five-year-old's mind could have prompted so insistently "ironic" and exotic a story, but it does reveal a certain ✻predilection for the extreme which has dogged me into adult life; perhaps if I were analytically inclined I would find it a truer story than any I might have told about Donald Johnson's birthday party or the day my cousin Brenda put Kitty Litter in the aquarium. *It's Not About Analysis — Just Impulse Thoughts*

So the point of my keeping a notebook has never been, nor is it now, to have an accurate factual record of what I have been doing or thinking. That would be a different impulse entirely, an instinct for reality which I sometimes envy but do not possess. At no point have I ever been able successfully to keep a diary; my approach to daily life ranges from the grossly negligent to the merely absent, and on those few occasions when I have tried dutifully to record a day's events, boredom has so overcome me that the results are mysterious at best. What is this business about "shopping, typing piece, dinner with E, depressed"? Shopping for what? Typing what piece? Who is E? Was this "E" depressed, or was I depressed? Who cares? *Don't Agree*

In fact I have abandoned altogether that kind of pointless entry; instead I tell what some would call lies. "That's simply not true," the members of my family frequently tell me when they come up against my memory of a shared event. "The party was not for you, the spider was not a black widow, it wasn't that way at all." Very likely they are right, for not only have I always had trouble distinguishing between what happened and what merely might have happened, but I remain unconvinced that the distinction, for my purposes, matters. The cracked crab that I recall having for lunch the day my father came home from Detroit in 1945 must certainly be embroidery, worked into the day's pattern to lend verisimilitude; I was ten years old and would not now remember the cracked crab. The day's events did not turn on cracked crab. And yet it is precisely that fictitious crab that makes me see the afternoon all over again, a home movie run all too often, the father bearing gifts, the child weeping, an exercise in family love and guilt. Or that is what it was to me. Similarly, perhaps it never did snow that August in Vermont; perhaps there never were flurries in the night wind, and maybe no one else felt the ground hardening and summer already dead even as we pretended to bask in it, but that was how it felt to me, and it might as well have snowed, could have snowed, did snow.

How it felt to me: that is getting closer to the truth about a notebook. I sometimes delude myself about why I keep a notebook, imagine that some thrifty virtue derives from preserving everything observed. See enough and write it down, I tell myself, and then some morning when the world seems drained of wonder, some day when I am only going through the motions of doing what I am supposed to do, which is write—on that bankrupt morning I will simply open my notebook and there it will all be, a forgotten account with accumulated interest, paid passage back to the world out there: dialogue overheard in hotels and elevators and at the hat-check counter in Pavillon (one middle-aged man shows his hat check to another and says, "That's my old football number"); impressions of Bettina Aptheker and Benjamin Sonnenberg and Teddy ("Mr. Acapulco") Stauffer; careful *aperçus* about tennis bums and failed fashion models and Greek shipping heiresses, one of whom taught me a significant lesson (a lesson I could have learned from F. Scott Fitzgerald, but perhaps we all must meet the very rich for ourselves) by asking, when I arrived to interview her in her orchid-filled sitting room on the second day of a paralyzing New York blizzard, whether it was snowing outside.

I imagine, in other words, that the notebook is about other people. But of course it is not. I have no real business with what one stranger said to another at the hat-check counter in Pavillon; in fact I suspect that the line "That's my old football number" touched not my own imagination at all, but merely some memory of something once read, probably "The Eighty-Yard Run." Nor is my concern with a woman in a dirty crepe-de-Chine wrapper in a Wilmington bar. My stake is always, of course, in the unmentioned girl in the plaid silk dress. *Remember what it was to be me*: that is always the point.

It is a difficult point to admit. We are brought up in the ethic that others, any others, all others, are by definition more interesting than ourselves; taught to be diffident, just this side of self-effacing. ("You're the least important person in the room and don't forget it," Jessica Mitford's governess would hiss in her ear on the advent of any social occasion; I copied that into my notebook because it is only recently that I have been able to enter a room without hearing some such phrase in my inner ear.) Only the very young and the very old may recount their dreams at breakfast, dwell upon self, interrupt with memories of beach picnics and favorite Liberty lawn dresses and the rainbow trout in a creek near Colorado Springs. The rest of us are expected, rightly, to affect absorption in other people's favorite dresses, other people's trout. *How It's All About Who We Are ↓ (Conclusion)*

And so we do. But our notebooks give us away, for however dutifully we record what we see around us, the common denominator of all we see is always, transparently, shamelessly, the implacable "I." We are not talking here about the kind of notebook that is patently for public consumption, a structural conceit for binding together a series of graceful *pensées*; we are talking about something private, about bits of the mind's string too short to use, an indiscriminate and erratic assemblage with meaning only for its maker.

And sometimes even the maker has difficulty with the meaning. There does not seem to be, for example, any point in my knowing for the rest of my life that, during 1964, 720 tons of soot fell on every square mile of New York City, yet there it is in my notebook, labeled "FACT." Nor do I really need to remember that Ambrose Bierce liked to spell Leland Stanford's name "£eland $tanford" or that "smart women almost always wear black in Cuba," a fashion hint without much potential for practical application. And does not the relevance of these notes seem marginal at best?:

> In the basement museum of the Inyo County Courthouse in Independence, California, sign pinned to a mandarin coat: "This MANDARIN COAT was often worn by Mrs. Minnie S. Brooks when giving lectures on her TEAPOT COLLECTION.
>
> Redhead getting out of car in front of Beverly Wilshire Hotel, chinchilla stole, Vuitton bags with tags reading:
>
> MRS LOU FOX
>
> HOTEL SAHARA
>
> VEGAS

Well, perhaps not entirely marginal. As a matter of fact, Mrs. Minnie S. Brooks and her MANDARIN COAT pull me back into my own childhood, for although I never knew Mrs. Brooks and did not visit Inyo County until I was thirty, I grew up in just such a world, in houses cluttered with Indian relics and bits of gold ore and ambergris and the souvenirs my Aunt Mercy Farnsworth brought back from the Orient. It is a long way from that world to

Mrs. Lou Fox's world, where we all live now, and is it not just as
well to remember that? Might not Mrs. Minnie S. Brooks help me
to remember what I am? Might not Mrs. Lou Fox help me to remember what I am not?

But sometimes the point is harder to discern. What exactly did I
have in mind when I noted down that it cost the father of someone
I know $650 a month to light the place on the Hudson in which he
lived before the Crash? What use was I planning to make of this
line by Jimmy Hoffa: "I may have my faults, but being wrong
ain't one of them"? And although I think it interesting to know
where the girls who travel with the Syndicate have their hair
done when they find themselves on the West Coast, will I ever
make suitable use of it? Might I not be better off just passing it on
to John O'Hara? What is a recipe for sauerkraut doing in my
notebook? What kind of magpie keeps this notebook? "He was
born the night the Titanic went down." That seems a nice enough
line, and I even recall who said it, but is it not really a better line in
life than it could ever be in fiction?

But of course that is exactly it: not that I should ever use the line,
but that I should remember the woman who said it and the afternoon I heard it. We were on her terrace by the sea, and we were
finishing the wine left from lunch, trying to get what sun there
was, a California winter sun. The woman whose husband was
born the night the Titanic went down wanted to rent her house,
wanted to go back to her children in Paris. I remember wishing
that I could afford the house, which cost $1,000 a month.
"Someday you will," she said lazily. "Someday it all comes." There
in the sun on her terrace it seemed easy to believe in someday, but
later I had a low-grade afternoon hangover and ran over a black
snake on the way to the supermarket and was flooded with inexplicable fear when I heard the checkout clerk explaining to the
man ahead of me why she was finally divorcing her husband. "He
left me no choice," she said over and over as she punched the
register. "He has a little seven-month-old baby by her, he left me
no choice." I would like to believe that my dread then was for the
human condition, but of course it was for me, because I wanted a
baby and did not then have one and because I wanted to own the
house that cost $1,000 a month to rent and because I had a
hangover.

It all comes back. Perhaps it is difficult to see the value in having
one's self back in that kind of mood, but I do see it; I think we are
well advised to keep on nodding terms with the people we used to

be whether we find them attractive company or not. Otherwise they turn up unannounced and surprise us, come hammering on the mind's door at 4 a.m. of a bad night and demand to know who deserted them, who betrayed them, who is going to make amends. We forget all too soon the things we thought we could never forget. We forget the loves and the betrayals alike, forget what we whispered and what we screamed, forget who we were. I have already lost touch with a couple of people I used to be; one of them, a seventeen-year-old, presents little threat, although it would be of some interest to me to know again what it feels like to sit on a river levee drinking vodka-and-orange-juice and listening to Les Paul and Mary Ford and their echoes sing "How High the Moon" on the car radio. (You see I still have the scenes, but I no longer perceive myself among those present, no longer could even improvise the dialogue.) The other one, a twenty-three-year-old, bothers me more. She was always a good deal of trouble, and I suspect she will reappear when I least want to see her, skirts too long, shy to the point of aggravation, always the injured party, full of recriminations and little hurts and stories I do not want to hear again, at once saddening me and angering me with her vulnerability and ignorance, an apparition all the more insistent for being so long banished.

It is a good idea, then, to keep in touch, and I suppose that keeping in touch is what notebooks are all about. And we are all on our own when it comes to keeping those lines open to ourselves: your notebook will never help me, nor mine you. "So what's new in the whiskey business?" What could that possibly mean to you? To me it means a blonde in a Pucci bathing suit sitting with a couple of fat men by the pool at the Beverly Hills Hotel. Another man approaches, and they all regard one another in silence for a while. "So what's new in the whiskey business?" one of the fat men finally says by way of welcome, and the blonde stands up, arches one foot and dips it in the pool, looking all the while at the cabaña where Baby Pignatari is talking on the telephone. That is all there is to that, except that several years later I saw the blonde coming out of Saks Fifth Avenue in New York with her California complexion and a voluminous mink coat. In the harsh wind that day she looked old and irrevocably tired to me, and even the skins in the mink coat were not worked the way they were doing them that year, not the way she would have wanted them done, and there is the point of the story. For a while after that I did not like to look in the mirror, and my eyes would skim the newspapers and

pick out only the deaths, the cancer victims, the premature coro-
naries, the suicides, and I stopped riding the Lexington Avenue
IRT because I noticed for the first time that all the strangers I had
seen for years—the man with the seeing-eye dog, the spinster
who read the classified pages every day, the fat girl who always
got off with me at Grand Central— looked older than they once
had.

It all comes back. Even that recipe for sauerkraut: even that
brings it back. I was on Fire Island when I first made that
sauerkraut, and it was raining, and we drank a lot of bourbon and
ate the sauerkraut and went to bed at ten, and I listened to the
rain and the Atlantic and felt safe. I made the sauerkraut again
last night and it did not make me feel any safer, but that is, as they
say, another story.

Anne (Student)

ON "ON KEEPING A NOTEBOOK"

Anne's essay in response to Didion's essay is an excellent response
to the difficult task of writing about writing. As you read Anne's
essay, think about how Didion's essay affected you.

Green couch, burnt orange carpeting, bright-orange lamp,
ginger ale. Late night. A boy I love reads me an essay that shows
me the limitless possibility of subjective prose. I love him even
more for doing this.

In Joan Didion's essay "On Keeping a Notebook," she reminds
us of the fragility of memory and the difficulty of recording history or "fact." While she writes down snippets of bar conversation
or words written on display cards at museums, she manages to
address also the difficulty of choosing what to remember and
what to dispose of in memory. What she retains is preserved and
what she jettisons becomes lost to time and space. (However,
Didion suggests that what she wants to remember is what her
notes suggest: the presence of the writer—herself—in a bar, on a
train, at an interview.)

About Learning Who We Are

As an essayist, Didion must listen carefully to every word, whether told directly to her or overheard. What she records, however, is not necessarily what "really" happening but "How it felt to me." On the surface, she describes "exactly" what she sees, but it is impossible for her to remove herself from her vision. In fact, it is impossible for any writer, even those who go by such titles as "journalist" or "historian" to remove themselves from the scene. Didion acknowledges that in describing what she sees, it is impossible for her to remove herself from what the scene; describing makes the describer part of the action.

Didion cites Jessica Mitford's governess as saying "You're the least important person in the room and don't you forget it" on any social occasion. Didion sympathizes with Mitford and rebels against this and other ways of playing down her presence—or anyone else's. For her, the notebook allows her to live out that rebellion; she can make herself the center of scenes that were important to her without failing to defer politely to another's point of view. She is the most important person in the notebook.

The occasions and conversations she notes down allow her to recall and recount moments of her life, which is in turn her reason for writing. The point of her keeping notebooks is not that she should note all the interesting parts and people of the world, but that she can relive her own life. Writing is, for her, both an act of selfishly pleasing herself and, indirectly, pleasing the world with her bright and cogent observations.

Rereading Didion, I relive my own life. A long time ago, I heard of Estelle from a boy I loved. Exact words fade, but the ideas remain clear, and that moment will stick with me forever. My subjective experience of the subjective experience of Joan Didion. . .

Matthew Arnold

LITERATURE AND SCIENCE

Matthew Arnold (1822-1888), literary critic, poet, and scholar, was educated in the best British schools and came to be known for his rigorously rational humanistic thought. Arnold here argues for the

supremacy of what he calls "humane letters" over natural science. He
is careful, however, not to condemn all science—indeed he believes
that any well-educated person should understand the theories of
Darwin, Galileo, and Copernicus. As you read, pay special attention
to the distinction Arnold makes between the science that every educated person should know and the science best left to specialists.

Practical people talk with a smile of Plato and of his absolute
ideas: and it is impossible to deny that Plato's ideas do often seem
unpractical and unpracticable, and especially when one views
them in connection with the life of a great work-a-day world like
the United States. The necessary staple of the life of such a world
Plato regards with disdain; handicraft and trade and the working
professions he regards with disdain; but what becomes of the life of
an industrial modern community if you take handicraft and
trade and the working professions out of it? The base mechanic
arts and handicrafts, says Plato, bring about a natural weakness
in the principle of excellence in a man, so that he cannot govern
the ignoble growths in him, but nurses them, and cannot understand fostering any other. Those who exercise such arts and
trades, as they have their bodies, he says, marred by their vulgar
businesses, so they have their souls, too, bowed and broken by
them. And if one of these uncomely people has a mind to seek self-
culture and philosophy, Plato compares him to a bald little tinker,
who has scraped together money and has got his release from
service, and has had a bath, and bought a new coat, and is rigged
out like a bridegroom about to marry the daughter of his master
who has fallen into poor and helpless estate.

Nor do the working professions fare any better than trade at the
hands of Plato. He draws for us an inimitable picture of the
working lawyer and of his life of bondage; he shows how this
bondage from his youth up has stunted and warped him, and
made him small and crooked of soul encompassing him with difficulties which he is not man enough to rely on justice and truth
as means to encounter, but has recourse, for help out of them, to
falsehood and wrong. And so, says Plato, this poor creature is bent
and broken, and grows up from boy to man without a particle of
soundness in him, although exceedingly smart and clever in his
own esteem.

One cannot refuse to admire the artist who draws these pictures. But we say to ourselves that his ideas show the influence of
a primitive and obsolete order of things, when the warrior caste

and the priestly caste were alone in honor, and the humble work of the world was done by slaves. We have now changed all that; the modern majesty consists in work, as Emerson declares; and in work, we may add, principally of such plain and dusty kind as the work of cultivators of the ground, handicraftsmen, men of trade and business, men of the working professions. Above all is this true in a great industrious community such as that of the United States.

Now education, many people go on to say, is still mainly governed by the ideas of men like Plato, who lived when the warrior caste and the priestly or philosophical class were alone in honor, and the really useful part of the community were slaves. It is an education fitted for persons of leisure in such a community. This education passed from Greece and Rome to the feudal communities of Europe, where also the warrior caste and the priestly caste were alone held in honor, and where the really useful and working part of the community, though not nominally slaves as in the pagan world, were practically not much better off than slaves, and not more seriously regarded. And how absurd it is, people end by saying, to inflict this education upon an industrious modern community, where very few indeed are persons of leisure, and the mass to be considered has not leisure, but is bound, for its own great good, and for the great good of the world at large, to plain labor and to industrial pursuits, and the education in question tends necessarily to make men dissatisfied with these pursuits and unfitted for them!

That is what is said. So far I must defend Plato, as to plead that his view of education and studies is in the general, as it seems to me, sound enough, and fitted for all sorts and conditions of men, whatever their pursuits may be. "An intelligent man," says Plato, "will prize those studies which result in his soul getting soberness, righteousness, and wisdom, and will less value the others." I cannot consider *that* a bad description of the aim of education, and of the motives which should govern us in the choice of studies, whether we are preparing ourselves for a hereditary seat in the English House of Lords or for the pork trade in Chicago.

Still I admit that Plato's world was not ours, that his scorn of trade and handicraft is fantastic, that he had no conception of a great industrial community such as that of the United States, and that such a community must and will shape its education to suit its own needs. If the usual education handed down to it from the past does not suit it, it will certainly before long drop this and try another. The usual education the past has been mainly literary. The question is whether the studies which were long supposed to be the best for all of us are practically the best now; whether others are not better. The tyranny of the past, many think, weighs on us injuriously in the predominance given to letters in education. The question is raised whether, to meet the needs of our modern life, the predominance ought not now to pass from letters to science, and naturally the question is nowhere raised with more energy than here in the United States. The design of abasing what is called "mere literary instruction and education," and of exalting what is called "sound, extensive, and practical scientific knowledge," is, in this intensely modern world of the United States, even more perhaps than in Europe, a very popular design, and makes great and rapid progress.

I am going to ask whether the present movement for ousting letters from their old predominance in education, and for transferring the predominance in education to the natural sciences, whether this brisk and flourishing movement ought to prevail, and whether it is likely that in the end it really will prevail. An objection may be raised which I will anticipate. My own studies have been almost wholly in letters, and my visits to the field of the natural sciences have been very slight and inadequate, although those sciences have always strongly moved my curiosity. A man of letters, it will perhaps be said, is not competent to discuss the comparative merits of letters and natural science as means of education. To this objection I reply, first of all, that his incompetence, if he attempts the discussion but is really incompetent for it, will be abundantly visible; nobody will be taken in; he will have plenty of sharp observers and critics to save mankind from that danger. But the line I am going to follow is, as you will soon discover, so extremely simple, that perhaps it may be followed without failure even by one who for a more ambitious line of discussion would be quite incompetent.

Some of you may possibly remember a phrase of mine which has been the object of a good deal of comment; an observation to the effect that in our culture, the aim being *to know ourselves and the world,* we have, as the means to this end, *to know the best which has been thought and said in the world.* A man of science, who is also an excellent writer and the very prince of debaters, Professor Huxley, in a discourse at the opening of Sir Josiah Mason's college at Birmingham, laying hold of this phrase, expanded it by quoting some more words of mine, which are these:

"The civilized world is to be regarded as now being, for intellectual and spiritual purposes, one great confederation, bound to a joint action and working to a common result; and whose members have for their proper outfit a knowledge of Greek, Roman, and Eastern antiquity and of one another. Special local and temporary advantages being put out of account, that modern nation will in the intellectual and spiritual sphere make most progress, which most thoroughly carries out this program."

Now on my phrase, thus enlarged, Professor Huxley remarks that when I speak of the above-mentioned knowledge as enabling us to know ourselves and the world, I assert *literature* to contain the materials which suffice for thus making us know ourselves and the world. But it is not by any means clear, says he, that after having learnt all which ancient and modern literatures have to tell us, we have laid a sufficiently broad and deep foundation for that criticism of life, that knowledge of ourselves and the world, which constitutes culture. On the contrary, Professor Huxley declares that he finds himself "wholly unable to admit that either nations or individuals will really advance, if their outfit draws nothing from the stores of physical science. An army without weapons of precision, and with no particular base of operations, might more hopefully enter upon a campaign on the Rhine, than a man, devoid of a knowledge of what physical science has done in the last century, upon a criticism of life."

This shows how needful it is for those who are to discuss any matter together, to have a common understanding as to the sense of the terms they employ—how needful, and how difficult. What Professor Huxley says, implies just the reproach which is so often brought against the study of belles-lettres, as they are called: that the study is an elegant one but slight and ineffectual; a smattering of Greek and Latin and other ornamental things, of little use for anyone whose object is to get at truth and to be a practical man. So, too, M. Renan talks of the "superficial humanism" of a school course which treats us as if we were all going to be poets, writers, preachers, orators, and he opposes this humanism to positive science, or the critical search after truth. And there is always a tendency in those who are remonstrating against the predominance of letters in education, to understand by letters belles-lettres, and by belles letters a superficial humanism, the opposite of science or true knowledge.

But when we talk of knowing Greek and Roman antiquity, for instance which is the knowledge people have called the humanities, I for my part mean a knowledge which is something more than a superficial humanism, mainly decorative. "I call all teaching *scientific*," says Wolf, the critic of Homer, "which is systematically laid out and followed up to its original sources. For example: a knowledge of classical antiquity is scientific when the remains of classical antiquity are correctly studied inthe original languages." There can be no doubt that Wolf is perfectly right; that all learning is scientific which is systematically laid out and followed up to its original sources, and that a genuine humanism is scientific.

When I speak of knowing Greek and Roman antiquity, therefore, as a help to knowing ourselves and the world, I mean more than a knowledge of so much vocabulary, so much grammar, so many portions of authors in the Greek and Latin languages, I mean knowing the Greeks and Romans, and their life and genius, and what they were and did in the world, what we get from them, and what is its value. That, at least, is the ideal; and when we talk of endeavoring to know Greek and Roman antiquity, as a help to knowing ourselves and the world, we mean endeavoring so to know them as to satisfy this ideal, however much we may still fall short of it.

The same also as to knowing our own and other modern nations, with the like aim of getting to understand ourselves and the world. To know the best that has been thought and said by the modern nations, is to know, says Professor Huxley, "only what modern *literatures* have to tell us, it is the criticism of life contained in modern literature." And yet "the distinctive character of our times," he urges, "lies in the vast and constantly increasing part which is played by natural knowledge." And how, therefore, can a man, devoid of knowledge of what physical science has done in the last century, enter hopefully upon a criticism of modern life?

Let us, I say, be agreed about the meaning of the terms we are using. I talk of knowing the best which has been thought and uttered in the world; Professor Huxley says this means knowing *literature*. Literature is a large word, it may mean everything written with letters or printed in a book. Euclid's *Elements* and Newton's *Principia* are thus literature. All knowledge that reaches us through books is literature. But by literature Professor Huxley means belles-lettres. He means to make me say, that knowing the best which has been thought and said by the modern nations is knowing their belles-lettres and no more. And this is no sufficient equipment, he argues, for a criticism of modern life. But as I do not mean, by knowing ancient Rome, knowing merely more or less of Latin belles-lettres, and taking no account of Rome's military, and political, and legal, and administrative work in the world; and as, by knowing ancient Greece, I understand knowing her as the giver of Greek art, and the guide to a free and right use of reason and to scientific method, and the founder of our mathematics and physics and astronomy and biology—I understand knowing her as all this, and not merely knowing certain Greek poems, and histories, and treatises, and speeches—so as to the knowledge of modern nations also. By knowing modern nations, I mean not merely knowing their belles-lettres, but knowing also what has been done by such men as Copernicus, Galileo, Newton, Darwin. "Our ancestors learned," says Professor Huxley, "that the earth is the center of the visible universe, and that man is the cynosure of things terrestrial; and more especially was it inculcated that the course of nature had no fixed order, but that it could be, and constantly was, altered." "But for us now," continues Professor Huxley, "the notions of the beginning and the end of the world entertained by our forefathers are no longer credible. It is very certain that the earth is not the chief body in the material universe, and that the world is not subordinated to man's use. It is even more certain that nature is the expression of a definite order, with which nothing interferes." "And yet," he cries, "the purely classical education advocated by the representatives of the humanists in our day gives no inkling of all this."

In due place and time I will just touch upon that vexed question of classical education; but at present the question is as to what is meant by knowing the best which modern nations have thought and said. It is not knowing their belles-lettres merely which is meant. To know Italian belles lettres is not to know Italy, and to know English belles-lettres is not to know England. Into knowing Italy and England there comes a great deal more, Galileo and Newton amongst it. The reproach of being a superficial humanism, a tincture of belles-lettres, may attach rightly enough to some other disciplines; but to the particular discipline recommended when I proposed knowing the best that has been thought and said in the world, it does not apply. In that best I certainly include what in modern times has been thought and said by the great observers and knowers of nature.

There is, therefore, really no question between Professor Huxley and me as to whether knowing the great results of the modern

scientific study of nature is not required as a part of our culture, as
well as knowing the products of literature and art. But to follow
the processes by which those results are reached, ought, say the
friends of physical science, to be made the staple of education for
the bulk of mankind. And here there does arise a question between
those whom Professor Huxley calls with playful sarcasm "the
Levites of culture," and those whom the poor humanist is sometimes apt to regard as its Nebuchadnezzars.

The great results of the scientific investigation of nature we are
agreed upon knowing, but how much of our study are we bound to
give to the processes by which those results are reached? The results have their visible bearing on human life. But all the processes, too, all the items of fact, by which those results are reached
and established, are interesting. All knowledge is interesting to a
wise man, and the knowledge of nature is interesting to all men. It
is very interesting to know, that, from the albuminous white of the
egg, the chick in the egg gets the materials for its flesh, bones,
blood, and feathers; while, from the fatty yolk of the egg it gets the
heat and energy which enable it at length to break its shell and
begin the world. It is less interesting, perhaps, but still it is interesting, to know that when a taper burns, the wax is converted into
carbonic acid and water. Moreover, it is quite true that the habit of
dealing with facts, which is given by the study of nature, is, as the
friends of physical science praise it for being, an excellent discipline. The appeal, in the study of nature, is constantly to observation and experiment; not only is it said that the thing is so, but
we can be made to see that it is so. Not only does a man tell us that
when a taper burns the wax is converted into carbonic acid and
water, as a man may tell us, if he likes, that Charon is punting his
ferry boat on the river Styx, or that Victor Hugo is a sublime poet,
or Mr. Gladstone the most admirable of statesmen; but we are
made to see that the conversion into carbonic acid and water does
actually happen. This reality of natural knowledge it is, which
makes the friends of physical science contrast it, as a knowledge
of things, with the humanist's knowledge, which is, say they, a
knowledge of words. And hence Professor Huxley is moved to lay
it down that, "for the purpose of attaining real culture, an exclusively scientific education is at least as effectual as an exclusively
literary education." And a certain President of the Section for
Mechanical Science in the British Association is, in Scripture
phrase, "very bold," and declares that if a man, in his mental
training, "has substituted literature and history for natural

science, he has chosen the less useful alternative." But whether we go these lengths or not, we must all admit that in natural science the habit gained of dealing with facts is a most valuable discipline, and that everyone should have some experience of it.

More than this, however, is demanded by the reformers. It is proposed to make the training in natural science the main part of education, for the great majority of mankind at any rate. And here, I confess, I part company with the friends of physical science, with whom up to this point I have been agreeing. In differing from them, however, I wish to proceed with the utmost caution and diffidence. The smallness of my own acquaintance with the disciplines of natural science is ever before my mind, and I am fearful of doing these disciplines an injustice. The ability and pugnacity of the partisans of natural science make them formidable persons to contradict. The tone of tentative inquiry, which befits a being of dim faculties and bounded knowledge, is the tone I would wish to take and not to depart from. At present it seems to me, that those who are for giving to natural knowledge, as they call it, the chief place in the education of the majority of mankind, leave one important thing out of their account: the constitution of human nature. But I put this forward on the strength of some facts not at all recondite, very far from it; facts capable of being stated in the simplest possible fashion, and to which, if I so state them, the man of science will, I am sure, be willing to allow their due weight.

Deny the facts altogether, I think, he hardly can. He can hardly deny that when we set ourselves to enumerate the powers which go to the building up of human life, and say that they are the power of conduct the power of intellect and knowledge, the power of beauty, and the power of social life and manners—he can hardly deny that this scheme, though drawn in rough and plain lines enough, and not pretending to scientific exactness, does yet give a fairly true representation of the matter. Human nature is built up by these powers; we have the need for them all. When we have rightly met and adjusted the claims of them all, we shall then be in a fair way for getting soberness and righteousness, with wisdom. This is evident enough, and the friends of physical science would admit it.

But perhaps they may not have sufficiently observed another thing: namely, that the several powers just mentioned are not isolated, but there is, in the generality of mankind, a perpetual tendency to relate them one to another in divers ways. With one such way of relating them I am particularly concerned now. Following our instinct for intellect and knowledge, we acquire pieces of knowledge; and presently, in the generality of men, there arises the desire to relate these pieces of knowledge to our sense for conduct, to our sense for beauty—and there is weariness and dissatisfaction if the desire is balked. Now in this desire lies, I think, the strength of that hold which letters have upon us.

All knowledge is, as I said just now, interesting; and even items of knowledge which from the nature of the case cannot well be related, but must stand isolated in our thoughts, have their interest. Even lists of exceptions have their interest. If we are studying Greek accents, it is interesting to know that *pais* and *pas,* and some other monosyllables of the same form of declension, do not take the circumflex upon the last syllable of the genitive plural, but vary, in this respect, from the common rule. If we are studying physiology, it is interesting to know that the pulmonary artery carries dark blood and the pulmonary vein carries bright blood, departing in this respect from the common rule for the division of labor between the veins and the arteries. But everyone knows how we seek naturally to combine the pieces of our knowledge together to bring them under general rules, to relate them to principles; and how unsatisfactory and tiresome it would be to go on forever learning lists of exceptions, or accumulating items of fact which must stand isolated.

Well, that same need of relating our knowledge, which operates here within the sphere of our knowledge itself, we shall find operating, also outside that sphere. We experience, as we go on learning and knowing—the vast majority of us experience—the need of relating what we have learnt and known to the sense which we have in us for conduct, to the sense which we have in us for beauty.

A certain Greek prophetess of Mantineia in Arcadia, Diotima by name, once explained to the philosopher Socrates that love, and impulse, and bent of all kinds, is, in fact, nothing else but the desire in men that good should forever be present to them. This desire for good, Diotima assured Socrates, is our fundamental desire, of which fundamental desire every impulse in us is only some one particular form. And therefore this fundamental desire it is, I suppose—this desire in men that good should be forever present to them—which acts in us when we feel the impulse for relating our knowledge to our sense for conduct and to our sense for beauty. At any rate, with men in general the instinct exists. Such is human nature. And the instinct, it will be admitted, is innocent, and human nature is preserved by our following the lead of its innocent instincts. Therefore, in seeking to gratify this instinct in question, we are following the instinct of self-preservation in humanity.

But, no doubt, some kinds of knowledge cannot be made to directly serve the instinct in question, cannot be directly related to the sense for beauty, to the sense for conduct. These are instrument knowledges; they lead on to other knowledges, which can. A man who passes his life in instrument knowledges is a specialist. They may be invaluable as instruments to something beyond, for those who have the gift thus to employ them; and they may be disciplines in themselves wherein it is useful for everyone to have some schooling. But it is inconceivable that the generality of men should pass all their mental life with Greek accents or with formal logic. My friend Professor Sylvester, who is one of the first mathematicians in the world, holds transcendental doctrines as to the virtue of mathematics, but those doctrines are not for common men. In the very Senate House and heart of our English Cambridge I once ventured though not without an apology for my profaneness, to hazard the opinion that for the majority of mankind a little of mathematics, even, goes a long way. Of course this is quite consistent with their being of immense importance as an instrument to something else; but it is the few who have the aptitude for thus using them, not the bulk of mankind.

The natural sciences do not, however, stand on the same footing with these instrument knowledges. Experience shows us that the generality of men will find more interest in learning that, when a taper burns, the wax is converted into carbonic acid and water, or in learning the explanation of the phenomenon of dew, or in learning how the circulation of the blood is carried on, than they find in learning that the genitive plural of *pais* and *pas* does not take the circumflex on the termination. And one piece of natural knowledge is added to another, and others are added to that, and at last we come to propositions so interesting as Mr. Darwin's famous proposition that "our ancestor was a hairy quadruped furnished with a tail and pointed ears, probably arboreal in his habits." Or we come to propositions of such reach and magnitude as those which Professor Huxley delivers, when he says that the notions of our forefathers about the beginning and the end of the world were all wrong, and that nature is the expression of a definite order with which nothing interferes.

Interesting, indeed, these results of science are, important they are, and we should all of us be acquainted with them. But what I now wish you to mark is, that we are still, when they are propounded to us and we receive them, we are still in the sphere of intellect and knowledge. And for the generality of men there will be found, I say, to arise, when they have duly taken in the proposition that their ancestor was "a hairy quadruped furnished with a tail and pointed ears, probably arboreal in his habits," there will be found to arise an invincible desire to relate this proposition to the sense in us for conduct, and to the sense in us for beauty. But this the men of science will not do for us, and will hardly even profess to do. They will give us other pieces of knowledge, other facts, about other animals and their ancestors, or about plants, or about stones, or about stars; and they may finally bring us to those great "general conceptions of the universe, which are forced upon us all," says Professor Huxley, "by the progress of physical science." But still it will be *knowledge* only which they give us; knowledge not put for us into relation with our sense for conduct, our sense for beauty, and touched with emotion by being so put; not thus put for us, and therefore, to the majority of mankind, after a certain while, unsatisfying, wearying.

Not to the born naturalist, I admit. But what do we mean by a born naturalist? We mean a man in whom the zeal for observing nature is so uncommonly strong and eminent, that it marks him off from the bulk of mankind. Such a man will pass his life happily in collecting natural knowledge and reasoning upon it, and will ask for nothing, or hardly anything, more. I have heard it said that the sagacious and admirable naturalist whom we lost not very long ago, Mr. Darwin, once owned to a friend that for his part he did not experience the necessity for two things which most men find so necessary to them—religion and poetry; science and the domestic affections, he thought, were enough. To a born naturalist, I can well understand that this should seem so. So absorbing is his occupation with nature, so strong his love for his occupation, that he goes on acquiring natural knowledge and reasoning upon it, and has little time or inclination for thinking about getting it related to the desire in man for conduct, the desire in man for beauty. He relates it to them for himself as he goes along, so far as he feels the need; and he draws from the domestic affections all the additional solace necessary. But then Darwins are extremely rare. Another great and admirable master of natural knowledge, Faraday, was a Sandemanian. That is to say he related his knowledge to his instinct for conduct and to his instinct for beauty, by the aid of that respectable Scottish sectary, Robert Sandeman. And so strong, in general, is the demand of religion and poetry to have their share in a man, to associate themselves with his knowing, and to relieve and rejoice it, that, probably, for one man amongst us with the disposition to do as Darwin did in this respect, there are at least fifty with the disposition to do as Faraday.

Education lays hold upon us, in fact, by satisfying this demand. Professor Huxley holds up to scorn medieval education, with its neglect of the knowledge of nature, its poverty even of literary studies, its formal logic devoted to "showing how and why that which the Church said was true must be true." But the great medieval Universities were not brought into being, we may be sure, by the zeal for giving a jejune and contemptible education. Kings have been their nursing fathers, and queens have been their nursing mothers, but not for this. The medieval Universities came into being, because the supposed knowledge, delivered by Scripture and the Church, so deeply engaged men's hearts, by so simply, easily, and powerfully relating itself to their desire for conduct, their desire for beauty. All other knowledge was dominated by this supposed knowledge and was subordinated to it, because of the surpassing strength of the hold which it gained upon the affections of men, by allying itself profoundly with their sense for conduct, their sense for beauty.

But now, says Professor Huxley, conceptions of the universe fatal to the notions held by our forefathers have been forced upon us by physical science. Grant to him that they are thus fatal, that the new conceptions must and will soon become current everywhere, and that everyone will finally perceive them to be fatal to the beliefs of our forefathers. The need of humane letters, as they are truly called, because they serve the paramount desire in men that good should be forever present to them—the need of humane letters, to establish a relation between the new conceptions, and our instinct for beauty, our instinct for conduct, is only the more visible. The Middle Age could do without humane letters, as it could do without the study of nature, because its supposed knowledge was made to engage its emotions so powerfully. Grant that the supposed knowledge disappears, its power of being made to engage the emotions will of course disappear along with it—but the emotions themselves, and their claim to be engaged and satisfied, will remain. Now if we find by experience that humane letters have an undeniable power of engaging the emotions, the importance of humane letters in a man's training becomes not less, but greater, in proportion to the success of modern science in extirpating what it calls "medieval thinking."

Have humane letters, then, have poetry and eloquence, the power here attributed to them of engaging the emotions, and do they exercise it? And if they have it and exercise it, *how* do they exercise it, so as to exert an influence upon man's sense for conduct, his sense for beauty? Finally, even if they both can and do exert an influence upon the senses in question, how are they to relate to them the results—the modern results—of natural science? All these questions may be asked. First, have poetry and eloquence the power of calling out the emotions? The appeal is to experience. Experience shows that for the vast majority of men, for mankind in general, they have the power. Next, do they exercise it? They do. But then, *how* do they exercise it so as to affect man's sense for conduct, his sense for beauty? And this is perhaps a case for applying the Preacher's words: "Though a man labor to seek it out, yet he shall not find it; yea, father, though a wise man think to know it, yet shall he not be able to find it." Why should it be one thing, in its effect upon the emotions, to say, "Patience is a virtue," and quite another thing, in its effect upon the emotions, to say with Homer. . . "for an enduring heart have the destinies appointed to the children of men"? Why should it be one thing, in its effect upon the emotions, to say with the philosopher Spinoza, *Felicitas in eo consistit quod homo suum esse conservare potest*— "Man's happiness consists in his being able to preserve his own essence," and quite another thing, in its effect upon the emotions, to say with the Gospel, "What is a man advantaged, if he gain the whole world, and lose himself, forfeit himself?" How does this difference of effect arise? I cannot tell, and I am not much concerned to know; the important thing is that it does arise, and that we can profit by it. But how, finally, are poetry and eloquence to exercise the power of relating the modern results of natural science to man's instinct for conduct, his instinct for beauty? And here again I answer that I do not know *how* they will exercise it, but that they can and will exercise it I am sure. I do not mean that modern philosophical poets and modern philosophical moralists are to come and relate for us, in express terms, the results of modern scientific research to our instinct for conduct, our instinct for beauty. But I mean that we shall find, as a matter of experience, if we know the best that has been thought and uttered in the world, we shall find that the art and poetry and eloquence of men who lived, perhaps long ago, who had the most limited natural knowledge, who had the most erroneous conceptions about many important matters, we shall find that this art, and poetry, and eloquence, have in fact not only the power of refreshing and delighting us, they have also the power—such is the strength and worth, in essentials, of their authors' criticism of life—they have a fortifying, and elevating, and quickening, and suggestive power, capable of wonderfully helping us to relate the results of modem science to our need for conduct, our need for beauty. Homer's conceptions of the physical universe were, I imagine, grotesque; but really, under the shock of hearing from modern science that "the world is not subordinated to man's use, and that man is not the cynosure of things terrestrial," I could, for my own part, desire no better comfort than Homer's line which I quoted just now, . . . "for an enduring heart have the destinies appointed to the children of men"!

And the more that men's minds are cleared, the more that the results of science are frankly accepted, the more that poetry and eloquence come to be received and studied as what in truth they really are—the criticism of life by gifted men, alive and active with extraordinary power at an unusual number of points—so much the more will the value of humane letters, and of art also, which is an utterance having a like kind of power with theirs, be felt and acknowledged, and their place in education be secured.

Susan (student)

MONKEY SEE, MONKEY DO

Though this essay seems mostly to complain about writing instructors, it also has a good point to make about writing: there is no one way to write well. Sometimes "I am going bananas" is just the right sentence for the situation.

During a recent workshop on grammar, a sentence—"I am going bananas"—was introduced for comment. A short poll of this class has rendered some suggestions about the kinds of responses a teacher would give if a student dared to write such a sentence.

"I am going bananas." The teacher will write "Slang. Please rewrite" in the margin. The student will obviously know what's slangy about the sentence, so no further comment is needed. This approach avoids the sticky question of verbs altogether and especially avoids discussion of intransitive, transitive, and linking verbs.

The teacher will probably get "I am going crazy" as the rewritten sentence. If this does indeed occur, the teacher can choose between two attacks: (1) Ignore it and go on, or (2) Mark "Too colloquial for Standard English models. Please rewrite." The latter is the more common, and certainly the preferred teacher response, since it affords her the opportunity to explain what colloquialisms are and why Standard English is *so* much better. After she has explained how "crazy" can be improved upon, she'll probably get the following rewrite: "I am losing my mind."

This sentence will really allow the teacher to deliver the *coup de grace* to the student! She'll simply write "Idiom" next to the sentence. After all, everyone knows you don't *really* lose your mind unless you have a particularly leaky cranium. If people really could lose their minds, others of us would find them lying around, wouldn't we? The student, of course, will believe this to be another error, and take one of two courses. He'll either give up, or produce an unsolicited rewrite.

The result might look like this: "As a response to certain unfavorable stimuli in an increasingly complex and hostile environment, this subject is developing a labile personality and is rapidly approaching an irrational state of mind." This, fellow writers, is a teacher's gold mine. She might begin with wordiness and jargon, but the majority of students polled (99.9%) felt that the following teacher comment would be most fitting and would help the student understand the intricacies of the English language more fully: "Jargon. Be concise and clear Why don't you just write, 'I'm going bananas'?"

Richard Wright

The Library Card

Richard Wright (1908-1960) started his life on a plantation in Mississippi. He lived in the South as a youth and worked his way through menial jobs until he found success as a writer. In this selection, from his autobiography, *Black Boy*, Wright becomes transformed through reading H.L. Mencken. The essay makes a powerful statement about the power of the pen. As you read this essay, consider how words—perhaps the words you are reading—can stir people to action.

One morning I arrived early at work and went into the bank lobby where the Negro porter was mopping. I stood at a counter and picked up the Memphis *Commercial Appeal* and began my free reading of the press. I came finally to the editorial page and saw an article dealing with one H. L. Mencken. I knew by hearsay that he was the editor of the *American Mercury,* but aside from that I knew nothing about him. The article was a furious denunciation of Mencken, concluding with one, hot, short sentence: Mencken is a fool.

I wondered what on earth this Mencken had done to call down upon him the scorn of the South. The only people I had ever heard denounced in the South were Negroes, and this man was not a Negro. Then what ideas did Mencken hold that made a newspaper like the *Commercial Appeal* castigate him publicly? Undoubtedly he must be advocating ideas that the South did not like. Were there, then, people other than Negroes who criticized the South? I knew that during the Civil War the South had hated northern whites, but I had not encountered such hate during my life. Knowing no more of Mencken than I did at that moment, I felt a vague sympathy for him. Had not the South, which had assigned me the role of a non-man, cast at him its hardest words?

Now, how could I find out about this Mencken? There was a huge library near the riverfront, but I knew that Negroes were not allowed to patronize its shelves any more than they were the parks and playgrounds of the city. I had gone into the library several times to get books for the white men on the job. Which of them would now help me to get books? And how could I read them without causing concern to the white men with whom I worked? I had so far been successful in hiding my thoughts and feelings from them, but I knew that I would create hostility if I went about the business of reading in a clumsy way.

I weighed the personalities of the men on the job. There was Don, a Jew; but I distrusted him. His position was not much better than mine and I knew that he was uneasy and insecure; he had always treated me in an offhand, bantering way that barely concealed his contempt. I was afraid to ask him to help me get books; his frantic desire to demonstrate a racial solidarity with the whites against Negroes might make him betray me.

Then how about the boss? No, he was a Baptist and I had the suspicion that he would not be quite able to comprehend why a black boy would want to read Mencken. There were other white men on the job whose attitudes showed clearly that they were Kluxers or sympathizers, and they were out of the question.

There remained only one man whose attitude did not fit into an anti-Negro category, for I had heard the white men refer to him as a "Pope lover." He was an Irish Catholic and was hated by the white Southerners. I knew that he read books, because I had got him volumes from the library several times. Since he, too, was an object of hatred, I felt that he might refuse me but would hardly betray me. I hesitated, weighing and balancing the imponderable realities.

One morning I paused before the Catholic fellow's desk.

"I want to ask you a favor," I whispered to him.

"What is it?"

"I want to read. I can't get books from the library. I wonder if you'd let me use your card?"

He looked at me suspiciously.

"My card is full most of the time," he said.

"I see," I said and waited, posing my question silently.

"You're not trying to get me into trouble, are you, boy?" he asked, staring at me.

"Oh, no, sir."

"What book do you want?"

"A book by H. L. Mencken."

"Which one?"

"I don't know. Has he written more than one?"

"He has written several."

"I didn't know that."

"What makes you want to read Mencken?"

"Oh, I just saw his name in the newspaper," I said.

"It's good of you to want to read," he said. "But you ought to read the right things."

I said nothing. Would he want to supervise my reading?

"Let me think," he said. "I'll figure out something."

I turned from him and he called me back. He stared at me quizzically.

"Richard, don't mention this to the other white men," he said.

"I understand," I said. "I won't say a word."

A few days later he called me to him.

"I've got a card in my wife's name," he said. "Here's mine."

"Thank you, sir."

"Do you think you can manage it?"

"I'll manage fine," I said.

"If they suspect you, you'll get in trouble," he said.

"I'll write the same kind of notes to the library that you wrote when you sent me for books," I told him. "I'll sign your name."

He laughed.

"Go ahead. Let me see what you get," he said.

That afternoon I addressed myself to forging a note. Now, what were the names of books written by H. L. Mencken? I did not know any of them. I finally wrote what I thought would be a foolproof note: *Dear Madam: Will you please let this nigger boy*—I used the word "nigger" to make the librarian feel that I could not possibly be the author of the note—*have some books by H. L. Mencken*—I forged the white man's name.

I entered the library as I had always done when on errands for whites, but I felt that I would somehow slip up and betray myself. I doffed my hat, stood a respectful distance from the desk, looked as unbookish as possible, and waited for the white patrons to be taken care of. When the desk was clear of people, I still waited. The white librarian looked at me.

"What do you want, boy?"

As though I did not possess the power of speech, I stepped forward and simply handed her the forged note, not parting my lips.

"What books by Mencken does he want?" she asked.

"I don't know, ma'am," I said, avoiding her eyes.

"Who gave you this card?"

"Mr. Falk," I said.

"Where is he?"

"He's at work, at the M——— Optical Company," I said. "I've been in here for him before."

"I remember," the woman said. "But he never wrote notes like this."

Oh, God, she's suspicious. Perhaps she would not let me have the books? If she had turned her back at that moment, I would have ducked out the door and never gone back. Then I thought of a bold idea.

"You can call him up, ma'am," I said, my heart pounding.

"You're not using these books, are you?" she asked pointedly.

"Oh, no, ma'am. I can't read."

"I don't know what he wants by Mencken," she said under her breath.

I knew now that I had won; she was thinking of other things and the race question had gone out of her mind. She went to the shelves. Once or twice she looked over her shoulder at me, as though she was still doubtful. Finally she came forward with two books in her hand.

"I'm sending him two books," she said. "But tell Mr. Falk to come in next time, or send me the names of the books he wants. I don't know what he wants to read."

I said nothing. She stamped the card and handed me the books. Not daring to glance at them, I went out of the library, fearing that the woman would call me back for further questioning. A block away from the library I opened one of the books and read a title: *A Book of Prefaces*. I was nearing my nineteenth birthday and I did not know how to pronounce the word "preface." I thumbed the pages and saw strange words and strange names. I shook my head, disappointed. I looked at the other book; it was called *Prejudices*. I knew what that word meant; I had heard it all my life. And right off I was on guard against Mencken's books. Why would a man want to call a book *Prejudices*? The word was so stained with all my memories of racial hate that I could not conceive of anybody using it for a title. Perhaps I had made a mistake about Mencken? A man who had prejudices must be wrong.

When I showed the books to Mr. Falk, he looked at me and frowned.

"That librarian might telephone you," I warned him.

"That's all right," he said. "But when you're through reading those books, I want you to tell me what you get out of them."

That night in my rented room, while letting the hot water run over my can of pork and beans in the sink, I opened *A Book of Prefaces* and began to read. I was jarred and shocked by the style, the clear, clean sweeping sentences. Why did he write like that? And how did one write like that? I pictured the man as a raging demon, slashing with his pen, consumed with hate, denouncing everything American, extolling everything European or German, laughing at the weaknesses of people, mocking God, authority. What was this? I stood up, trying to realize what reality lay behind the meaning of the words. . . . Yes, this man was fighting, fighting with words. He was using words as a weapon, using them as one would use a club. Could words be weapons? Well, yes, for here they were. Then, maybe, perhaps, I could use them as a weapon? No. It frightened me. I read on and what amazed me was not what he said, but how on earth anybody had the courage to say it.

Occasionally I glanced up to reassure myself that I was alone in the room. Who were these men about whom Mencken was talking so passionately? Who was Anatole France? Joseph Conrad? Sinclair Lewis, Sherwood Anderson, Dostoevski, George Moore, Gustave Flaubert, Maupassant, Tolstoy, Frank Harris, Mark Twain, Thomas Hardy, Arnold Bennett, Stephen Crane, Zola, Norris, Gorky, Bergson, Ibsen, Balzac, Bernard Shaw, Dumas, Poe, Thomas Mann, O. Henry, Dreiser, H. G. Wells, Gogol, T. S. Eliot, Gide, Baudelaire, Edgar Lee Masters, Stendhal, Turgenev, Huneker, Nietzsche, and scores of others? Were these men real? Did they exist or had they existed? And how did one pronounce their names?

I ran across many words whose meanings I did not know, and I either looked them up in a dictionary or, before I had a chance to do that, encountered the word in a context that made its meaning clear. But what strange world was this? I concluded the book with the conviction that I had somehow overlooked something terribly important in life. I had once tried to write, had once reveled in feeling, had let my crude imagination roam, but the impulse to dream had been slowly beaten out of me by experience. Now it surged up again and I hungered for books, new ways of looking and seeing. It was not a matter of believing or disbelieving what I read, but of feeling something new, of being affected by something that made the look of the world different.

As dawn broke I ate my pork and beans, feeling dopey, sleepy. I went to work, but the mood of the book would not die; it lingered, coloring everything I saw, heard, did. I now felt that I knew what the white men were feeling. Merely because I had read a book that had spoken of how they lived and thought, I identified myself with that book. I felt vaguely guilty. Would I, filled with bookish notions, act in a manner that would make the whites dislike me?

I forged more notes and my trips to the library became frequent. Reading grew into a passion. My first serious novel was Sinclair Lewis's *Main Street*. It made me see my boss, Mr. Gerald, and identify him as an American type. I would smile when I saw him lugging his golf bags into the office. I had always felt a vast distance separating me from the boss, and now I felt closer to him, though still distant. I felt now that I knew him, that I could feel the very limits of his narrow life. And this had happened because I had read a novel about a mythical man called George F. Babbitt.

The plots and stories in the novels did not interest me so much as the point of view revealed. I gave myself over to each novel without reserve, without trying to criticize it; it was enough for me to see and feel something different. And for me, everything was something different. Reading was like a drug, a dope. The novels created moods in which I lived for days. But I could not conquer my sense of guilt, my feeling that the white men around me knew that I was changing, that I had begun to regard them differently.

Whenever I brought a book to the job, I wrapped it in newspaper—a habit that was to persist for years in other cities and under other circumstances. But some of the white men pried into my packages when I was absent and they questioned me.

"Boy, what are you reading those books for?"

"Oh, I don't know, sir."

"That's deep stuff you're reading, boy."

"I'm just killing time, sir."

"You'll addle your brains if you don't watch out." I read Dreiser's *Jennie Gerhardt* and *Sister Carrie* and they revived in me a vivid sense of my mother's suffering; I was overwhelmed. I grew silent, wondering about the life around me. It would have been impossible for me to have told anyone what I derived from these novels, for it was nothing less than a sense of life itself. All my life had shaped me for the realism, the naturalism of the modern novel, and I could not read enough of them.

Steeped in new moods and ideas, I bought a ream of paper and tried to write; but nothing would come, or what did come was flat beyond telling. I discovered that more than desire and feeling were necessary to write and I dropped the idea. Yet I still wondered how it was possible to know people sufficiently to write about them? Could I ever learn about life and people? To me, with my vast ignorance, my Jim Crow station in life, it seemed a task impossible of achievement. I now knew what being a Negro meant. I could endure the hunger. I had learned to live with hate. But to feel that there were feelings denied me, that the very breadth of life itself was beyond my reach, that more than anything else hurt, wounded me. I had a new hunger.

In buoying me up, reading also cast me down, made me see what was possible, what I had missed. My tension returned, new, terrible, bitter, surging, almost too great to be contained. I no longer *felt* that the world about me was hostile, killing; I *knew* it. A million times I asked myself what I could do to save myself, and there were no answers. I seemed forever condemned, ringed by walls.

I did not discuss my reading with Mr. Falk, who had lent me his library card; it would have meant talking about myself and that would have been too painful. I smiled each day, fighting desperately to maintain my old behavior, to keep my disposition seemingly sunny. But some of the white men discerned that I had begun to brood.

"Wake up there, boy!" Mr. Olin said one day.

"Sir!" I answered for the lack of a better word.

"You act like you've stolen something," he said.

I laughed in the way I knew he expected me to laugh, but I resolved to be more conscious of myself, to watch my every act, to guard and hide the new knowledge that was dawning within me. If I went north, would it be possible for me to build a new life then? But how could a man build a life upon vague, unformed yearnings? I wanted to write and I did not even know the English language. I bought English grammars and found them dull. I felt that I was getting a better sense of the language from novels than from grammars. I read hard, discarding a writer as soon as I felt that I had grasped his point of view. At night the printed page stood before my eyes in sleep.

Mrs. Moss, my landlady, asked me one Sunday morning:

"Son, what is this you keep on reading?"

"Oh, nothing. Just novels."

"What you get out of 'em?"

"I'm just killing time," I said.

"I hope you know your own mind," she said in a tone which implied that she doubted if I had a mind.

I knew of no Negroes who read the books I liked and I wondered if any Negroes ever thought of them. I knew that there were Negro doctors, lawyers, newspapermen, but I never saw any of them. When I read a Negro newspaper I never caught the faintest echo of my preoccupation in its pages. I felt trapped and occasionally, for a few days, I would stop reading. But a vague hunger would come over me for books, books that opened up new avenues of feeling and seeing, and again I would forge another note to the white librarian. Again I would read and wonder as only the naive and unlettered can read and wonder, feeling that I carried a secret, criminal burden about with me each day.

That winter my mother and brother came and we set up housekeeping, buying furniture on the installment plan, being cheated and yet knowing no way to avoid it. I began to eat warm food and to my surprise found that regular meals enabled me to read faster. I may have lived through many illnesses and survived them, never suspecting that I was ill. My brother obtained a job and we began to save toward the trip north, plotting our time, setting tentative dates for departure. I told none of the white men on the job that I was planning to go north; I knew that the moment they felt I was thinking of the North they would change toward me. It would have made them feel that I did not like the life I was living, and because my life was completely conditioned by what they said or did, it would have been tantamount to challenging them.

I could calculate my chances for life in the South as a Negro fairly clearly now.

I could fight the Southern whites by organizing with other Negroes, as my grandfather had done. But I knew that I could never win that way; there were many whites and there were but few blacks. They were strong and we were weak. Outright black rebellion could never win. If I fought openly I would die and I did not want to die. News of lynchings were frequent.

I could submit and live the life of a genial slave, but that was impossible. All my life had shaped me to live by my own feelings, and thoughts. I could make up to Bess and marry her and inherit the house. But that, too, would be the life of a slave; if I did that, I would crush to death something within me, and I would hate myself as much as I knew the whites already hated those who had submitted. Neither could I ever willingly present myself to be kicked, as Shorty had done. I would rather have died than do that.

I could drain off my restlessness by fighting with Shorty and Harrison. I had seen many Negroes solve the problem of being black by transferring their hatred of themselves to others with a black skin and fighting them. I would have to be cold to do that, and I was not cold and I could never be.

I could, of course, forget what I had read, thrust the whites out of my mind, forget them; and find release from anxiety and longing in sex and alcohol. But the memory of how my father had conducted himself made that course repugnant. If I did not want others to violate my life, how could I voluntarily violate it myself?

I had no hope whatever of being a professional man. Not only had I been so conditioned that I did not desire it, but the fulfillment of such an ambition was beyond my capabilities. Well-to-do Negroes lived in a world that was almost as alien to me as the world inhabited by whites.

What, then, was there? I held my life in my mind, in my consciousness each day, feeling at times that I would stumble and drop it, spill it forever. My reading had created a vast sense of distance between me and the world in which I lived and tried to make a living, and that sense of distance was increasing each day. My days and nights were one long, quiet, continuously contained dream of terror, tension, and anxiety. I wondered how long I could bear it.

Mary Wollstonecraft Shelley

INTRODUCTION TO *FRANKENSTEIN*

Mary Wollstonecraft Shelley (1797-1851), herself a great novelist, spent her life in the company of other great literary figures. Her mother, Mary Wollstonecraft (who died in childbirth), was a pioneer feminist; her husband, Percy Bysshe Shelley, a renowned poet. Though in this preface she is quite modest about the accomplishment of writing *Frankenstein*, giving much credit to her husband, the novel *she* wrote is today regarded as one of the greatest of all time. Here she describes the moment of inspiration that produced *Frankenstein*. As you read, consider the horror typically felt (even today in the case of genetic engineering) at the thought of people creating new forms of life.

The Publishers of the Standard Novels, in selecting "Frankenstein" for one of their series, expressed a wish that I should furnish them with some account of the origin of the story. I am the more willing to comply, because I shall thus give a general answer to the question, so very frequently asked me—"How I, then a young girl, came to think of, and to dilate upon, so very hideous an idea?" It is true that I am very averse to bringing myself forward in print; but as my account will only appear as an appendage to a former production, and as it will be confined to such topics as have connection with my authorship alone, I can scarcely accuse myself of a personal intrusion.

It is not singular that, as the daughter of two persons of distinguished literary celebrity, I should very early in life have thought of writing. As a child I scribbled; and my favourite pastime, during the hours given me for recreation, was to "write stories." Still I had a dearer pleasure than this, which was the formation of castles in the air—the indulging in waking dreams—the following up trains of thought, which had for their subject the formation of a succession of imaginary incidents. My dreams were at once more fantastic and agreeable than my writings. In the latter I was a close imitator—rather doing as others had done, than putting down the suggestions of my own mind. What I wrote was intended at least for one other eye—my childhood's companion and friend; but my dreams were all my own; I accounted for them to nobody; they were my refuge when annoyed—my dearest pleasure when free.

I lived principally in the country as a girl, and passed a considerable time in Scotland. I made occasional visits to the more picturesque parts; but my habitual residence was on the blank and dreary northern shores of the Tay, near Dundee. Blank and dreary on retrospection I call them; they were not so to me then. They were the eyry of freedom, and the pleasant region where unheeded I could commune with the creatures of my fancy. I wrote then—but in a most common-place style. It was beneath the trees of the grounds belonging to our house, or on the bleak sides of the woodless mountains near, that my true compositions, the airy flights of my imagination, were born and fostered. I did not make myself the heroine of my tales. Life appeared to me too common-place an affair as regarded myself. I could not figure to myself that romantic woes or wonderful events would ever be my lot; but I was not confined to my own identity; and I could people the hours with creations far more interesting to me at that age, than my own sensations.

After this my life became busier, and reality stood in place of fiction. My husband, however, was, from the first, very anxious that I should prove myself worthy of my parentage, and enrol myself on the page of fame. He was for ever inciting me to obtain literary reputation, which even on my own part I cared for then, though since I have become infinitely indifferent to it. At this time he desired that I should write, not so much with the idea that I could produce any thing worthy of notice, but that he might himself judge how far I possessed the promise of better things hereafter. Still I did nothing. Travelling, and the cares of a family, occupied my time; and study, in the way of reading, or improving my ideas in communication with his far more cultivated mind, was all of literary employment that engaged my attention.

In the summer of 1816, we visited Switzerland, and became the neighbours of Lord Byron. At first we spent our pleasant hours on the lake, or wandering on its shores; and Lord Byron, who was writing the third canto of Childe Harold, was the only one among us who put his thoughts upon paper. These, as he brought them successively to us,clothed in all the light and harmony of poetry, seemed to stamp as divine the glories of heaven and earth, whose influences we partook with him.

But it proved a wet, ungenial summer, and incessant rain often confined us for days to the house. Some volumes of ghost stories, translated from the German into French, fell into our hands. There was the History of the Inconstant Lover, who, when he thought to clasp the bride to whom he had pledged his vows, found himself in the arms of the pale ghost of her whom he had deserted. There was the tale of the sinful founder of his race, whose miserable doom it was to bestow the kiss of death on all the younger sons of his fated house, just when they reached the age of promise. His gigantic, shadowy form, clothed like the ghost in Hamlet, in complete armour, but with the beaver up, was seen at midnight, by the moon's fitful beams, to advance slowly along the gloomy avenue. The shape was lost beneath the shadow of the castle walls; but soon a gate swung back, a step was heard, the door of the chamber opened, and he advanced to the couch of the blooming youths, cradled in healthy sleep. Eternal sorrow sat upon his face as he bent down and kissed the forehead of the boys, who from that hour withered like flowers snapt upon the stalk. I have not seen these stories since then, but their incidents are as fresh in my mind as if I had read them yesterday.

"We will each write a ghost story," said Lord Byron; and his proposition was acceded to. There were four of us. The noble author began a tale, a fragment of which he printed at the end of his poem of Mazeppa. Shelley, more apt to embody ideas and sentiments in the radiance of brilliant imagery, and in the music of the most melodious verse that adorns our language, than to invent the machinery of a story, commenced one founded on the experiences of his early life. Poor Polidori had some terrible idea about a skull-headed lady, who was so punished for peeping through a keyhole—what to see I forget—something very shocking and wrong of course; but when she was reduced to a worse condition than the renowned Tom of Coventry, he did not know what to do with her, and was obliged to despatch her to the tomb of the Capulets, the only place for which she was fitted. The illustrious poets also, annoyed by the platitude of prose, speedily relinquished their uncongenial task.

I busied myself to *think of a story,*—a story to rival those which had excited us to this task. One which would speak to the mysterious fears of our nature, and awaken thrilling horror—one to make the reader dread to look round, to curdle the blood, and quicken the beatings of the heart. If I did not accomplish these things, my ghost story would be unworthy of its name. I thought and pondered—vainly. I felt that blank incapability of invention which is the greatest misery of authorship, when dull Nothing replies to our anxious invocations. *Have you thought of a story?* I was asked each morning, and each morning I was forced to reply with a mortifying negative.

Every thing must have a beginning, to speak in Sanchean phrase, and that beginning must be linked to something that went before. the Hindoos give the world an elephant to support it, but they make the elephant stand upon a tortoise. Invention, it must be humbly admitted, does not consist in creating out of void, but out of chaos; the materials must, in the first place, be afforded: it can give form to dark, shapeless substances, but cannot bring into being the substance itself. In all matters of discovery and invention, even of those that appertain to the imagination, we are continually reminded of the story of Columbus and his egg. Invention consists in the capacity of seizing on the capabilities of a subject, and in the power of moulding and fashioning ideas suggested to it.

Many and long were the conversations between Lord Byron and Shelley, to which I was a devout but nearly silent listener. During one of these, various philosophical doctrines were discussed, and among others the nature of the principle of life, and whether there was any probability of its ever being discovered and communicated. They talked of the experiments of Dr. Darwin, (I speak not of what the Doctor really did,or said that he did, but, as more to my purpose, of what was then spoken of as having been done by him,) who preserved a piece of vermicelli in a glass case, till by some extraordinary means it began to move with voluntary motion. Not thus, after all, would life be given. Perhaps a corpse would be re-animated, galvanism had given token of such things:perhaps the component parts of a creature might be manufactured, brought together, and endued with vital warmth.

Night waned upon this talk, and even the witching hour had gone by, before we retired to rest. When I placed my head on my pillow, I did not sleep, nor could I be said to think. My imagination, unbidden, possessed and guided me, gifting the successive images that arose in my mind with a vividness far beyond the usual bounds of reverie. I saw—with shut eyes, but acute mental vision,—I saw the pale student of unhallowed arts kneeling beside the thing he had put together. I saw the hideous phantasm of a man stretched out, and then, on the working of some powerful engine, show signs of life and stir with an uneasy, half vital motion. Frightful must it be; for supremely frightful would be the effect of any human endeavour to mock the stupendous mechanism of the Creator of the world. His success would terrify the artist, he would rush away from his odious handywork, horror-stricken. He would hope that, left to itself, the slight spark of life which he had communicated would fade; that this thing, which had received such imperfect animation, would subside into dead matter; and he might sleep in the belief that the silence of the grave would quench for ever the transient existence of the hideous corpse which he had looked upon as the cradle of life. He sleeps; but he is awakened; he opens his eyes; behold the horrid thing stands at his bedside, opening his curtains, and looking on him with yellow, watery, but speculative eyes.

I opened mine in terror. The idea so possessed my mind, that a thrill of fear ran through me, and I wished to exchange the ghastly image of my fancy for the realities around. I see them still, the very room, the dark *parquet,* the closed shutters, with the moonlight struggling through and the sense I had that the glassy lake and white high Alps were beyond. I could not so easily get rid of my hideous phantom; still it haunted me. I must try to think of something else. I recurred to my ghost story,—my tiresome unlucky ghost story! O! if I could only contrive one which would frighten my reader as I myself had been frightened that night!

Swift as light and as cheering was the idea that broke in upon me. "I have found it! What terrified me will terrify others; and I need only describe the spectre which had haunted my midnight pillow." On the morrow I announced that I had *thought of a story.* I began that day with the words, *It was on a dreary night of November,* making only a transcript of the grim terrors of my waking dream.

At first I thought but of a few pages—of a short tale; but Shelley urged me to develope the idea at greater length. I certainly did not owe the suggestion of one incident, nor scarcely of one train of feeling, to my husband, and yet but for his incitement, it would never have taken the form in which it was presented to the world. From this declaration I must except the preface. As far as I can recollect, it was entirely written by him.

And now, once again, I bid my hideous progeny go forth and prosper. I have an affection for it, for it was the offspring of happy days, when death and grief were but words, which found no true echo in my heart. Its several pages speak of many a walk, many a drive, and many a conversation, when I was not alone; and my companion was one who, in this world, I shall never see more. But this is for myself; my readers have nothing to do with these associations.

I will add but one word as to the alterations I have made. They are principally those of style. I have changed no portion of the story, nor introduced any new ideas or circumstances. I have mended the language where it was so bald as to interfere with the interest of the narrative; and these changes occur almost exclusively in the beginning of the first volume. Throughout they are entirely confined to such parts as are mere adjuncts to the story, leaving the core and substance of it untouched.

M.W.S.

Beth (student)

WRITING AND LIVER

Frustration with writing is nearly universal. If you can't write about something, often good writing can be produced by writing about your frustration. Beware, though: a lot of bad writing has been produced in this way as well. As you read this essay, see how Beth has used her bad feelings to help her write. Instead of writing just one sentence "I hate writing," Beth thought of something that made her feel just as bad (liver), and turned two bad ideas into one good essay.

As I sit down to write this essay, one specific part of my childhood comes to mind. Growing up included rules and regulations requiring me to obey my parents. One rule I detested the most required me to eat liver. Comparing the writing of essays to eating liver may seem questionable, even impossible, yet the comparison directly relates to my experiences as a writer.

When I woke up in the morning and saw the raw, limp meat thawing for dinner, knowing I must consume it, I moped the rest of the day. Liver had a way of spoiling my day because I dwelled on the thought of eating the horrible, brown substance. Despite my protesting and raving temper tantrums, complete with breath-holding and floor-pounding, my parents ruthlessly forced me to eat the iron-filled meat. Their rationale for this insane cruelty never appealed to me; they always said, "Eat it, it's good for you. It will make you strong and healthy." I always thought I would rather die from drinking milkshakes than live and eat the unsightly organs of some animal. The mere sight of it made my stomach churn and my heart drop into the pit of my stomach.

Writing essays brings back the memory of eating liver because I have the same skeptical attitude about it. The assignment sits heavily in the back of my mind throughout the week, and a knot forms in the pit of my stomach when I think about writing. First, I complain about the assignment to others or to myself to vent frustration and make me feel better. These fits of frustration, however, do me no good because I still must write the paper.

Although I know writing is "good for me" because it builds, develops, and strengthens writing skills, the necessary steps I must suffer through do not seem worth the trouble. Anxiety attacks and sleepless nights invade my life each time the professor assigns another essay.

Often I remained alone at the dinner table after the rest of the family finished eating. Most of the time I would put off eating the liver until the last possible moment, hoping my parents would either forget about it or decide to have mercy on me and give me dessert instead. The more I stared at the brown, lifeless, and somewhat shriveled portion on my plate, the more the idea of eating it repulsed me. Delaying only made me hate the liver more and love my life less. My sisters kept telling me to just eat it and get it over with. But that first step seemed impossible and I wanted to keep it that way.

Every time I think of writing an essay, I cringe and decide to put it off for a few more days. However, when I hesitate too long to begin writing, the assignment haunts me and I feel tortured until I finally produce it. For some unknown reason, I feel the teacher may show compassion for me and change or even cancel the assignment if I wait long enough to start it. Unfortunately, the professor never cancels the essay, and I am left staring at a blank piece of paper. Putting off writing only intensifies my anxiety, especially when the due date becomes nearer and my mind more blank. Sentence structure, word choice, creativity, and punctuation take so much concentration: I hate the thought of suffering through it, so I prolong taking the first step as long as possible.

Sitting alone at the dinner table, I thought of ways to escape my ill-fated circumstances. Perhaps I should run away, or join the army. But with those last moments and increasing threats from Mom and Dad, I held my nose, closed my eyes, and consumed the dreaded meat, secretly hoping I would die to show my parents that their cruelty had killed me. The first bite validated all my deepest fears—it tasted even worse than I imagined. The remaining bites did not get any easier, and I felt sicker with each one.

When I begin to compose an essay, ideas to avoid it wrack my brain. My thoughts include dropping out of composition class, dropping out of school, and dropping dead. As the pressure increases and fears of failing to receive a degree because of one paper surround me, I sit down to write. Solitarily secured in my room, I take pen in hand, a deep breath, and write the entire paper all at once to get it over with. With every sentence written, I doubt my writing skills even more but hope I satisfy my professor with the final product.

After the nightmare ended and I could enjoy a sweet dessert to wash away the repugnant taste of the meat, I wondered when the next time would come to undergo the terrible task of devouring liver. I fantasized liver would become nonexistent or inessential in my mother's diet plan for our family. But somehow I knew this could not happen and I would probably get the leftovers for lunch the next day.

I feel a great sense of relief after I complete a paper and can rest in peace for awhile. Again, I wish the impossible—that universities will ban essay writing from their requirements. However, I know I must enjoy my time off while I can, for soon I must begin the endless process of writing all over again.

Oscar Wilde

PREFACE TO *THE PICTURE OF DORIAN GRAY*

Oscar Wilde (1854-1900), an outspoken novelist, poet, playwright, and conversationalist, shocked Victorian England with his non-traditional lifestyle. A homosexual relationship landed him in prison and disrepute, effectively ending his career. Soon after he died in poverty and exile in Paris. As you read this selection, consider the way you in which you want people to read your own writing. Would you ever consider telling people how to read your work? Why or why not?

The artist is the creator of beautiful things.
To reveal art and conceal the artist is art's aim.
The critic is he who can translate into another manner or a new material his impression of beautiful things.
> The highest, as the lowest, form of criticism is a mode of autobiography.
Those who find ugly meaning in beautiful things are corrupt without being charming. This is a fault.

Those who find beautiful meanings in beautiful things are the cultivated. For these there is hope.

They are the elect to whom beautiful things mean only Beauty.

There is no such thing as a moral or an immoral book. Books are well written, or badly written. That is all.

The nineteenth-century dislike of Realism is the rage of Caliban seeing his own face in a glass.

The nineteenth-century dislike of Romanticism is the rage of Caliban not seeking his own face in a glass.

The moral life of man forms part of the subject matter of the artist, but the morality of art consists in the perfect use of an imperfect medium. No artist desires to prove anything. Even things that are true can be proved.

No artist has ethical sympathies. An ethical sympathy in an artist is an unpardonable mannerism of style.

No artist is ever morbid. The artist can express everything.

Thought and language are to the artist instruments of an art.

Vice and Virtue are to the artist materials for an art.

From the point of view of form, the type of all the arts is the art of the musician. From the point of view of feeling, the actor's craft is the type.

All art is at once surface and symbol.

Those who go beneath the surface do so at their peril.

Those who read the symbol do so at their peril.

It is the spectator, and not life, that art really mirrors.

Diversity of opinion about a work of art shows that the work is new, complex, and vital.

When critics disagree the artist is in accord with himself.

We can forgive a man for making a useful thing as long as he does not admire it. The only excuse for making a useless thing is that one admires it intensely.

All art is quite useless.

John O'Hayre

A FIRST LOOK AT GOBBLEDYGOOK

This essay is taken from a United States Department of The Interior, Bureau of Land Management, publication *Gobbledygook Has Gotta Go*. The author, John O'Hayre, is an employee of the Bureau. In his preface, O'Hayre says, "If we are to succeed in these times of new technologies, new demands, and new attitudes, we must improve our communications radically. We must abandon soggy formality and incoherence in favor of modern personal communications. No longer can gobbledygook be allowed to clog communication lines." This work was published in 1966. If we can believe what we read about the proliferation of "officialese," we can only conclude that O'Hayre's crusade has made little progress in more than twenty years.

A disgruntled State director tossed a copy of a memo on our desk some time back. "Here's a lusty sample of what good writing ain't," he said. "Maybe you can use it to show some of our staff how not to write."

He picked up the memo and rattled it, saying: "All I did was write this solicitor a short memo. I told him I thought we could solve a nasty trespass case we'd both been working on. We suggested we give this trespasser a special-use permit and make him legal. That way we'd all get off the hook. All I asked the solicitor was, 'is this okay with you?'"

He threw the memo on the desk and scowled. "Cripes! All he had to do was say 'yes' or 'no.' But look what he sends me!"

Properly meek by this time, I asked: "Did the solicitor say 'yes' or 'no'?"

The state director whirled: "How the heck do I know! I've only read it twice!"

There was no doubt about it, that State director had a problem; he simply couldn't get readable writing out of his staff, or, more important this day, his solicitor.

Our distressed State director wasn't alone in his sweat over unreadable writing. Leaders in government, business, and industry have had the same feverish feeling for years. One chemical company executive put it this way: "If our antifreeze had the same quality as our writing, we'd rust out half the radiators in the country in 6 months."

A study showed executives in one company used 200 words to write 125-word memos, 8 paragraphs for 4-paragraph letters, and nearly 200 pages for 100 page reports. Another corporation finally got so frustrated it quit trying to hire writers and started training the ones it already had. Most big corporations are doing this now; they have to. This way they get good writing and save good money—lots of it. An average letter's cost varies from $6 for top executives to $2—lower levels.

Let's read the memo that shook up the State director:

To: State Director
From: John Lawbook, Solicitor
Subject: Roland Occupancy Trespass

This responds to your memorandum dated February 21,1964, requesting that we review and comment concerning the subject Roland trespass on certain lands under reclamation withdrawal.

We appreciate your apprising us of this matter and we certainly concur that appropriate action is in order to protect the interests of the United States.

We readily recognize the difficult problem presented by this situation, and if it can be otherwise satisfactorily resolved, we would prefer to avoid trespass action. If you determine it permissible to legalize the Roland occupancy and hay production by issuance of a special use permit, as suggested in your memorandum, we have no objection to that procedure.

Any such permit should be subject to cancellation when the lands are actively required for reclamation purposes and should provide for the right of the officers, agents, and employees of the United States at all times to have unrestricted access and ingress to, passage over, and egress from all said lands, to make investigations of all kinds, dig test pits and drill test holes, to survey for reclamation and irrigation works, and to perform any and all necessary soil and moisture conservation work.

If we can be of any further assistance in this matter, please advise. We would appreciate being informed of the disposition of this problem.

Before we edit the solicitor's memo, let's look at two of its weak points:

1. *False Opening:* The solicitor starts his memo by telling the State director; "This is my memo to you, answering your memo to me." Who could care less? Openings like this tell nobody nothing. Yet many memos and letters start in this word-wasteful manner.

2. *Writer's Grade:** The solicitor's memo has 217 words, 44 difficult words, 3 syllables or over, and a writer's grade of 53; it should grade out at 70 or above to be reasonably readable. A high grade means that, even if you're not saying what you mean, you're saying it readably well. Your sentences are short, your constructions simple, and your words are not painfully syllabic. A high writer's grade is a guarantee of readable writing. With it you're in business as a writer; without it you're in trouble with the reader.

A basic rule for all writing is: Have something to say; say it simply; quit! The next rule is: After you've quit, go over it again with a harsh pencil and a vengeance, crossing out everything that isn't necessary.

Let's see if the solicitor's memo takes well to the pencil. On our first trip through, in order to be fair to the solicitor, we won't change any of his words or word order.

Let's start penciling out:

"~~This responds to your memorandum dated February 21,1964, requesting that we review and comment~~ concerning the ~~subject~~ Roland trespass ~~on certain lands under reclamation withdrawal.~~

"~~We appreciate your apprising us of this matter and~~ we ~~certainly~~ concur that ~~appropriate~~ action is in order ~~to protect the interests of the United States.~~

"~~We readily recognize the difficult problem presented by this situation, and if it can be otherwise satisfactorily resolved,~~ we would prefer to avoid trespass action. If you determine it permissible to legalize the Roland occupancy ~~and hay production~~ by issuance of a special use permit, ~~as suggested in your memorandum,~~ we have no objection ~~to that procedure.~~

"Any such permit should be subject to cancellation ~~when the lands are actively required for reclamation purposes~~ and should provide for the right of ~~the officers, agents, and employees of the~~ United States at all times ~~to have unrestricted access and ingress to, passage over, and egress from all said lands, to make investigations of all kinds, dig test pits and drill test holes, to survey for reclamation and irrigation works, and~~ to perform any ~~and all~~ necessary ~~soil and moisture conservation~~ work.

---

* Refers to the *Lensear Write Formula,* a system for grading effective writing used by this author.

"If we can be of any further assistance in this matter, please advise. We would appreciate being informed of the disposition of this problem."

What did we accomplish in this quick trip? Well, let's see. We cut the number of words from 217 to 75, cut the difficult words from 44 to 10, and raised the writer's grade from 53 (difficult) to 60 (acceptable).

Can we cut more yet? Let's go over it again and see, still without changing the solicitor's words or word order.

First sentence: Concerning the Roland Trespass case, we concur that action is in order.

We can throw this whole sentence out, because: (1) the subject heading of the memo clearly states what the memo concerns; and (2) both knew "action was in order." That's why they had been writing each other.

Second and third sentences: We would prefer to avoid trespass action. If you determine it permissible to legalize Roland's occupancy by issuance of a special use permit, we have no objection.

Let's leave this for now; it contains the essence of the memo; it's the answer.

Fourth sentence: Any such permit should be subject to cancellation and should provide for the right of the United States at all times to perform all necessary work.

Let's throw this out, too. The State director and his staff issue special use permits as a matter of routine. They know what cancellation clauses and special-use provisions these have to carry. Why tell them what they already know?

Fifth sentence: We would appreciate being informed of the disposition of this problem.

Let's leave this sentence as it is and see what we have left after two editings.

> We would prefer to avoid trespass action. If you determine it permissible to legalize Roland's occupancy by issuance of a special use permit, we have no objection.
> We would appreciate being informed of the disposition of the problem.

A recount shows we're now down to 38 words, 8 difficult words, and have a writer's grade of 68.

The question now is: Does the edited memo carry the essential message and does it read easily? It does both pretty well. However, it could have a little more clarity and a little less pretension if it said simply:

> We'd like to avoid trespass action, if possible. So, if you can settle this case by issuing Roland a special use permit, go ahead.
> Please keep us informed.

This is the way we would have written the memo had we been in the solicitor's seat. The memo now has 28 words, 2 difficult words, and a writer's grade of 70. That's good writing.

Let's go back to the original memo. What we did first was to concentrate on axing out empty words and phrases. Note how they strain to sound unnatural—and succeed. Note how they can be replaced with simple, direct words.

First and second sentences: This responds to your memorandum dated February 21, 1964, requesting that we review and comment concerning the subject Roland trespass on certain lands under reclamation withdrawal. We appreciate your apprising us of this matter, and we certainly concur that appropriate action is in order to protect the interests of the United States.

How much better had he said: "Got your memo on the Roland trespass case. You're right; action is needed."

Third sentence: We readily recognize the difficult problem presented by this situation, and if it can be otherwise satisfactorily resolved, we would prefer to avoid trespass action.

Why didn't he just say, "The problem is tough, and we'd like to avoid trespass action if we can."?

Fourth sentence: If you determine it permissible to legalize Roland's occupancy by issuance of a special use permit, as suggested in your memorandum, we have no objection to that procedure.

It's a lot clearer this way: "If you can solve this problem by issuing Roland a special use permit, go ahead."

Fifth sentence: Any such permit should be subject to cancellation when the lands are actively required for reclamation purposes and should provide for the right of officers, agents and employees of the United States at all times to have unrestricted access and ingress to, passage over, and egress from all said lands, to make investigations of all kinds, dig test pits and drill test holes, to survey for reclamation and irrigation works, and to perform any and all necessary soil and moisture conservation work.

Such a lawyerish enumeration belongs, if it belongs at all, in a legal contract, not in an inner-office memo. If the solicitor felt an obligation to give the State director a reminder, he might have said: "Please spell out the Government's cancellation rights and right-to-use provisions in the permit."

Sixth and seventh sentences (adequate but somewhat high-blown): If we can be of any further assistance in this matter, please advise. We would appreciate being informed of the disposition of this problem.

It's somewhat better, at least shorter, this way: "If we can be of further help, please call. Keep us informed."

How does the whole, empty-word-less memo read now? Would it, too, be satisfactory? Let's look:

> Got your memo on the Roland trespass case. You're right; action is needed. The problem *is* tough, and we'd like to avoid trespass action if we can. So, if you can settle this case by issuing Roland a special-use permit, go ahead. Please spell out the Government's cancellation rights and right-to-use provisions in the permit.
> If we can be of further help, please call. Keep us informed.

In this version we have 70 words, only four difficult words, and a writer's grade of 69.

Moreover, we've said everything the solicitor said in his original memo, even the stuff that didn't need saying. The only difference is that we threw out the empty words, shortened the sentences, changed the passive to the active, and generally tried to say things simply, directly and clearly. The gobbledygook is gone!

Virginia Woolf

IF SHAKESPEARE HAD HAD A SISTER

Virginia Woolf (1882-1941) was a poet, essayist, editor, and most notably, a novelist. She was the focus of the "Bloomsbury Group," a gathering of important thinkers, including T.S. Eliot, John Maynard Keynes, and E.M. Forster, who had wide influence in the early part of this century. In this passage from *A Room of One's Own* (1929), she builds a convincing case that a woman in Elizabethan England would never have been allowed the opportunity to create works like Shakespeare's plays. As you read this excerpt, consider how important your environment is to your success in school. If you didn't have an adequate place (or time) to study, how would it affect your grades? Your life?

It is a perennial puzzle why no woman wrote a word of that extraordinary [Elizabethan] literature when every other man, it seemed, was capable of song or sonnet. What were the conditions in which women lived, I asked myself; for fiction, imaginative work that is, is not dropped like a pebble upon the ground, as science may be; fiction is like a spider's web, attached ever so lightly perhaps, but still attached to life at all four corners. Often the attachment is scarcely perceptible; Shakespeare's plays, for instance, seem to hang there complete by themselves. But when the web is pulled askew, hooked up at the edge, torn in the middle, one remembers that these webs are not spun in midair by incorporeal creatures, but are the work of suffering human beings, and are attached to grossly material things, like health and money and the house we live in. . . .

But what I find. . .is that nothing is known about women before the eighteenth century. I have no model in my mind to turn about this way and that. Here am I asking why women did not write poetry in the Elizabethan age, and I am not sure how they were educated; whether they were taught to write; whether they had sitting-rooms to themselves; how many women had children before they were twenty-one; what, in short, they did from eight in the morning till eight at night. They had no money, evidently; according to Professor Trevelyan they were married whether they liked it or not before they were out of the nursery, at fifteen or sixteen very likely. It would have been extremely odd, even upon this showing, had one of them suddenly written the plays of Shakespeare, I concluded, and I thought of that old gentleman, who is dead now, but was a bishop, I think, who declared that it was impossible for any woman, past, present, or to come, to have the genius of Shakespeare. He wrote to the papers about it. He also told a lady who applied to him for information that cats do not as a matter of fact go to heaven, though they have, he added, souls of a sort. How much thinking those old gentlemen used to save one! How the borders of ignorance shrank back at their approach! Cats do not go to heaven. Women cannot write the plays of Shakespeare.

Be that as it may, I could not help thinking, as I looked at the works of Shakespeare on the shelf, that the bishop was right at least in this; it would have been impossible, completely and en-

tirely, for any woman to have written the plays of Shakespeare in
the age of Shakespeare. Let me imagine, since facts are so hard to
come by, what would have happened had Shakespeare had a
wonderfully gifted sister, called Judith, let us say. Shakespeare
himself went, very probably—his mother was an heiress—to the
grammar school, where he may have learnt Latin—Ovid, Virgil
and Horace—and the elements of grammar and logic. He was, it
is well known, a wild boy who poached rabbits, perhaps shot a
deer, and had, rather sooner than he should have done, to marry a
woman in the neighbourhood, who bore him a child rather
quicker than was right. That escapade sent him to seek his fortune in London. He had, it seemed, a taste for the theatre; he began by holding horses at the stage door. Very soon he got work in
the theatre, became a successful actor, and lived at the hub of the
universe, meeting everybody, knowing everybody, practising his
art on the boards, exercising his wits in the streets, and even getting access to the palace of the queen. Meanwhile his extraor-
dinarily gifted sister, let us suppose, remained at home. She was as
adventurous, as imaginative, as agog to see the world as he was.
But she was not sent to school. She had no chance of learning
grammar and logic, let alone of reading Horace and Virgil. She
picked up a book now and then, one of her brother's perhaps, and
read a few pages. But then her parents came in and told her to
mend the stockings or mind the stew and not moon about with
books and papers. They would have spoken sharply but kindly, for
they were substantial people who knew the conditions of life for a
woman and loved their daughter—indeed, more likely than not
she was the apple of her father's eye. Perhaps she scribbled some
pages up in an apple loft on the sly, but was careful to hide them or
set fire to them. Soon, however, before she was out of her teens, she
was to be betrothed to the son of a neighbouring wool-stapler. She
cried out that marriage was hateful to her, and for that she was
severely beaten by her father. Then he ceased to scold her. He
begged her instead not to hurt him, not to shame him in this matter of her marriage. He would give her a chain of beads or a fine
petticoat, he said; and there were tears in his eyes. How could she
disobey him? How could she break his heart? The force of her own
gift alone drove her to it. She made up a small parcel of her
belongings, let herself down by a rope one summer's night and
took the road to London. She was not seventeen. The birds that
sang in the hedge were not more musical than she was. She had
the quickest fancy, a gift like her brother's, for the tune of words.

Like him, she had a taste for the theatre. She stood at the stage door; she wanted to act, she said. Men laughed in her face. The manager—a fat, loose-lipped man—guffawed. He bellowed something about poodles dancing and women acting—no woman, he said, could possibly be an actress. He hinted—you can imagine what. She could get no training in her craft. Could she even seek her dinner in a tavern or roam the streets at midnight? Yet her genius was for fiction and lusted to feed abundantly upon the lives of men and women and the study of their ways. At last—for she was very young, oddly like Shakespeare the poet in her face, with the same grey eyes and rounded brows—at last Nick Greene the actor-manager took pity on her; she found herself with child by that gentleman and so—who shall measure the heat and violence of the poet's heart when caught and tangled in a woman's body?—killed herself one winter's night and lies buried at some cross-roads where the omnibuses now stop outside the Elephant and Castle.

That, more or less, is how the story would run, I think, if a woman in Shakespeare's day had had Shakespeare's genius. But for my part, I agree with the deceased bishop, if such he was—it is unthinkable that any woman in Shakespeare's day should have had Shakespeare's genius. For genius like Shakespeare's is not born among labouring, uneducated, servile people. It was not born in England among the Saxons and the Britons. It is not born today among the working classes. How, then, could it have been born among women whose work began, according to Professor Trevelyan, almost before they were out of the nursery, who were forced to it by their parents and held to it by all the power of law and custom?

Chapter 2:
Humanity and Nature

Chief Seattle

ADDRESS

Chief Seattle (1786?-1866) was chief of the Duwamish and other tribes when the United States took possession of what are now the states of Washington and Oregon. His tribes' situation when he made this speech was similar to what had already been the fate of hundreds of tribes across America: faced with the overwhelming might and numbers of Americans, they were forced into signing disadvantageous treaties—eventually losing almost everything they had. Seattle's speech was made in response to Governor Isaac Stevens' offer to purchase two million acres of Duwampo territory. As Seattle's speech implies, his tribe in fact had little choice in the matter. As you read the passage, try to put yourself in Seattle's position. What were his realistic options at the time, and why did he choose to respond in the he manner he did?

The Governor made a fine speech, but he was outranged and outclassed that day. Chief Seattle, who answered on behalf of the Indians, towered a foot above the Governor. He wore his blanket like the toga of a Roman senator, and he did not have to strain his famous voice, which everyone agreed was audible and distinct at a distance of half a mile. Seattle's oration was in Duwamish. Doctor Smith, who had learned the language, wrote it down; under the flowery garlands of his translation the speech rolls like an articulate iron engine, grim with meanings that outlasted his generation and may outlast all the generations of men. As the amiable follies of the white race become less amiable, the iron rumble of old Seattle's speech sounds louder and more ominous. Standing in front of Doctor Maynard's office in the stumpy clearing, with his hand on the little Governor's head, the white invaders about him and his people before him, Chief Seattle said:

"Yonder sky that has wept tears of compassion upon my people for centuries untold, and which to us appears changeless and eternal, may change. Today is fair. Tomorrow may be overcast with clouds. My words are like the stars that never change. Whatever Seattle says the great chief at Washington can rely upon with as much certainty as he can upon the return of the sun or the seasons. The White Chief says that Big Chief at Washington sends us greetings of friendship and goodwill. That is kind of him for we know he has little need of our friendship in return. His people are many. They are like the grass that covers vast prairies. My people are few. They resemble the scattering trees of a storm-swept plain. The great, and—I presume—good, White Chief sends us word that he wishes to buy our lands but is willing to allow us enough to live comfortably. This indeed appears just, even generous, for the Red Man no longer has rights that he need respect, and the offer may be wise also, as we are no longer in need of an extensive country. . . . I will not dwell on, nor mourn over, our untimely decay, nor reproach our paleface brothers with hastening it, as we too may have been somewhat to blame.

"Youth is impulsive. When our young men grow angry at some real or imaginary wrong, and disfigure their faces with black paint, it denotes that their hearts are black, and then they are often cruel and relentless, and our old men and old women are unable to restrain them. Thus it has ever been. Thus it was when the white men first began to push our forefathers further westward. But let us hope that the hostilities between us may never return. We would have everything to lose and nothing to gain. Revenge by young men is considered gain, even at the cost of their own lives, but old men who stay at home in times of war, and mothers who have sons to lose, know better.

"Our good father at Washington—for I presume he is now our father as well as yours, since King George has moved his boundaries further north—our great good father, I say, sends us word that if we do as he desires he will protect us. His brave warriors will be to us a bristling wall of strength, and his wonderful ships of war will fill our harbors so that our ancient enemies far to the northward—the Hydas and Tsimpsians—will cease to frighten our women, children, and old men. Then in reality will he be our father and we his children. But can that ever be? Your God is not our God! Your God loves your people and hates mine. He folds his strong and protecting arms lovingly about the paleface and leads him by the hand as a father leads his infant son—but He has forsaken His red children—if they really are his. Our God, the Great Spirit, seems also to have forsaken us. Your God makes your people wax strong every day. Soon they will fill the land. Our people are ebbing away like a rapidly receding tide that will never return. The white man's God cannot love our people or He would protect them. They seem to be orphans who can look nowhere for help. How then can we be brothers? How can your God become our God and renew our prosperity and awaken in us dreams of returning greatness? If we have a common heavenly father He must be partial—for He came to his paleface children. We never saw Him. He gave you laws but He had no word for His red children whose teeming multitudes once filled this vast continent as stars fill the firmament. No; we are two distinct races with separate origins and separate destinies. There is little in common between us.

"To us the ashes of our ancestors are sacred and their resting place is hallowed ground. You wander far from the graves of your ancestors and seemingly without regret. Your religion was written upon tables of stone by the iron finger of your God so that you could not forget. The Red Man could never comprehend nor remember it. Our religion is the traditions of our ancestors—the dreams of our old men, given them in solemn hours of night by the Great Spirit; and the visions of our sachems; and it is written in the hearts of our people.

"Your dead cease to love you and the land of their nativity as soon as they pass the portals of the tomb and wander way beyond the stars. They are soon forgotten and never return. Our dead never forget the beautiful world that gave them being.

"Day and night cannot dwell together. The Red Man has ever fled the approach of the White Man, as the morning mist flees before the morning sun. However, your proposition seems fair and I think that my people will accept it and will retire to the reservation you offer them. Then we will dwell apart in peace, for the words of the Great White Chief seem to be the words of nature speaking to my people out of dense darkness.

"It matters little where we pass the remnant of our days. They will not be many. A few more moons; a few more winters—and not one of the descendants of the mighty hosts that once moved over this broad land or lived in happy homes, protected by the Great Spirit, will remain to mourn over the graves of a people once more powerful and hopeful than yours. But why should I mourn at the untimely fate of my people? Tribe follows tribe, and nation follows nation, like the waves of the sea. It is the order of nature, and regret is useless. Your time of decay may be distant, but it will surely come, for even the White Man whose God walked and talked with him as friend with friend, cannot be exempt from the common destiny. We may be brothers after all. We will see.

"We will ponder your proposition, and when we decide we will let you know. But should we accept it, I here and now make this condition that we will not be denied the privilege without molestation of visiting at any time the tombs of our ancestors, friends and children. Every part of this soil is sacred in the estimation of my people. Every hillside, every valley, every plain and grove, has been hallowed by some sad or happy event in days long vanished. . . . The very dust upon which you now stand responds more lovingly to their footsteps than to yours, because it is rich with the blood of our ancestors and our bare feet are conscious of the sympathetic touch. . . . Even the little children who lived here and rejoiced here for a brief season will love these somber solitudes and at eventide they greet shadowy returning spirits. And when the last Red Man shall have perished, and the memory of my tribe shall have become a myth among the White Men, these shores will swarm with the invisible dead of my tribe, and when your children's children think themselves alone in the field, the store, the shop, upon the highway, or in the silence of the pathless woods, they will not be alone. . . . At night when the streets of your cities and villages are silent and you think them deserted, they will throng with the returning hosts that once filled and still love this beautiful land. The White Man will never be alone.

"Let him be just and deal kindly with my people, for the dead are not powerless. Dead, did I say? There is no death, only a change of worlds."

Henry David Thoreau

WHERE I LIVED, AND WHAT I LIVED FOR

Henry David Thoreau (1817-1862) was a philosopher and writer who sought to live purely by renouncing "civilization. In this selection, he explains why he avoids seeking "news" and other products of a civilized, industrialized society

I went to the woods because I wished to live deliberately, to front only the essential facts of life, and see if I could not learn what it had to teach, and not, when I came to die, discover that I had not lived. I did not wish to live what was not life, living is so dear, nor did I wish to practice resignation, unless it was quite necessary. I wanted to live deep and suck out all the marrow of life, to live so sturdily and Spartan-like as to put to rout all that was not life, to cut a broad swath and shave close, to drive life into a corner, and reduce it to its lowest terms, and, if it proved to be mean, why then to get the whole and genuine meanness of it, and publish its meanness to the world; or if it were sublime, to know it by experience, and be able to give a true account of it in my next excursion. For most men, it appears to me, are in a strange uncertainty about it, whether it is of the devil or of God and have *somewhat hastily* concluded that it is the chief end of man here to "glorify God and enjoy him forever."

Still we live meanly, like ants; though the fable tells us that we were long ago changed into men; like pygmies we fight with cranes; it is error upon error, and clout upon clout, and our best virtue has for its occasion a superfluous and evitable wretchedness. Our life is frittered away by detail. An honest man has hardly need to count more than his ten fingers, or in extreme cases he may add his ten toes, and lump the rest. Simplicity, simplicity, simplicity! I say, let your affairs be as two or three, and not a hundred or a thousand; instead of a million count half a dozen, and keep your accounts on your thumb-nail. In the midst of this chopping sea of civilized life, such are the clouds and storms and quicksands and thousand-and-one items to be allowed for, that a man has to live, if he would not founder and go to the bottom and not make his port at all, by dead reckoning, and he must be a great calculator indeed who succeeds. Simplify, simplify. Instead of three meals a day, if it be necessary eat but one; instead of a hundred dishes, five; and reduce other things in proportion. Our life is like a German Confederacy, made up of petty states, with its boundary forever fluctuating, so that even a German cannot tell you how it is bounded at any moment. The nation itself, with all its so-called internal improvements, which, by the way, are all external and superficial, is just such an unwieldy and overgrown establishment, cluttered with furniture and tripped up by its own traps, ruined by luxury and heedless expense, by want of calculation and a worthy aim, as the million households in the land; and the only cure for it, as for them, is in a rigid economy, a stern and more than Spartan simplicity of life and elevation of purpose. It lives too fast. Men think that it is essential that the *Nation* have commerce, and export ice, and talk through a telegraph, and ride thirty miles an hour, without a doubt, whether *they* do or not; but whether we should live like baboons or like men, is a little uncertain. If we do not get out sleepers, and forge rails, and devote days and nights to the work, but go to tinkering upon our *lives* to improve *them,* who will build railroads? And if railroads are not built, how shall we get to Heaven in season? But if we stay at home and mind our business, who will want railroads? We do not ride on the railroad; it rides upon us. Did you ever think what those sleepers are that underlie the railroad? Each one is a man, an Irishman, or a Yankee man. The rails are laid on them, and they are covered with sand, and the cars run smoothly over them. They are sound sleepers, I assure you. And every few years a new lot is laid down and run over; so that, if some have the pleasure of riding on a rail, others have the misfortune to be ridden upon. And when they run over a man that is walking in his sleep, a supernumerary sleeper in the wrong position, and wake him up, they suddenly stop the cars, and make a hue and cry about it, as if this were an exception. I am glad to know that it takes a gang of men for every five miles to keep the sleepers down and level in their beds as it is, for this is a sign that they may sometime get up again.

Why should we live with such hurry and waste of life? We are determined to be starved before we are hungry. Men say that a stitch in time saves nine, and so they take a thousand stitches today to save nine tomorrow. As for *work,* we haven't any of any consequence. We have the Saint Vitus' dance, and cannot possibly keep our heads still. If I should only give a few pulls at the parish bell-rope, as for a fire, that is, without setting the bell, there is hardly a man on his farm in the outskirts of Concord, notwithstanding that press of engagements which was his excuse so many times this morning, nor a boy, nor a woman, I might almost say, but would forsake all and follow that sound, not mainly to save property from the flames, but, if we will confess the truth, much more to see it burn, since burn it must, and we, be it known, did not set it on fire,—or to see it put out, and have a hand in it, if that is done as handsomely; yes, even if it were the parish church itself. Hardly a man takes a half-hour's nap after dinner, but when he wakes he holds up his head and asks, "What's the news?" as if the rest of mankind had stood his sentinels. Some give directions to be waked every half-hour, doubtless for no other purpose; and then, to pay for it, they tell what they have dreamed. After a night's sleep the news is as indispensable as the breakfast. "Pray tell me anything new that has happened to a man anywhere on this globe,"—and he reads it over his coffee and rolls, that a man has had his eyes gouged out this morning on the Wachito River, never dreaming the while that he lives in the dark unfathomed mammoth cave of this world, and has but the rudiment of an eye himself

For my part, I could easily do without the post-office. I think that there are very few important communications made through it. To speak critically, I never received more than one or two letters in my life—I wrote this some years ago—that were worth the postage. The penny-post is, commonly, an institution through which you seriously offer a man that penny for his thoughts which is so often safely offered in jest. And I am sure that I never read any memorable news in a newspaper. If we read of one man robbed, or murdered, or killed by accident, or one house burned, or one vessel wrecked, or one steamboat blown up, or one cow run over on the Western Railroad, or one mad dog killed, or one lot of grasshoppers in the winter,—we never need read of another. One is enough. If you are acquainted with the principle, what do you care for a myriad instances and applications? To a philosopher all news, as it is called, is gossip and they who edit and read it are old women over their tea. Yet not a few are greedy after this gossip. There was such a rush, as I hear, the other day at one of the offices to learn the foreign news by the last arrival, that several large squares of plate glass belonging to the establishment were broken by the pressure,—news which I seriously think a ready wit might write a twelvemonth, or twelve years, beforehand with sufficient accuracy. As for Spain, for instance, if you know how to throw in Don Carlos and the Infanta, and Don Pedro and Seville and Granada, from time to time in the right proportions,—they may have changed the names a little since I saw the papers,—and serve up a bull-fight when other entertainments fail, it will be true to the letter, and give us as good an idea of the exact state or ruin of things in Spain as the most succinct and lucid reports under this head in the newspapers: and as for England, almost the last significant scrap of news from that quarter was the revolution of 1649, and if you have learned the history of her crops for an average year, you never need attend to that thing again, unless your speculations are of a merely pecuniary character. If one may judge who rarely looks into the newspapers, nothing new does ever happen in foreign parts, a French revolution not excepted.

What news! how much more important to know what that is which was never old! "Kieou-he-yu (great dignitary of the state of Wei) sent a man to Khoung-tseu to know his news. Khoung-tseu caused the messenger to be seated near him, and questioned him in these terms: What is your master doing? The messenger answered with respect: My master desires to diminish the number of his faults, but he cannot come to the end of them. The messenger being gone, the philosopher remarked: What a worthy messenger! What a worthy messenger!" The preacher, instead of vexing the ears of drowsy farmers on their day of rest at the end of the week,—for Sunday is the fit conclusion of an ill-spent week, and not the fresh and brave beginning of a new one,—with this one other draggle-tail of a sermon, should shout with thundering voice, "Pause! Avast! Why so seeming fast, but deadly slow?"

Shams and delusions are esteemed for soundest truths, while reality is fabulous. If men would steadily observe realities only, and not allow themselves to be deluded, life, to compare it with such things as we know, would be like a fairy tale and the Arabian Nights' Entertainments. If we respected only what is inevitable and has a right to be, music and poetry would resound along the streets. When we are unhurried and wise, we perceive that only great and worthy things have any permanent and absolute existence, that petty fears and petty pleasures are but the shadow of the reality. This is always exhilarating and sublime. By closing the eyes and slumbering, and consenting to be deceived by shows, men

establish and confirm their daily life of routine and habit everywhere, which still is built on purely illusory foundations. Children,
who play life, discern its true law and relations more clearly than
men, who fail to live it worthily, but who think that they are wiser
by experience, that is, by failure. I have read in a Hindoo book, that
"there was a king's son, who, being expelled in infancy from his
native city, was brought up by a forester, and growing up to
maturity in that state, imagined himself to belong to the barbarous race with which he lived. One of his father's ministers
having discovered him, revealed to him what he was, and the
misconception of his character was removed, and he knew himself to be a prince. So soul," continues the Hindoo philosopher,
"from the circumstances in which it is placed, mistakes its own
character, until the truth is revealed to it by some holy teacher,
and then it knows itself to be *Brahma."* I perceive that we inhabitants of New England live this mean life that we do because our
vision does not penetrate the surface of things. We think that that
is which *appears* to be. If a man should walk through this town
and see only the reality, where, think you, would the "Mill-dam"
go to? If he should give us an account of the realities he beheld
there, we should not recognize the place in his description. Look at
a meeting-house, or a court-house, or a jail, or a shop, or a
dwelling-house, and say what that thing really is before a true
gaze, and they would all go to pieces in your account of them. Men
esteem truth remote, in the outskirts of the system, behind the
farthest star, before Adam and after the last man. In eternity
there is indeed something true and sublime. But all these times
and places and occasions are now and here. God himself cul-
minates in the present moment, and will never be more divine in
the lapse of all the ages. And we are enabled to apprehend at all
what is sublime and noble only by the perpetual instilling and
drenching of the reality that surrounds us. The universe constantly and obediently answers to our conceptions; whether we
travel fast or slow, the track is laid for us. Let us spend our lives in
conceiving then. The poet or the artist never yet had so fair and
noble a design but some of his posterity at least could accomplish it.

  Let us spend one day as deliberately as Nature, and not be
thrown off the track by every nutshell and mosquito's wing that
falls on the rails. Let us rise early and fast, or break fast, gently
and without perturbation; let company come and let company go,
let the bells ring and the children cry,—determined to make a day
of it. Why should we knock under and go with the stream? Let us

not be upset and overwhelmed in that terrible rapid and whirlpool called a dinner, situated in the meridian shallows. Weather this danger and you are safe, for the rest of the way is down hill. With unrelaxed nerves, with morning vigor, sail by it, looking another way, tied to the mast like Ulysses. If the engine whistles, let it whistle till it is hoarse for its pains. If the bell rings, why should we run? We will consider what kind of music they are like. Let us settle ourselves, and work and wedge our feet downward through the mud and slush of opinion, and prejudice, and tradition, and delusion, and appearance, that alluvion which covers the globe, through Paris and London, through New York and Boston and Concord, through Church and State, through poetry and philosophy and religion, till we come to a hard bottom and rocks in place, which we can call *reality*, and say, This is, and no mistake; and then begin, having a *point d'appui*, below freshet and frost and fire, a place where you might found a wall or a state, or set a lamp-post safely, or perhaps a gauge, not a Nilometer, but a Realometer, that future ages might know how deep a freshet of shams and appearances had gathered from time to time. If you stand right fronting and face to face to a fact, you will see the sun glimmer on both its surfaces, as if it were a cimeter, and feel its sweet edge dividing you through the heart and marrow, and so you will happily conclude your mortal career. Be it life or death, we crave only reality. If we are really dying, let us hear the rattle in our throats and feel cold in the extremities; if we are alive, let us go about our business.

Time is but the stream I go a-fishing in. I drink at it; but while I drink I see the sandy bottom and detect how shallow it is. Its thin current slides away, but eternity remains. I would drink deeper; fish in the sky, whose bottom is pebbly with stars. I cannot count one. I know not the first letter of the alphabet. I have always been regretting that I was not as wise as the day I was born. The intellect is a cleaver; it discerns and rifts its way into the secret of things. I do not wish to be any more busy with my hands than is necessary. My head is hands and feet. I feel all my best faculties concentrated in it. My instinct tells me that my head is an organ for burrowing, as some creatures use their snout and fore paws, and with it I would mine and burrow my way through these hills. I think that the richest vein is somewhere hereabouts; so by the divining-rod and thin rising vapors I judge; and here I will begin to mine.

Nathaniel Hawthorne

JOURNAL NOTES ON THOREAU

Following his graduation from Bowdoin College in 1825, Nathaniel Hawthorne (1804-1864) returned to live with his widowed mother and began his literary career. After sixteen years of producing work that was unsatisfactory to him, Hawthorne purchased a share in the transcendentalists' Brook Farm utopian community. In less than two years he found communal living unattractive; married his fiancee, Sophia Peabody; and established a home in West Roxbury, Massachusetts, once owned by Ralph Waldo Emerson. It was then that he abandoned his English Gothic style and began to write as an American about the American experience. When he lost his job in the Boston Customs House because of politics, he turned full-time to his writing and in the next five to six years produced the bulk of his total output—including *The Scarlet Letter, The House of the Seven Gables,* and *Twice-Told Tales.* This character study of Thoreau was written less than two months after Hawthorne's marriage. Could Thoreau have been the newlyweds' first guest?

Mr. Thoreau dined with us yesterday. He is a singular character—a young man with much of wild original nature still remaining in him; and so far as he is sophisticated, it is in a way and method of his own. He is as ugly as sin, long-nosed, queermouthed, and with uncouth and rustic, although courteous manners, corresponding very well with such an exterior. But his ugliness is of an honest and agreeable fashion, and becomes him much better than beauty. He was educated, I believe, at Cambridge, and formerly kept school in this town; but for two or three years back, he has repudiated all regular modes of getting a living, and seems inclined to lead a sort of Indian life among civilized men—an Indian life, I mean, as respects the absence of any systematic effort for a livelihood. He has been for some time an inmate of Mr. Emerson's family; and, in requital, he labors in the garden, and performs such other offices as may suit him—being entertained by Mr. Emerson for the sake of what true manhood there is in him. Mr. Thoreau is a keen and delicate observer of nature—a genuine observer—which, I suspect, is almost as rare a character as even an original poet; and Nature, in return for his love, seems to adopt him as her especial child, and shows him secrets which few others are allowed to witness. He is familiar with beast, fish, fowl, and reptile, and has strange stories to tell of adventures and friendly passages with these lower brethren of mortality. Herb and flower, likewise, wherever they grow, whether in garden or wildwood, are his familiar friends. He is also on intimate terms with the clouds, and can tell the portents of storms. It is a characteristic trait, that he has great regard for the memory of the Indian tribes, whose wild life would have suited him so well; and, strange to say, he seldom walks over a ploughed field without picking up an arrowpoint, spearhead, or other relic of the red man, as if their spirits willed him to be the inheritor of their wealth.

With all this he has more than a tincture of literature—a deep and true taste for poetry, especially the elder poets, although more exclusive than is desirable, like all other Transcendentalists, so far as I am acquainted with them. He is a good writer—at least he has written one good article, a rambling disquisition on Natural History, in the last *Dial*, which, he says, was chiefly made up from journals of his own observations. Methinks this article gives a very fair image of his mind and character—so true, innate, and literal in observation, yet giving the spirit as well as the letter of what he sees, even as a lake reflects its wooded banks, showing every leaf, yet giving the wild beauty of the whole scene. Then there are passages in the article of cloudy and dreamy metaphysics, partly affected, and partly the natural exhalations of his intellect; and also passages where his thoughts seem to measure and attune themselves into spontaneous verse, as they rightfully may, since there is real poetry in him. There is a basis of good sense and of moral truth, too, throughout the article, which also is a reflection of his character; for he is not unwise to think and feel, however imperfect is his own mode of action. On the whole, I find him a healthy and wholesome man to know.

After dinner (at which we cut the first watermelon and muskmelon that our garden has grown), Mr. Thoreau and I walked up the bank of the river, and at a certain point he shouted for his boat. Forthwith a young man paddled it across, and Mr. Thoreau and I voyaged farther up the stream, which soon became more beautiful than any picture, with its dark and quiet sheet of water, half shaded, half sunny, between high and wooded banks. The late rains have swollen the stream so much that many trees are standing up to their knees, as it were, in the water, and boughs, which lately swung high in air, now dip and drink deep of the passing wave. As to the poor cardinals which glowed upon the bank a few days since, I could see only a few of their scarlet caps, peeping above the tide. Mr. Thoreau managed the boat so perfectly, either with two paddles or with one, that it seemed instinct with his own will, and to require no physical effort to guide it. He said that, when some Indians visited Concord a few years ago, he found that he had acquired, without a teacher, their precise method of propelling and steering a canoe. Nevertheless being in want of money, the poor fellow was desirous of selling the boat of which he was so fit a pilot, and which was built by his own hands; so I agreed to give him his price (only seven dollars), and accordingly became the possessor of the Musketaquid. I wish I could acquire the aquatic skill of the original owner at as reasonable a rate.

Diana Peck (Student)

THE SHELLFISH OF AREY'S POND

The quintessential *bad* essay topic is "What I did during my summer vacation." It has gotten such a bad reputation that few students are even assigned it anymore, leaving elementary school teachers across the nation struggling to come up with adequate lesson plans for the first day of school. Yet even topics like this one can be turned into great essays if the recollections are described with a fond realism and the whole piece makes a good point. Diana Peck does precisely that in this essay, progressing in an anxious manner from descriptions of the most common shellfish of her pond to the most coveted. A simple description becomes a quest, and in the end becomes a comment on the relationship of humanity and nature.

The Atlantic Ocean pounding the Cape Cod shoreline finds a break in the dunes just north of Monomoy Point. Here, it can enter the calm, shallow waters of Pleasant Bay, separated from the ocean's surf by the outsized sand dune named Nauset. Continuing a tidal journey, some ocean water finds its way to the northern reaches of the bay and sidetracks into a small channel called Namequoit. Twice a day, every day, ocean water completes its journey down this channel and fills Arey's Pond, one of the many ponds that terminate similar channels. Nursed by this fresh supply of nutrient-rich waters, Arey's Pond, small though it is, has until recently provided the spawning grounds for a rich variety of marine fauna. When I was a child, many a summer day's activities revolved around the shellfish life of the pond.

The periwinkle was both the most common and the most useless shellfish in the pond. Hundreds of these small black snails, the size of lima beans, littered our tiny beach at low tide. As we stepped on them, unable to avoid them, they squashed into the wet sand, emerging undaunted a moment later. Although edible, they were useless as food since it would have taken a dozen of their soft black insides to produce a thimbleful of escargots. Adults ignored periwinkles, and even children quickly tired of picking them up, waiting for them to stick their bodies out of the shell, then poking them to watch them disappear inside their shells. Sometimes, picking up these shells, we were surprised to find the tiniest fiddler crab had made an empty shell its home. Struggling to pull its right claw, equal in size to the rest of its body, inside the borrowed shell, the crab entertained us for a few moments. We enjoyed it far more, however, when an adult fiddler crab, accidentally shellless, would run frantically around the beach, terrorized by its vulnerability.

Less common were the horseshoe crabs which the tide brought to our beach. Often they were paired, the male glued to the back of the female, and it thrilled us to pick up one spiny tail and lift up the two helpless, heavy bodies, their dozens of small underlegs thrashing the air. The dark brown armored semicircles of their bodies, often about ten inches in width, were too heavy for us to hold for long, and so they would usually be freed within a half-minute. Meatless, they had only one use: sometimes my father split a female horseshoe crab with one blow of his axe, put each of her halves in an eel pot, and attracted eels for miles around with her roe.

An animal which was not particularly common but could be found accidentally was the blue crab. The big brother of the Maryland soft-shell crab, this species offered little meat and was therefore usually ignored except at a clambake where the joy of cracking open the shells excused the meagre store of meat. The only aggressive variety of shellfish we encountered, this type of crab would endlessly surprise us, pinching our toes as we waded in the water, gripping our drop lines as we pulled up what we thought was a flounder, staring at us through the wires as we hauled up our eel pots.

But hiding in the mud of the pond were the rare bivalves with edible meat, especially sought-after by adults who, aided by curious children, spent whole afternoons searching for them, spurred on by my father's enthusiasm. The most common of the bivalves were clams, called soft-shell clams by the tourists but just plain clams by Cape Codders. My father led the expeditions at dead-low tide, armed with a shovel and a bucket. In the sand near the water, he looked for telltale air holes, then dug a shovelful of mud and dumped it out on the beach. The children, responsible for combing the mud with their fingers to find the smooth, oval bodies of the clams, usually squeezed each clam, watching it squirt a last stream of water through its long, thick neck, then tossed it unceremoniously into the waiting bucket. We worked our way down the shoreline until, as the tide started in, we stood in a few inches of water. Over and over, my father dug into the muck, sending swirls of black grit into the water, raising the pungent smell of disturbed compost, dumping shovelfuls of oozing mud into the shallow water for us to search. Over and over we gushed the mud through our fingers, plucked out the clams, and moved on to the next shovelful, often stepping into the soft warm muck up to our ankles, hearing the "pop" of the suction as we pulled out our feet. The clams, hard-won from the mud, would provide a feast of steamers for all the relatives as well as bait for the next days fishing.

More difficult to find were the quahogs, and not until we were older did my father teach us, one by one, how to find them. Adults considered them more of a delicacy than the clams and either ate the meat raw or ground it for chowder. A hard-shelled clam, quahogs have no necks and keep their mantles inside their tightly-closed shells. They, too, burrow in the mud, but they keep a ridge of shell just above the surface. To find quahogs, my father, in goggles and bathing suit, floated face down along the shoreline where the water was about a foot deep. The water being too murky to see through, he pulled himself along, feeling the mud with his hands for the telltale ridge. When he found one, he loosened the surrounding mud with his fingers and pulled the quahog out of its hiding place. This was a slow, arduous process, demanding too much patience for most of us children. But my father was motivated by his love for the result of his labors, especially enjoying the sweet flavor of the small quahogs' meat, called cherrystones, as he swallowed them raw.

Even more treasured than quahogs and more difficult to find were the jewels of Arey's Pond: the oysters. Even my father, experienced shellfisherman as he was, had a special smile as he emerged from the water with an oyster. Hiding in their sharp, blotchy, irregularly shaped shells amidst the roots of the eel grass at the shore's edge, oysters were impossible to see. Feeling for them was difficult, because the edges of the eel grass felt similar to the layered edges of the oyster's shell. The grass eventually yielded to pressure, while the oyster remained firm, but anyone pressing hard enough to distinguish the difference was sure to cut his fingers on the reedy edge of the grass or the sharp edge of a shell. Wearing gloves made the hands too clumsy to detect the difference. For my father it was a labor of love. The scores of tiny cuts on his fingers were small payment for the joy of eating a raw oyster, captured only minutes before. Children were never offered oysters, and those adults fortunate enough to be present when my father caught some usually mirrored his sublime expression as they swallowed the fresh meat. Even the oyster's shell had value, serving as bureau-top catch-alls, as ash trays, or as a decorative border for the garden.

We still visit Arey's Pond whenever we can, my father still digging for clams and searching for quahogs. But some years ago, the channel to the bay was deepened to provide access for pleasure boats. The shellfish never recovered. After two or three years some of the clams came back and a few quahogs can still be found, but the oysters are gone and none of the crabs can negotiate the channel. Only the periwinkles remain in abundance to remind us of how it once was.

Mark Twain

TWO VIEWS OF THE MISSISSIPPI

This unusual essay reveals none of the wry wit usually associated with Mark Twain (1835-1910). It is, instead, a lyrical, pensive reflection on his view of the river before and after he was trained as a riverboat pilot. As you read the essay, notice the use of analogy, description, and comparison and contrast the author makes to help his reader see and understand the thesis of the work. This excerpt is taken from Twain's *Life on the Mississippi*.

The face of the water, in time, became a wonderful book-a book that was a dead language to the uneducated passenger, but which told its mind to me without reserve, delivering its most cherished secrets as clearly as if it uttered them with a voice. And it was not a book to be read once and thrown aside, for it had a new story to tell every day. Throughout the long twelve hundred miles there was never a page that was void of interest, never one that you could leave unread without loss, never one that you would want to skip, thinking you could find higher enjoyment in some other thing. There never was so wonderful a book written by man; never one whose interest was so absorbing, so unflagging, so sparklingly renewed with every reperusal. The passenger who could not read it was charmed with a peculiar sort of faint dimple on its surface (on the rare occasions when he did not overlook it altogether); but to the pilot that was an *italicized* passage; indeed, it was more than that, it was a legend of the largest capitals, with a string of shouting exclamation points at the end of it; for it meant that a wreck or a rock was buried there that could tear the life out of the strongest vessel that ever floated. It is the faintest and simplest expression the water ever makes, and the most hideous to a pilot's eye. In truth, the passenger who could not read this book saw nothing but all manner of pretty pictures in it, painted by the sun and shaded by the clouds, whereas to the trained eye these were not pictures at all, but the grimmest and most dead-earnest of reading matter.

Now when I had mastered the language of this water and had come to know every trifling feature that bordered the great river as familiarly as I knew the letters of the alphabet, I had made a valuable acquisition. But I had lost something, too. I had lost something which could never be restored to me while I lived. All the grace, the beauty, the poetry had gone out of the majestic river! I still keep in mind a certain wonderful sunset which I witnessed when steamboating was new to me. A broad expanse of the river was turned to blood; in the middle distance the red hue brightened into gold, through which a solitary log came floating, black and conspicuous; in one place a long, slanting mark lay sparkling upon the water; in another the surface was broken by boiling, tumbling rings, that were as many-tinted as an opal; where the ruddy flush was faintest, was a smooth spot that was covered with graceful circles and radiating lines, ever so delicately traced; the shore on our left was densely wooded, and the somber shadow that fell from this forest was broken in one place by a long, ruffled trail that shone like silver; and high above the forest wall a clean-stemmed dead tree waved a single leafy bough that glowed like a flame in the unobstructed splendor that was flowing from the sun. There were graceful curves, reflected images, woody heights, soft distances; and over the whole scene, far and near, the dissolving lights drifted steadily, enriching it, every passing moment, with new marvels of coloring.

I stood like one bewitched. I drank it in, in a speechless rapture. The world was new to me, and I had never seen anything like this at home. But as I have said, a day came when I began to cease from noting the glories and the charms which the moon and the sun and the twilight wrought upon the river's face; another day came when I ceased altogether to note them. Then, if that sunset scene had been repeated, I should have looked upon it without rapture, and should have commented upon it, inwardly, after this fashion: This sun means that we are going to have wind tomorrow; that floating log means that the river is rising, small thanks to it; that slanting mark on the water refers to a bluff reef which is going to kill somebody's steamboat one of these nights, if it keeps on stretching out like that; those tumbling "boils" show a dissolving bar and a changing channel there; the lines and circles in the slick water over yonder are a warning that that troublesome place is shoaling up dangerously; that silver streak in the shadow of the forest is the "break" from a new snag, and he has located himself in the very best place he could have found to fish for steamboats; that tall dead tree, with a single living branch, is not going to last long, and then how is a body ever going to get through this blind place at night without the friendly landmark?

No, the romance and the beauty were all gone from the river. All the value any feature of it had for me now was the amount of usefulness it could furnish toward compassing the safe piloting of a steamboat. Since those days, I have pitied doctors from my heart. What does the lovely flush in a beauty's cheek mean to a doctor but a "break" that rippled above some deadly disease? Are not all her visible charms sown thick with what are to him the signs and symbols of hidden decay? Does he ever see her beauty at all, or doesn't he simply view her professionally, and comment upon her unwholesome condition all to himself? And doesn't he sometimes wonder whether he had gained most or lost most by learning his trade?

Troyce Nolan (student)

A BATTLE FOR EXISTENCE

In this short research paper, Troyce was required to describe the efforts to preserve an endangered species. Troyce decided to discuss the whooping crane, which meets the demands of the assignment quite well—it is one of the rarest species on the continent. He briefly describes the problem in a straightforward manner, and then explains in detail specific programs to revitalize the species. It would be tempting with an assignment of this kind to stray from the topic and discuss the problem of endangered species in broad terms, but by sticking closely to the topic he has chosen, Troyce shows how difficult the effort to save this one species can be. He leaves it to the reader to see how big the problem is by considering the growing number of endangered species.

Because cities across the nation are growing, more and more land once occupied by wild animals is being developed from wilderness to metropolis. Developing the animals' wild habitat is causing overcrowding and a shortage of food and shelter. Because of the crowding and shortages, many animals are dwindling in numbers and others are becoming extinct. *Editorial Research Reports* estimates nearly 250,000 species are endangered in the world today. According to the same report, "In this country, no fewer than 181 species—including 36 mammals, 68 birds, 30 fishes, 10 reptiles, and 4 amphibians—fall into the endangered species category" (Gimlin et al. 683). According to the Endangered Species Act of 1973, an animal is considered endangered when it appears close to extinction throughout its livable habitat (Gimlin et al. 683). One such endangered animal is the whooping crane. With the help of man and a cross-fostering program, however, the number of whooping cranes can be replenished.

Scientifically known as the *Grus americana,* the whooper is "the rarest North American species" (Peterson 79). The bird gets its name from its most distinguishing characteristic, its call, which resembles a loud whoop, and it is easily recognized by its white body feathers, red skin around the face, and black wing feathers (Peterson 79). The whooping crane is America's largest bird, averaging from four to five feet high and having a seven-foot wingspan (Harmon 41).

The whooping crane's summer habitat once covered much of northern Canada, and a section of the United States including northern Illinois, Minnesota, and North Dakota. Their wintering grounds were found all along the Gulf of Mexico. Also, there was a non-migratory flock in southwestern Louisiana. The population within this entire range peaked between 1,300 and 1,500 whoopers (Hamilton 56). But, between 1800 and 1920 the whoopers began to disappear (Drewein 682). Construction in the prairie wetlands and hunting quickly thinned out the crane's population. Also, in 1940, a hurricane wiped out the Louisiana flock. Of the thirteen birds in the flock, seven of them were killed during the storm, and the remaining six had all disappeared by 1949 (Mackenzie 124).

By 1936 man was trying to help the struggling cranes because of their inability to reproduce steadily in the wild (Zimmerman, *Peril* 75). During 1936 the U.S. Fish and Wildlife Service established a 47,000 acre refuge near Aransas pass in Texas called the

Aransas Pass National Wildlife Refuge, where the last surviving flock spends its winters (Zimmerman, "Technique" 54). But, because their nesting grounds had not been discovered, the flock dwindled down to a record low of fifteen in 1948 (Harmon 41). Finally, the long-sought-after nesting grounds were found at Wood Buffalo National Park (W.B.N.P.) in a remote section of Canada's Northwest Territories (Drewein 682).

Once scientists discovered Wood Buffalo, they began attempts to rebuild the whooper's population. Scientists working for the Endangered Wildlife Research Program first attempted to form a captive flock at Patuxent Wildlife Research Center in Laural, Maryland (Zimmerman, *Peril* 75-76). These captive cranes failed to mate on their own, so artificial insemination was used. Fertile eggs were produced through this technique, but the chicks did not survive because of physical disorders. The next attempt at helping the whoopers was to collect eggs from W.B.N.P. and let the Patuxent whoopers hatch and raise them. Unfortunately, the results of this experiment were much the same as those from earlier attempts (Drewein 683).

Still using the egg collecting idea, scientists decided to try having sandhill cranes acting much like foster parents hatch and raise the eggs (Drewein 683). As Lee Harmon explains in *Sunset:*

> The foster parent plan is a joint American-Canadian experiment. It uses the sandhill cranes as foster parents. For three years now, eggs of northern California whoopers have been transferred to sandhill nests at Gray's Lake National Wildlife Refuge in southeastern Idaho. The sandhill cranes have adopted the whoopers, even bringing them along their own 800 mile winter migration to Bosque del Apache (41).

In the *National Geographic* Roderick Drewein reports that the foster parent sandhill cranes behaved much like the whoopers. Like whoopers, sandhills lay two eggs that require a thirty day incubation period, the chicks are identical to those of the whooper, and the adult cranes did not abandon the nest if an egg was taken or switched. Also, like the whoopers, of the two layed eggs, very seldom do two offspring survive due to sibling rivalries. Therefore, even if the collected eggs do not hatch, the birds' normal evolutionary cycle is not upset. In fact, the number of chicks that reached maturity increased during the egg collection process (684).

The first trial with egg-fostering produced ten chicks from fourteen transported eggs. Three died at birth, two were lost, and five migrated south to winter in Bosque del Apache with their fostering sandhills (Zimmerman, "Cranes" 132). The whoopers were compatible with their foster parents, but were very aggressive towards sandhill chicks, a sign of species recognition that will help them when they begin mating (Zimmerman, "Cranes" 132).

Bruce Hamilton writing in *Sierra* reports that, "To date the foster parent program is highly successful. However, it will be several years before researchers know if the fostered juveniles will mate, breed and establish a second stable flock" (58). The wait is because whooping cranes do not become sexually mature until the age of five or six (Drewein 692). Despite the wait for maturity, progress can already be seen. In 1980 there were just over 90 whoopers wintering on the Gulf Coast (Jonsgard 74). Maybe, with the help of man and the cross-fostering program, the whooping crane can once again live without the danger of extinction.

Works Cited

Derwein, Roderick C. "Teamwork Helps the Whooping Crane." *National Geographic* May 1979: 680+.

Gimlin, Hoyt et al. *Editorial Research Reports.* Washington, D.C.: Congressional Quarterly, 1977.

Hamilton, Druce. "The Whooping Crane a Success Story." *Sierra* May/June 1979: 56.

Harmon, Lee. "The Whoopers at Bosque del Apache." *Sunset* Dec. 1978: 41.

Jonsgard, Paul A. "Whooper Recount." *Natural History* Feb. 1982: 70.

Mackenzie, John. *Birds in Peril.* Boston: Houghton, 1977.

Peterson, Roger Torey. *A Field Guide to the Birds of Texas.* Boston: Houghton, 1960.

Zimmerman, David R. "A Technique Called Cross-Fostering May Help to Save the Whooping Crane." *Smithsonian* Sept. 1978: 52.

———— *To Save a Bird in Peril.* New York: Coward, 1975.

———— "Whooping Cranes." *Audubon* Mar. 1976: 132.

Herman Melville

THE LINE

In this excerpt from *Moby Dick,* Herman Melville recreates, in fine
detail, the scene on board a whaling ship as the whale-line is brought
in and stored away for its next use. The author is so skilled at writing
descriptive prose that the reader almost feels himself or herself to be
an eyewitness to the event. This ability to describe an event so vividly is
one of the reasons that Melville is considered to be among the world's
great novelists.

With reference to the whaling scene shortly to be described, as
well as for the better understanding of all similar scenes elsewhere presented, I have here to speak of the magical, sometimes
horrible whale-line.

The line originally used in the fishery was of the best hemp,
slightly vapoured with tar, not impregnated with it, as in the case
of ordinary rope; for while tar, as ordinarily used, makes the
hemp more pliable to the rope-maker, and also renders the rope
itself more convenient to the sailor for common ship use; yet, not
only would the ordinary quantity too much stiffen the whale-line
for the close coiling to which it must be subjected; but as most
seamen are beginning to learn, tar in general by no means adds to
the rope's durability or strength, however much it may give it
compactness and gloss.

Of late years the Manilla rope has in the American fishery almost entirely superseded hemp as a material for whale-line; for,
though not so durable as hemp, it is stronger, and far more soft
and elastic; and I will add (since there is an aesthetic in all things),
is much more handsome and becoming to the boat than hemp.
Hemp is a dusky, dark fellow, a sort of Indian; but Manilla is a
golden-haired Circassian to behold.

The whale-line is only two-thirds of an inch in thickness. At first
sight, you would not think it so strong as it really is. By experiment
its one and fifty yarns will each suspend a weight of one hundred
and twenty pounds; so that the whole rope will bear a strain

nearly equal to three tons. In length, the common sperm whale-line measures something over two hundred fathoms. Towards the stern of the boat it is spirally coiled away in the tub, not like the worm-pip of a still, though, but so as to form one round, cheese-shaped mass of densely bedded "sheaves," or layers of concentric spiralisations, without any hollow but the "heart," or minute vertical tube formed at the axis of the cheese. As the least tangle or kink in the coiling would, in running out, infallibly take somebody's arm, leg, or entire body off, the utmost precaution is used in stowing the line in its tub. Some harpooneers will consume almost an entire morning in this business, carrying the line high aloft and then reeving it downwards through a block towards the tub, so as in the act of coiling to free it from all possible wrinkles and twists.

In the English boats two tubs are used instead of one; the same line being continuously coiled in both tubs. There is some advantage in this; because these twin-tubs being so small they fit more readily into the boat, and do not strain it so much, whereas, the American tub, nearly three feet in diameter and of proportionate depth, makes a rather bulky freight for a craft whose planks are but one half-inch in thickness; for the bottom of the whaleboat is like critical ice, which will bear up a considerable distributed weight, but not very much of a concentrated one. When the painted canvas cover is clapped on the American line-tub, the boat looks as if it were pulling off with a prodigious great wedding-cake to present to the whales.

Both ends of the line are exposed; the lower end terminating in an eye-splice or loop coming up from the bottom against the side of the tub, and hanging over its edge completely disengaged from everything. This arrangement of the lower end is necessary on two accounts. First: In order to facilitate the fastening to it of an additional line from a neighbouring boat, in case the stricken whale should sound so deep as to threaten to carry off the entire line originally attached to the harpoon. In these instances, the whale of course is shifted like a mug of ale, as it were, from the one boat to the other; though the first boat always hovers at hand to assist its consort. Second: This arrangement is indispensable for common safety's sake; for were the lower end of the line in any way attached to the boat, and were the whale then to run the line out to the end almost in a single, smoking minute as he sometimes does, he would not stop there, for the doomed boat would infallibly be dragged down after him into the profundity of the sea; and in that case no town-crier would ever find her again.

Before lowering the boat for the chase, the upper end of the line is taken aft from the tub, and passing round the loggerhead there, is again carried forward the entire length of the boat, resting crosswise upon the loom or handle of every man's oar, so that it jogs against his wrist in rowing; and also passing between the men, as they alternately sit at the opposite gunwales, to the leaded chocks or grooves in the extreme pointed prow of the boat, where a wooden pin or skewer the size of a common quill, prevents it from slipping out. From the chocks it hangs in a slight festoon over the bows, and is then passed inside the boat again; and some ten or twenty fathoms (called box-line) being coiled upon the box, in the bows, it continues its way to the gunwale still a little farther aft, and is then attached to the shortwarp—the rope which is immediately connected with the harpoon; but previous to that connection, the short-warp goes through sundry mystifications too tedious to detail.

Thus the whale-line folds the whole boat in its complicated coils, twisting and writhing around it in almost every direction. All the oarsmen are involved in its perilous contortions; so that to the timid eye of the landsman, they seem as Indian jugglers, with the deadliest snakes sportively festooning their limbs. Nor can any son of mortal woman, for the first time, seat himself amid those hempen intricacies, and while straining his utmost at the oar, bethink him that at any unknown instant the harpoon may be darted, and all these horrible contortions be put in play like ringed lightnings; he cannot be thus circumstanced without a shudder that makes the very marrow in his bones to quiver in him like a shaken jelly. Yet habit—strange thing! what cannot habit accomplish?—Gayer sallies, more merry mirth, better jokes, and brighter repartees, you never heard over your mahogany, than you will hear over the half-inch white cedar of the whale boat, when thus hung in hangman's nooses; and, like the six burghers of Calais before King Edward, the six men composing the crew pull into the jaws of death, with a halter around every neck, as you may say.

Perhaps a very little thought will now enable you to account for those repeated whaling disasters—some few of which are casually chronicled—of this man or that man being taken out of the boat by the line, and lost. For, when the line is darting out, to be seated then in the boat, is like being seated in the midst of the

manifold whizzings of a steam-engine in full play, when every
flying beam, and shaft, and wheel, is grazing you. It is worse; for
you cannot sit motionless in the heart of these perils, because the
boat is rocking like a cradle, and you are pitched one way and the
other, without the slightest warning, and only by a certain self-
adjusting buoyancy and simultaneousness of volition and action,
can you escape being made a Mazeppa of, and run away with
where the all-seeing sun himself could never pierce you out.

Again: as the profound calm which only apparently precedes
and prophesies of the storm, is perhaps more awful than the
storm itself; for, indeed, the calm is but the wrapper and envelope
of the storm; and contains it in itself, as the seemingly harmless
rifle holds the fatal powder, and the ball, and the explosion; so the
graceful repose of the line, as it silently serpentines about the
oarsmen before being brought into actual play—this is a thing
which carries more of true terror than any other aspect of this
dangerous affair. But why say more? All men live enveloped in
whale-lines. All are born with halters round their necks; but it is
only when caught in the swift, sudden turn of death, that mortals
realise the silent, subtle, ever-present perils of life. And if you be a
philosopher, though seated in the whale-boat, you would not at
heart feel one whit more of terror than though seated before your
evening fire with a poker, and not a harpoon, by your side.

E. B. White

DEATH OF A PIG

E.B. White (1899-1985) is known by writers for his classic guide, *The
Elements of Style*, by children for his book, *Charlotte's Web*, and by
readers of *The New Yorker* for his brilliant essays. In this essay he
chronicles the passing of his pig, and manages to make it a sentimental telling even though he readily admits that his plan was to
"murder" the pig.

I spent several days and nights in mid-September with an ailing
pig and I feel driven to account for this stretch of time, more par-

ticularly since the pig died at last, and I lived, and things might
easily have gone the other way round and none left to do the accounting. Even now, so close to the event, I cannot recall the hours
sharply and am not ready to say whether death came on the third
night or the fourth night. This uncertainty afflicts me with a
sense of personal deterioration; if I were in decent health I would
know how many nights I had sat up with a pig. The scheme of
buying a spring pig in blossomtime, feeding it through summer
and fall, and butchering it when the solid cold weather arrives, is a
familiar scheme to me and follows an antique pattern. It is a
tragedy enacted on most farms with perfect fidelity to the original
script. The murder, being premeditated, is in the first degree but is
quick and skillful, and the smoked bacon and ham provide a cer-
emonial ending whose fitness is seldom questioned.

Once in a while something slips—one of the actors goes up in his
lines and the whole performance stumbles and halts. My pig
simply failed to show up for a meal. The alarm spread rapidly.
The classic outline of the tragedy was lost. I found myself cast
suddenly in the role of pig's friend and physician—a farcical
character with an enema bag for a prop. I had a presentiment, the
very first afternoon, that the play would never regain its balance
and that my sympathies were now wholly with the pig. This was
slapstick—the sort of dramatic treatment that instantly appealed
to my old dachshund, Fred, who joined the vigil, held the bag, and,
when all was over, presided at the interment. When we slid the
body into the grave, we both were shaken to the core. The loss we
felt was not the loss of ham but the loss of pig. He had evidently become precious to me, not that he represented a distant nourishment in a hungry time, but that he had suffered in a suffering
world. But I'm running ahead of my story and shall have to go
back. My pigpen is at the bottom of an old orchard below the
house. The pigs I have raised have lived in a faded building that
once was an icehouse. There is a pleasant yard to move about in,
shaded by an apple tree that overhangs the low rail fence. A pig
couldn't ask for anything better—or none has, at any rate. The
sawdust in the icehouse makes a comfortable bottom in which to
root, and a warm bed. This sawdust, however, came under suspicion when the pig took sick. One of my neighbors said he thought
the pig would have done better on new ground—the same principle that applies in planting potatoes. He said there might be
something unhealthy about that sawdust, that he never thought
well of sawdust. It was about four o'clock in the afternoon when I

first noticed that there was something wrong with the pig. He failed to appear at the trough for his supper, and when a pig (or a child) refuses supper a chill wave of fear runs through any household, or ice-household. After examining my pig, who was stretched out in the sawdust inside the building, I went to the phone and cranked it four times. Mr. Dameron answered. "What's good for a sick pig?" I asked. (There is never any identification needed on a country phone; the person on the other end knows who is talking by the sound of the voice and by the character of the question.)

"I don't know, I never had a sick pig," said Mr. Dameron, "but I can find out quick enough. You hang up and I'll call Henry."

Mr. Dameron was back on the line again in five minutes. "Henry says roll him over on his back and give him two ounces of castor oil or sweet oil, and if that doesn't do the trick give him an injection of soapy water. He says he's almost sure the pig's plugged up, and even if he's wrong, it can't do any harm." I thanked Mr. Dameron. I didn't go right down to the pig, though. I sank into a chair and sat still for a few minutes to think about my troubles, and then I got up and went to the barn, catching up on some odds and ends that needed tending to. Unconsciously I held off, for an hour, the deed by which I would officially recognize the collapse of the performance of raising a pig; I wanted no interruption in the regularity of feeding, the steadiness of growth, the even succession of days. I wanted no interruption, wanted no oil, no deviation. I just wanted to keep on raising a pig, full meal after full meal, spring into summer into fall. I didn't even know whether there were two ounces of castor oil on the place.

Shortly after five o'clock I remembered that we had been invited out to dinner that night and realized that if I were to dose a pig there was no time to lose. The dinner date seemed a familiar conflict: I move in a desultory society and often a week or two will roll by without my going to anybody's house to dinner or anyone's coming to mine, but when an occasion does arise, and I am summoned, something usually turns up (an hour or two in advance) to make all human intercourse seem vastly inappropriate. I have come to believe that there is in hostesses a special power of divination, and that they deliberately arrange dinners to coincide with pig failure or some other sort of failure. At any rate, it was after five o'clock and I knew I could put off no longer the evil hour.

When my son and I arrived at the pigyard, armed with a small bottle of castor oil and a length of clothesline, the pig had emerged from his house and was standing in the middle of his yard, listlessly. He gave us a slim greeting. I could see that he felt uncomfortable and uncertain. I had brought the clothesline thinking I'd have to tie him (the pig weighed more than a hundred pounds) but we never used it. My son reached down, grabbed both front legs, upset him quickly, and when he opened his mouth to scream I turned the oil into his throat—a pink, corrugated area I had never seen before. I had just time to read the label while the neck of the bottle was in his mouth. It said Puretest. The screams, slightly muffled by oil, were pitched in the hysterically high range of pig-sound, as though torture were being carried out, but they didn't last long: It was all over rather suddenly, and, his legs released, the pig righted himself.

In the upset position the corners of his mouth had been turned down, giving him a frowning expression. Back on his feet again, he regained the set smile that a pig wears even in sickness. He stood his ground, sucking slightly at the residue of oil; a few drops leaked out of his lips while his wicked eyes, shaded by their coy little lashes, turned on me in disgust and hatred. I scratched him gently with oily fingers and he remained quiet, as though trying to recall the satisfaction of being scratched when in health, and seeming to rehearse in his mind the indignity to which he had just been subjected. I noticed, as I stood there, four or five small dark spots on his back near the tail end, reddish brown in color, each about the size of a housefly. I could not make out what they were. They did not look troublesome but at the same time they did not look like mere surface bruises or chafe marks. Rather they seemed blemishes of internal origin. His stiff white bristles almost completely hid them and I had to part the bristles with my fingers to get a good look.

Several hours later, a few minutes before midnight, having dined well and at someone else's expense, I returned to the pighouse with a flashlight. The patient was asleep. Kneeling, I felt his ears (as you might put your hand on the forehead of a child) and they seemed cool, and then with the light made a careful examination of the yard and the house for sign that the oil had worked. I found none and went to bed.

We had been having an unseasonable spell of weather—hot, close days, with the fog shutting in every night, scaling for a few hours in midday, then creeping back again at dark, drifting in first over the trees on the point, then suddenly blowing across the fields, blotting out the world and taking possession of houses, men, and animals. Everyone kept hoping for a break, but the break failed to come. Next day was another hot one. I visited the pig before breakfast and tried to tempt him with a little milk in his trough. He just stared at it, while I made a sucking sound through my teeth to remind him of past pleasures of the feast. With very small, timid pigs, weanlings, this ruse is often quite successful and will encourage them to eat; but with a large, sick pig the ruse is senseless and the sound I made must have made him feel, if anything, more miserable. He not only did not crave food, he felt a positive revulsion to it. I found a place under the apple tree where he had vomited in the night.

At this point, although a depression had settled over me, I didn't suppose that I was going to lose my pig. From the lustiness of a healthy pig a man derives a feeling of personal lustiness; the stuff that goes into the trough and is received with such enthusiasm is an earnest of some later feast of his own, and when this suddenly comes to an end and the food lies stale and untouched, souring in the sun, the pig's imbalance becomes the man's, vicariously, and life seems insecure, displaced, transitory.

As my own spirits declined, along with the pig's, the spirits of my vile old dachshund rose. The frequency of our trips down the footpath through the orchard to the pigyard delighted him, although he suffers greatly from arthritis, moves with difficulty, and would be bedridden if he could find anyone willing to serve him meals on a tray.

He never missed a chance to visit the pig with me, and he made many professional calls on his own. You could see him down there at all hours, his white face parting the grass along the fence as he wobbled and stumbled about, his stethoscope dangling—a happy quack, writing his villainous prescriptions and grinning his corrosive grin. When the enema bag appeared, and the bucket of warm suds, his happiness was complete, and he managed to squeeze his enormous body between the two lowest rails of the yard and then assumed full charge of the irrigation. Once, when I lowered the bag to check the flow, he reached in and hurriedly drank a few mouthfuls of the suds to test their potency. I have noticed that Fred will feverishly consume any substance that is associated with trouble—the bitter flavor is to his liking. When the bag was above reach, he concentrated on the pig and was everywhere at once, a tower of strength and inconvenience. The pig, curiously enough, stood rather quietly through this colonic carnival, and the enema, though ineffective, was not as difficult as I had anticipated.

I discovered, though, that once having given a pig an enema there is no turning back, no chance of resuming one of life's more stereotyped roles. The pig's lot and mine were inextricably bound now, as though the rubber tube were the silver cord. From then until the time of his death I held the pig steadily on the bowl of my mind; the task of trying to deliver him from his misery became a strong obsession. His suffering soon became the embodiment of all earthly wretchedness. Along toward the end of the afternoon, defeated in physicking, I phoned the veterinary twenty miles away and placed the case formally in his hands. He was full of questions, and when I casually mentioned the dark spots on the pig's back, his voice changed its tone.

"I don't want to scare you," he said, "but when there are spots, erysipelas has to be considered."

Together we considered erysipelas, with frequent interruptions from the telephone operator, who wasn't sure the connection had been established.

"If a pig has erysipelas can he give it to a person?" I asked.

"Yes, he can," replied the vet.

"Have they answered?" asked the operator.

"Yes, they have," I said. Then I addressed the vet again.

"You better come over here and examine this pig right away."

"I can't come myself," said the vet, "but McFarland can come this evening if that's all right. Mac knows more about pigs than I do anyway. You needn't worry too much about the spots. To indicate erysipelas they would have to be deep hemorrhagic infarcts."

"Deep hemorrhagic what?" I asked.

"Infarcts," said the vet.

"Have they answered?" asked the operator.

"Well," I said, "I don't know what you'd call these spots, except they're about the size of a housefly. If the pig has erysipelas I guess I have it, too, by this time, because we've been very close lately."

"McFarland will be over," said the vet. I hung up. My throat felt dry and I went to the cupboard and got a bottle of whiskey. Deep hemorrhagic infarcts—the phrase began fastening its hooks in my head. I had assumed that there could be nothing much wrong with a pig during the months it was being groomed for murder; my confidence in the essential health and endurance of pigs had been strong and deep, particularly in the health of pigs that belonged to me and that were part of my proud scheme. The awakening had been violent and I minded it all the more because I knew that what could be true of my pig could be true also of the rest of my tidy world. I tried to put this distasteful idea from me, but it kept recurring. I took a short drink of the whiskey and then, although I wanted to go down to the yard and look for fresh signs, I was scared to. I was certain I had erysipelas. It was long after dark and the supper dishes had been put away when a car drove in and McFarland got out. He had a girl with him. I could just make her out in the darkness—she seemed young and pretty. "This is Miss Owen," he said. "We've been having a picnic supper on the shore, that's why I'm late." McFarland stood in the driveway and stripped off his jacket, then his shirt. His stocky arms and capable hands showed up in my flashlight's gleam as I helped him find his coverall and get zipped up. The rear seat of his car contained an astonishing amount of paraphernalia, which he soon overhauled, selecting a chain, a syringe, a bottle of oil, a rubber tube, and some other things I couldn't identify. Miss Owen said she'd go along with us and see the pig. I led the way down the warm slope of the orchard, my light picking out the path for them, and we all climbed the fence, entered the pighouse, and squatted by the pig while McFarland took a rectal reading. My flashlight picked up the glitter of an engagement ring on the girl's hand.

"No elevation," said McFarland, twisting the thermometer in the light. "You needn't worry about erysipelas." He ran his hand slowly over the pig's stomach and at one point the pig cried out in pain. "Poor piggledy-wiggledy!" said Miss Owen. The treatment I had been giving the pig for two days was then repeated, somewhat more expertly, by the doctor, Miss Owen and I handing him things as he needed them—holding the chain that he had looped around the pig's upper jaw, holding the syringe, holding the bottle stopper, the end of the tube, all of us working in darkness and in comfort, working with the instinctive teamwork induced by emergency conditions, the pig unprotesting, the house shadowy, protecting, intimate. I went to bed tired but with a feeling of relief that I had turned over part of the responsibility of the case to a licensed doctor. I was beginning to think, though, that the pig was not going to live.

He died twenty-four hours later, or it might have been forty-eight—there is a blur in time here, and I may have lost or picked up a day in the telling and the pig one in the dying. At intervals during the last day I took cool fresh water down to him and at such times as he found the strength to get to his feet he would stand with head in the pail and snuffle his snout around. He drank a few sips but no more; yet it seemed to comfort him to dip his nose in water and bobble it about, sucking in and blowing out through his teeth. Much of the time, now, he lay indoors half buried in sawdust. Once, near the last, while I was attending him I saw him try to make a bed for himself but he lacked the strength, and when he set his snout into the dust he was unable to plow even the little furrow he needed to lie down in.

He came out of the house to die. When I went down, before going to bed, he lay stretched in the yard a few feet from the door. I knelt, saw that he was dead, and left him there: His face had a mild look, expressive neither of deep peace nor of deep suffering, although I think he had suffered a good deal. I went back up to the house and to bed, and cried internally—deep hemorrhagic in tears. I didn't wake till nearly eight the next morning, and when I looked out the open window the grave was already being dug, down beyond the dump under a wild apple. I could hear the spade strike against the small rocks that blocked the way. Never send to know for whom the grave is dug, I said to myself, it's dug for thee. Fred, I well knew, was supervising the work of digging, so I ate breakfast slowly.

It was a Saturday morning. The thicket in which I found the gravediggers at work was dark and warm, the sky overcast. Here, among alders and young hackmatacks, at the foot of the apple tree, Lennie had dug a beautiful hole, five feet long, three feet wide, three feet deep. He was standing in it, removing the last spadefuls of earth while Fred patrolled the brink in simple but impressive circles, disturbing the loose earth of the mound so that it trickled back in. There had been no rain in weeks and the soil, even three feet down, was dry and powdery. As I stood and stared, an enormous earthworm which had been partially exposed by the spade at the bottom dug itself deeper and made a slow withdrawal, seeking even remoter moistures at even lonelier depths. And just as Lennie stepped out and rested his spade against the tree and lit a cigarette, a small green apple separated itself from a branch overhead and fell into the hole. Everything about this last scene seemed overwritten—the dismal sky, the shabby woods, the imminence of rain, the worm (legendary bedfellow of the dead), the apple (conventional garnish of a pig). But even so, there was a directness and dispatch about animal burial, I thought, that made it a more decent affair than human burial: There was no stopover in the undertaker's foul parlor, no wreath nor spray; and when we hitched a line to the pig's hind legs and dragged him swiftly from his yard, throwing our weight into the harness and leaving a wake of crushed grass and smoothed rubble over the dump, ours was a businesslike procession, with Fred, the dishonorable pall-bearer, staggering along in the rear, his perverse bereavement showing in every seam in his face; and the postmortem performed handily and swiftly right at the edge of the grave, so that the inwards that had caused the pig's death preceded him into the ground and he lay at last resting squarely on the cause of his own undoing.

I threw in the first shovelful, and then we worked rapidly and without talk, until the job was complete. I picked up the rope, made it fast to Fred's collar (he is a notorious ghoul), and we all three filed back up the path to the house, Fred bringing up the rear and holding back every inch of the way, feigning unusual stiffness. I noticed that although he weighed far less than the pig, he was harder to drag, being possessed of the vital spark. The news of the death of my pig traveled fast and far, and I received many expressions of sympathy from friends and neighbors, for no one took the event lightly and the premature expiration of a pig is, I soon discovered, a departure which the community marks solemnly on its calendar, a sorrow in which it feels fully involved. I have written this account in penitence and in grief, as a man who failed to raise his pig, and to explain my deviation from the classic course of so many raised pigs. The grave in the woods is unmarked, but Fred can direct the mourner to it unerringly and with immense good will, and I know he and I shall often revisit it, singly and together, in seasons of reflection and despair, on flag-less memorial days of our own choosing.

Edith Wharton

THE VALLEY OF CHILDISH THINGS

Edith Wharton (1862-1937) began her life as the daughter of wealthy New York socialites, who expected her to become one herself. She performed as required for a time, but became bored with social obligations. Around the turn of the century, she disappointed her family by becoming a writer. Her first novel, The House of Mirth (1905), established her as one of America's finest writers. As you read this story, see if you can guess how Wharton's family might have reacted to it.

Once upon a time a number of children lived together in the Valley of Childish Things, playing all manner of delightful games, and studying the same lesson books. But one day a little girl, one of their number, decided that it was time to see something of the world about which the lesson books had taught her; and as none of the other children cared to leave their games, she set out alone to climb the pass which led out of the valley.

It was a hard climb, but at length she reached a cold, bleak tableland beyond the mountains. Here she saw cities and men, and learned many useful arts, and in so doing grew to be a woman. But the tableland was bleak and cold, and when she had served her apprenticeship she decided to return to her old companions in the Valley of Childish Things, and work with them instead of with strangers.

It was a weary way back, and her feet were bruised by the stones, and her face was beaten by the weather; but halfway down the pass she met a man, who kindly helped her over the roughest places. Like herself, he was lame and weather-beaten; but as soon as he spoke she recognized him as one of her old playmates. He too had been out in the world, and was going back to the valley; and on the way they talked together of the work they meant to do there. He had been a dull boy, and she had never taken much notice of him; but as she listened to his plans for building bridges and draining swamps and cutting roads through the jungle, she thought to herself, "Since he has grown into such a fine fellow, what splendid men and women my other playmates must have become!"

But what was her surprise to find, on reaching the valley, that her former companions, instead of growing into men and women, had all remained little children. Most of them were playing the same old games, and the few who affected to be working were engaged in such strenuous occupations as building mudpies and sailing paper boats in basins. As for the lad who had been the favorite companion of her studies, he was playing marbles with all the youngest boys in the valley.

At first the children seemed glad to have her back, but soon she saw that her presence interfered with their games; and when she tried to tell them of the great things that were being done on the tableland beyond the mountains, they picked up their toys and went farther down the valley to play.

Then she turned to her fellow traveler, who was the only grown man in the valley; but he was on his knees before a dear little girl with blue eyes and a coral necklace, for whom he was making a garden out of cockleshells and bits of glass and broken flowers stuck in sand.

The little girl was clapping her hands and crowing (she was too young to speak articulately); and when she who had grown to be a woman laid her hand on the man's shoulder, and asked him if he did not want to set to work with her building bridges, draining swamps, and cutting roads through the jungle, he replied that at that particular moment he was too busy.

And as she turned away, he added in the kindest possible way, "Really, my dear, you ought to have taken better care of your complexion."

Chapter 3: Changing Perspectives on Women

Mary Wollstonecraft

From A VINDICATION OF THE RIGHTS OF WOMAN

Mary Wollstonecraft (1759-1797), a novelist and translator, helped found the feminist movement with the publication in 1792 of *A Vindication of the Rights of Woman*. Unfortunately, after her death, when her husband published the details of their passionate pre-marital affair, her work was largely discredited. Wollstonecraft was not given the recognition she deserved until over a century later. As you read the excerpt, ask yourself if any of Wollstonecraft's complaints about the condition of women are still relevant today.

After considering the historic page, and viewing the living world with anxious solicitude, the most melancholy emotions of sorrowful indignation have depressed my spirits, and I have sighed when obliged to confess, that either nature has made a great difference between man and man, or that the civilization which has hitherto taken place in the world has been very partial. I have turned over various books written on the subject of education, and patiently observed the conduct of parents and the management of schools; but what has been the result?—a profound conviction that the neglected education of my fellow-creatures is the grand source of the misery I deplore; and that women, in particular, are rendered weak and wretched by a variety of concurring causes, originating from one hasty conclusion. The conduct and manners of women, in fact, evidently prove that their minds are not in a healthy state; for, like the flowers which are planted in too rich a soil, strength and usefulness are sacrificed to beauty; and the flaunting leaves, after having pleased a fastidious eye, fade, disregarded on the stalk, long before the season when they ought to have arrived at maturity. One cause of this barren blooming I attribute to a false system of education, gathered from the books written on this sub-ject by men who, considering females rather as women than hu-man creatures, have been more anxious to make them alluring mistresses than affectionate wives and rational mothers; and the understanding of the sex has been so bubbled by this specious homage, that the civilized women of the present century, with a few exceptions, are only anxious to inspire love, when they ought to cherish a nobler ambition, and by their abilities and virtues ex-act respect. In a treatise, therefore, on female rights and manners, the works which have been particularly written for their im-provement must not be overlooked; especially when it is asserted, in direct terms, that the minds of women are enfeebled by false refinement; that the books of instruction, written by men of ge-nius, have had the same tendency as more frivolous productions; and that, in the true style of Mahometanism, they are treated as a kind of subordinate beings, and not as a part of the human species, when improvable reason is allowed to be the dignified distinction which raises men above the brute creation, and puts a natural sceptre in a feeble hand.

Yet, because I am a woman, I would not lead my readers to sup-pose that I mean violently to agitate the contested question re-specting the equality or inferiority of the sex; but as the subject lies in my way, and I cannot pass it over without subjecting the main tendency of my reasoning to misconstruction, I shall stop a mo-ment to deliver, in a few words, my opinion.—In the government of the physical world it is observable that the female in point of strength is, in general, inferior to the male. This is the law of na-ture; and it does not appear to be suspended or abrogated in favour

1st Point

of woman. A degree of physical superiority cannot, therefore, be denied—and it is a noble prerogative! But not content with this natural pre-eminence, men endeavour to sink us still lower, merely to render us alluring objects for a moment; and women, intoxicated by the adoration which men, under the influence of their senses, pay them, do not seek to obtain a durable interest in their hearts, or to become the friends of the fellow creatures who find amusement in their society. I am aware of an obvious inference:—from every quarter have I heard exclamations against masculine women; but where are they to be found? If by this appellation men mean to inveigh against their ardour in hunting, shooting, and gaming, I shall most cordially join in the cry; but if it be against the imitation of many virtues, or, more properly speaking, the attainment of those talents and virtues, the exercise of which ennobles the human character, and which raise females in the scale of animal being, when they are comprehensively termed mankind, all those who view them with a philosophic eye must, I should think, wish with me, that they may every day grow more and more masculine. This discussion naturally divides the subject. I shall first consider women in the grand light of human creatures, who, in common with men, are placed on this earth to unfold their faculties; and afterwards I shall more particularly point out their peculiar designation. I wish also to steer clear of an error which many respectable writers have fallen into; for the instruction which has hitherto been addressed to women, has rather been applicable to *ladies,* if the little indirect advice, that is scattered through Sandford and Merton, be excepted; but, addressing my sex in a firmer tone, I pay particular attention to those in the middle class, because they appear to be in the most natural state.

Perhaps the seeds of false refinement, immorality, and vanity, have ever been shed by the great. Weak, artificial beings, raised above the common wants and affections of their race, in a premature unnatural manner, undermine the very foundation of virtue, and spread corruption through the whole mass of society! As a class of mankind they have the strongest claim to pity; the education of the rich tends to render them vain and helpless, and the unfolding mind is not strengthened by the practice of those duties which dignify the human character.—They only live to amuse themselves, and by the same law which in nature invariably produces certain effects, they soon only afford barren amusement.

But as I purpose taking a separate view of the different ranks of society, and of the moral character of women, in each, this hint is, for the present, sufficient, and I have only alluded to the subject, because it appears to me to be the very essence of an introduction to give a cursory account of the contents of the work it introduces. My own sex, I hope, will excuse me, if I treat them like rational creatures, instead of flattering their fascinating graces, and viewing them as if they were in a state of perpetual childhood, unable to stand alone. I earnestly wish to point out in what true dignity and human happiness consists—I wish to persuade women to endeavour to acquire strength, both of mind and body, and to convince them that the soft phrases, susceptibility of heart, delicacy of sentiment, and refinement of taste, are almost synonymous with epithets of weakness, and that those beings who are only the objects of pity and that kind of love, which has been termed its sister, will soon become objects of contempt. Dismissing then those pretty feminine phrases, which the men condescendingly use to soften our slavish dependence, and despising that weak elegancy of mind, exquisite sensibility, and sweet docility of manners, supposed to be the sexual characteristics of the weaker vessel, I wish to shew that elegance is inferior to virtue, that the first object of laudable ambition is to obtain a character as a human being, regardless of the distinction of sex; and that secondary views should be brought to this simple touchstone. This is a rough sketch of my plan; and should I express my conviction with the energetic emotions that I feel whenever I think of the subject, the dictates of experience and reflection will be felt by some of my readers. Animated by this important object, I shall disdain to cull my phrases or polish my style,—I aim at being useful, and sincerity will render me unaffected; for, wishing rather to persuade by the force of my arguments, than dazzle by the elegance of my language, I shall not waste my time in rounding periods, or in fabricating the turgid bombast of artificial feelings, which, coming from the head, never reach the heart. I shall be employed about things, not words!—and, anxious to render my sex more respectable members of society, I shall try to avoid that flowery diction which has slided from essays into novels, and from novels into familiar letters and conversation

These pretty superlatives, dropping glibly from the tongue, vitiate the taste, and create a kind of sickly delicacy that turns away from simple unadorned truth; and a deluge of false sentiments and overstretched feelings, stifling the natural emotions of the heart, render the domestic pleasures insipid, that ought to sweeten the exercise of those severe duties which educate a rational and immortal being for a nobler field of action. The education of women has, of late, been more attended to than formerly; yet they are still reckoned a frivolous sex, and ridiculed or pitied by the writers who endeavour by satire or instruction to improve them. It is acknowledged that they spend many of the first years of their lives in acquiring a smattering of accomplishments; meanwhile strength of body and mind are sacrificed to libertine notions of beauty, to the desire of establishing themselves,—the only way women can rise in the world,—by marriage. And this desire making mere animals of them when they marry they act as such children may be expected to act:—they dress; they paint, and nickname God's creatures.—Surely these weak beings are only fit for a seraglio!—Can they be expected to govern a family with judgment, or take care of the poor babes whom they bring into the world? If then it can be fairly deduced from the present conduct of the sex, from the prevalent fondness for pleasure which takes place of ambition and those nobler passions that open and enlarge the soul, that the instruction which women have hitherto received has only tended, with the constitution of civil society, to render them insignificant objects of desire—mere propagators of fools!—if it can be proved that in aiming to accomplish them, without cultivating their understandings, they are taken out of their sphere of duties, and made ridiculous and useless when the short-lived bloom of beauty is over, I presume that *rational* men will excuse me for endeavouring to persuade them to become more masculine and respectable. Indeed the word masculine is only a bugbear: there is little reason to fear that women will acquire too much courage or fortitude; for their apparent inferiority with respect to bodily strength, must render them, in some degree, dependent on men in the various relations of life, but why should it be increased by prejudices that give a sex to virtue, and confound simple truths with sensual reveries? Women are, in fact, so much degraded by mistaken notions of female excellence, that I do not mean to add a paradox when I assert, that this artificial weakness produces a propensity to tyrannize, and gives birth to cunning, the natural opponent of strength, which leads them to play off those contemptible infantine airs that undermine esteem even whilst they excite desire. Let men become more chaste and modest, and if women do not grow wiser in the same ratio it will be clear that they have weaker understandings. It seems scarcely

necessary to say, that I now speak of the sex in general. Many individuals have more sense than their male relatives, and, as
nothing preponderates where there is a constant struggle for an
equilibrium, without it has naturally more gravity, some women
govern their husbands without degrading themselves, because
intellect will always govern.

John Stuart Mill

From THE SUBJECTION OF WOMEN

John Stuart Mill (1806-1873), philosopher and political economist,
was given an accelerated education by his father James Mill, an important utilitarian thinker. Later in life, he departed from his father's
philosophy, and generated many important works of his own. In this
selection, Mill describes his theory of the cause of the subjection of
women. He must make a lengthy argument to dismiss the idea that
the subordination of women to men reflects the natural order of
things. His explanation of why women continue to be suppressed continues to have value today. As you read this piece, pay special attention to the rights Mill seeks for women, and how they differ from those
Wollstonecraft sought for women half a century earlier.

The object of this Essay is to explain as clearly as I am able, the
grounds of an opinion which I have held from the very earliest
period when I had formed any opinions at all on social or political
matters, and which, instead of being weakened or modified, has
been constantly growing stronger by the progress of reflection and
the experience of life: That the principle which regulates the existing social relations between the two sexes—the legal subordination of one sex to the other—is wrong in itself, and now one of
the chief hindrances to human improvement; and that it ought to
be replaced by a principle of perfect equality, admitting no power
or privilege on the one side, nor disability on the other. . . .

Some will object, that a comparison cannot fairly be made between the government of the male sex and the forms of unjust
power which I have adduced in illustration of it, since these are
arbitrary, and the effect of mere usurpation, while it on the con-

trary is natural. But was there ever any domination which did not appear natural to those who possessed it? There was a time when the division of mankind into two classes, a small one of masters and a numerous one of slaves, appeared, even to the most cultivated minds, to be a natural, and the only natural, condition of the human race. No less an intellect, and one which contributed no less to the progress of human thought, than Aristotle, held this opinion without doubt or misgiving; and rested it on the same premises on which the same assertion in regard to the dominion of men over women is usually based, namely that there are different natures among mankind, free natures, and slave natures; that the Greeks were of a free nature, the barbarian races of Thracians and Asiatics of a slave nature. But why need I go back to Aristotle? Did not the slaveowners of the Southern United States maintain the same doctrine, with all the fanaticism with which men cling to the theories that justify their passions and legitimate their personal interests? Did they not call heaven and earth to witness that the dominion of the white man over the black is natural, that the black race is by nature incapable of freedom, and marked out for slavery? some even going so far as to say that the freedom of manual laborers is an unnatural order of things anywhere. Again, the theorists of absolute monarchy have always affirmed it to be the only natural form of government; issuing from the patriarchal, which was the primitive and spontaneous form of society, framed on the model of the paternal, which is anterior to society itself, and, as they contend, the most natural authority of all. Nay, for that matter, the law of force itself, to those who could not plead any other, has always seemed the most natural of all grounds for the exercise of authority. Conquering races hold it to be Nature's own dictate that the conquered should obey the conquerors or, as they euphoniously paraphrase it, that the feebler and more unwarlike races should submit to the braver and manlier. The smallest acquaintance with human life in the middle ages, shows how supremely natural the dominion of the feudal nobility over men of low condition appeared to the nobility themselves, and how unnatural the conception seemed, of a person of the inferior class claiming equality with them, or exercising authority over them. It hardly seemed less so to the class held in subjection. The emancipated serfs and burgesses, even in their most vigorous struggles, never made any pretension to a share of authority; they only demanded more or less of limitation to the power of tyrannizing over them. So true is it that unnatural generally means only uncustomary, and that everything which is usual appears natural. The subjection of women to men being a universal custom, any departure from it quite naturally appears unnatural. But how entirely, even in this case, the feeling Is dependent on custom, appears by ample experience. Nothing so much astonishes the people of distant parts of the world, when they first learn anything about England, as to be told that it is under a queen: the thing seems to them so unnatural as to be almost incredible. To Englishmen this does not seem in the least degree unnatural, because they are used to it; but they do feel it unnatural that women should be soldiers or members of Parliament. In the feudal ages, on the contrary, war and politics were not thought unnatural to women, because not unusual; it seemed natural that women of the privileged classes should be of manly character, inferior in nothing but bodily strength to their husbands and fathers. The independence of women seemed rather less unnatural to the Greeks than to other ancients, on account of the fabulous Amazons (whom they believed to be historical), and the partial example afforded by the Spartan women; who, though no less subordinate by law than in other Greek states, were more free in fact, and being trained to bodily exercises in the same manner with men, gave ample proof that they were not naturally disqualified for them. There can be little doubt that Spartan experience suggested to Plato, among many other of his doctrines, that of the social and political equality of the two sexes. But, it will be said, the rule of men over women differs from all these others in not being a rule of force: it is accepted voluntarily; women make no complaint, and are consenting parties to it. In the first place, a great number of women do not accept it. Ever since there have been women able to make their sentiments known by their writings (the only mode of publicity which society permits to them), an increasing number of them have recorded protests against their present social condition: and recently many thousands of them, headed by the most eminent women known to the public, have petitioned Parliament for their admission to the Parliamentary Suffrage. The claim of women to be educated as solidly, and in the same branches of knowledge, as men, is urged with growing intensity, and with a great prospect of success; while the demand for their admission into professions and occupations hitherto closed against them, becomes every year more urgent. Though there are not in this country, as there are in the United States, periodical Conventions and an organized party to agitate for the Rights of

Women, there is a numerous and active Society organized and
managed by women, for the more limited object of obtaining the
political franchise. Nor is it only in our own country and in
America that women are beginning to protest, more or less collectively, against the disabilities under which they labor. France, and
Italy, and Switzerland, and Russia now afford examples of the
same thing. How many more women there are who silently
cherish similar aspirations, no one can possibly know; but there
are abundant tokens how many *would* cherish them, were they
not so strenuously taught to repress them as contrary to the pro-
prieties of their sex. It must be remembered, also, that no enslaved
class ever asked for complete liberty at once. When Simon de
Montforts called the deputies of the commons to sit for the first
time in Parliament, did any of them dream of demanding that an
assembly, elected by their constituents, should make and destroy
ministries, and dictate to the king in affairs of state? No such
thought entered into the imagination of the most ambitious of
them. The nobility had already these pretensions; the commons
pretended to nothing but to be exempt from arbitrary taxation,
and from the gross individual oppression of the king's officers. It is
a political law of nature that those who are under any power of
ancient origin, never begin by complaining of the power itself, but
only of its oppressive exercise. There is never any want of women
who complain of ill usage by their husbands. There would be infinitely more, if complaint were not the greatest of all provocatives
to a repetition and increase of the ill usage. It is this which frus-
trates all attempts to maintain the power but protect the woman
against its abuses. In no other case (except that of a child) is the
person who has been proved judicially to have suffered an injury,
replaced under the physical power of the culprit who inflicted it.
Accordingly wives, even in the most extreme and protracted cases
of bodily ill usage, hardly ever dare avail themselves of the laws
made for their protection: and if, in a moment of irrepressible
indignation, or by the interference of neighbors, they are induced
to do so, their whole effort afterward is to disclose as little as they
can, and to beg off their tyrant from his merited chastisement.

All causes, social and natural, combine to make it unlikely that
women should be collectively rebellious to the power of men. They
are so far in a position different from all other subject classes, that
their masters require something more from them than actual
service. Men do not want solely the obedience of women, they
want their sentiments. All men, except the most brutish, desire to

have, in the woman most nearly connected with them, not a forced slave but a willing one, not a slave merely, but a favorite. They have therefore put everything in practice to enslave their minds. The masters of all other slaves rely, for maintaining obedience, on fear; either fear of themselves or religious fears. The masters of women wanted more than simple obedience, and they turned the whole force of education to effect their purpose. All women are brought up from the very earliest years in the belief that their ideal of character is the very opposite to that of men; not self-will, and government by self-control but submission, and yielding to the control of others. All the moralities tell them that it is the duty of women, and all the current sentimentalities that it is their nature, to live for others, to make complete abnegation of themselves, and to have no life but in their affections. And by their affections are meant the only ones they are allowed to have—those to the men with whom they are connected, or to the children who constitute an additional and indefeasible tie between them and a man. When we put together three things—first, the natural attraction between opposite sexes; secondly, the wife's entire dependence on the husband, every privilege or pleasure she has being either his gift, or depending entirely on his will; and lastly, that the principal object of human pursuit, consideration, and all objects of social ambition, can in general be sought or obtained by her only through him, it would be a miracle if the object of being attractive to men had not become the polar star of feminine education and formation of character. And, this great means of influence over the minds of women having been acquired, an instinct of selfishness made men avail themselves of it to the utmost as a means of holding women in subjection, by representing to them meekness, submissiveness, and resignation of all individual will into the hands of a man, as an essential part of sexual attractiveness. Can it be doubted that any of the other yokes which mankind have succeeded in breaking, would have subsisted till now if the same means had existed, and had been as sedulously used, to bow down their minds to it? If it had been made the object of the life of every young plebeian to find personal favor in the eyes of some patrician, of every young serf with some seigneur; if domestication with him, and a share of his personal affections, had been held out as the prize which they all should look out for, the most gifted and aspiring being able to reckon on the most desirable prizes; and if, when this prize had been obtained, they had been shut out by a wall of brass from all interests not centering in him, all feelings and desires but those which he shared or inculcated; would not serfs and seigneurs, plebeians and patricians, have been as broadly distinguished at this day as men and women are? and would not all but a thinker here and there, have believed the distinction to be a fundamental and unalterable fact in human nature?

The preceding considerations are amply sufficient to show that custom, however universal it may be, affords in this case no presumption, and ought not to create any prejudice, in favor of the arrangements which place women in social and political subjection to men. But I may go farther, and maintain that the course of history, and the tendencies of progressive human society, afford not only no presumption in favor of this system of inequality of rights, but a strong one against it; and that, so far as the whole course of human improvement up to this time, the whole stream of modern tendencies, warrants any inference on the subject, it is, that this relic of the past is discordant with the future, and must necessarily disappear.

For, what is the peculiar character of the modern world—the difference which chiefly distinguishes modern institutions, modern social ideas, modern life itself, from those of times long past? It is, that human beings are no longer born to their place in life, and chained down by an inexorable bond to the place they are born to, but are free to employ their faculties, and such favourable chances as offer, to achieve the lot which may appear to them most desirable.

Elizabeth Cady Stanton

DECLARATION OF SENTIMENTS AND RESOLUTIONS

Elizabeth Cady Stanton (1815-1902) lead the women's movement in the United States in the 19th century. She was an organizer of the Seneca Falls Convention in 1848, where this declaration and resolutions were adopted. The convention has come to be recognized as the start of the women's movement in America, and many similar conventions were held until women finally gained suffrage in 1920. The

Declaration imitates the Declaration of Independence because at the time, opponents of the women's movement liked to quote the line, "all *men* are created equal." As you read this selection, think about how often the use of the word, "men" to mean "people" can cause confusion and misinterpretation.

When, in the course of human events, it becomes necessary for one portion of the family of man to assume among the people of the earth a position different from that which they have hitherto occupied, but one to which the laws of nature and of nature's God entitle them, a decent respect to the opinions of mankind requires that they should declare the causes that impel them to such a course.

We hold these truths to be self-evident: that all men and women are created equal; that they are endowed by their Creator with certain inalienable rights; that among these are life, liberty, and the pursuit of happiness; that to secure these rights governments are instituted, deriving their just powers from the consent of the governed. Whenever any form of government becomes destructive of these ends, it is the right of those who suffer from it to refuse allegiance to it, and to insist upon the institution of a new government, laying its foundation on such principles, and organizing its powers in such form, as to them shall seem most likely to effect their safety and happiness. Prudence, indeed, will dictate that governments long established should not be changed for light and transient causes; and accordingly all experience hath shown that mankind are more disposed to suffer, while evils are sufferable, than to right themselves by abolishing the forms to which they were accustomed. But when a long train of abuses and usurpations, pursuing invariably the same object, evinces a design to reduce them under absolute despotism, it is their duty to throw off such government, and to provide new guards for their future security. Such has been the patient sufferance of the women under this government, and such is now the necessity which constrains them to demand the equal station to which they are entitled.

The history of mankind is a history of repeated injuries and usurpations on the part of man toward woman, having in direct object the establishment of an absolute tyranny over her. To prove this, let facts be submitted to a candid world.

He has never permitted her to exercise her inalienable right to the elective franchise.

He has compelled her to submit to laws, in the formation of which she had no voice.

He has withheld from her rights which are given to the most ignorant and degraded men—both natives and foreigners.

Having deprived her of this first right of a citizen, the elective franchise, thereby leaving her without representation in the halls of legislation, he has oppressed her on all sides.

He has made her, if married, in the eye of the law, civilly dead. He has taken from her all right in property, even to the wages she earns.

He has made her, morally, an irresponsible being, as she can commit many crimes with impunity, provided they be done in the presence of her husband. In the covenant of marriage, she is compelled to promise obedience to her husband, he becoming to all intents and purposes, her master—the law giving him power to deprive her of her liberty, and to administer chastisement.

He has so framed the laws of divorce, as to what shall be the proper causes, and in case of separation, to whom the guardianship of the children shall be given, as to be wholly regardless of the happiness of women—the law, in all cases, going upon a false supposition of the supremacy of man, and giving all power into his hands.

After depriving her of all rights as a married woman, if single, and the owner of property, he has taxed her to support a government which recognizes her only when her property can be made profitable to it.

He has monopolized nearly all the profitable employments, and from those she is permitted to follow, she receives but a scanty remuneration. He closes against her all the avenues to wealth and distinction which he considers most honorable to himself. As a teacher of theology, medicine, or law, she is not known.

He has denied her the facilities for obtaining a thorough education, all colleges being closed against her.

He allows her in Church, as well as State, but a subordinate position, claiming Apostolic authority for her exclusion from the ministry, and, with some exceptions, from any public participation in the affairs of the Church.

He has created a false public sentiment by giving to the world a different code of morals for men and women, by which moral delinquencies which exclude women from society, are not only tolerated, but deemed of little account in man.

He has usurped the prerogative of Jehovah himself, claiming it as his right to assign for her a sphere of action, when that belongs to her conscience and to her God.

He has endeavored, in every way that he could, to destroy her confidence in her own powers, to lessen her self-respect, and to make her willing to lead a dependent and abject life.

Now, in view of this entire disfranchisement of one-half the people of this country, their social and religious degradation—in view of the unjust laws above mentioned, and because women do feel themselves aggrieved, oppressed, and fraudulently deprived of their most sacred rights, we insist that they have immediate admission to all the rights and privileges which belong to them as citizens of the United States.

In entering upon the great work before us, we anticipate no small amount of misconception, misrepresentation, and ridicule; but we shall use every instrumentality within our power to effect our object. We shall employ agents, circulate tracts, petition the State and National legislatures, and endeavor to enlist the pulpit and the press in our behalf. We hope this Convention will be followed by a series of Conventions embracing every part of this country.

[The following resolutions were discussed by Lucretia Mott, Thomas and Mary Ann McClintock, Amy Post, Catharine A. F. Stebbins, and others, and were adopted:]

Whereas, The great precept of nature is conceded to be, that "man shall pursue his own true and substantial happiness." Blackstone in his Commentaries remarks, that this law of Nature being coeval with mankind, and dictated by God himself, is of course superior in obligation to any other. It is binding over all the globe, in all countries, and at all times; no human laws are of any validity if contrary to this, and such of them as are valid, derive all their force, and all their validity, and all their authority, mediately and immediately, from this original; therefore,

Resolved, That such laws as conflict, in any way, with the true and substantial happiness of woman, are contrary to the great precept of nature and of no validity, for this is "superior in obligation to any other."

Resolved, That all laws which prevent woman from occupying such a station in society as her conscience shall dictate, or which place her in a position inferior to that of man, are contrary to the great precept of nature, and therefore of no force or authority.

Resolved, That woman is man's equal—was intended to be so by the Creator, and the highest good of the race demands that she should be recognized as such.

Resolved, That the women of this country ought to be enlightened in regard to the laws under which they live, that they may no longer publish their degradation by declaring themselves satisfied with their present position, nor their ignorance, by asserting that they have all the rights they want.

Resolved, That inasmuch as man, while claiming for himself intellectual superiority, does accord to woman moral superiority, it is preeminently his duty to encourage her to speak and teach, as she has an opportunity, in all religious assemblies.

Resolved, That the same amount of virtue, delicacy, and refinement of behavior that is required of woman in the social state, should also be required of man, and the same transgressions should be visited with equal severity on both man and woman.

Resolved, That the objection of indelicacy and impropriety, which is so often brought against woman when she addresses a public audience, comes with a very ill-grace from those who encourage, by their attendance, her appearance on the stage, in the concert, or in feats of the circus.

Resolved, That woman has too long rested satisfied in the circumscribed limits which corrupt customs and a perverted application of the Scriptures have marked out for her, and that it is time she should move in the enlarged sphere which her great Creator has assigned her.

Resolved, That it is the duty of the women of this country to secure to themselves their sacred right to the elective franchise.

Resolved, That the equality of human rights results necessarily from the fact of the identity of the race in capabilities and responsibilities.

Resolved, therefore, That, being invested by the Creator with the same capabilities, and the same consciousness of responsibility for their exercise, it is demonstrably the right and duty of woman, equally with man, to promote every righteous cause by every righteous means; and especially in regard to the great subjects of morals and religion, it is self-evidently her right to participate with her brother in teaching them, both in private and in public, by writing and by speaking, by any instrumentalities proper to be used, and in any assemblies proper to be held; and this being a self-evident truth growing out of the divinely implanted principles of human nature, any custom or authority adverse to it, whether modern or wearing the hoary sanction of antiquity, is to be regarded as a self-evident falsehood, and at war with mankind.

[At the last session Lucretia Mott offered and spoke to the following resolution:]

Resolved, That the speedy success of our cause depends upon the zealous and untiring efforts of both men and women, for the overthrow of the monopoly of the pulpit, and for the securing to woman an equal participation with men in the various trades, professions, and commerce.

Olive Schreiner

SEX-PARASITISM

South African novelist Olive Schreiner was the daughter of a missionary father and a stern and rigid Victorian mother who believed in the superiority of the British over native black Africans and the Boers. Schreiner's parents met any show of sympathy for those two groups with severe punishment. Rather than adopt the same views, Schreiner resolved to spend her life defending the weak against the strong. In 1889 she met and married a cattle rancher, Samuel Cronwright, another anti-imperialist who, at her request, took her name when they married. The first novel Schreiner published, *The Story of an African Farm,* was an immediate best-seller. Her 1911 work *Women and Labour* is the volume from which this selection is taken. In this work Schreiner outlines the history and fate of any nation in which prosperity, because of the subjugation of a slavery class, leads to its women becoming useless except as vessels in which to breed the next generation.

There never has been, and as far as can be seen, there never will be, a time when the majority of the males in any society will be supported by the rest of the males in a condition of perfect mental and physical inactivity. *"Find labour or die,"* is the choice ultimately put before the human male today, as in the past; and *this* constitutes his labour problem.

The labour of the man may not always be useful in the highest sense to his society, or it may even be distinctly harmful and anti-social, as in the case of the robber-barons of the Middle Ages, who lived by capturing and despoiling all who passed by their castles; or as in the case of the share speculators, stockjobbers, ring-and-corner capitalists, and monopolists of the present day, who feed upon the productive labours of society without contributing any-thing to its welfare. But even males so occupied are compelled to expend a vast amount of energy and even a low intelligence in their callings; and, however injurious to their societies, they run no personal risk of handing down effete and enervated consti-tutions to their race. Whether beneficially or unbeneficially, the human male must, generally speaking, employ his intellect, or his muscle, or die.

The position of the unemployed modern female is one wholly different. The choice before her, as her ancient fields of domestic labour slip from her, is not generally or often at the present day the choice between finding new fields of labour, or death; but one far more serious in its ultimate reaction on humanity as a whole—it is the choice between finding new forms of labour or sinking into a condition of more or less complete and passive *sex-parasitism!*

Again and again in the history of the past, when among human creatures a certain stage of material civilization has been reached, a curious tendency has manifested itself for the human female to become more or less parasitic; social conditions tend to rob her of all forms of active conscious social labour, and to reduce her, like the field-bug, to the passive exercise of her sex functions alone. And the result of this parasitism has invariably been the de-cay in vitality and intelligence of the female, followed after a longer or shorter period by that of her male descendants and her entire society.

Nevertheless, in the history of the past the dangers of the sex-parasitism have never threatened more than a small section of the females of the human race, those exclusively of some domi-nant race or class; the mass of women beneath them being still compelled to assume many forms of strenuous activity. It is at the present day, and under the peculiar conditions of our modern civilization, that for the first time sex-parasitism has become a danger, more or less remote, to the mass of civilized women, perhaps ultimately to all.

In the very early stages of human growth, the sexual parasitism and degeneration of the female formed no possible source of social danger. Where the conditions of life rendered it inevitable that all the labour of a community should be performed by the members of that community for themselves, without the assistance of slaves or machinery, the tendency has always been rather to throw an excessive amount of social labour on the female. Under no conditions, at no time, in no place, in the history of the world have the males of any period, of any nation, or of any class, shown the slightest inclination to allow their own females to become inactive or parasitic, so long as the actual muscular labour of feeding and clothing them would in that case have devolved upon *themselves*!

The parasitism of the human female becomes a possibility only when a point in civilization is reached (such as that which was attained in the ancient civilizations of Greece, Rome, Persia, Assyria, India, and such as today exists in many of the civilizations of the East, such as those of China and Turkey), when, owing to the extensive employment of the labour of slaves, or of subject races or classes, the dominant race or class has become so liberally supplied with the material goods of life that mere physical toil on the part of its own females members has become unnecessary.

It is when this point has been reached, and never before, that the symptoms of female parasitism have in the past almost invariably tended to manifest themselves, and have become a social danger. The males of the dominant class have almost always contrived to absorb to themselves the new intellectual occupations, which the absence of necessity for the old forms of physical toil made possible in their societies and the females of the dominant class or race, for whose muscular labours there was now also no longer any need, not succeeding grasping or attaining to these new forms of labour, have sunk into a state in which, performing no species of active social duty, they have existed through the passive performance of sexual functions alone, with how much or how little of discontent will now never be known, since no literary record has been made by the woman of the past, of her desires or sorrows. Then, in place of the active labouring woman, upholding society—by her toil, has come the effete wife, concubine or prostitute, clad in fine raiment, the work of others' fingers; fed on luxurious viands, the result of others' toil, waited on and tended by the labour of others. The need for her physical labour having gone, and mental industry not having taken its place, she bedecked and scented her person, or had it bedecked and scented for her, she lay upon her sofa, or drove or was carried out in her vehicle, and, loaded with jewels, she sought by dissipations and amusements to fill up the inordinate blank left by the lack of productive activity. And the hand whitened and frame softened, till, at last, the very duties of motherhood, which were all the constitution of her life left her, became distasteful, and, from the instant when her infant came damp from her womb, it passed into the hands of others, to be tended and reared by them; and from youth to age her offspring often owed nothing to her personal toil. In many cases so complete was her enervation, that at last the very joy of giving life, the glory and beatitude of a virile womanhood, became distasteful; and she sought to evade it, not because of its interference with more imperious duties to those already born of her, or to her society, but because her existence of inactivity had robbed her of all joy in strenuous exertion and endurance in any form. Finely clad, tenderly housed, life became for her merely the gratification of her own physical and sexual appetites, and the appetites of the male, through the stimulation of which she could maintain herself. And, whether as kept wife, kept mistress, or prostitute, she contributed nothing to the active and sustaining labours of her society. She had attained to the full development of that type which, whether in modern Paris or New York or London, or in ancient Greece, Assyria, or Rome, is essentially one in its features, its nature, and its results. She was the "fine lady," the human female parasite—the most deadly microbe which can make its appearance on the surface of any social organism.

Wherever in the history of the past this type has reached its full development and has comprised the bulk of the females belonging to any dominant class or race, it has heralded its decay. In Assyria, Greece, Rome, Persia, as in Turkey today, the same material conditions have produced the same social disease among wealthy and dominant races and again and again when the nation so affected has come into contact with nations more healthily constituted, the diseased condition has contributed to its destruction.

D. H. Lawrence

PORNOGRAPHY

Though D.H. Lawrence (1885-1930) was often criticized for descriptions of sex in his novels, the passages in question are actually quite tame by today's standards. Here he defends his work by constructing a definition of pornography which carefully excludes his novels. As you read his essay, ask yourself whether today's R-rated movies, or even some television commercials, might be considered pornographic by Lawrence.

What is pornography to one man is the laughter of genius to another. The word itself, we are told, means "pertaining to harlots"—the graph of the harlot. But nowadays, what is a harlot? If she was a woman who took money from a man in return for going to bed with him—really, most wives sold themselves, in the past, and plenty of harlots gave themselves, when they felt like it, for nothing. If a woman hasn't got a tiny streak of harlot in her, she's a dry stick as a rule. And probably most harlots had somewhere a streak of womanly generosity. Why be so cut and dried? The law is a dreary thing, and its judgments have nothing to do with life. . . .

One essay on pornography, I remember, comes to the conclusion that pornography in art is that which is calculated to arouse sexual desire, or sexual excitement. And stress is laid on the fact, whether the author or artist *intended* to arouse sexual feelings. It is the old vexed question of intention, become so dull today, when we know how strong and influential our unconscious intentions are. And why a man should be held guilty of his conscious intentions, and innocent of his unconscious intentions, I don't know, since every man is more made up of unconscious intentions than of conscious ones. I am what I am, not merely what I think I am.

However! We take it, I assume, that *pornography* is something base, something unpleasant. In short, we don't like it. And why don't we like it? Because it arouses sexual feelings?

I think not. No matter how hard we may pretend otherwise, most of us rather like a moderate rousing of our sex. It warms us, stimulates us like sunshine on a grey day. After a century or two of Puritanism, this is still true of most people. Only the mob-habit of condemning any form of sex is too strong to let us admit it naturally. And there are, of course, many people who are genuinely repelled by the simplest and most natural stirrings of sexual feeling. But these people are perverts who have fallen into hatred of their fellow men; thwarted, disappointed, unfulfilled people, of whom, alas, our civilisation contains so many. And they nearly always enjoy some unsimple and unnatural form of sex excitement, secretly.

Even quite advanced art critics would try to make us believe that any picture or book which had "sex appeal" was *ipso facto* a bad book or picture. This is just canting hypocrisy. Half the great poems, pictures, music, stories, of the whole world are great by virtue of the beauty of their sex appeal. Titian or Renoir, the Song of Solomon or *Jane Eyre,* Mozart or "Annie Laurie," the loveliness is all interwoven with sex appeal, sex stimulus, call it what you will. Even Michelangelo, who rather hated sex, can't help filling the Cornucopia with phallic acorns. Sex is a very powerful, beneficial and necessary stimulus in human life, and we are all grateful when we feel its warm, natural flow through us, like a form of sunshine. . . .

Then what is pornography, after all this? It isn't sex appeal or sex stimulus in art. It isn't even a deliberate intention on the part of the artist to arouse or excite sexual feelings. There's nothing wrong with sexual feelings in themselves, so long as they are straightforward and not sneaking or sly. The right sort of sex stimulus is invaluable to human daily life. Without it the world grows grey. I would give everybody the gay Renaissance stories to read; they would help to shake off a lot of grey self-importance, which is our modern civilised disease.

But even I would censor genuine pornography, rigorously. It would not be very difficult. In the first place, genuine pornography is almost always underworld, it doesn't come into the open. In the second, you can recognise it by the insult it offers, invariably, to sex and to the human spirit.

Pornography is the attempt to insult sex, to do dirt on it. This is unpardonable. Take the very lowest instance, the picture postcard sold underhand, by the underworld, in most cities. What I have seen of them have been of an ugliness to make you cry. The insult to the human body, the insult to a vital human relationship! Ugly and cheap they make the human nudity, ugly and degraded they make the sexual act, trivial and cheap and nasty.

It is the same with the books they sell in the underworld. They are either so ugly they make you ill, or so fatuous you can't imagine anybody but a cretin or a moron reading them, or writing them.

It is the same with the dirty limericks that people tell after dinner, or the dirty stories one hears commercial travellers telling each other in a smoke-room. Occasionally there is a really funny one, that redeems a great deal. But usually they are just ugly and repellent, and the so-called "humour" is just a trick of doing dirt on sex.

Now the human nudity of a great many modern people is just ugly and degraded, and the sexual act between modern people is just the same, merely ugly and degrading. But this is nothing to be proud of. It is the catastrophe of our civilisation. I am sure no other civilisation, not even the Roman, has showed such a vast proportion of ignominious and degraded nudity, and ugly, squalid dirty sex. Because no other civilisation has given sex into the underworld, and nudity to the w.c.

The intelligent young, thank heaven, seem determined to alter in these two respects. They are rescuing their young nudity from the stuffy, pornographical hole-and-corner underworld of their elders, and they refuse to sneak about the sexual relation. This is a change the elderly grey ones of course deplore, but it is in fact a very great change for the better, and a real revolution.

But it is amazing how strong is the will in ordinary, vulgar people, to do dirt on sex. It was one of my fond illusions, when I was young, that the ordinary healthy-seeming sort of men in railway carriages, or the smoke-room of an hotel or a pullman, were healthy in their feelings and had a wholesome rough devil-may-care attitude towards sex. All wrong! All wrong! Experience teaches that common individuals of this sort have a disgusting attitude towards sex, a disgusting contempt of it, a disgusting desire to insult it. If such fellows have intercourse with a woman, they triumphantly feel that they have done her dirt, and now she is lower, cheaper, more contemptible than she was before.

It is individuals of this sort that tell dirty stories, carry indecent picture postcards, and know the indecent books. This is the great pornographical class—the really common men-in-the-street and women-in-the-street. They have as great a hate and contempt of sex as the greyest Puritan, and when an appeal is made to them, they are always on the side of the angels. They insist that a film heroine shall be a neuter, a sexless thing of washed-out purity. They insist that real sex-feeling shall only be shown by the villain or villainess, low lust. They find a Titian or a Renoir really indecent, and they don't want their wives and daughters to see it.

Why? Because they have the grey disease of sex-hatred, coupled with the yellow disease of dirt-lust. The sex functions and the excrementory functions in the human body work so close together, yet they are, so to speak, utterly different in direction. Sex is a creative flow, the excrementory flow is towards dissolution, decreation, if we may use such a word. In the really healthy human being the distinction between the two is instant, our profoundest instincts are perhaps our instincts of opposition between the two flows. But in the degraded human being the deep instincts have gone dead, and then the two flows become identical. *This is* the secret of really vulgar and of pornographical people: the sex flow and the excrement flow is the same to them. It happens when the psyche deteriorates, and the profound controlling instincts collapse. Then sex is dirt and dirt is sex, and sexual excitement becomes a playing with dirt, and any sign of sex in a woman becomes a show of her dirt. This is the condition of the common, vulgar human being whose name is legion, and who lifts his voice and it is the *Vox populi, vox Dei.* And this is the source of all pornography.

Gloria Steinem

MARILYN MONROE: THE WOMAN WHO DIED TOO SOON

Gloria Steinem (1934-   ), feminist, writer, and editor, helped found two magazines and has written several books. In this piece, she analyzes the life of Marilyn Monroe—a woman whose name is not often uttered in the same sentence with "feminism." Nonetheless, Steinem points to the many ways in which Monroe helped the women's movement, and the many more ways in which she was a victim of circumstances. Before you read, make a list of words you associate with

"Marilyn Monroe." After you read the essay, does the list still seem
appropriate?

Saturday afternoon movies—no matter how poorly made or incredible the plot, they were a refuge from my neighborhood and
all my teenage miseries. Serials that never ended, Doris Day, who
never capitulated, cheap travelogues, sci-fi features with zippers
in the monster suits: I loved them all, believed them all, and never
dreamed of leaving until the screen went sickeningly blank.

But I walked out on Marilyn Monroe. I remember her on the
screen, huge as a colossus doll, mincing and whispering and simply hoping her way into total vulnerability. Watching her, I felt
angry, even humiliated, but I didn't understand why.

After all, Jane Russell was in the movie, too (a very bad-taste
version of *Gentlemen Prefer Blondes*), so it wasn't just the vulnerability that all big-breasted women seem to share. (If women
viewers prefer actresses who are smaller, neater—the Audrey
Hepburns of the world—it is not because we're jealous of the *zoftig*
ones as men suppose. It's just that we would rather identify with a
woman we don't have to worry about, someone who doesn't seem
in constant danger.) Compared to Marilyn, Jane Russell seemed
in control of her body and even of the absurd situations in this
movie.

Perhaps it was the uncertainty in the eyes of this big, blond
child-woman; the terrible desire for approval that made her different from Jane Russell. How dare she express the neediness that
so many women feel, but try so hard to hide? How dare she, a
movie star, be just as unconfident as I was?

So I disliked her and avoided her movies, as we avoid that which
reflects our fears about ourselves. If there were jokes made on her
name and image when I was around, I joined in. I contributed to
the laughing, the ridicule, the put-downs, thus proving that I was
nothing like her. Nothing at all.

I, too, got out of my neighborhood in later years, just as she had
escaped from a much worse life of lovelessness, child abuse, and
foster homes. I didn't do it, as she did, through nude calendar
photographs and starlet bits. (Even had there been such opportunities for mildly pretty girls in Toledo, Ohio, I would never have
had the courage to make myself so vulnerable.) Yes, I was
American enough to have show-business dreams. The boys in my
neighborhood hoped to get out of a lifetime in the factories
through sports; the girls, if we imagined anything other than

marrying a few steps up in the world, always dreamed of show-business careers. But after high-school years as a dancer on the Toledo show-business circuit, or what passed for show business there, it seemed hopeless even to me. In the end, it was luck and an encouraging mother and a facility with words that got me out; a facility that helped me fake my way through the college entrance exams for which I was totally unprepared.

But there's not much more confidence in girls who scrape past college boards than there is in those who, like Marilyn, parade past beauty-contest judges. By the time I saw her again, I was a respectful student watching the celebrated members of the Actors Studio do scenes from what seemed to me very impressive and highbrow plays (Arthur Miller and Eugene O'Neill were to be served up that day). She was a student, too, a pupil of Lee Strasberg, leader of the Actors Studio and American guru of the Stanislavski method, but her status as a movie star and sex symbol seemed to keep her from being taken seriously even there. She was allowed to observe, but not to do scenes with her colleagues.

So the two of us sat there, mutually awed, I think, in the presence of such theater people as Ben Gazzara and Rip Torn, mutually insecure in the masculine world of High Culture, mutually trying to fade into the woodwork.

I remember thinking that Strasberg and his actors seemed to take positive pleasure in their power to ignore this great and powerful movie star who had come to learn. Their greetings to her were a little too studiously casual, their whispers to each other about her being there a little too self-conscious and condescending. Though she stayed in the back of the room, her blond head swathed in a black scarf and her body hidden in a shapeless black sweater and slacks, she gradually became a presence, if only because the group was trying so hard *not* to look, to remain oblivious and cool.

As we filed slowly out of the shabby room after the session was over, Marilyn listened eagerly to the professional postmortem being carried on by Ben Gazzara and others who walked ahead of us, her fingers nervously tracing a face that was luminous and without makeup, as if she were trying to hide herself, to apologize for being there. I was suddenly glad she hadn't participated and hadn't been subjected to the criticisms of this rather vulturous group. (Perhaps it was an unschooled reaction, but I hadn't enjoyed watching Strasberg encourage an intimate love scene between an actor and actress, and then pick them apart with humiliating authority.) Summoning my nerve, I did ask the shy, blond woman in front of me if she could imagine playing a scene for this group.

"Oh, no," Marilyn said, her voice childish, but much less whispery than on the screen, "I admire all these people so much. I'm just not good enough." Then, after a few beats of silence: "Lee Strasberg is a genius, you know. I plan to do what he says."

Her marriage to Arthur Miller seemed quite understandable to me and to other women, even those who were threatened by Miller's casting off of a middle-aged wife to take a younger, far more glamorous one. If you can't be taken seriously in your work, if you have an emotional and intellectual insecurity complex, then marry a man who has the seriousness you've been denied. It's a traditional female option—far more acceptable than trying to achieve that identity on one's own.

Of course, Marilyn's image didn't really gain seriousness and intellectuality. Women don't gain serious status by sexual association any more easily than they do by hard work. (At least, not unless the serious man dies and we confine ourselves to being keepers of the flame. As Margaret Mead has pointed out, widows are almost the only women this country honors in authority.) Even Marilyn's brave refusal to be intimidated by threats that she would never work in films again if she married Miller, who was then a "subversive" called to testify before the House Un-American Activities Committee, was considered less brave than Miller's refusal to testify. Indeed, it was barely reported at all.

Perhaps she didn't take her own bravery seriously either. She might be giving up her livelihood, the work that meant so much to her, but she was about to give that up for marriage anyway. As Mrs. Arthur Miller, she retired to a Connecticut farm and tried to limit her life to his solitary work habits, his friends, and his two children. Only when they badly needed money did she come out of retirement again, and that was to act in *The Misfits,* a film written by her husband.

On the other hand, the public interpretation was very different. She was an egocentric actress forcing one of America's most important playwrights to tailor a screenplay to her inferior talents: that was the gossip-column story here and in Europe. But her own pattern argues the case for her. In two previous marriages, to an aircraft factory worker at the age of sixteen and later to Joe DiMaggio, she had cut herself off from the world and put all her energies into being a housewife. When it didn't work out, she

blamed herself, not the role, and added one more failure to her list
of insecurities. "I have too many fantasies to be a housewife," she
told a woman friend sadly. And finally, to an interviewer: "I guess
I *am* a fantasy."

The Misfits seemed to convey some facets of the real Marilyn:
honesty, an innocence and belief that survived all experience to
the contrary, kindness toward other women, a respect for the life
of plants and animals. Because for the first time she wasn't only a
sex object and victim, I also was unembarrassed enough to notice
her acting ability. I began to see her earlier movies—those in
which, unlike *Gentlemen Prefer Blondes,* she wasn't called upon
to act the female impersonator.

For me as for so many people, she was a presence in the world, a
life force.

Over the years, I heard other clues to her character. When Ella
Fitzgerald, a black artist and perhaps the greatest singer of popular songs, hadn't been able to get a booking at an important Los
Angeles nightclub in the fifties, it was Marilyn who called the
owner and promised to sit at a front table every night while she
sang. The owner hired Ella, Marilyn was faithful to her promise
each night, the press went wild, and, as Ella remembers with
gratitude, "After that, I never had to play a small jazz club again."

Even more movingly, there was her last interview. She pleaded
with the reporter to end with "What I really want to say: That
what the world really needs is a real feeling of kinship. Everybody:
stars, laborers, Negroes, Jews, Arabs. We are all brothers.... Please
don't make me a joke. End the interview with what I believe."

And then she was gone. I remember being told, in the middle of
a chaotic student meeting in Europe, that she was dead. I remember that precise moment on August 5, 1962—the people around
me, what the room looked like—and I've discovered that many
other people remember that moment of hearing the news, too. It's
a phenomenon usually reserved for the death of family and presidents.

She was an actress, a person on whom no one's fate depended,
and yet her energy and terrible openness to life had made a connection to strangers. Within days after her body was discovered,
eight young and beautiful women took their lives in individual
incidents clearly patterned after Marilyn Monroe's death. Some
of them left notes to make that connection clear.

Two years later, Arthur Miller's autobiographical play, *After
the Fall,* brought Marilyn back to life in the character of Maggie.

But somehow that Maggie didn't seem the same. She had Marilyn's pathetic insecurity, the same need to use her sexual self as her only way of getting recognition and feeling alive. But, perhaps naturally, the play was about Miller's suffering, not Marilyn's. He seemed honestly to include some of his own destructive acts. (He had kept a writer's diary of his movie-star wife, for instance, and Marilyn's discovery of it was an emotional blow, the beginning of the end for that marriage. It made her wonder: Was her husband exploiting her, as most men had done, but in a more intellectual way?) Nonetheless, the message of the play was mostly Miller's view of his attempts to shore up a creature of almost endless insecurities; someone doomed beyond his helping by a mysterious lack of confidence.

To women, that lack was less mysterious. Writer Diana Trilling, who had never met Marilyn, wrote an essay just after her death that some of Marilyn's friends praised as a more accurate portrayal than Miller's. She described the public's "mockery of [Marilyn's] wish to be educated"; the sexual awareness that came only from outside, from men's reactions, "leaving a great emptiness where a true sexuality would have supplied her with a sense of herself as a person with connection and content." She questioned whether Marilyn had really wanted to die, or only to be asleep, not to be conscious through the loneliness of that particular Saturday night.

Trilling also recorded that feeling of connection to Marilyn's loneliness felt by so many strangers ("especially women to whose protectiveness her extreme vulnerability spoke so directly"), so much so that we fantasized our ability to save her, if only we had been there. "But we were the friends," as Trilling wrote sadly, "of whom she knew nothing."

"She was an unusual woman—a little ahead of her times," said Ella Fitzgerald. "And she didn't know it."

Now that women's self-vision is changing, we are thinking again about the life of Marilyn Monroe. Might our new confidence in women's existence with or without the approval of men have helped a thirty-six-year-old woman of talent to stand on her own? To resist the insecurity and ridicule? To stop depending on sexual attractiveness as the only proof that she was alive—and therefore to face aging with confidence? Because the ability to bear a child was denied to her, Could these new ideas have helped her to know that being a woman included much more? Could she have challenged the Freudian analysts to whom she turned in her suffering?

Most of all, we wonder if the support and friendship of other women could have helped. Her early experiences of men were not good. She was the illegitimate daughter of a man who would not even contribute for her baby clothes; her mother's earliest memory of her own father, Marilyn's grandfather, was his smashing a pet kitten against the fireplace in a fit of anger; Marilyn herself said she was sexually attacked by a foster father while still a child; and she was married off at sixteen because another foster family could not take care of her. Yet she was forced always to depend for her security on the goodwill and recognition of men; even to be interpreted by them in writing because she feared that sexual competition made women dislike her. Even if they had wanted to, the women in her life did not have the power to protect her. In films, photographs, and books, even after her death as well as before, she has been mainly seen through men's eyes.

We are too late. We cannot know whether we could have helped Norma Jean Baker or the Marilyn Monroe she became. But we are not too late to do as she asked. At last, we can take her seriously.

Margaret Atwood

PORNOGRAPHY

Margaret Atwood (1939-   ), a novelist, poet, and essayist, is best known as the author of novels such as *The Handmaid's Tale* (1986) and *Cat's Eye* (1989). In this essay, Atwood clearly has a much narrower definition of pornography than D.H. Lawrence. Instead of merely defining pornography, however, she is more interested in determining how to regulate it. The issues she brings up are not without consequence: how can we balance the need for freedom of expression against the rights of potential victims of rape or incest? If pornography incites people to violence, shouldn't it be banned? Should we define a movie depicting the horrible consequences of rape as "pornography" or "education"?

When I was in Finland a few years ago for an international writers' conference, I had occasion to say a few paragraphs in public on the subject of pornography. The context was a discussion of political repression, and I was suggesting the possibility of a link between the two. The immediate result was that a male journalist took several large bites out of me. Prudery and pornography are two halves of the same coin, said he, and I was clearly a prude. What could you expect from an Anglo-Canadian? Afterward, a couple of pleasant Scandinavian men asked me what I had been so worked up about. All "pornography" means, they said, is graphic depictions of whores, and what was the harm in that?

Not until then did it strike me that the male journalist and I had two entirely different things in mind. By "pornography," he meant naked bodies and sex. I, on the other hand, had recently been doing the research for my novel *Bodily Harm,* and was still in a state of shock from some of the material I had seen, including the Ontario Board of Film Censors' "outtakes." By "pornography," I meant women getting their nipples snipped off with garden shears, having meat hooks stuck into their vaginas, being disemboweled; little girls being raped; men (yes, there are some men) being smashed to a pulp and forcibly sodomized. The cutting edge of pornography, as far as I could see, was no longer simple old copulation, hanging from the chandelier or otherwise: it was death, messy, explicit and highly sadistic. I explained this to the nice Scandinavian men. "Oh, but that's just the United States," they said. "Everyone knows they're sick." In their country, they said, violent "pornography" of that kind was not permitted on television or in movies; indeed, excessive violence of any kind was not permitted. They had drawn a clear line between erotica, which earlier studies had shown did not incite men to more aggressive and brutal behavior toward women, and violence, which later studies indicated did. Some time after that I was in Saskatchewan, where, because of the scenes in *Bodily Harm, I* found myself on an open-line radio show answering questions about "pornography." Almost no one who phoned in was in favor of it, but again they weren't talking about the same stuff I was, because they hadn't seen it. Some of them were all set to stamp out bathing suits and negligees, and, if possible, any depictions of the female body whatsoever. God, it was implied, did not approve of female bodies, and sex of any kind, including that practised by bumblebees, should be shoved back into the dark, where it belonged. I had more than a suspicion that *Lady Chatterley's Lover,*

Margaret Laurence's *The Diviners,* and indeed most books by
most serious modern authors would have ended up as confetti if
left in the hands of these callers. For me, these two experiences illustrate the two poles of the emotionally heated debate that is now
thundering around this issue. They also underline the desirability
and even the necessity of defining the terms. "Pornography" is
now one of those catchalls, like "Marxism" and "feminism," that
have become so broad they can mean almost anything, ranging
from certain verses in the Bible, ads for skin lotion and sex tests
for children to the contents of Penthouse, Naughty '90s postcards
and films with titles containing the word *Nazi* that show vicious
scenes of torture and killing. It's easy to say that sensible people
can tell the difference. Unfortunately, opinions on what constitutes a sensible person vary. But even sensible people tend to lose
their cool when they start talking about this subject. They soon
stop talking and start yelling, and the name calling begins. Those
in favor of censorship (which may include groups not noticeably
in agreement on other issues, such as some feminists and religious
fundamentalists) accuse the others of exploiting women through
the use of degrading images, contributing to the corruption of
children, and adding to the general climate of violence and threat
in which both women and children live in this society; or, though
they may not give much of a hoot about actual women and children, they invoke moral standards and God's supposed aversion to
"filth," "smut" and deviated *preversion,* which may mean ankles.
The camp in favor of total "freedom of expression" often comes
out howling as loud as the Romans would have if told they could
no longer have innocent fun watching the lions eat up Christians.
It too may include segments of the population who are not natural
bedfellows: those who proclaim their God-given right to freedom,
including the freedom to tote guns, drive when drunk, drool over
chicken porn and get off on videotapes of women being raped and
beaten, may be waving the same anticensorship banner as responsible liberals who fear the return of Mrs. Grundy, or gay
groups for whom sexual emancipation involves the concept of
"sexual theatre." *Whatever turns you on* is a handy motto, as is *A
man's home is his castle* (and if it includes a dungeon with beautiful maidens strung up in chains and bleeding from every pore,
that's his business).

Meanwhile, theoreticians theorize and speculators speculate. Is
today's pornography yet another indication of the hatred of the
body, the deep mind-body split, which is supposed to pervade

Western Christian society? Is it a backlash against the women's movement by men who are threatened by uppity female behavior in real life, so like to fantasize about women done up like outsize parcels, being turned into hamburger, kneeling at their feet in slavelike adoration or sucking off guns? Is it a sign of collective impotence, of a generation of men who can't relate to real women at all but have to make do with bits of celluloid and paper? Is the current flood just a result of smart marketing and aggressive promotion by the money men in what has now become a multi billion dollar industry? If they were selling movies about men getting their testicles stuck full of knitting needles by women with swastikas on their sleeves, would they do as well, or is this penchant somehow peculiarly male? If so, why? Is pornography a power trip rather than a sex one? Some say that those ropes, chains, muzzles and other restraining devices are an argument for the immense power female sexuality still wields in the male imagination: you don't put these things on dogs unless you're afraid of them. Others, more literary, wonder about the shift from the 19th-century Magic Woman or Femme Fatale image to the lollipop-licker, airhead or turkey-carcass treatment of women in porn today. The proporners don't care much about theory; they merely demand product. The antiporners don't care about it in the final analysis either; there's dirt on the street, and they want it cleaned up, now. It seems to me that this conversation, with its *You're-a-prude*/*You're-a-pervert* dialectic, will never get anywhere as long as we continue to think of this material as just "entertainment." Possibly we're deluded by the packaging, the format: magazine, book, movie, theatrical presentation. We're used to thinking of these things as part of the "entertainment industry," and we're used to thinking of ourselves as free adult people who ought to be able to see any kind of "entertainment" we want to. That was what the First Choice pay-TV debate was all about. After all, it's only entertainment, right? Entertainment means fun, and only a killjoy would be antifun. What's the harm? This is obviously the central question: *What's the harm?* If there isn't any real harm to any real people, then the antiporners can tsk-tsk and/or throw up as much as they like, but they can't rightfully expect more legal controls or sanctions. However, the no harm position is far from being proven. (For instance, there's a clear-cut case for banning—as the federal government has proposed—movies, photos and videos that depict children engaging in sex with adults: real children are used to make the movies, and

hardly anybody thinks this is ethical. The possibilities for coercion
are too great.) To shift the viewpoint, I'd like to suggest three
other models for looking at "pornography"—and here I mean the
violent kind. Those who find the idea of regulating pornographic
materials repugnant because they think it's Fascist or
Communist or otherwise not in accordance with the principles of
an open democratic society should consider that Canada has
made it illegal to disseminate material that may lead to hatred
toward any group because of race or religion. I suggest that if
pornography of the violent kind depicted these acts being done
predominantly to Chinese, to blacks, to Catholics, it would be off
the market immediately, under the present laws. Why is hate literature illegal? Because whoever made the law thought that such
material might incite real people to do real awful things to other
real people. The human brain is to a certain extent a computer:
garbage in, garbage out. We only hear about the extreme cases
(like that of American multimurderer Ted Bundy) in which
pornography has contributed to the death and/or mutilation of
women and/or men. Although pornography is not the only factor
involved in the creation of such deviance, it certainly has upped
the ante by suggesting both a variety of techniques and the social
acceptability of such actions. Nobody knows yet what effect this
stuff is having on the less psychotic. Studies have shown that a
large part of the market for all kinds of porn, soft and hard, is
drawn from the 16-to-21-year-old population of young men. Boys
used to learn about sex on the street, or (in Italy, according to
Fellini movies) from friendly whores, or, in more genteel sur-
roundings, from girls, their parents, or, once upon a time, in
school, more or less. Now porn has been added, and sex education
in the schools is rapidly being phased out. The buck has been
passed, and boys are being taught that all women secretly like to
be raped and that real men get high on scooping out women's di-
gestive tracts. Boys learn their concept of masculinity from other
men: is this what most men want them to be learning? If word
gets around that rapists are "normal" and even admirable men,
will boys feel that in order to be normal, admirable and masculine
they will have to be rapists? Human beings are enormously flexible, and how they turn out depends a lot on how they're educated,
by the society in which they're immersed as well as by their
teachers. In a society that advertises and glorifies rape or even
implicitly condones it, more women get raped. It becomes socially
acceptable. And at a time when men and the traditional male role

have taken a lot of flak and men are confused and casting around for an acceptable way of being male (and, in some cases, not getting much comfort from women on that score), this must be at times a pleasing thought. It would be naive to think of violent pornography as just harmless entertainment. It's also an educational tool and a powerful propaganda device. What happens when boy educated on porn meets girl brought up on Harlequin romances? The clash of expectations can be heard around the block. She wants him to get down on his knees with a ring, he wants her to get down on all fours with a ring in her nose. Can this marriage be saved? Pornography has certain things in common with such addictive substances as alcohol and drugs: for some, though by no means for all, it induces chemical changes in the body, which the user finds exciting and pleasurable. It also appears to attract a "hard core" of habitual users and a penumbra of those who use it occasionally but aren't dependent on it in any way. There are also significant numbers of men who aren't much interested in it, not because they're undersexed but because real life is satisfying their needs, which may not require as many appliances as those of users. For the "hard core," pornography may function as alcohol does for the alcoholic: tolerance develops, and a little is no longer enough. This may account for the short viewing time and fast turnover in porn theatres. Mary Brown, chairwoman of the Ontario Board of Film Censors, estimates that for every one mainstream movie requesting entrance to Ontario, there is one porno flick. Not only the quantity consumed but the quality of explicitness must escalate, which may account for the growing violence: once the big deal was breasts, then it was genitals, then copulation, then that was no longer enough and the hard users had to have more. The ultimate kick is death, and after that, as the Marquis de Sade so boringly demonstrated, multiple death. The existence of alcoholism has not led us to ban social drinking. On the other hand, we do have laws about drinking and driving, excessive drunkenness and other abuses of alcohol that may result in injury or death to others. This leads us back to the key question: what's the harm? Nobody knows, but this society should find out fast, before the saturation point is reached. The Scandinavian studies that showed a connection between depictions of sexual violence and increased impulse toward it on the part of male viewers would be a starting point, but many more questions remain to be raised as well as answered. What, for instance, is the crucial difference between men who are users and

men who are not? Does using affect a man's relationship with
actual women, and, if so, adversely? Is there a clear line between
erotica and violent pornography, or are they on an escalating
continuum? Is this a "men versus women" issue, with all men secretly siding with the proporners and all women secretly siding
against? (I think not; there *are* lots of men who don't think that
running their true love through the Cuisinart is the best way they
can think of to spend a Saturday night, and they're just as nau-
seated by films of someone else doing it as women are.) Is pornography merely an expression of the sexual confusion of this age or
an active contributor to it? Nobody wants to go back to the age of
official repression, when even piano legs were referred to as
"limbs" and had to wear pantaloons to be decent. Neither do we
want to end up in George Orwell's 1984, in which pornography is
turned out by the State to keep the proles in a state of torpor, sex itself is considered dirty and the approved practise it only for repro-
duction. But Rome under the emperors isn't such a good model
either. If all men and women respected each other, if sex were
considered joyful and life-enhancing instead of a wallow in germ-
filled glop, if everyone were in love all the time, if, in other words,
many people's lives were more satisfactory for them than they
appear to be now, pornography might just go away on its own. But
since this is obviously not happening, we as a society are going to
have to make some informed and responsible decisions about how
to deal with it.

Lisa (Student)

RESPONSE TO ATWOOD AND LAWRENCE ON PORNOGRAPHY

Between Atwood and Lawrence's definitions of pornography, there
is a lot of gray area. Lisa's essay explores that gray area and attempts
a reconciliation—and a questioning—of both essays.

Margaret Atwood and D. H. Lawrence, two of the twentieth
century's most respected and sensuous writers, both have a lot to

say on the subject of pornography. For each of them, the question of definition is central, and they both make a distinction between pornography, and depictions of sex and bodies.

For Atwood, real pornography is found in violence and sadism used as entertainment, in depictions of "women getting their nipples sheared off. . . little girls being raped. . . men. . . being smashed to a pulp and forcibly sodomized." To her, this is hate literature, and as such, should be banished (as racially-based hate literature is currently banned in Canada). Too often, she says, people either think of pornography as graphic depictions of whores or "naked bodies and sex" or "bathing suits and negligees."

Atwood would probably take exception with Lawrence when he says "If a woman hasn't got a tiny streak of harlot in her, she's a dry stick as a rule," but she might agree with him that literature that arouses sexual feelings is a good thing, and quite different from literature which "does dirt to sex." Pornography, he says, occurs when people want to hide sex, to keep in underground, when people confuse sex functions with excretory functions. He want to suppress this kind of thinking and celebrate the body.

The question of suppression is one of the key questions surrounding the issue of pornography today. For Atwood, the question boils down to "What is the harm?" which comes off as a question that is both sardonically rhetorical and straightforwardly serious. A variety of studies involving showing pornographic movies and magazines to men to determine the answer to this question has produced an inconclusive bunch of conclusions, and we end up forced to make a decision based on our original position. If pornography does affect men's ability to see women as human, then there is great harm, and that window of possibility is enough for Atwood to suggest that certain pornographic works be classed as hate literature and censored if not banned.

According to Lawrence, the harm is done in pornography's "attempt to insult sex." Sex is big and beautiful and people want to make it small and dirty. Sex should be celebrated; it is and should be found in great literature and great paintings. Lawrence is something of a snob; first by giving too much credit to the common men and women in the street, believing them to be more in touch with the earth and therefore aware of and happy with the earthy, then by seeing those common people as the ones responsible for cheapening and dirtying sex.

Though both writers bring up the question of what to do about pornography, neither one has an ultimate or fully satisfactory an-

swer. I would say that pornography isn't found in those kitten-
ishly cute photos of prom queens in Playboy—except possibly
insofar as those are by nature embarrassing, to both the women
who pose and the men who buy. But at this point there seems to be
nothing to do about such degradation. Atwood would get rid of the
violent and sadistic, Lawrence would get rid of the degrading and
dirtying. My own fear is that by getting rid of potentially pornographic material you allow for suppression of all material that
mentions sex—including Atwood's and Lawrence's works.
Including, in fact, this essay—and I would hate to see that happen.

Felicia (student)

WHY I AM NOT A FEMINIST

Growing up in the '70s and '80s means growing up *after* the '60s,
when many of American society's attitudes were turned upside-down.
Suddenly, it was OK for a man to stay home and raise children.
Suddenly, it was OK for a woman to have a career. Felicia grew up in
the '70s, and the result has been perhaps somewhat different than expected. As you read, consider how the times you grew up in have
affected your politics.

Where I come from, I could get in big trouble saying that. My
mother, while never exactly an agitator, was a divorced mother
from about 1970 on, and she found herself in a position of
"liberating" the men around her. She gender-integrated a men's
exercise class, she learned (and taught) that women could pick up
the check in a restaurant without castrating men, and she was a
charter subscriber to *Ms.* magazine. Yet I am not a feminist—so
where did she fail?

I guess she made the world too easy, too much better for her
daughters. Nobody could get away with telling me or my sister
that we couldn't take shop or try out for the football team or join
the Boy Scouts of America—but we never wanted those things.
Nobody ever told my brother that he should be "manly" and avoid
cooking or housework for more masculine activities like lawn-
mowing and watching televised sports—he just ended up inept at

all those skills. Without an atmosphere of denial, suppression, obviously unfair rules or social structures inhibiting us, my brother and sister and I grew up expecting the world to treat us fairly, or each as fairly as the others, and it always has.

Well, fair-to-middling. I have noticed that my sister and I, having followed my mother's wishes for *all* her children, became proficient typists and have been able to get secretarial jobs in a flash. My brother, on the other hand, graduated from college with a B.A. in English and no such manual skills, only intellectual ones, and was able to begin work immediately as a paralegal, earning $23,000 a year to start. He never had to type after that; all his typing was done by a secretary, also with a B.A., who earned $17,000 a year, probably because she had listened to her mother and excelled at typing.

Granted, both of those positions are dead-end. The difference between them is primarily status, and kind of work required. I don't point this out because I'm a feminist, because I'm not, merely because it's true.

On the other hand, my mother managed, over the course of 20 years, to parlay her typing skills and a B.A. in English into a career in city government, in which she earned $48,000 a year. My father, on the other hand, never much of a typist but armed with an M.S. in mathematics, plateaued at around $36,000 a year in software engineering. It's hard to see any systematic forces at work here. I see instead two personalities, two different lives lived differently. My mother likes work and my father doesn't. My mother raised three children (not without my father's help, but as primary caregiver), while my father began ten years ago to raise his fourth. My father is intensely involved in his leisure activities; my mother prefer work activity. Perhaps the discrepancy in my brother's office between his earnings and the earnings of a similarly qualified woman is due to an ambition discrepancy as well. I point this out because I'm not a feminist, because a feminist would never bother to point this out.

I'll bet you my brother will never be asked to take a typing test. And neither will my father. But though I try to, I can't begin to feel outraged at this. I have the same opportunity to go to college as my mother and her mother, the same as my father and brother and sister. I can take exercise classes with men (even at formerly all-male clubs), I can buy a man dinner, and I can get a job using my mind. I thank my mother for these opportunities, but I have always been secure that they will be there. No one has ever suggested otherwise to me. If anyone did, I'd black his eye—with my typing hand.

Lester C. Thurow

WHY WOMEN ARE PAID LESS THAN MEN

Lester Thurow (1938-   ) is an economist at the Massachusetts Institute of Technology. In this aptly titled analysis, Thurow gives his explanation of why women are paid less than men. As you read, see if you can answer these questions: If his explanation is correct, then who is to blame? Is it the women who stay home to raise children? Is it the men who don't? Is it the "system" that governs the success or failure of workers?

In the 40 years from 1939 to 1979 white women who work full time have with monotonous regularity made slightly less than 60 percent as much as white men. Why? Over the same time period, minorities have made substantial progress in catching up with whites, with minority women making even more progress than minority men. Black men now earn 72 percent as much as white men (up 16 percentage points since the mid-1950's) but black women earn 92 percent as much as white women. Hispanic men make 71 percent of what their white counterparts do, but Hispanic women make 82 percent as much as white women. As a result of their faster progress, fully employed black women make 75 percent as much as fully employed black men while Hispanic women earn 68 percent as much as Hispanic men. This faster progress may, however, end when minority women finally catch up with white women. In the bible of the New Right, George Gilder's *Wealth and Poverty,* the 60 percent is just one of Mother Nature's constants like the speed of light or the force of gravity. Men are programmed to provide for their families economically while women are programmed to take care of their families emotionally and physically. As a result men put more effort into their jobs than women. The net result is a difference in work intensity that leads to that 40 percent gap in earnings. But there is no discrimination against women—only the biological facts of life.

The problem with this assertion is just that. It is an assertion with no evidence for it other than the fact that white women have made 60 percent as much as men for a long period of time. "Discrimination against women" is an easy answer but it also has its problems as an adequate explanation. Why is discrimination against women not declining under the same social forces that are leading to a lessening of discrimination against minorities? In recent years women have made more use of the enforcement provisions of the Equal Employment Opportunities Commission and the courts than minorities. Why do the laws that prohibit discrimination against women and minorities work for minorities but not for women? When men discriminate against women, they run into a problem. To discriminate against women is to discriminate against your own wife and to lower your own family income. To prevent women from working is to force men to work more. When whites discriminate against blacks, they can at least think that they are raising their own incomes. When men discriminate against women they have to know that they are lowering their own family income and increasing their own work effort. While discrimination undoubtedly explains part of the male-female earnings differential, one has to believe that men are monumentally stupid or irrational to explain all of the earnings gap in terms of discrimination. There must be something else going on. Back in 1939 it was possible to attribute the earnings gap to large differences in educational attainments. But the educational gap between men and women has been eliminated since World War II. It is no longer possible to use education as an explanation for the lower earnings of women. Some observers have argued that women earn less money since they are less reliable workers who are more apt to leave the labor force. But it is difficult to maintain this position since women are less apt to quit one job to take another and as a result they tend to work as long, or longer, for any one employer. From any employer's perspective they are more reliable, not less reliable, than men. Part of the answer is visible if you look at the lifetime earnings profile of men. Suppose that you were asked to predict which men in a group of 25-year-olds would become economically successful. At age 25 it is difficult to tell who will be economically successful and your predictions are apt to be highly inaccurate. But suppose that you were asked to predict which men in a group of 35-year-olds would become economically successful. If you are successful at age 35, you are very likely to remain successful for the rest of your life. If you have not become economically successful by age 35, you are very unlikely to do so later. The decade between 25 and 35 is when men either succeed or fail. It is the decade when lawyers become partners in the good firms, when business managers make it onto the "fast track," when academics get tenure at good universities, and when blue collar workers find the job opportunities that will lead to training opportunities and the skills that will generate high earnings. If there is any one decade when it pays to work hard and to be consistently in the labor force, it is the decade between 25 and 35. For those who succeed, earnings will rise rapidly. For those who fail, earnings will remain flat for the rest of their lives. But the decade between 25 and 35 is precisely the decade when women are most apt to leave the labor force or become part-time workers to have children. When they do, the current system of promotion and skill acquisition will extract an enormous lifetime price. This leaves essentially two avenues for equalizing male and female earnings. Families where women who wish to have successful careers, compete with men, and achieve the same earnings should alter their family plans and have their children either before 25 or after 35. Or society can attempt to alter the existing promotion and skill acquisition system so that there is a longer time period in which both men and women can attempt to successfully enter the labor force. Without some combination of these two factors, a substantial fraction of the male-female earnings differentials are apt to persist for the next 40 years, even if discrimination against women is eliminated.

Chapter 4:
Customs and Habits

Jane Austen

From PRIDE AND PREJUDICE

A novelist and social critic, Jane Austen (1775-1817) wrote most often about society and marriage. Ironically, she never married herself, and kept herself quite removed from society. This excerpt from her novel, *Pride and Prejudice*, offers a penetrating description of the relationship between the Bennets, and the urgency which accompanied the custom of marriage. It might be helpful for you to compare this selection to John Stuart Mill's discussion of marriage.

It is a truth universally acknowledged that a single man in possession of a good fortune must be in want of a wife.

However little known the feelings or views of such a man may be on his first entering a neighbourhood, this truth is so well fixed in the minds of the surrounding families that he is considered as the rightful property of some one or other of their daughters.

"My dear Mr. Bennet," said his lady to him one day, "have you heard that Netherfield Park is let at last?"

Mr. Bennet replied that he had not.

"But it is," returned she; "for Mrs. Long has just been here, and she told me all about it."

Mr. Bennet made no answer.

"Do not you want to know who has taken it?" cried his wife impatiently.

"*You* want to tell me, and I have no objection to hearing it."

This was invitation enough.

"Why, my dear, you must know, Mrs. Long says that Netherfield is taken by a young man of large fortune from the north of England; that he came down on Monday in a chaise and four to see the place, and was so much delighted with it that he agreed with Mr. Morris immediately; that he is to take possession before Michaelmas*, and some of his servants are to be in the house by the end of next week."

"What is his name?"

"Bingley."

"Is he married or single?"

"Oh! single, my dear, to be sure! A single man of large fortune; four or five thousand a year. What a fine thing for our girls!"

"How so? How can it affect them?"

"My dear Mr. Bennet," replied his wife, "how can you be so tiresome! You must know that I am thinking of his marrying one of them."

"Is that his design in settling here?"

"Design! nonsense, how can you talk so! But it is very likely that he *may* fall in love with one of them, and therefore you must visit him as soon as he comes."

"I see no occasion for that. You and the girls may go, or you may send them by themselves, which perhaps will be still better, for as you are as handsome as any of them, Mr. Bingley might like you the best of the party."

"My dear, you flatter me. I certainly *have* had my share of beauty, but I do not pretend to be anything extraordinary now. When a woman has five grown up daughters, she ought to give over thinking of her own beauty."

"In such cases, a woman has not often much beauty to think of."

"But, my dear, you must indeed go and see Mr. Bingley when he comes into the neighbourhood."

"It is more than I engage for, I assure you."

---

* a religious holiday celebrated on September 29, the end of summer

"But consider your daughters. Only think what an establishment it would be for one of them. Sir William and Lady Lucas are determined to go, merely on that account, for in general you know they visit no newcomers. Indeed you must go, for it will be impossible for us to visit him if you do not."

"You are over scrupulous surely. I dare say Mr. Bingley will be very glad to see you; and I will send a few lines by you to assure him of my hearty consent to his marrying whichever he chooses of the girls; though I must throw in a good word for my little Lizzy."

"I desire you will do no such thing. Lizzy is not a bit better than the others; and I am sure she is not half so handsome as Jane, nor half so good-humoured as Lydia. But you are always giving *her* the preference."

"They have none of them much to recommend them," replied he; "they are all silly and ignorant like other girls; but Lizzy has something more of quickness than her sisters."

"Mr. Bennet, how can you abuse your own children in such a way? You take delight in vexing me. You have no compassion on my poor nerves."

"You mistake me, my dear. I have a high respect for your nerves. They are my old friends. I have heard you mention them with consideration these twenty years at least."

"Ah! you do not know what I suffer."

"But I hope you will get over it, and live to see many young men of four thousand a year come into the neighbourhood."

"It will be no use to us if twenty such should come since you will not visit them."

"Depend upon it, my dear, that when there are twenty, I will visit them all."

Mr. Bennet was so odd a mixture of quick parts, sarcastic humour, reserve, and caprice, that the experience of three and twenty years had been insufficient to make his wife understand his character. *Her* mind was less difficult to develop. She was a woman of mean understanding, little information, and uncertain temper. When she was discontented she fancied herself nervous. The business of her life was to get her daughters married; its solace was visiting and news.

James Thurber

COURTSHIP THROUGH THE AGES

James Thurber (1894-1961) an essayist, cartoonist, and short story
writer, gained notoriety when he joined the staff of *The New Yorker* at
the urging of E.B. White. Though his essays and cartoons often made
important social or political points, they were almost always pervaded
by Thurber's extraordinary wit. Here, he finds humor in the comparison of some of nature's most unusual courtship rituals with some of
man's most usual ones. As you read this essay, try to remember (if
you can bear it) your most embarrassing attempt to lure a member of
the desired sex.

Surely nothing in the astonishing scheme of life can have non-
plussed Nature so much as the fact that none of the females of
any of the species she created really cared very much for the
male, as such. For the past ten million years Nature has been
busily inventing ways to make the male attractive to the female,
but the whole business of courtship, from the marine annelids up
to man, still lumbers heavily along, like a complicated musical
comedy. I have been reading the sad and absorbing story in
Volume 6 (Cole to Dama) of the *Encyclopaedia Britannica.* In this
volume you can learn all about cricket, cotton, costume designing,
crocodiles, crown jewels, and Coleridge, but none of these subjects
is so interesting as the Courtship of Animals, which recounts the
sorrowful lengths to which all males must go to arouse the interest of a lady.

We all know, I think, that Nature gave man whiskers and a
mustache with the quaint idea in mind that these would prove
attractive to the female. We all know that, far from attracting
her, whiskers and mustaches only made her nervous and gloomy,
so that man had to go in for somersaults, tilting and lances, and
performing feats of parlor magic to win her attention; he also had
to bring her candy, flowers, and the furs of animals. It is common
knowledge that in spite of all these "love displays" the male is
constantly being turned down, insulted, or thrown out of the

house. It is rather comforting, then, to discover that the peacock, for all his gorgeous plumage, does not have a particularly easy time in courtship; none of the males in the world do. The first peahen, it turned out, was only faintly stirred by her suitor's beautiful train. She would often go quietly to sleep while he was whisking it around. The *Britannica* tells us that the peacock actually had to learn a certain little trick to wake her up and revive her interest: he had to learn to vibrate his quills so as to make a rustling sound. In ancient times man himself, observing the ways of the peacock, probably tried vibrating his whiskers to make a rustling sound; if so, it didn't get him anywhere. He had to go in for something else; so, among other things, he went in for gifts. It is not unlikely that he got this idea from certain flies and birds who were making no headway at all with rustling sounds.

One of the flies of the family Empidae, who had tried everything finally hit on something pretty special. He contrived to make a glistening transparent balloon which was even larger than himself. Into this he would put sweetmeats and tidbits and he would carry the whole elaborate envelope through the air to the lady of his choice. This amused her for a time, but she finally got bored with it. She demanded silly little colorful presents, something that you couldn't eat but that would look nice around the house. So the male Empis had to go around gathering flower petals and pieces of bright paper to put into his balloon. On a courtship flight a male Empis cuts quite a figure now, but he can hardly be said to be happy. He never knows how soon the female will demand heavier presents, such as Roman coins and gold collar buttons. It seems probable that one day the courtship of the Empidae will fall down, as man's occasionally does, of its own weight.

The bowerbird is another creature that spends so much time courting the female that he never gets any work done. If all the male bowerbirds became nervous wrecks within the next ten or fifteen years, it would not surprise me. The female bowerbird insists that a playground be built for her with a specially constructed bower at the entrance. This bower is much more elaborate than an ordinary nest and is harder to build; it costs a lot more, too. The female will not come to the playground until the male has filled it up with a great many gifts: silvery leaves, red leaves, rose petals, shells, beads, berries, bones, dice, buttons, cigar bands, Christmas seals, and the Lord knows what else. When the female finally condescends to visit the playground, she is in a coy and silly mood and has to be chased in and out of the bower and up and down the

playground before she will quit giggling and stand still long
enough even to shake hands. The male bird is, of course, pretty
well done in before the chase starts, because he has worn himself
out hunting for eyeglass lenses and begonia blossoms. I imagine
that many a bowerbird, after chasing a female for two or three
hours, says the hell with it and goes home to bed. Next day, of
course, he telephones someone else and the same trying ritual is
gone through with again. A male bowerbird is as exhausted as a
night-club habitue before he is out of his twenties.

The male fiddler crab has a somewhat easier time, but it can
hardly be said that he is sitting pretty. He has one enormously
large and powerful claw, usually brilliantly colored, and you
might suppose that all he had to do was reach out and grab some
passing cutie. The very earliest fiddler crabs may have tried this,
but, if so, they got slapped for their pains. A female fiddler crab will
not tolerate any caveman stuff; she never has and she doesn't intend to start now. To attract a female, a fiddler crab has to stand
on tiptoe and brandish his claw in the air. If any female in the
neighborhood is interested—and you'd be surprised how many
are not—she comes over and engages in light badinage, for which
he is not in the mood. As many as a hundred females may pass the
time of day with him and go on about their business. By night-fall
of an average courting day, a fiddler crab who has been standing
on tiptoe for eight or ten hours waving a heavy claw in the air is in
pretty sad shape. As in the case of the males of all species, however, he gets out of bed next morning, dashes some water on his
face, and tries again.

The next time you encounter a male web-spinning spider, stop
and reflect that he is too busy worrying about his love life to have
any desire to bite you. Male web-spinning spiders have a tougher
life than any other males in the animal kingdom. This is because
the female web-spinning spiders have very poor eyesight. If a
male lands on a female's web, she kills him before he has time to
lay down his cane and gloves, mistaking him for a fly or a bum-
blebee who has tumbled into her trap. Before the species figured
out what to do about this, millions of males were murdered by
ladies they called on. It is the nature of spiders to perform a little
dance in front of the female, but before a male spinner could get
near enough for the female to see who he was and what he was up
to, she would lash out at him with a flat-iron or a pair of garden
shears. One night, nobody knows when, a very bright male spinner lay awake worrying about calling on a lady who had been

killing suitors right and left. It came to him that this business of dancing as a love display wasn't getting anybody anywhere except the grave. He decided to go in for web-twitching, or strand-vibrating. The next day he tried it on one of the nearsighted girls. Instead of dropping in on her suddenly, he stayed outside the web and began monkeying with one of its strands. He twitched it up and down and in and out with such a lilting rhythm that the female was charmed. The serenade worked beautifully; the female let him live. The *Britannica's* spider-watchers, however, report that this system is not always successful. Once in a while, even now, a female will fire three bullets into a suitor or run him through with a kitchen knife. She keeps threatening him from the moment he strikes the first low notes on the outside strings, but usually by the time he has got up to the high notes played around the center of the web, he is going to town and she spares his life.

Even the butterfly, as handsome a fellow as he is, can't always win a mate merely by fluttering around and showing off. Many butterflies have to have scent scales on their wings. Hepialus carries a powder puff in a perfumed pouch. He throws perfume at the ladies when they pass. The male tree cricket, Oecanthus, goes Hepialus one better by carrying a tiny bottle of wine with him and giving drinks to such doxies as he has designs on. One of the male snails throws darts to entertain the girls. So it goes, through the long list of animals, from the bristle worm and his rudimentary dance steps to man and his gift of diamonds and sapphires. The golden-eye drake raises a jet of water with his feet as he flies over a lake; Hepialus has his powder puff, Oecanthus his wine bottle, man his etchings. It is a bright and melancholy story, the age-old desire of the male for the female, the age-old desire of the female to be amused and entertained. Of all the creatures on earth, the only males who could be figured as putting any irony into their courtship are the grebes and certain other diving birds. Every now and then a courting grebe slips quietly down to the bottom of a lake and then, with a mighty "Whoosh!," pops out suddenly a few feet from his girl friend, splashing water all over her. She seems to be persuaded that this is a purely loving display, but I like to think that the grebe always has a faint hope of drowning her or scaring her to death.

I will close this investigation into the mournful burdens of the male with the *Britannica's* story about a certain Argus pheasant. It appears that the Argus displays himself in front of a female who stands perfectly still without moving a feather. . . . The male Argus the *Britannica* tells about was confined in a cage with a female of another species, a female who kept moving around, emptying ashtrays and fussing with lampshades all the time the male was showing off his talents. Finally, in disgust, he stalked away and began displaying in front of his water trough. He reminds me of a certain male (Homo sapiens) of my acquaintance who one night after dinner asked his wife to put down her detective magazine so that he could read a poem of which he was very fond. She sat quietly enough until he was well into the middle of the thing, intoning with great ardor and intensity. Then suddenly there came a sharp, disconcerting slap! It turned out that all during the male's display, the female had been intent on a circling mosquito and had finally trapped it between the palms of her hands. The male in this case did not stalk away and display in front of a water trough; he went over to Tim's and had a flock of drinks and recited the poem to the fellas. I am sure they all told bitter stories of their own about how their displays had been interrupted by females. I am also sure that they all ended up singing "Honey, Honey, Bless Your Heart."

Leah Neuman (student)

CALLING A "BOY" FOR A "DATE"

We've all experienced it (men, still, probably more than women)—the anxiety about asking a potential love-interest on a date. Here, Leah Neuman (yes, the names have been changed to protect the innocent) tells all about one such experience. As you read, notice how much easier—and more fun—it is to read about these awkward moments than it would be to actually go through them yourself.

The first time I called up a "boy" ("a male human of almost any age whom I would consider going out with") to ask for a "date" ("an specified romantic activity that two people who don't know each other very well participate in"), I wrote down everything I wanted to say on a scrap of paper, so I wouldn't flub it. My cues went through several revisions before I settled on: "You are Daniel Clark. I am Leah Neuman. We know each other. I was wondering if you'd like to have dinner with me on Saturday." I wasn't planning to actually say the first three sentences; probably something like "Hello, Daniel? This is Leah Neuman. Yeah, that's right..." would come out. The last sentence, though, seemed to me to strike a perfect balance among all the necessary elements:

    a) It didn't end in a question mark;
    b) It referred to a specific activity;
    c) It referred to a specific day;
    d) It referred to a potentially romantic activity.

All these elements were necessary in order to make it easy for him to answer either yes or no graciously, without making me feel personally rejected. A question like "Do you want to go out with me?" for example, would leave not enough room for doubt. (Several desperate-but-charming young men I know have actually used this ploy with moderate, or at least temporary, success; it makes them look desperate-but-charming, neurotic in the way that certain neurotic hearers respond to very well indeed.)

Now that I had rehearsed and paced for a few hours, all that was left was to place the call. I figured that there were three possible desirable outcomes to dialing: Busy, no answer, or CONTACT! I received, on this call, the second-best option: CONTACT!, but with a brother—Argh! Daniel wasn't home, I left a message, Daniel would call back tonight; time for a new plan of attack. All that rehearsal time out the window. Now I had to re-shape my evening, around the central theme of Waiting for the Return Call—Without Sounding Like You're Waiting.

Let me step aside for a moment to tell you how I felt about Daniel. I knew him barely, briefly, but I had talked to him twice, at two different parties, once before Christmas vacation and once after. At the party before Christmas I had sprained my ankle and was sitting on a couch, trying to look as if I had chosen my fate, as if I liked to sit alone, as if all I was there for was people-watching, anyway. All of a sudden, a gorgeous stranger walked across the room, said hello, introduced himself, and sat beside me on the couch for fifteen minutes! I kept my cool, and we had a conversation about writing (mine) and painting (his). At the exact appropriate time, he excused himself, and a friend of mined eagerly filled his place to pump me for information. The next time I saw him, I walked by him several times (proving just how much more mobile I'd become since last we spoke), before I saw him alone and moved in for the kill—which turned out to be a conversation about painting (his) and writing (mine). Even so, I continued to find him charming, handsome, and friendly. In other words, good enough for a stranger.

So I got his number from my brother who knows his brother, who of course told him that somebody's brother had asked him for the phone number for her—so he had advance warning. However, I did not let advance warning take the place of proper rehearsal. Nosiree. He was a little older, he knew the score, and rehearsing my lines was the only way I could think of to equalize us at all. And now, waiting for his call, I had to devise a new plan that would serve the same equalizing function.

Simplicity was the answer. I would wait to pick up the phone until the middle of the third ring (time enough to clear my throat, not enough time to frustrate him), say hello, act unsurprised that he'd returned my call, and go directly from "Howareyougreatiamfine" to "I was wondering if you'd like to have dinner with me on Saturday night."

He called, I answered, it actually worked. I chose the restaurant; turns out he loves Thai! Great! Everything worked perfectly, charmingly, and we had a perfectly charming date. Over shrimp dumplings and sweet ice coffee, we discoursed at length on the topics of writing (mine) and painting (his). Our first, best, and only date.

Adam (student)

TIME TORTURE

In this essay, Adam describes what truly must be every students' object of hatred—the clock/radio. Notice how he uses the device of personification to make his loathing of his clock seem more. . . well, personal. Adam uses hyperbole—like the "millions" of dials—to excellent comic effect. You must be brave to use comedy well, though, since there are many situations where it may be seen as inappropriate.

Don't get me wrong—I'm really not paranoid. I mean, my alarm clock looks like a typical generic style clock/radio. Nothing appears outwardly abnormal at all. In fact, it doesn't have any truly distinguishing features at all, and I'm tempted to say that it's an average, run-of-the-mill, nondescript clock/radio. But, since it's a cop-out to describe something as "nondescript" (if not outright contradictory), I'll give a quick rundown of it. I've owned this clock/radio, a Realistic Chronomatic 213, for a month now, and it's still difficult to remember exactly what it looks like. There it is, a rectangular box sitting on my desk in the corner, six feet from my bed, with a bright red digital readout saying 9:39. The colon between the 9 and the 39—no, now 40—flashes on and off once per second, 24 hours a day. To the right of the time display is the radio tuning dial, set near 97 FM, probably KBCO Boulder. Also on the rectangular front face, just below the clock display and the radio tuning dial, is a row of four small round switches, used to set the time and the alarm. The top and the sides of the radio are an artificial wood-grain finish, trimmed with black and separated from the front panel by a chrome strip. Centered on its top is a small square speaker grill.

Yeah, this alarm clock would seem like a normal, well-adjusted appliance to most people, but that's because they don't have to live with it. Just by looking at it, a person wouldn't sense that this clock/radio carried a grudge and had general anti-social tendencies. Even I didn't notice anything strange until recently. First, small irritating things became apparent. For instance, the way it stares at night, annoyingly blinking its stupid red colon. After a half-hour of watching the clock gaze back, it's obvious that the stare isn't a benign one; it has the qualities of an unpleasant sneer, that certain executioner's look of someone in ultimate control. Then, I noticed how time always seemed to speed up at night while I slept. I could almost hear that damn blood-red colon flashing faster and faster, but as soon as I would open my eyes it would skid back down to once per second, once per second. The unnerving part, though, is that the clock speeds up in direct proportion to the amount of sleep that I need—so even if I go to bed early the night before a big exam, I still wake up with severe jetlag.

This clock's attitude problem doesn't become blatantly apparent until early morning, however. The hours of darkness slowly convert it into a remorseless predatory creature, primed to terrorize. Yes, terrorize. Remaining utterly silent and motionless so as not to stir its unsuspecting comatose victim, the clock waits. Mercilessly it savors its position of power as the final seconds slip by. And then it strikes. Noise and chaos, resembling the detonation of a medium-sized nuclear device in the corner of my room, slam out of its tiny speaker. At five in the morning. Actually, at five in the morning, the sound has more of a physical quality, roughly equivalent to a chainsaw being started in the left ear while a rake crashes into the jaw. Instinctively, my body, instantly brought from suspended animation to adrenalin overload, lunges in the general direction of the demonic box on the desk. My hand swats at every small knob—there are now millions of them—until it slaps the right switch in the right direction, snuffing out the noise and the pain.

Every morning, as I lie limply on the floor, I can see the clock display staring straight ahead, blinking its damn red colon in the morning sun, once per second, once per second, and I know it's trying not to snicker. I'm not paranoid—the clock really does hate me.

Maya Angelou

GRADUATION

Maya Angelou (1928-   ), an actress, editor, and poet, is best known for her autobiographical works. This selection is taken from her first such book, *I Know Why the Caged Bird Sings* (1969). As you read, ask yourself why celebrations such as graduation are so important to us. Why does it comfort us to sing the same songs (like the *Negro National Anthem*) over and over again? Why does *The Star Spangled Banner* make us cry during a war but make us bored at a sporting event?

The children in Stamps trembled visibly with anticipation. Some adults were excited too, but to be certain the whole young population had come down with graduation epidemic. Large classes were graduating from both the grammar school and the high school. Even those who were years removed from their own day of glorious release were anxious to help with preparations as a kind of dry run. The junior students who were moving into the vacating classes' chairs were tradition-bound to show their talents for leadership and management. They strutted through the school and around the campus exerting pressure on the lower grades. Their authority was so new that occasionally if they pressed a little too hard it had to be overlooked. After all, next term was coming, and it never hurt a sixth grader to have a play sister in the eighth grade, or a tenth-year student to be able to call a twelfth grader Bubba. So all was endured in a spirit of shared understanding. But the graduating classes themselves were the nobility. Like travelers with exotic destinations on their minds, the graduates were remarkably forgetful. They came to school without their books, or tablets or even pencils. Volunteers fell over themselves to secure replacements for the missing equipment. When accepted, the willing workers might or might not be thanked, and it was of no importance to the pregraduation rites. Even teachers were respectful of the now quiet and aging seniors, and tended to speak to them, if not as equals, as beings only slightly lower than themselves. After tests were returned and grades given, the student body, which acted like an extended family, knew who did well, who excelled, and what piteous ones had failed.

Unlike the white high school, Lafayette County Training School distinguished itself by having neither lawn, nor hedges, nor tennis court, nor climbing ivy. Its two buildings (main classrooms, the grade school and home economics) were set on a dirt hill with no fence to limit either its boundaries or those of bordering farms. There was a large expanse to the left of the school which was used alternately as a baseball diamond or a basketball court. Rusty hoops on the swaying poles represented the permanent recreational equipment, although bats and balls could be borrowed from the P.E. teacher if the borrower was qualified and if the diamond wasn't occupied. Over this rocky area relieved by a few shady tall persimmon trees the graduating class walked. The girls often held hands and no longer bothered to speak to the lower students. There was a sadness about them, as if this old world was not their home and they were bound for higher ground. The boys, on the other hand, had become more friendly, more outgoing. A decided change from the closed attitude they projected while studying for finals. Now they seemed not ready to give up the old school, the familiar paths and classrooms. Only a small percentage would be continuing on to college—one of the South's A & M (agricultural and mechanical) schools, which trained Negro youths to be carpenters, farmers, handymen, masons, maids, cooks and baby nurses. Their future rode heavily on their shoulders, and blinded them to the collective joy that had pervaded the lives of the boys and girls in the grammar school graduating class.

Parents who could afford it had ordered new shoes and ready-made clothes for themselves from Sears and Roebuck or Montgomery Ward. They also engaged the best seamstresses to make the floating graduating dresses and to cut down second-hand pants which would be pressed to a military slickness for the important event.

Oh, it was important, all right. Whitefolks would attend the ceremony, and two or three would speak of God and home, and the Southern way of life, and Mrs. Parsons, the principal's wife, would play the graduation march while the lower-grade graduates paraded down the aisles and took their seats below the platform. The high school seniors would wait in empty classrooms to make their dramatic entrance.

In the Store I was the person of the moment. The birthday girl. The center. Bailey had graduated the year before, although to do so he had had to forfeit all pleasures to make up for his time lost in Baton Rouge.

My class was wearing butter-yellow piqué dresses, and Momma launched out on mine. She smocked the yoke into tiny crisscrossing puckers, then shirred the rest of the bodice. Her dark fingers ducked in and out of the lemony cloth as she embroidered raised daisies around the hem. Before she considered herself finished she had added a crocheted cuff on the puff sleeves, and a pointy crocheted collar.

I was going to be lovely. A walking model of all the various styles of fine hand sewing and it didn't worry me that I was only twelve years old and merely graduating from the eighth grade. Besides, many teachers in Arkansas Negro schools had only that diploma and were licensed to impart wisdom.

The days had become longer and more noticeable. The faded beige of former times had been replaced with strong and sure colors. I began to see my classmates' clothes, their skin tones, and the dust that waved off pussy willows. Clouds that lazed across the sky were objects of great concern to me. Their shiftier shapes might have held a message that in my new happiness and with a little bit of time I'd soon decipher. During that period I looked—at the arch of heaven so religiously my neck kept a steady ache. I had taken to smiling more often, and my jaws hurt from the unaccustomed activity. Between the two physical sore spots, I suppose I could have been uncomfortable, but that was not the case. As a member of the winning team (the graduating class of 1940) I had outdistanced unpleasant sensations by miles. I was headed for the freedom of open fields.

Youth and social approval allied themselves with me and we trammeled memories of slights and insults. The wind of our swift passage remodeled my features. Lost tears were pounded to mud and then to dust. Years of withdrawal were brushed aside and left behind, as hanging ropes of parasitic moss.

My work alone had awarded me a top place and I was going to be one of the first called in the graduating ceremonies. On the classroom blackboard, as well as on the bulletin board in the auditorium, there were blue stars and white stars and red stars. No absences, no tardinesses, and my academic work was among the best of the year. I could say the preamble to the Constitution even faster than Bailey. We timed ourselves often: "Wethepeopleofthe-UnitedStatesinordertoformamoreperfectunion. . ." I had memorized the Presidents of the United States from Washington to Roosevelt in chronological as well as alphabetical order.

My hair pleased me, too. Gradually the black mass had lengthened and thickened, so that it kept at last to its braided pattern, and I didn't have to yank my scalp off when I tried to comb it.

Louise and I had rehearsed the exercises until we tired out ourselves. Henry Reed was class valedictorian. He was a small, very black boy with hooded eyes, a long, broad nose and an oddly shaped head. I had admired him for years because each term he and I vied for the best grades in our class. Most often he bested me, but instead of being disappointed I was pleased that we shared top places between us. Like many Southern Black children, he lived with his grandmother, who was as strict as Momma and as kind as she knew how to be. He was courteous, respectful and soft-spoken to elders, but on the play-ground he chose to play the roughest games. I admired him. Anyone, I reckoned, sufficiently afraid or sufficiently dull could be polite. But to be able to operate at a top level with both adults and children was admirable.

His valedictory speech was entitled "To Be or Not to Be." The rigid tenth-grade teacher had helped him to write it. He'd been working on the dramatic stresses for months.

The weeks until graduation were filled with heady activities. A group of small children were to be presented in a play about buttercups and daisies and bunny rabbits. They could be heard throughout the building practicing their hops and their little songs that sounded like silver bells. The older girls (non-graduates, of course) were assigned the task of making refreshments for the night's festivities. A tangy scent of ginger, cinnamon, nutmeg and chocolate wafted around the home economics building as the budding cooks made samples for themselves and their teachers.

In every corner of the workshop, axes and saws split fresh timber as the woodshop boys made sets and stage scenery. Only the graduates were left out of the general bustle. We were free to sit in the library at the back of the building or look in quite detachedly, naturally, on the measures being taken for our event.

Even the minister preached on graduation the Sunday before. His subject was, "Let your light so shine that men will see your good works and praise your father, Who is in Heaven." Although the sermon was purported to be addressed to us, he used the occasion to speak to backsliders, gamblers, and general ne'er-do-wells. But since he had called our names at the beginning of the service we were mollified.

Among Negroes the tradition was to give presents to children going only from one grade, to another. How much more important this was when the person was graduating at the top of the class. Uncle Willie and Momma had sent away for a Mickey Mouse watch like Bailey's. Louise gave me four embroidered handkerchiefs. (I gave her three crocheted doilies.) Mrs. Sneed, the minister's wife, made me an underskirt to wear for graduation, and nearly every customer gave me a nickel or maybe even a dime with the instruction "Keep on moving to higher ground," or some such encouragement.

Amazingly the great day finally dawned and I was out of bed before I knew it. I threw open the back door to see it more clearly, but Momma said, "Sister, come away from that door and put your robe on."

I hoped the memory of that morning would never leave me. Sunlight was itself still young, and the day had none of the insistence maturity would bring it in a few hours. In my robe and barefoot in the backyard, under cover of going to see about my new beans, I gave myself up to the gentle warmth and thanked God that no matter what evil I had done in my life He had allowed me to live to see this day. Somewhere in my fatalism I had expected to die, accidentally, and never have the chance to walk up the stairs in the auditorium and gracefully receive my hard-earned diploma. Out of God's merciful bosom I had won reprieve.

Bailey came out in his robe and gave me a box wrapped in Christmas paper. He said he had saved his money for months to pay for it. It felt like a box of chocolates, but I knew Bailey wouldn't save money to buy candy when we had all we could want under our noses.

He was as proud of the gift as I. It was a soft-leather-bound copy of a collection of poems by Edgar Allan Poe, or, as Bailey and I called him, "Eap." I turned to "Annabel Lee" and we walked up and down the garden rows, the cool dirt between our toes, reciting the beautifully sad lines.

Momma made a Sunday breakfast although it was only Friday. After we finished the blessing, I opened by eyes to find the watch on my plate. It was a dream of a day. Everything went smoothly and to my credit. I didn't have to be reminded or scolded for anything. Near evening I was too jittery to attend to chores, so Bailey volunteered to do all before his bath.

Days before, we had made a sign for the Store and as we turned out the lights Momma hung the cardboard over the doorknob. It read clearly: CLOSED. GRADUATION.

My dress fitted perfectly and everyone said that I looked like a sunbeam in it. On the hill, going toward the school, Bailey walked behind with Uncle Willie, who muttered, "Go on, Ju." He wanted him to walk ahead with us because it embarrassed him to have to walk so slowly. Bailey said he'd let the ladies walk together, and the men would bring up the rear. We all laughed, nicely.

Little children dashed by out of the dark like fireflies. Their crepe-paper dresses and butterfly wings were not made for running and we heard more than one rip, dryly, and the regretful "uh uh" that followed.

The school blazed without gaiety. The windows seemed cold and unfriendly from the lower hill. A sense of ill-fated timing crept over me, and if Momma hadn't reached for my hand I would have drifted back to Bailey and Uncle Willie, and possibly beyond. She made a few slow jokes about my feet getting cold, and tugged me along to the now-strange building.

Around the front steps, assurance came back. There were my fellow "greats," the graduating class. Hair brushed back, legs oiled, new dresses and pressed pleats, fresh pocket handkerchiefs and little handbags, all homesewn. Oh, we were up to snuff, all

right. I joined my comrades and didn't even see my family go in to
find seats in the crowded auditorium.

The school band struck up a march and all classes filed in as
had been rehearsed. We stood in front of our seats, as assigned,
and on a signal from the choir director, we sat. No sooner had this
been accomplished that the band started to play the national anthem. We rose again and sang the song, after which we recited
the pledge of allegiance. We remained standing for a brief minute
before the choir director and the principal signaled to us, rather
desperately I thought, to take our seats. The command was so
unusual that our carefully rehearsed and smooth-running machine was thrown off. For a full minute we fumbled for our chairs
and bumped into each other awkwardly. Habits change or solidify
under pressure, so in our state of nervous tension we had been
ready to follow our usual assembly pattern: the American
National Anthem, then the pledge of allegiance, then the song every Black person I knew called the Negro National Anthem. All
done in the same key, with the same passion and most often
standing on the same foot.

Finding my seat at last, I was overcome with a presentiment of
worse things to come. Something unrehearsed, unplanned, was
going to happen, and we were going to be made to look bad. I distinctly remember being explicit in the choice of pronoun. It was
"we," the graduating class, the unit, that concerned me then.

The principal welcomed "parents and friends" and asked the
Baptist minister to lead us in prayer. His invocation was brief and
punchy, and for a second I thought we were getting back on the
high road to right action. When the principal came back to the
dais, however, his voice had changed. Sounds always affected me
profoundly and the principal's voice was one of my favorites.
During assembly it melted and lowed weakly into the audience. It
had not been in my plan to listen to him, but my curiosity was
piqued and I straightened up to give him my attention.

He was talking about Booker T. Washington, our "late great
leader," who said we can be as close as the fingers on the hand,
etc. . . . Then he said a few vague things about friendship and the
friendship of kindly people to those less fortunate than themselves.
With that his voice nearly faded, thin, away. Like a river diminishing to a stream and then to a trickle. But he cleared his throat
and said, "Our speaker tonight, who is also our friend, came from
Texarkana to deliver the commencement address, but due to the
irregularity of the train schedule, he's going to, as they say, 'speak

and run.'" He said that we understood and wanted the man to know that we were most grateful for the time he was able to give us and then something about how we were willing always to adjust to another's program, and without more ado—"I give you Mr. Edward Donleavy."

Not one but two white men came through the door offstage. The shorter one walked to the speaker's platform, and the tall one moved over to the center seat and sat down. But that was our principal's seat, and already occupied. The dislodged gentleman bounced around for a long breath or two before the Baptist minister gave him his chair, then with more dignity than the situation deserved, the minister walked off the stage.

Donleavy looked at the audience once (on reflection, I'm sure that he wanted only to reassure himself that we were really there), adjusted his glasses and began to read from a sheaf of papers.

He was glad "to be here and to see the work going on just as it was in the other schools."

At the first "Amen" from the audience I willed the offender to immediate death by choking on the word. But Amen's and Yes, sir's began to fall around the room like rain through a ragged umbrella.

He told us of the wonderful changes we children in Stamps had in store. The Central School (naturally, the white school was Central) had already been granted improvements that would be in use in the fall. A well-known artist was coming from Little Rock to teach art to them. They were going to have the newest microscopes and chemistry equipment for their laboratory. Mr. Donleavy didn't leave us long in the dark over who made these improvements available to Central High. Nor were we to be ignored in the general betterment scheme he had in mind.

He said that he had pointed out to people at a very high level that one of the first-line football tacklers at Arkansas Agricultural and Mechanical College had graduated from good old Lafayette County Training School. Here fewer Amen's were heard. Those few that did break through lay dully in the air with the heaviness of habit.

He went on to praise us. He went on to say how he had bragged that "one of the best basketball players at Fisk sank his first ball right here at Lafayette County Training School."

The white kids were going to have a chance to become Galileos and Madame Curies and Edisons and Gauguins, and our boys

(the girls weren't even in on it) would try to be Jesse Owenses and
Joe Louises.

Owens and the Brown Bomber were great heroes in our world,
but what school official in the white-goddom of Little Rock had
the right to decide that those two men must be our only heroes?
Who decided that for Henry Reed to become a scientist he had to
work like George Washington Carver, as a bootblack, to buy a
lousy microscope? Bailey was obviously always going to be small to
be an athlete, so which concrete angel glued to what country seat
had decided that if my brother wanted to become a lawyer he had
to first pay penance for his skin by picking cotton and hoeing corn
and studying correspondence books at night for twenty years?

The man's dead words fell like bricks around the auditorium
and too many settled in my belly. Constrained by hard-learned
manners I couldn't look behind me, but to my left and right the
proud graduating class of 1940 had dropped their heads. Every
girl in my row had found something new to do with her handkerchief. Some folded the tiny squares into love knots, some into
triangles, but most were wadding them, then pressing them flat
on their yellow laps.

On the dais, the ancient tragedy was being replayed. Professor
Parsons sat, a sculptor's reject, rigid. His large, heavy body
seemed devoid of will or willingness, and his eyes said he was no
longer with us. The other teachers examined the flag (which was
draped stage right) or their notes, or the windows which opened
on our now-famous playing diamond.

Graduation, the hush-hush magic time of frills and gifts and
congratulations and diplomas, was finished for me before my
name was called. The accomplishment was nothing. The metic-
ulous maps, drawn in three colors of ink, learning and spelling
decasyllabic words, memorizing the whole of *The Rape of
Lucrece*—it was nothing. Donleavy had exposed us.

We were maids and farmers, handymen and washerwomen,
and anything higher that we aspired to was farcical and pre-
sumptuous. Then I wished that Gabriel Prosser and Nat Turner
had killed all whitefolks in their beds and that Abraham Lincoln
had been assassinated before the signing of the Emancipation
Proclamation, and that Harriet Tubman had been killed by that
blow on her head and Christopher Columbus had drowned in the
Santa Maria.

It was awful to be Negro and have no control over my life. It
was brutal to be young and already trained to sit quietly and listen

to charges brought against my color with no chance of defense. We should all be dead. I thought I should like to see us all dead, one on top of the other. A pyramid of flesh with the whitefolks on the bottom, as the broad base, then the Indians with their silly toma- hawks and teepees and wigwams and treaties, the Negroes with their mops and recipes and cotton sacks and spirituals sticking out of their mouths. The Dutch children should all stumble in their wooden shoes and break their necks. The French should choke to death on the Louisiana Purchase (1803) while silk- worms ate all the Chinese with their stupid pigtails. As a species, we were an abomination. All of us.

Donleavy was running for election, and assured our parents that if he won we could count on having the only colored paved playing field in that part of Arkansas. Also—he never looked up to acknowledge the grunts of acceptance—also, we were bound to get some new equipment for the home economics building and the workshop.

He finished, and since there was no need to give any more than the most perfunctory thank-you's, he nodded to the men on the stage, and the tall white man who was never introduced joined him at the door. They left with the attitude that now they were off to something really important. (The graduation ceremonies at Lafayette County Training School had been a mere preliminary.)

The ugliness they left was palpable. An uninvited guest who wouldn't leave. The choir was summoned and sang a modern ar- rangement of "Onward, Christian Soldiers," with new words pertaining to graduates seeking their place in the world. But it didn't work. Elouise, the daughter of the Baptist minister, recited "Invictus," and I could have cried at the impertinence of "I am the master of my fate, I am the captain of my soul."

My name had lost its ring of familiarity and I had to be nudged to go and receive my diploma. All my preparations had fled. I neither marched up to the stage like a conquering Amazon, nor did I look in the audience for Baileys nod of approval. Marguerite Johnson, I heard the name again, my honors were read, there were noises in the audience of appreciation, and I took my place on the stage as rehearsed.

I thought about colors I hated: ecru, puce, lavender, beige and black.

There was shuffling and rustling around me, then Henry Reed was giving his valedictory address, "To Be or Not to Be." Hadn't he heard the whitefolks? We couldn't *be*, so the question was a

waste of time. Henry's voice came out clear and strong. I feared to
look at him. Hadn't he got the message? There was no "nobler in
the mind" for Negroes because the world didn't think we had
minds, and they let us know it. "Outrageous fortune"? Now, that
was a joke. When the ceremony was over I had to tell Henry Reed
some things. That is, if I still cared. Not "rub," Henry, "erase."
"Ah, there's the erase." Us.

Henry had been a good student in elocution. His voice rose on
tides of promise and fell on waves of warnings. The English
teacher had helped him to create a sermon winging through
Hamlet's soliloquy. To be a man, a doer, a builder, a leader, or to be
a tool, an unfunny joke, a crusher of funky toadstools. I marveled
that Henry could go through with the speech as if we had a choice.

I had been listening and silently rebutting each sentence with
my eyes closed; then there was a hush, which in an audience
warns that something unplanned is happening. I looked up and
saw Henry Reed, the conservative, the proper, the A student, turn
his back to the audience and turn to us (the proud graduating
class of 1940) and sing, nearly speaking,

> Lift ev'ry voice and sing
> Till earth and heaven ring
> Ring with the harmonies of Liberty . . .

It was the poem written by James Weldon Johnson. It was the
music composed by J. Rosamond Johnson. It was the Negro
National Anthem. Out of habit we were singing it. Our mothers
and fathers stood in the dark hall and joined the hymn of encouragement. A kindergarten teacher led the small children onto the
stage and the buttercups and daisies and bunny rabbits marked
time and tried to follow:

> Stony the road we trod
> Bitter the chastening rod
> Felt in the days when hope, unborn, had died.
> Yet with a steady beat
> Have not our weary feet
> Come to the place for which our fathers sighed?

Every child I knew had learned that song with his ABC's and
along with "Jesus Loves Me This I Know." But I personally had
never heard it before. Never heard the words, despite the thousands of times I had sung them. Never thought they had anything
to do with me.

On the other hand, the words of Patrick Henry had made such an impression on me that I had been able to stretch myself tall and trembling and say, "I know not what course others may take, but as for me, give me liberty or give me death."

And now I heard, really for the first time:

We have come over a way that with tears has been watered,
We have come, trading our path through the blood of the slaughtered.

While echoes of the song shivered in the air, Henry Reed bowed his head, said "Thank you," and returned to his place in the line. The tears that slipped down many faces were not wiped away in shame.

We were on top again. As always, again. We survived. The depths had been icy and dark, but now a bright sun spoke to our souls. I was no longer simply a member of the proud graduating class of 1940; I was a proud member of the wonderful, beautiful Negro race.

Oh, Black known and unknown poets, how often have your auctioned pains sustained us? Who will compute the lonely nights made less lonely by your songs, or the empty pots made less tragic by your tales?

If we were a people much given to revealing secrets, we might raise monuments and sacrifice to the memories of our poets, but slavery cured us of that weakness. It may be enough, however, to have it said that we survive in exact relationship to the dedication of our poets (include preachers, musicians and blues singers).

W. E. B. DuBois

THE SOULS OF WHITE FOLK

William Edgar Burghardt DuBois was a descendant of a French Huguenot and an African slave. He received B.A. degrees from both Fisk and Harvard Universities and a Ph.D. from the University of Berlin. He taught, at various times, at Wilberforce, the University of Pennsylvania, and Atlanta University, holding professorships in Greek, Latin, Sociology, Economics, and History. In addition, he edited many publications, including *Crisis*, the journal of the

National Association for the Advancement of Colored People, from
1910 to 1934. One of his most famous works was *The Souls of Black
Folks*—both a fine piece of English prose and a plea for greater understanding of blacks by whites. Seven years later, in 1910, he wrote this
essay as a plea to whites to understand themselves.

High in the tower where I sit beside the loud complaining of the
human sea I know many souls that toss and whirl and pass, but
none there are that puzzle me more than the Souls of White Folk.
Not, mind you, the souls of them that are white, but souls of them
that have become painfully conscious of their whiteness; those in
whose minds the paleness of their bodily skins is fraught with
tremendous and eternal significance.

Forgetting (as I can at times forget) the meaning of this singular obsession to me and my folk, I become the more acutely
sensitive to the marvelous part this thought is playing today, and
to the way it is developing the Souls of White Folk, and I wonder
what the end will be.

The discovery of personal whiteness among the world's people is
a very modern thing—a nineteenth- and twentieth-century
matter, indeed. The ancient world would have laughed at such a
distinction. The Middle Ages regarded it with mild curiosity, and
even up into the eighteenth century we were hammering our national manikins into one great Universal Man with fine frenzy,
which ignored color and race as well as birth. Today we have
changed all that, and the world, in sudden emotional conversation, has discovered that it is white, and, by that token,
wonderful.

When I seek to explain this, to me, inexplicable phenomenon,
there always creeps first to my mind the analogy of the child and
his candy. To every child there comes a time when the tooth-
someness of his sweets is strangely enhanced by the thought that
his playmate has none. Further than this, however, the analogy
fails, for with one accord the mother world seeks to teach this
child the third new joy of sharing. Any thought, however, of
sharing their color is to white folk not simply unthinkable, but its
mention is liable to lead to violent explosions of anger and vitu-
peration. Not only is there this unrebuked and vociferously ap-
plauded greediness, but something that sounds like: "I shall keep
my candy and you shall not have yours." Or, in other words, it is
not the obvious proposition: "I am white and you are black," but
the astonishing declaration, "I am white and you are nothing."

This assumption that of all the hues of God, whiteness alone is candy to the world child—is inherently and obviously better than brownness or tan—leads to curious acts; even the sweeter souls of the dominant world, as they discourse with me on weather, weal and woe, are continually playing above their actual words an obligato of turn and tone, saying:

"My poor unwhite thing! Weep not nor rage. I know, too well, that the curse of God lies heavy on you. Why? That is not for me to say; but be brave! Do your work in your lowly sphere, praying the good Lord that into heaven above, where all is love, you may one day, be born—white!"

At such times I have an unholy desire to laugh, and to ask with seemingly irrelevance and certain irreverence: "But what on earth is whiteness, that one should so desire it?"

Then always somehow, some way, silently but clearly, I am given to understand that whiteness is the ownership of the earth, forever and ever, Amen!

Now, what is the effect on a man or a nation when it comes passionately to believe such an extraordinary dictum as this? That nations are coming to believe it is manifest daily. Wave on wave, each with increasing virulence, is dashing this new religion of whiteness on the shores of our time. Its first effects are funny; the strut of the Southerner, the arrogance of the Englishman amuck, the whoop of the hoodlum who vicariously leads your mob. Next it appears dampening generous enthusiasm in what we once counted glorious: To free the slave is discovered to be tolerable only insofar as it freed his master. Do we sense somnolent writhings in black Africa, or angry groans in India, or triumphant "banzais" in Japan? "To your tents, O Israel!" These nations are not white. Build warships and heft the Big Stick.

After the more comic manifestations and chilling of generous enthusiasm, come subtler, darker deeds. Everything considered, the title to the universe claimed by white folk is faulty. It ought at least to look plausible. How easy, then, by emphasis and omission, to make every child believe that every great soul the world ever saw was a white man's soul; that every great thought the world ever knew was a white man's thought; that every great deed the world ever did was a white man's deed; that every great dream the world ever sang was a white man's dream. In fine, that if from the world were dropped everything that could not fairly be attributed to white folk the world would, if anything, be even

greater, truer, better than now. And if all this be a lie, is it not a lie
in a great cause?

Here it is that the comedy verges to tragedy. The fist minor note
is struck all unconsciously by those worthy souls in whom consciousness of high descent brings burning desire to spread the gift
abroad—the obligation of nobility to the ignoble. Such sense of duty
assumes two things: A real possession of the heritage and its frank
appreciation by the humbly born. So long, then, as humble black
folk, voluble with thanks, receive barrels of old clothes from lordly
and generous whites, there is much mental peace and moral satisfaction. But when the black man begins to dispute the white
man's title to certain alleged bequests of the Father's in wage and
position, authority and training; and when his attitude toward
charity is sullen anger rather than humble jollity; when he insists
on his human rights to swagger and swear and waste—then the
spell is suddenly broken and the philanthropist is apt to be ready to
believe that Negroes are impudent, that the South is right, and
that Japan wants to fight us.

Mentally the blight has fallen on American science. The race
problem is not insoluble if the correct answer is sought. It is insoluble if the wrong answer is insisted upon as it has been insisted
upon for thrice a hundred years. A very moderate brain can show
that two and two is four. But no human ingenuity can make that
sum three or five. This American science has long attempted to
do. It has made itself the handmaid of a miserable prejudice. In its
attempt to justify the treatment of black folk it has repeatedly
suppressed evidence, misquoted authority, distorted fact and deliberately lied. It is wonderful that in the very lines of social study,
where America should shine, it has done nothing.

Worse than this is our moral and religious plight. We profess a
religion of high ethical advancement, a spiritual faith, of respect
for truth, despising of personal riches, a reverence for humility,
and not simply justice to our fellows, but personal sacrifice of our
good for theirs. It is a high aim, so high that we ought not utterly
to be condemned for not reaching it, so long as we strive bravely
toward it. Do we, as a people? On the contrary, we have injected
into our creed a gospel of human hatred and prejudice, a despising
of our less fortunate fellows, not to speak of our reverence for
wealth, which flatly contradicts the Christian ideal. Granting all
that American Christianity has done to educate and uplift black
men, it must be frankly admitted that there is absolutely no logical
method by which the treatment of black folk by white folk in this

land can be squared with any reasonable statement or practice of the Christian ideal.

What is the result? It is either the abandonment of the Christian ideal or hypocrisy. Some frankly abandon Christianity when it comes to the race problem and say: Religion does not enter here. They then retire to some more primitive paganism and live there, enlightened by such prejudices as they adopt or inherit. This is retrogression toward barbarism, but it is at least honest. It is infinitely better than its widely accepted alternative, which attempts to reconcile color caste and Christianity, and sees or affects to see no incongruity. What ails the religion of a land when its strongholds of orthodoxy are to be found in those regions where race prejudice is most uncompromising, vindictive, and cruel; where human brotherhood is a lie?

The one great moral issue of America upon which the Church of Christ comes nearest being dumb is the question as to the application of the golden rule between white and black folk.

All this I see and hear up in my tower above the thunder of the seven seas. From my narrowed windows I stare into the night that looms beneath the cloud-swept stars. Eastward and westward storms are brewing great, ugly whirlwinds of hatred and blood and cruelty. I will not believe them inevitable. I will not believe that all that was must be—that all the shameful drama of the past must be done again today before the sunlight sweeps the silver seas.

If I cry amid this roar of elemental forces, must my cry be vain because it is but a cry—a small and human cry amid Promethean gloom?

Back beyond the world and swept by these wild white faces of the awful dead, why will this Soul of the White Folk, this modern Prometheus, hang bound by his own binding, tethered by a labor of the past? I hear his mighty cry reverberating through the world, I am white!" Well and good, O Prometheus, divine thief! The world is wide enough for two colors, two little shinings of the sun; why then devour your own vitals when I answer, "I am black"?

Tom (student)

THE ACCIDENT

Tom has managed to turn an essay that could easily been just hero-worship into something more. His father assisted two badly injured people at the scene of an accident, an act worthy of considerable praise. Tom simply describes what he saw, but when he contrasts the inaction of the crowd with his father's bravery, the result is a poignant statement about society, instead of simply empty praise for his father. As you read the essay, ask yourself what you would have done if you were driving by.

The summer of '74 contained more than its share of excitement. My family had decided to move from a small, friendly community to a larger, more vibrant city. At the time, I was only ten years old and could hardly wait to meet new friends and move into a new house. This experience did not prove to be the highlight of my summer. Of far greater significance, I witnessed a near-fatal automobile accident. Never before had I been exposed to such pain and suffering.

The accident occurred on the sixty-mile stretch of highway connecting our town to the city. It was my Dad's day off, and he had asked me to accompany him as he drove the old Ford truck, loaded down with furniture, to our new home. I couldn't pass up the offer. Riding in the truck with my father was always enjoyable, even though I had become bored with the monotonous scenery of the trip. The traffic on the narrow two-lane highway was heavier than usual for a Saturday afternoon, but it did not seem to diminish Dad's ability to talk and drive at the same time.

Roughly forty miles into the journey the real action began. Several hundred yards ahead of us was the junction of our highway with the interstate that led into the city. As we entered the approach ramp, I remember Dad commenting on the excessive speed of a red car traveling in front of us. Out of reflex I turned my head to face the front window. It was at this time that a cold chill of fright grabbed my body. I froze to my seat, watching the same red car mysteriously vault from the highway, fly over the long, steep embankment, and vanish from my field of vision.

Without a blink of hesitation or fear, Dad slammed on our brakes, sending the truck into a controlled skid. We came to an abrupt stop on the shoulder of the road in the vicinity of where the car had become momentarily airborne. Several other cars also stopped, but I saw no one advancing to the wreckage. Then Dad turned in my direction, instructing me to stay close to the truck. Filled with fear, I watched as he fled from our vehicle and descended the steep embankment, twice losing balance and landing on his back. As Dad made his way to the crushed automobile, not one of the other bystanders responded in a similar manner. They all remained on the highway, watching the action from a distance.

A cloud of smoke and dust surrounded the site where the car had landed. From my location I could smell the fumes of gasoline and burning rubber, though I could neither see nor hear any signs of life. As Dad approached the smoldering wreckage, however, I became aware of the deathly scream of a young girl trapped within. Dad reacted quickly, attempting to jar one of the twisted doors open. Being unsuccessful, he then crawled beneath the inverted car and pulled her to safety through the opening that had once been occupied by the front windshield. She appeared to be holding her left knee as she squirmed frantically on the ground. Hearing her screams, I could tell she was in great pain.

The driver had miraculously been thrown clear of the automobile, possibly escaping death by the shattered front window. I watched as he attempted to stand up, his face and chest dripping with blood. This attempt ended instantly as his wobbly body collapsed to the earth. He had lost consciousness. I began to panic as not one of the adults standing next to me responded to the crisis. Out of instinct I yelled at my Dad. Hearing my screams, he immediately switched his attention from the girl to the unconscious man. By applying pressure to the open wounds, he was able to stabilize the excessive bleeding.

Within a few minutes an ambulance arrived at the scene. The paramedics rushed down the embankment with their first-aid equipment and began emergency care of the victims. Sensing he was no longer needed, Dad made his way back to our truck. His previously clean shirt was now filthy with blood and dirt, and his face was sticky with sweat.

I had observed everyone's reaction to the accident from my position on the highway. I was amazed at how quickly my Dad had reacted. He had possibly saved another person's life. What confused me, however, was the reaction of the other adults who were standing alongside me. Why, I wondered, had not one of them offered assistance to my Dad? I could not understand how they could simply watch and not respond when other human beings were desperately in need of help. Perhaps they had been overcome with fear, momentarily paralyzed. Or maybe they preferred not to get involved, assuming my Dad had the situation under control. Whatever their reasons, I was perplexed at their behavior. If I had been older, I surely would have attempted to help.

I remember how proud I was as I watched Dad climb back into the truck. His shirt was ruined, but he did not seem to mind. As we drove the remaining twenty miles to the city, I sensed he was satisfied with how he had responded to the emergency; I know I was. From that day on I wanted to grow up to be just like him.

Shana Alexander

FASHIONS IN FUNERALS

Have you ever considered why we bury our dead? Does it really make any more sense than cutting them up and serving them for dinner? The only explanation is that it's what we're comfortable doing, just like natives of New Guinea are comfortable eating roasted thigh. Shana Alexander (1925-   ) chews on that thought in this excerpt from *Talking Woman*. As you read it, think about how you'd like to be treated when you've passed on.

A man in the remote jungles of New Guinea not long ago murdered another man with an ax. Tribal justice ensued. First the murderer was shot and killed with an arrow, and then seven other members of the tribe cut him up and ate him.

When word of the feast reached civilization, the authorities concluded that on this occasion justice had literally been served, and perhaps a bit too swiftly, so they hauled the seven cannibals into court, where a wise Australian judge dismissed all the charges, and acquitted the seven men. "The funerary customs of the people of Papua and New Guinea," he explained, "have been, and in many cases remain, bizarre in the extreme."

What, I wonder, would the judge have to say about the new, high-rise mausoleum now under construction in Nashville, Tennessee? When completed, this model of modern funerary design will be twenty stories high, fully air-conditioned, and capable of holding 65,000 bodies. A second slightly less deluxe tower on an adjoining site will have facilities to entomb 63,500 more. Nashville's enterprising mortician entrepreneur points out that his high-rise mortuary will be self-contained on only 14 acres, whereas it would require 129 acres to contain all these caskets in the, uh, conventional manner.

Well, not exactly caskets. In the new-style funeral, you will be laid out—after embalming, of course—on something called a "repose," described as a "bedlike structure," complete with white sheets, pillow, and blanket. When the ceremonies are ended, bed, pillow, sheet, and blanket are all whisked away; a fiberglass lid snaps down over what remains; and—zap—it's into the wall, stacked seven-high, with a neat bronze marker attached to the face of the crypt.

The forward-looking undertaker who thought all this up is already respected, in the trade, for bringing to Nashville the one-stop funeral.

But the most important advantage of the high-rise mausoleum is that by putting everything-but-everything under one roof you cut down on the high cost of dying. Maybe so, maybe so. But I can't help thinking it would be even cheaper to die in New Guinea, where the funerary customs are certainly no less bizarre, and a lot more practical.

William Raspberry

THE HANDICAP OF DEFINITION

William Raspberry (1935-   ) is a journalist who writes frequently about the issues of race and discrimination. In this essay, he comments on the problems created by society's narrow definition of "black." Before you read this essay, ask yourself what things black people do especially well.

I know all about bad schools, mean politicians, economic deprivation and racism. Still, it occurs to me that one of the heaviest burdens black Americans—and black children in particular—have to bear is the handicap of definition: the question of what it means to be black.

Let me explain quickly what I mean. If a basketball fan says that the Boston Celtics' Larry Bird plays "black," the fan intends it—and Bird probably accepts it—as a compliment. Tell pop singer Tom Jones he moves "black" and he might grin in appreciation. Say to Teena Marie or The Average White Band that they sound "black" and they'll thank you.

But name one pursuit, aside from athletics, entertainment or sexual performance in which a white practitioner will feel complimented to be told he does it "black." Tell a white broadcaster he talks "black" and he'll sign up for diction lessons. Tell a white reporter he writes "black" and he'll take a writing course. Tell a white lawyer he reasons "black" and he might sue you for slander.

What we have here is a tragically limited definition of blackness, and it isn't only white people who buy it.

Think of all the ways black children can put one another down with charges of "whiteness." For many of these children, hard study and hard work are "white." Trying to please a teacher might be criticized as acting "white." Speaking correct English is "white." Scrimping today in the interest of tomorrow's goals is "white." Educational toys and games are "white."

An incredible array of habits and attitudes that are conducive to success in business, in academia, in the non-entertainment professions are likely to be thought of as somehow "white." Even economic success, unless it involves such "black" undertakings as numbers banking, is defined as "white."

And the results are devastating. I wouldn't deny that blacks often are better entertainers and athletes. My point is the harm that comes from too narrow a definition of what is black.

One reason black youngsters tend to do better at basketball, for instance, is that they assume they can learn to do it well, and so they practice constantly to prove themselves right.

Wouldn't it be wonderful if we could infect black children with the notion that excellence in math is "black" rather than white, or possibly Chinese? Wouldn't it be of enormous value if we could create the myth that morality, strong families, determination, courage and love of learning are traits brought by slaves from Mother Africa and therefore quintessentially black?

There is no doubt in my mind that most black youngsters could develop their mathematical reasoning, their elocution and their attitudes the way they develop their jump shots and their dance steps: by the combination of sustained, enthusiastic practice and the unquestioned belief that they can do it.

In one sense, what I am talking about is the importance of developing positive ethnic traditions. Maybe Jews have an innate talent for communication; maybe the Chinese are born with a gift for mathematical reasoning; maybe blacks are naturally blessed with athletic grace. I doubt it. What is at work, I suspect, is assumption, inculcated early in their lives, that this is a thing our people do well.

Unfortunately, many of the things about which blacks make this assumption are things that do not contribute to their career success—except for that handful of the truly gifted who can make it as entertainers and athletes. And many of the things we concede to whites are the things that are essential to economic security. So it is with a number of assumptions black youngsters make about what it is to be a "man": physical aggressiveness, sexual prowess, the refusal to submit to authority. The prisons are full of people who, by this perverted definition, are unmistakably men.

But the real problem is not so much that the things defined as "black" are negative. The problem is that the definition is much too narrow.

Somehow, we have to make our children understand that they are intelligent, competent people, capable of doing whatever they put their minds to and making it in the American mainstream, not just in a black subculture.

What we seem to be doing, instead, is raising up yet another generation of young blacks who will be failures—by definition.

Melvin Konner

KICK OFF YOUR HEELS

Melvin Konner, an M.D. and anthropologist, occasionally writes essays for popular consumption. In this essay, he examines the allure and the dangers of high-heeled shoes. As you read this essay, think about the painful things you do to make yourself attractive—from plucking eyebrows to exercise to wearing uncomfortable clothes—how much of it is really necessary and how much is just for show?

A friend of mine, a sedate historian, allows how he used to sit in the library as a graduate student at Princeton trying to bury his thoughts in some thick tome. In those bad old days, when Princeton was all-male, the appearance of a female visitor would sometimes be signaled by a sound outside the window in the summer evening: the unmistakable click, click of high heels on the garden walk. Like the bell that made Pavlov's dog salivate, the mere sound of the walk triggered a physiological cascade. Such is the drift of the male brain that it can be drawn off course, for at least minutes, by the sound of a symbol of sexuality.

Yet consider what those heels do with the female form. The legs are slimmed and lengthened; this makes them what students of animal behavior call a supernormal stimulus—recalling, yet exaggerating the lengthening that occurs at puberty. (Pin-up drawings always exaggerate length.) At the same time, the feet are shortened—daintier? For some reason, both men and women seem to prefer smaller feet. Heels tighten the calves and make them prominent. The buttocks are thrown up and out (a distant echo, perhaps, of the sexual "presenting" of female mammals) and the bosom thrust forward, producing the S-curve for which women bustled and corseted brutally in time past. That certain something—not a ponytail—that sways when she walks (because women's hips are wider and not poised over the knees) sways more than usual. And she is hobbled. She is charmingly (to him) off-balance on her pedestal, and unable to flee. (A convicted mugger has said, "We would wait under a stairwell in the subway station and, when we heard the click of the wobbly spiked heel, we knew we had one.")

The message is not unambiguous helplessness. The heels just about abolish the average male advantage in height. The points of the heels and the toes are suitable weapons. But regardless of ambiguity, they convey a message: Look at me; get close if you can—or, if you haven't the courage, try to go back to your book.

Courting creatures signal sex in myriad ways. Often the males do the strutting. The peacock spreads his magnificent eyed feathers, and antelope like the Uganda kob prance and clang great antlers against each other. Other species leave some posing to the female. In the 10-spined stickleback, a little fresh-water fish of the British Isles, the female flashes a bit of swollen silver belly and triggers the male's courtship dance. The female zebra finch, an Australian perching bird, sits on a branch and stretches in a horizontal posture. While the male watches nearby, she bends her legs, sleeks her gray feathers and flutters her black-and-white tail. The female great crested grebe, ordinarily a graceful diving waterbird, assumes an even more awkward posture, sitting on the water with her wings spread and shoulders pointing down.

Humans are no slouches when it comes to sexual signaling. On the contrary, we take the signals nature has given us—an arched brow, a descending eyelid, a smile—and embellish them with every conceivable cultural brush stroke. Draping or painting or piercing or molding the body has gone on for millenniums. New Guinea men paint themselves dramatically for dancing, and marriageable Papuan maidens bear elegant tattoos. Extensive, patterned scars variously signified femininity and manliness in many African cultures. Lip plugs, head molding, circumcision, ear stretching, tooth filing—the list goes on.

Fewer than a hundred years ago, Western women tied themselves in corsets that damaged abdominal organs and made them respiratory wrecks. At the same time, the Chinese were still practicing the extraordinary 1,000-year-old tradition of footbinding. The resulting foot was shortened, with all toes but the first curled under and the arch drastically raised—essentially, high heels made of bone. This distortion was a matter of pride, a sign of nobility and allure.

How close do our own artificial high heels come to that old Chinese ideal? Not very, but there are similarities. Both signify sex and class, and achieve femininity. And both, to different degrees, result in impairment.

Orthopedists and chiropractors see the consequences in backache and knee problems. One orthopedics textbook describes the gait in such shoes as "ungainly" and "mincing," and notes that the normal cushioning is lost. Authorities agree that the toes and balls of the feet in high heels must bear too much weight in striking the ground, and that they transmit the shock upward. After prolonged wearing of high heels, the calf muscles and the Achilles' tendon may permanently contract. Robert Donatelli, a physical therapist, says shortened calf muscles may cause the knees to be slightly flexed; this in turn may cause chronic flection of hips. The ultimate result may produce a shape of buttocks suggestive to the male, but at the cost of increased lumbar lordosis, harmful pressure on the lumbar discs that can cause low-back pain.

Richard Benjamin, a podiatrist at the Greater Southeastern Hospital in Washington, says, too, that throwing the weight on the ball of the foot diminishes the normal roles of both heel and big toe. Incorrect turning of the foot throws the knee out, affecting the hip and back. Like the S-shaped stance, the exaggerated pelvic sway provides allure at a cost in physical damage.

Podiatrists do see several times more women than men, primarily because of high-heeled shoes with pointed toes. Pain in foot bones is almost inevitable, but this is only the beginning. Abrasions, calluses, bunions *(hallux valgus),* tendinitis, ingrown toenails and serious bone deformities such as hammer toes and "pump bump"—a bony enlargement of the heel where the shoe rim bites into it—are frequent. Bunions can be serious; they can force the joint between the big toe and the adjacent metatarsal bone to become so bent for so long that calcium buildup renders it permanently and painfully deviated. The ratio of women to men who have this disorder is estimated to be 40-to-1. High heels also cause abnormal thickening of skin and bone at the ball of the foot, and this can force the small toes under the foot, crushing them, in some rare cases. Sheldon Flaxman, a foot surgeon, concludes: "These shoes should be worn for special occasions only." Even then, he says, they should not be pointed and the heels should be as low as possible.

High heels are, after all, relatively new in Western tradition. In the 16th century, the elegant—men and women alike—began to like upward-tilting footwear. Before the Elizabethan period in England, flatness in shoes was consistent with both elegance and sex. One will search in vain in earlier paintings and sculpture for evidence of shoes that lever people off the ground. By the mid-18th century, men's shoes had returned to normalcy, but women were stuck on their awkward platforms, and there they have remained. The most extreme form—the stiletto of the 1950's—was often banned, to prevent damage to floors. No laws, written or unwritten, prevent damage to feet—or to women's sense of freedom.

Why do we have such an attachment to this hurtful fashion? The Freudians have had a field day with it, likening it to a mild version of the condition in which a fetishist (always a man) can be aroused only by a shoe. They even invoke sadomasochism as well, and in this explanation the pain and harm are no longer incidental. As I get older, the pain is what I most often see. But I have to admit that a woman will sometimes take me by surprise—dressed to the nines, high-heeled shoes and all.

I'm fighting it though, the part of it that comes from bad shoes. I expect to win. I think of adjectives that apply to women in flat shoes: lithe, graceful, earthy, athletic, sensible, fleet, dancing, practical, fresh, nimble, strong—and sexy, definitely sexy. (Don't look for logic here, we're talking about hormones.) I think of the women depicted by Greek and Roman art—they didn't need to be hobbled to interest men. I think of the polka and the hora instead of the waltz and the tango—and as for whatever it is we do to rock music, that works just as well in flats.

Still, it's hard to visualize a great formal party without stylish women kicking up their high heels. Like some of the other indulgences of that and like occasions, they're probably O.K. in moderation. But for everyday wear they make as little sense as a three-martini lunch. They're a relatively recent innovation. They've wormed their way into our sexual imagery. But it's hard to see why they have to stay there.

Chapter 5:
Politics and Belief

C. S. Lewis

WHAT CHRISTIANS BELIEVE

C.S. Lewis (1898-1963), an essayist, literary critic and prominent Christian, is most famous in America for his series of children's books, *The Chronicles of Narnia.* After his own conversion to Christianity, Lewis spent much of his life trying to convert others to his faith. Here, he explains the complexities of belief and disbelief in a Christian God. The apparent seamlessness of his argument makes it quite difficult to dispute. As you read, try to bring up objections to his reasoning. Does Lewis counter your responses?

THE RIVAL CONCEPTIONS OF GOD

I have been asked to tell you what Christians believe, and I am going to begin by telling you one thing that Christians do not need to believe. If you are a Christian you do not have to believe that all the other religions are simply wrong all through. If you are an atheist you do have to believe that the main point in all the religions of the whole world is simply one huge mistake. If you are a Christian, you are free to think that all these religions, even the

AIDS Deaths and New AIDS Cases in the U.S., 1985-94

Source: *Health United States 1994*, National Center for Health Statistics, U.S. Dept. of Health and Human Services

	All years[1]	1985	1988	1989	1990	1991	1992	1993	1994[2]
TOTAL DEATHS	284,249	6,961	21,019	27,653	31,339	36,246	40,072	42,572	44,052[3]
NEW AIDS CASES									
All races	410,532	8,160	30,716	33,643	41,761	43,771	45,961	103,463	61,301
Male									
All males, 13 years and older	352,092	7,539	27,106	29,666	36,475	37,722	39,223	86,469	49,887
White, not Hispanic	192,158	4,781	16,041	17,543	21,000	20,675	20,899	43,892	18,089
Black, not Hispanic	106,167	1,713	7,188	8,055	10,300	11,149	12,209	28,714	23,211
Hispanic	49,786	986	3,637	3,737	4,773	5,467	5,625	12,782	18,089
American Indian[2]	841	6	38	61	78	84	102	289	7,954
Asian or Pacific Islander[4]	2,528	49	162	216	262	259	285	670	135
13-19 years	1,184	31	84	92	106	98	94	362	397
20-29 years	61,926	1,471	5,393	5,694	6,813	6,457	6,387	14,456	186
30-39 years	162,922	3,619	12,699	13,940	16,885	17,481	18,014	39,513	7,622
40-49 years	89,238	1,656	6,127	6,846	8,977	9,657	10,392	23,382	22,932
50-59 years	27,047	602	1,993	2,247	2,664	2,909	3,097	6,590	13,750
60 years and over	9,775	160	840	847	1,030	1,120	1,239	2,166	4,031
Female									
All females, 13 years and over	52,778	520	3,040	3,380	4,560	5,373	5,980	16,113	10,693
White, not Hispanic	13,448	141	860	944	1,225	1,352	1,479	4,077	2,437
Black, not Hispanic	30,092	280	1,655	1,903	2,561	3,110	3,409	9,193	6,318
Hispanic	8,728	96	492	499	736	863	1,023	2,670	1,854
American Indian[3]	152	2	6	9	9	11	17	57	35
Asian or Pacific Islander[4]	279	1	22	16	19	25	39	96	40
13-19 years	586	4	22	29	63	55	55	194	134
20-29 years	12,462	174	768	889	1,105	1,219	1,381	3,692	2,308
30-39 years	24,657	233	1,512	1,625	2,109	2,542	2,747	7,654	4,838
40-49 years	10,194	45	412	506	787	998	1,244	3,269	2,524
50-59 years	2,941	27	151	171	276	338	338	871	610
60 years and over	1,938	37	175	160	220	221	215	433	279
Children									
All children, under 13 years	5,662	131	570	597	726	676	758	881	721
White, not Hispanic	1,122	26	148	114	160	147	129	146	102
Black, not Hispanic	3,348	86	307	339	389	408	483	538	478
Hispanic	1,130	19	111	137	169	114	139	184	131
American Indian[4]	17	–	–	2	4	2	3	3	–
Asian or Pacific Islander[5]	32	–	4	3	4	4	1	5	8
Under 1 year	2,183	56	192	241	288	255	318	324	233
1-12 years	3,479	75	378	356	438	421	440	557	488

Note: The AIDS case definition was changed in 1985, 1987, and 1993, as more was learned about AIDS-associated diseases and conditions and to expand the spectrum of human immunodeficiency virus-associated diseases reportable as AIDS. Excludes residents of U.S. territories. Data are updated periodically because of reporting delays. Data for all years have been updated through Sept. 30, 1994. (1) Includes cases and deaths prior to 1985 and years not shown. (2) Jan. to Sept. 1994 unless otherwise noted. (3) Jan. to Dec. 1994. (4) Includes Aleut and Eskimo. (5) Includes Chinese, Japanese, Filipino, Hawaiian and part-Hawaiian and other Asian or Pacific Islander.

New AIDS Cases in the U.S., 1985-94, by Transmission Category

Source: *Health United States 1994*, National Center for Health Statistics. U.S. Dept. of Health and Human Services

Sex and transmission category	All years[1]	1985	1988	1989	1990	1991	1992	1993	1994[2]
Male	352,092	7,539	27,106	29,666	36,475	37,722	39,223	86,469	49,887
Men who have sex with men	218,587	5,393	17,794	19,668	23,966	24,020	24,509	49,756	26,711
Injecting drug use	72,203	1,102	5,236	5,427	7,001	7,684	8,073	20,227	11,959
Men who have sex with men and injecting drug use	26,290	643	2,209	2,382	2,681	2,884	2,904	6,311	2,843
Hemophilia/coagulation disorder	3,431	68	294	278	330	304	319	1,063	401
Heterosexual contact[3]	9,004	32	328	492	712	878	1,270	3,103	1,959
Sex with injecting drug user	4,262	25	226	359	460	503	652	1,217	655
Transfusion[4]	3,888	105	485	425	462	404	366	639	357
Undetermined[5]	18,689	196	760	994	1,323	1,548	1,782	5,320	5,657
Female	52,778	520	3,040	3,380	4,560	5,373	5,980	16,113	10,693
Injecting drug use	25,464	282	1,641	1,799	2,321	2,752	2,879	7,752	4,431
Hemophilia/coagulation disorder	95	1	4	7	11	10	5	26	17
Heterosexual contact[3]	18,417	116	874	1,001	1,536	1,883	2,304	6,007	3,861
Sex with injecting drug user	9,760	82	637	704	1,040	1,188	1,328	2,718	1,489
Transfusion[4]	2,670	63	329	291	338	241	265	517	256
Undetermined[5]	6,132	58	192	282	354	487	527	1,811	2,128

Note: The AIDS case definition was changed in 1985, 1987, and 1993, as more was learned about AIDS-associated diseases and conditions and to expand the spectrum of human immunodeficiency virus-associated diseases reportable as AIDS. Excludes residents of U.S. territories. Data are updated periodically because of reporting delays. Data for all years have been updated through Sept. 30, 1994. (1) Includes cases prior to 1985 and years not shown. (2) Jan. to Sept. 1994. (3) Includes persons who have had heterosexual contact with a person with human immunodeficiency virus (HIV) infection or at risk of HIV infection. (4)

Estimated HIV Infection and Reported AIDS Cases

Source: World Health Organization

The interval between infection with the human immunodeficiency virus (HIV) and development of acquired immune deficiency syndrome (AIDS) is estimated to be 7-10 years. The actual number of AIDS cases worldwide is estimated to be more than 4.5 million—4 times the number of reported cases—because of underdiagnosis, underreporting, and the use of different definitions of AIDS in different countries. As of June 30, 1995, a total of 1,169,811 AIDS cases had been reported to the World Health Organization, a 19% increase from the 985,119 reported on July 1, 1994.

Estimated Total HIV[1] Cases by Region, Mid-1995

Region	Est. cases	Region	Est. cases	Region	Est. cases
Sub-Saharan Africa	11,000,000+	North America	1,100,000	E. Europe/Central Asia	50,000+
South/Southeast Asia	3,500,000	Western Europe	600,000	Australasia	25,000+
Latin America/Caribbean	2,000,000	North Africa/Middle East	150,000	East Asia/Pacific	50,000+
				World	18,500,000+

(1) Estimated cumulative HIV prevalence in adults. The WHO estimated more than 1.5 million children had also been infected with HIV by mid-1995.

Cumulative Reported AIDS Cases by Continent, 1980-95

Year	Africa	America[1]	Asia	Europe	Oceania[2]	World
1980	0	187	1	17	0	205
1985	744	24,379	46	2,457	315	27,941
1990	130,100	245,385	1,226	58,713	3,030	438,454
1995 (midyear)	418,051	580,129	23,912	141,275	6,444	1,169,811

(1) Includes North and South America and the Caribbean. (2) Includes Australia.

Highest mortality There are no reported recoveries from the disease AIDS (Acquired Immune Deficiency Syndrome), which was first reported in 1981. The virus that causes it, HIV, attacks the body's immune defense system, leaving the body wide open to attack from infections which in a healthy person would be fought off without any problems. Many people who are carriers of HIV may have none of the signs or symptoms of the disease AIDS, which may develop later. The World Health Organization (WHO) reported 611,589 HIV positive cases worldwide by 31 Jan 1993. WHO estimates that there are actually 2.5 million AIDS cases worldwide.

By 31 Mar 1993 the total number of HIV positive cases in the United States was 289,320. This total included 284,840 adults and 4,480 children under 13. The total number of deaths was 182,275. By the end of 1994, the United States can expect to reach 415,000 AIDS cases and 385,000 AIDS deaths.

AIDS STATISTICS

State	Cases
New York	55,154
California	53,851
Florida	28,376
Texas	20,662
New Jersey	16,171

Metropolitan Areas	Cases
New York	54,516
Los Angeles	18,900
San Francisco	15,329
Miami	8,295
Houston	8,261
Washington, D.C.	8,051
Chicago	8,023

Data: Centers for Disease Control (31 Mar 1993)

queerest ones, contain at least some hint of the truth. When I was an atheist I had to try to persuade myself that most of the human race have always been wrong about the question that mattered to them most; when I became a Christian I was able to take a more liberal view. But, of course, being a Christian does mean thinking that where Christianity differs from other religions, Christianity is right and they are wrong. As in arithmetic—there is only one right answer to a sum, and all other answers are wrong: but some of the wrong answers are much nearer being right than others.

The first big division of humanity is into the majority, who believe in some kind of God or gods, and the minority who do not. On this point, Christianity lines up with the majority—lines up with ancient Greeks and Romans, modern savages, Stoics, Platonists, Hindus, Mohammedans [Muslims], etc., against the modern Western European materialist.

Now I go on to the next big division. People who all believe in God can be divided according to the sort of God they believe in. There are two very different ideas on this subject. One of them is the idea that He is beyond good and evil. We humans call one thing good and another thing bad. But according to some people that is merely our human point of view. These people would say that the wiser you become the less you would want to call anything good or bad, and the more clearly you would see that everything is good in one way and bad in another, and that nothing could have been different. Consequently, these people think that long before you got anywhere near the divine point of view the distinction would have disappeared altogether. We call a cancer bad, they would say, because it kills a man; but you might just as well call a successful surgeon bad because he kills a cancer. It all depends on the point of view. The other and opposite idea is that God is quite definitely "good" or "righteous," a God who takes sides, who loves love and hates hatred, who wants us to behave in one way and not in another. The first of these views—the one that thinks God beyond good and evil—is called Pantheism. It was held by the great Prussian philosopher Hegel and, as far as I can understand them, by the Hindus. The other view is held by Jews, Mohammedans and Christians.

And with this big difference between Pantheism and the Christian idea of God, there usually goes another. Pantheists usually believe that God, so to speak, animates the universe as you animate your body: that the universe almost *is* God, so that if it did not exist He would not exist either, and anything you find in the universe is a part of God. The Christian[s'] idea is quite different. They think God invented and made the universe—like a man making a picture or composing a tune. A painter is not a picture, and he does not die if his picture is destroyed. You may say, "He's put a lot of himself into it," but you only mean that all its beauty and interest has come out of his head. His skill is not in the picture in the same way that it is in his head, or even in his hands. I expect you see how this difference between Pantheists and Christians hangs together with the other one. If you do not take the distinction between good and bad very seriously, then it is easy to say that anything you find in this world is a part of God. But, of course, if you think some things really bad, and God really good, then you cannot talk like that. You must believe that God is separate from the world and that some of the things we see in it are contrary to His will. Confronted with a cancer or a slum the Pantheist can say, "If you could only see it from the divine point of view, you would realise that this also is God." The Christian replies, "Don't talk damned nonsense."* For Christianity is a fighting religion. It thinks God made the world—that space and time, heat and cold, and all the colours and tastes, and all the animals and vegetables, are things that God "made up out of His head" as a man makes up a story. But it also thinks that a great many things have gone wrong with the world that God made and that God insists, and insists very loudly, on our putting them right again.

And, of course, that raises a very big question. If a good God made the world why has it gone wrong? And for many years I simply refused to listen to the Christian answers to this question, because I kept on feeling "whatever you say, and however clever your arguments are, isn't it much simpler and easier to say that the world was not made by any intelligent power? Aren't all your arguments simply a complicated attempt to avoid the obvious?" But then that threw me back into another difficulty.

My argument against God was that the universe seemed so cruel and unjust. But how had I got this idea of *just* and *unjust?* A man does not call a line crooked unless he has some idea of a straight line. What was I comparing this universe with when I called it unjust? If the whole show was bad and senseless from A to Z, so to speak, why did I, who was supposed to be part of the show, find myself in such violent reaction against it? A man feels wet

---

* One listener complained of the word *damned* as frivolous swearing. But I mean exactly what I say—nonsense that is *damned* is under God's curse, and will (apart from God's grace) lead those who believe it to eternal death. [Lewis's note.]

when he falls into water, because man is not a water animal: a fish would not feel wet. Of course I could have given up my idea of justice by saying it was nothing but a private idea of my own. But if I did that, then my argument against God collapsed too—for the argument depended on saying that the world was really unjust, not simply that it did not happen to please my private fancies. Thus in the very act of trying to prove that God did not exist—in other words, that the whole of reality was senseless—I found I was forced to assume that one part of reality—namely my idea of justice—was full of sense. Consequently atheism turns out to be too simple. If the whole universe has no meaning, we should never have found out that it has no meaning: just as, if there were no light in the universe and therefore no creatures with eyes, we should never know it was dark. *Dark* would be without meaning.

THE INVASION

Very well then, atheism is too simple. And I will tell you another view that is also too simple. It is the view I call Christianity-and-water, the view which simply says there is a good God in Heaven and everything is all right—leaving out all the difficult and terrible doctrines about sin and hell and the devil, and the redemption. Both these are boys' philosophies.

It is no good asking for a simple religion. After all, real things are not simple. They look simple, but they are not. The table I am sitting at looks simple: but ask a scientist to tell you what it is really made of—all about the atoms and how the light waves rebound from them and hit my eye and what they do to the optic nerve and what it does to my brain—and, of course, you find that what we call "seeing a table" lands you in mysteries and complications which you can hardly get to the end of. A child saying a child's prayer looks simple. And if you are content to stop there, well and good. But if you are not—and the modern world usually is not—if you want to go on and ask what is really happening—then you must be prepared for something difficult. If we ask for something more than simplicity, it is silly then to complain that the something more is not simple.

Very often, however, this silly procedure is adopted by people who are not silly, but who, consciously or unconsciously, want to destroy Christianity. Such people put up a version of Christianity suitable for a child of six and make that the object of their attack. When you try to explain the Christian doctrine as it is really held

by an instructed adult, they then complain that you are making
their heads turn round and that it is all too complicated and that if
there really were a God they are sure He would have made
"religion" simple, because simplicity is so beautiful, etc. You must
be on your guard against these people for they will change their
ground every minute and only waste your time. Notice, too, their
idea of God "making religion simple": as if "religion" were something God invented, and not His statement to us of certain quite
unalterable facts about His own nature.

Besides being complicated, reality, in my experience, is usually
odd. It is not neat, not obvious, not what you expect. For instance,
when you have grasped that the earth and the other planets all go
round the sun, you would naturally expect that all the planets
were made to match—all at equal distances from each other, say,
or distances that regularly increased, or all the same size, or else
getting bigger or smaller as you go farther from the sun. In fact,
you find no rhyme or reason (that we can see) about either the
sizes or the distances; and some of them have one moon, one has
four, one has two, some have none, and one has a ring.

Reality, in fact, is usually something you could not have guessed.
That is one of the reasons I believe Christianity. It is a religion you
could not have guessed. If it offered us just the kind of universe we
had always expected, I should feel we were making it up. But, in
fact, it is not the sort of thing anyone would have made up. It has
just that queer twist about it that real things have. So let us leave
behind all these boys' philosophies—these oversimple answers.
The problem is not simple and the answer is not going to be simple
either.

What is the problem? A universe that contains much that is obviously bad and apparently meaningless, but containing creatures
like ourselves who know that it is bad and meaningless. There are
only two views that face all the facts. One is the Christian view
that this is a good world that has gone wrong, but still retains the
memory of what it ought to have been. The other is the view called
Dualism. Dualism means the belief that there are two equal and
independent powers at the back of everything, one of them good
and the other bad, and that this universe is the battlefield in which
they fight out an endless war. I personally think that next to
Christianity Dualism is the manliest and most sensible creed on
the market. But it has a catch in it.

The two powers, or spirits, or gods—the good one and the bad
one—are supposed to be quite independent. They both existed

from all eternity. Neither of them made the other, neither of them has any more right than the other to call itself God. Each presumably thinks it is good and thinks the other bad. One of them likes hatred and cruelty, the other likes love and mercy, and each backs its own view. Now what do we mean when we call one of them the Good Power and the other the Bad Power? Either we are merely saying that we happen to prefer the one to the other—like preferring beer to cider—or else we are saying that, whatever the two powers think about it, and whichever we humans, at the moment, happen to like, one of them is actually wrong, actually mistaken, in regarding itself as good. Now if we mean merely that we happen to prefer the first, then we must give up talking about good and evil at all. For good means what you ought to prefer quite regardless of what you happen to like at any given moment. If "being good" meant simply joining the side you happened to fancy, for no real reason, then good would not deserve to be called good. So we must mean that one of the two powers is actually wrong and the other actually right.

But the moment you say that, you are putting into the universe a third thing in addition to the two Powers: some law or standard or rule of good which one of the powers conforms to and the other fails to conform to. But since the two powers are judged by this standard, then this standard, or the Being who made this standard, is farther back and higher up than either of them, and He will be the real God. In fact, what we meant by calling them good and bad turns out to be that one of them is in a right relation to the real ultimate God and the other in a wrong relation to Him.

The same point can be made in a different way. If Dualism is true, then the bad Power must be a being who likes badness for its own sake. But in reality we have no experience of anyone liking badness just because it is bad. The nearest we can get to it is in cruelty. But in real life people are cruel for one of two reasons—either because they are sadists, that is, because they have a sexual perversion which makes cruelty a cause of sensual pleasure to them, or else for the sake of something they are going to get out of it—money, or power, or safety. But pleasure, money, power, and safety are all, as far as they go, good things. The badness consists in pursuing them by the wrong method, or in the wrong way, or too much. I do not mean, of course, that the people who do this are not desperately wicked. I do mean that wickedness, when you examine it, turns out to be the pursuit of some good in the wrong way. You can be good for the mere sake of goodness: you cannot be bad for the mere sake of badness. You can do a kind action when you are not feeling kind and when it gives you no pleasure, simply because kindness is right; but no one ever did a cruel action simply because cruelty is wrong—only because cruelty was pleasant or useful to him. In other words badness cannot succeed even in being bad in the same way in which goodness is good. Goodness is, so to speak, itself: badness is only spoiled goodness. And there must be something good first before it can be spoiled. We called sadism a sexual perversion; but you must first have the idea of a normal sexuality before you can talk of its being perverted; and you can see which is the perversion, because you can explain the perverted from the normal, and cannot explain the normal from the perverted. It follows that this Bad Power, who is supposed to be on an equal footing with the Good Power, and to love badness in the same way as the Good Power loves goodness, is a mere bogy. In order to be bad he must have good things to want and then to pursue in the wrong way: he must have impulses which were originally good in order to be able to pervert them. But if he is bad he cannot supply himself either with good things to desire or with good impulses to pervert. He must be getting both from the Good Power. And if so, then he is not independent. He is part of the Good Power's world: he was made either by the Good Power or by some power above them both.

Put it more simply still. To be bad, he must exist and have intelligence and will. But existence, intelligence and will are in themselves good. Therefore he must be getting them from the Good Power: even to be bad he must borrow or steal from his opponent. And do you now begin to see why Christianity has always said that the devil is a fallen angel? That is not a mere story for the children. It is a real recognition of the fact that evil is a parasite, not an original thing. The powers which enable evil to carry on are powers given it by goodness. All the things which enable a bad man to be effectively bad are in themselves good things—resolution, cleverness, good looks, existence itself. That is why Dualism, in a strict sense, will not work.

But I freely admit that real Christianity (as distinct from Christianity-and-water) goes much nearer to Dualism than people think. One of the things that surprised me when I first read the New Testament seriously was that it talked so much about a Dark Power in the universe—a mighty evil spirit who was held to be the Power behind death and disease, and sin. The difference is that Christianity thinks this Dark Power was created by God, and was good when he was created, and went wrong. Christianity agrees with Dualism that this universe is at war. But it does not think this is a war between independent powers. It thinks it is a civil war, a rebellion, and that we are living in a part of the universe occupied by the rebel.

Enemy-occupied territory—that is what this world is. Christianity is the story of how the rightful king has landed, you might say landed in disguise, and is calling us all to take part in a great campaign of sabotage. When you go to church you are really listening-in to the secret wireless from our friends: that is why the enemy is so anxious to prevent us from going. He does it by playing on our conceit and laziness and intellectual snobbery. I know someone will ask me, "Do you really mean, at this time of day, to re-introduce our old friend the devil—hoofs and horns and all?" Well, what the time of day has to do with it I do not know. And I am not particular about the hoofs and horns. But in other respects my answer is "Yes, I do." I do not claim to know anything about his personal appearance. If anybody really wants to know him better I would say to that person, "Don't worry. If you really want to, you will. Whether you'll like it when you do is another question."

THE SHOCKING ALTERNATIVE

Christians, then, believe that an evil power has made himself for the present the Prince of this World. And, of course, that raises problems. Is this state of affairs in accordance with God's will or not? If it is, He is a strange God, you will say: and if it is not, how can anything happen contrary to the will of a being with absolute power?

But anyone who has been in authority knows how a thing can be in accordance with your will in one way and not in another. It may be quite sensible for a mother to say to the children, "I'm not going to go and make you tidy the schoolroom every night. You've got to learn to keep it tidy on your own." Then she goes up one night and finds the Teddy bear and the ink and the French Grammar all lying in the grate. That is against her will. She would prefer the children to be tidy. But on the other hand, it is her will which has left the children free to be untidy. The same thing arises in any regiment, or trade union, or school. You make a thing voluntary and then half the people do not do it. That is not what you willed, but your will has made it possible.

It is probably the same in the universe. God created things which had free will. That means creatures which can go either wrong or right. Some people think they can imagine a creature which was free but had no possibility of going wrong; I cannot. If a thing is free to be good it is also free to be bad. And free will is what has made evil possible. Why, then, did God give them free will? Because free will, though it makes evil possible, is also the only thing that makes possible any love or goodness or joy worth having. A world of automata—of creatures that worked like machines—would hardly be worth creating. The happiness which God designs for His higher creatures is the happiness of being freely, voluntarily united to Him and to each other in an ecstasy of love and delight compared with which the most rapturous love between a man and a woman on this earth is mere milk and water. And for that they must be free.

Of course God knew what would happen if they used their freedom the wrong way: apparently He thought it worth the risk. Perhaps we feel inclined to disagree with Him. But there is a difficulty about disagreeing with God. He is the source from which all your reasoning power comes: you could not be right and He wrong any more than a stream can rise higher than its own source. When you are arguing against Him you are arguing against the very power that makes you able to argue at all: it is like cutting off the branch you are sitting on. If God thinks this state of war in the universe a price worth paying for free will— that is, for making a live world in which creatures can do real good or harm and something of real importance can happen, instead of a toy world which only moves when He pulls the strings—then we may take it it is worth paying.

When we have understood about free will, we shall see how silly it is to ask, as somebody once asked me: "Why did God make a creature of such rotten stuff that it went wrong?" The better stuff a creature is made of—the cleverer and stronger and freer it is— then the better it will be if it goes right, but also the worse it will be if it goes wrong. A cow cannot be very good or very bad; a dog can be both better and worse; a child better and worse still; an ordinary man, still more so; a man of genius, still more so; a superhuman spirit best—or worst—of all.

How did the Dark Power go wrong? Here, no doubt, we ask a question to which human beings cannot give an answer with any certainty. A reasonable (and traditional) guess, based on our own experiences of going wrong, can, however, be offered. The moment you have a self at all, there is a possibility of putting yourself first—wanting to be the centre—wanting to be God, in fact. That was the sin of Satan: and that was the sin he taught the human race. Some people think the fall of man had something to do with sex, but that is a mistake. (The story in the Book of Genesis rather suggests that some corruption in our sexual nature followed the fall and was its result, not its cause.) What Satan put into the heads of our remote ancestors was the idea that they could "be like gods"—could set up on their own as if they had created themselves—be their own masters—invent some sort of happiness for themselves outside God, apart from God. And out of that hopeless attempt has come nearly all that we call human history—money, poverty, ambition, war, prostitution, classes, empires, slavery— the long terrible story of man trying to find something other than God which will make him happy.

The reason why it can never succeed is this. God made us: invented us as a man invents an engine. A car is made to run on gasoline, and it would not run properly on anything else. Now God designed the human machine to run on Himself. He Himself is the fuel our spirits were designed to burn, or the food our spirits were designed to feed on. There is no other. That is why it is just no good asking God to make us happy in our own way without bothering about religion. God cannot give us a happiness and peace apart from Himself, because it is not there. There is no such thing.

That is the key to history. Terrific energy is expended—civilisations are built up—excellent institutions devised; but each time something goes wrong. Some fatal flaw always brings the selfish and cruel people to the top and it all slides back into misery and ruin. In fact, the machine conks. It seems to start up all right and runs a few yards, and then it breaks down. They are trying to run it on the wrong juice. That is what Satan has done to us humans.

And what did God do? First of all He left us conscience, the sense of right and wrong: and all through history there have been people trying (some of them very hard) to obey it. None of them ever quite succeeded. Secondly, He sent the human race what I call good dreams: I mean those queer stories scattered all through the heathen religions about a god who dies and comes to life again and, by his death, has somehow given new life to men. Thirdly, He selected one particular people and spent several centuries hammering into their heads the sort of God He was—that there was only one of Him and that He cared about right conduct. Those people were the Jews, and the Old Testament gives an account of the hammering process.

Then comes the real shock. Among these Jews there suddenly turns up a man who goes about talking as if He was God. He claims to forgive sins. He says He has always existed. He says He is coming to judge the world at the end of time. Now let us get this clear. Among Pantheists, like the Indians, anyone might say that he was a part of God, or one with God: there would be nothing very odd about it. But this man, since He was a Jew, could not mean that kind of God. God, in their language, meant the Being outside the world Who had made it and was infinitely different from anything else. And when you have grasped that, you will see that what this man said was, quite simply, the most shocking thing that has ever been uttered by human lips.

One part of the claim tends to slip past us unnoticed because we have heard it so often that we no longer see what it amounts to. I mean the claim to forgive sins: any sins. Now unless the speaker is God, this is really so preposterous as to be comic. We can all understand how a man forgives offences against himself. You tread on my toe and I forgive you, you steal my money and I forgive you. But what should we make of a man, himself unrobbed and untrodden on, who announced that he forgave you for treading on other men's toes and stealing other men's money? Asinine fatuity is the kindest description we should give of his conduct. Yet this is what Jesus did. He told people that their sins were forgiven, and never waited to consult all the other people whom their sins had undoubtedly injured. He unhesitatingly behaved as if He was the party chiefly concerned, the person chiefly offended in all offences. This makes sense only if He really was the God whose laws are broken and whose love is wounded in every sin. In the mouth of any speaker who is not God, these words would imply what I can only regard as a silliness and conceit unrivalled by any other character in history.

Yet (and this is the strange, significant thing) even His enemies, when they read the Gospels, do not usually get the impression of silliness and conceit. Still less do unprejudiced readers. Christ says that He is "humble and meek" and we believe Him; not noticing that, if He were merely a man, humility and meekness are the very last characteristics we could attribute to some of His sayings.

I am trying here to prevent anyone saying the really foolish thing that people often say about Him: "I'm ready to accept Jesus as a great moral teacher, but I don't accept His claim to be God."

That is the one thing we must not say. A man who was merely a man and said the sort of things Jesus said would not be a great moral teacher. He would either be a lunatic—on a level with the man who says he is a poached egg—or else he would be the Devil of Hell. You must make your choice. Either this man was, and is, the Son of God: or else a madman or something worse. You can shut Him up for a fool, you can spit at Him and kill Him as a demon; or you can fall at His feet and call Him Lord and God. But let us not come with any patronising nonsense about His being a great human teacher. He has not left that open to us. He did not intend to.

Barbara Tuchman

from A DISTANT MIRROR

Barbara Tuchman (1912-1989), a journalist and historian, was convinced that history could tell us much about the present. In *A Distant Mirror*, she chronicled the plagues and famines of the 14th century, but always with an eye to how the "mirror" of the past reflects society today. In this passage, she details the impact of the Church on daily life. As you read, see if you can find places where Tuchman shows how 14th century life "reflects" our times.

In daily life the Church was comforter, protector, physician. The Virgin and patron saints gave succor in trouble and protection against the evils and enemies that lurked along every man's path. Craft guilds, towns, and functions had patron saints, as did individuals. Archers and crossbowmen had St. Sebastian, martyr of the arrows; bakers had St. Honore, whose banner bore an oven shovel argent and three loaves gules; sailors had St. Nicholas with the three children he saved from the sea; travelers had St. Christopher carrying the infant Jesus on his shoulder; charitable brotherhoods usually chose St. Martin, who gave half his cloak to the poor man; unmarried girls had St. Catherine, supposed to have been very beautiful. The patron saint was an extra companion through life who healed hurts, soothed distress, and in extremity could make miracles. His image was carried on banners in processions, sculpted over the entrance to town halls and chapels, and worn as a medallion on an individual's hat. Above all, the Virgin was the ever-merciful, ever-dependable source of comfort, full of compassion for human frailty, caring nothing for laws and judges, ready to respond to anyone in trouble; amid all the inequities, injuries, and senseless harms, the one never-failing figure. She frees the prisoner from his dungeon, revives the starving with milk from her own breasts. When a peasant mother takes her son, blinded by a thorn in his eye, to the Church of St. Denis, kneels before Our Lady, recites an Ave Maria, and makes the sign of the cross over the child with a sacred relic, the nail of the Saviour, "at once," reports the chronicler, "the thorn falls out, the inflammation disappears, and the mother in joy returns home with her son no longer blind." A hardened murderer has no less access. No matter what crime a person has committed, though every man's hand be against him, he is still not cut off from the Virgin. In the *Miracles of Notre Dame,* a cycle of popular plays performed in the towns, the Virgin redeems every kind of malefactor who reaches out to her through the act of repentance. A woman accused of incest with her son-in-law has procured his assassination by two hired men and is about to be burned at the stake. She prays to Notre Dame, who promptly appears and orders the fire not to burn. Convinced of a miracle, the magistrates free the condemned woman, who, after distributing her goods and money to the poor, enters a convent. The act of faith through prayer was what counted. It was not justice one received from the Church but forgiveness.

More than comfort, the Church gave answers. For nearly a thousand years it had been the central institution that gave meaning and purpose to life in a capricious world. It affirmed that man's life on earth was but a passage in exile on the way to God and the New Jerusalem, "our other home." Life was nothing, wrote Petrarch to his brother, but "a hard and weary journey toward the eternal home for which we look; or, if we neglect our salvation, an equally pleasureless way to eternal death." What the Church offered was salvation, which could be reached only through the rituals of the established Church and by the permission and aid of its ordained priests. *"Extra ecclesium nulla salus"* (No salvation outside the Church) was the rule.

Salvation's alternative was Hell and eternal torture, very realistically pictured in the art of the time. In Hell the damned hung by their tongues from trees of fire, the impenitent burned in furnaces, unbelievers smothered in foul smelling smoke. The wicked fell into the black waters of an abyss and sank to a depth proportionate to their sins; fornicators up to the nostrils, persecutors of their fellow man up to the eyebrows. Some were swallowed by monstrous fish, some gnawed by demons, tormented by serpents, by fire or ice or fruits hanging forever out of the reach of the starving. In Hell men were naked, nameless, and forgotten. No wonder salvation was important and the Day of Judgment present in every mind. Over the doorway in every cathedral it was carved in vivid reminder, showing the numerous sinners roped and led off by devils toward a flaming cauldron while angels led the fewer elect to bliss in the opposite direction.

No one doubted in the Middle Ages that the vast majority would be eternally damned. *Salvandorum paucitas, damnandorum multitudo* (Few saved, many damned) was the stern principle maintained from Augustine to Aquinas. Noah and his family were taken to indicate the proportion of the saved, usually estimated at one in a thousand or even one in ten thousand. No matter how few were to be chosen, the Church offered hope to all. Salvation was permanently closed to non-believers in Christ, but not to sinners, for sin was an inherent condition of life which could be canceled as often as necessary by penitence and absolution. "Turn thee again, turn thee again, thou sinful soul," spoke a Lollard preacher, "for God knoweth thy misgovernance and will not forsake thee. Turn thou to me saith the Lord and I shall receive thee and take thee to grace."

The Church gave ceremony and dignity to lives that had little of either. It was the source of beauty and art to which all had some access and which many helped to create. To carve the stone folds of an apostle's gown, to paste with infinite patience the bright mosaic chips into a picture of winged angels in a heavenly chorus, to stand in the towering space of a cathedral nave amid pillars rising and rising to an almost invisible vault and know this to be man's work in honor of God, gave pride to the lowest and could make the least man an artist.

The Church, not the government, sponsored the care of society's helpless—the indigent and sick, orphan and cripple, the leper, the blind, the idiot—by indoctrinating the laity in the belief that alms bought them merit and a foothold in Heaven. Based on this principle, the impulse of Christian charity was self-serving but effective. Nobles gave alms daily at the castle gate to all comers, in coin and in leftover food from the hall. Donations from all sources poured into the hospitals, favorite recipients of Christian charity. Merchants bought themselves peace of mind for the non-Christian business of making profit by allocating a regular percentage to charity. This was entered in the ledger under the name of God as the poor's representative. A Christian duty of particular merit was the donation of dowries to enable poor girls to marry, as in the case of a Gascon seigneur of the 14th century who left 100 livres to "Those whom I deflowered, if they can be found."

Corporate bodies accepted the obligation to help the poor as a religious duty. The statutes of craft guilds set aside a penny for charity, called "God's penny," from each contract of sale or purchase. Parish councils of laymen superintended maintenance of the "table of the Poor" and of a bank for alms. On feast days it was a common practice to invite twelve poor to the banquet table, and on Holy Thursday, in memory of Christ, the mayor of a town or other notable would wash the feet of a beggar. When St. Louis conducted the ceremony, his companion and biographer, the Sire de Joinville, refused to participate, saying it would make him sick to touch the feet of such villains. It was not always easy to love the poor.

The clergy on the whole were probably no more lecherous or greedy or untrustworthy than other men, but because they were supposed to be better or nearer to God than other men, their failings attracted more attention. If Clement VI was luxury-loving, he was also generous and warm-hearted. The Parson among the Canterbury pilgrims is as benign and admirable as the Pardoner is repulsive, always ready to visit on foot the farthest and poorest house of his parish, undeterred by thunder or rain.

Nevertheless, a wind of discontent was rising. Papal tax-collectors were attacked and beaten, and even bishops were not safe. In 1326, in a burst of anti-clericalism, a London mob beheaded the Bishop and left his body naked in the street. In 1338 two "rectors of churches" joined two knights and a "great crowd of country folk" in attacking the Bishop of Constance, severely wounding several of his retinue, and holding him in prison. Among the religious themselves, the discontent took serious form. In Italy arose the Fraticelli, a sect of the Franciscan order, in another of the poverty-embracing movements that periodically tormented the Church by wanting to disendow it. The Fraticelli or spiritual Franciscans insisted that Christ had lived without possessions, and they preached a return to that condition as the only true "imitation of Christ."

The poverty movements grew out of the essence of Christian doctrine: renunciation of the material world—the idea that made the great break with the classical age. It maintained that God was positive and life on earth negative, that the world was incurably bad and holiness achieved only through renunciation of earthly pleasures, goods, and honors. To gain victory over the flesh was the purpose of fasting and celibacy, which denied the pleasures of this world for the sake of reward in the next. Money was evil, beauty vain, and both were transitory. Ambition was pride, desire for gain was avarice, desire of the flesh was lust, desire for honor, even for knowledge and beauty, was vainglory. Insofar as these diverted man from seeking the life of the spirit, they were sinful. The Christian ideal was ascetic: the denial of sensual man. The result was that, under the sway of the Church, life became a continual struggle against the senses and a continual engagement in sin, accounting for the persistent need for absolution. Repeatedly, mystical sects arose in an effort to sweep away the whole detritus of the material world, to become nearer to God by cutting the earth-binding chains of property. Embedded in its hands and buildings, the Church could only react by renouncing the sects as heretical. The Fraticelli's stubborn insistence on the absolute poverty of Christ and his twelve Apostles was acutely inconvenient for the Avignon papacy, which condemned their doctrine as "false and pernicious" heresy in 1315 and, when they refused to desist, excommunicated them and other associated sects at various times during the next decade. Twenty-seven members of a particularly stubborn group of Spiritual Franciscans of Provence were tortured by the Inquisition and four of them burned at the stake at Marseille in 1318. The wind of temporal challenge to papal supremacy was rising too, focusing on the Pope's right to crown the Emperor, and setting the claims of the state against those of the Church. The Pope tried to excommunicate this temporal spirit in the person of its boldest exponent, Marsilius of Padua, whose *Defensor Pacis* in 1324 was a forthright assertion of the supremacy of the state. Two years later the logic of the struggle led John XXII to excommunicate William of Ockham, the English Franciscan, known for his forceful reasoning as "the invincible doctor." In expounding a philosophy called "nominalism," Ockham opened a dangerous door to direct intuitive knowledge of the physical world. He was in a sense a spokesman for intellectual freedom, and the Pope recognized the implications by his ban. In reply to the excommunication, Ockham promptly charged John XXII with seventy errors and seven heresies.

Frances FitzGerald

From REWRITING AMERICAN HISTORY

Journalist Frances FitzGerald (1940-   ) has won critical acclaim for her poignant investigation and analysis of issues at the heart of American culture. In *Rewriting American History*, she examines the changing ways in which American history is taught. In this excerpt, she laments the loss of "permanence" in textbooks as perceived by students of her generation. As you read, ask yourself if the history books you used in elementary and high school were like the ones FitzGerald derides in this passage. What about *this* book? Who does she blame? Do you agree with her?

Those of us who grew up in the fifties believed in the permanence of our American-history textbooks. To us as children, those texts were the truth of things: they were American history. It was not just that we read them before we understood that not everything that is printed is the truth, or the whole truth. It was that they, much more than other books, had the demeanor and trappings of authority. They were weighty volumes. They spoke in measured cadences: imperturbable, humorless, and as distant as Chinese emperors. Our teachers treated them with respect, and we paid them abject homage by memorizing a chapter a week. But now the textbook histories have changed, some of them to such an extent that an adult would find them unrecognizable.

One current junior-high-school American history begins with a story about a Negro cowboy called George McJunkin. It appears that when McJunkin was riding down a lonely trail in New Mexico one cold spring morning in 1925 he discovered a mound containing bones and stone implements, which scientists later proved belonged to an Indian civilization ten thousand years old. The book goes on to say that scientists now believe there were people in the Americas at least twenty thousand years ago. It discusses the Aztec, Mayan, and Incan civilizations and the meaning of the word "culture" before introducing the European explorers.

Another history text—this one for the fifth grade—begins with the story of how Henry B. Gonzalez, who is a member of Congress from Texas, learned about his own nationality. When he was ten years old, his teacher told him he was an American because he was born in the United States. His grandmother, however, said, "The cat was born in the oven. Does that make him bread?" After reporting that Mr. Gonzalez eventually went to college and law school, the book explains that "the melting pot idea hasn't worked out as some thought it would," and that now "some people say that the people of the United States are more like a salad bowl than a melting pot."

Poor Columbus! He is a minor character now, a walk-on in the middle of American history. Even those books that have not replaced his picture with a Mayan temple or an Iroquois mask do not credit him with discovering America—even for the Europeans. The Vikings, they say, preceded him to the New World, and after that the Europeans, having lost or forgotten their maps, simply neglected to cross the ocean again for five hundred years. Columbus is far from being the only personage to have suffered from time and revision. Captain John Smith, Daniel Boone, and Wild Bill Hickok—the great self-promoters of American history—have all but disappeared, taking with them a good deal of the romance of the American frontier. General Custer has given way to Chief Crazy Horse; General Eisenhower no longer liberates Europe single-handed; and, indeed, most generals, even to Washington and Lee, have faded away, as old soldiers do, giving place to social reformers such as William Lloyd Garrison and Jacob Riis. A number of black Americans have risen to prominence: not only George Washington Carver but Frederick Douglass and Martin Luther King, Jr. W. E. B. Du Bois now invariably accompanies Booker T. Washington. In addition, there is a mystery man called Crispus Attucks, a fugitive slave about whom nothing seems to be known for certain except that he was a victim of the Boston Massacre and thus became one of the first casualties of the American Revolution. Thaddeus Stevens has been reconstructed—his character changed, as it were, from black to white, from cruel and vindictive to persistent and sincere. As for Teddy Roosevelt, he now champions the issue of conservation instead of charging up San Juan Hill. No single President really stands out as a hero, but all Presidents—except certain

unmentionables in the second half of the nineteenth century—
seem to have done as well as could be expected, given difficult circumstances.

Of course, when one thinks about it, it is hardly surprising that
modern scholarship and modern perspectives have found their
way into children's books. Yet the changes remain shocking.
Those who in the sixties complained of the bland optimism, the
chauvinism, and the materialism of their old civics texts did so in
the belief that, for all their protests, the texts would never change.
The thought must have had something reassuring about it, for
that generation never noticed when its complaints began to take
effect and the songs about radioactive rainfall and houses made of
ticky-tacky began to appear in the textbooks. But this is what
happened.

The history texts now hint at a certain level of unpleasantness
in American history. Several books, for instance, tell the story of
Ishi, the last "wild" Indian in the continental United States, who,
captured in 1911 after the massacre of his tribe, spent the final
four and a half years of his life in the University of California's
museum of anthropology, in San Francisco. At least three books
show the same stunning picture of the breaker boys, the child coal
miners of Pennsylvania—ancient children with deformed bodies
and blackened faces who stare stupidly out from the entrance to a
mine. One book quotes a soldier on the use of torture in the
American campaign to pacify the Philippines at the beginning of
the century. A number of books say that during the American
Revolution the patriots tarred and feathered those who did not
support them, and drove many of the loyalists from the country.
Almost all the present-day history books note that the United
States interned Japanese-Americans in detention camps during
the Second World War.

Ideologically speaking, the histories of the fifties were implacable, seamless. Inside their covers, America was perfect: the
greatest nation in the world, and the embodiment of democracy,
freedom, and technological progress. For them, the country never
changed in any important way; its values and its political institutions remained constant from the time of the American
Revolution. To my generation—the children of the fifties—these
texts appeared permanent just because they were so self-contained. Their orthodoxy, it seemed, left no handholds for attack, no
lodging for decay. Who, after all, would dispute the wonders of
technology or the superiority of the English colonists over the

Spanish? Who would find fault with the pastorale of the West or the Old South? Who would question the anti-Communist crusade? There was, it seemed, no point in comparing these visions with reality, since they were the public truth and were thus quite irrelevant to what existed and to what anyone privately believed. They were—or so it seemed—the permanent expression of mass culture in America.

But now the texts have changed, and with them the country that American children are growing up into. The society that was once uniform is now a patchwork of rich and poor, old and young, men and women, blacks, whites, Hispanics, and Indians. The system that ran so smoothly by means of the Constitution under the guidance of benevolent conductor Presidents is now a rattletrap affair. The past is no highway to the present; it is a collection of issues and events that do not fit together and that lead in no single direction. The word "progress" has been replaced by the word "change": children, the modern texts insist, should learn history so that they can adapt to the rapid changes taking place around them. History is proceeding in spite of us. The present, which was once portrayed in the concluding chapters as a peaceful haven of scientific advances and Presidential inaugurations, is now a tangle of problems: race problems, urban problems, foreign-policy problems, problems of pollution, poverty, energy depletion, youthful rebellion, assassination, and drugs. Some books illustrate these problems dramatically. One, for instance, contains a picture of a doll half buried in a mass of untreated sewage; the caption reads, "Are we in danger of being overwhelmed by the products of our society and wastage created by their production? Would you agree with this photographer's interpretation?" Two books show the same picture of an old black woman sitting in a straight chair in a dingy room, her hands folded in graceful resignation; the surrounding text discusses the problems faced by the urban poor and by the aged who depend on Social Security. Other books present current problems less starkly. One of the texts concludes sagely:

> Problems are part of life. Nations face them, just as people face them, and try to solve them. And today's Americans have one great advantage over past generations. Never before have Americans been so well equipped to solve their problems. They have today the means to conquer poverty, disease, and ignorance. The technetronic age has put that power into their hands.

Such passages have a familiar ring. Amid all the problems, the deus ex machina of science still dodders around in the gloaming of pious hope.

Even more surprising than the emergence of problems is the discovery that the great unity of the texts has broken. Whereas in the fifties all texts represented the same political view, current texts follow no pattern of orthodoxy. Some books, for instance, portray civil-rights legislation as a series of actions taken by a wise, paternal government; others convey some suggestion of the social upheaval involved and make mention of such people as Stokely Carmichael and Malcolm X. In some books, the Cold War has ended; in others, it continues, with Communism threatening the free nations of the earth.

The political diversity in the books is matched by a diversity of pedagogical approach. In addition to the traditional narrative histories, with their endless streams of facts, there are so-called "discovery," or "inquiry," texts, which deal with a limited number of specific issues in American history. These texts do not pretend to cover the past; they focus on particular topics, such as "stratification in Colonial society" or "slavery and the American Revolution," and illustrate them with documents from primary and secondary sources. The chapters in these books amount to something like case studies, in that they include testimony from people with different perspectives or conflicting views on a single subject. In addition, the chapters provide background information, explanatory notes, and a series of questions for the student. The questions are the heart of the matter, for when they are carefully selected they force students to think much as historians think: to define the point of view of the speaker, analyze the ideas presented, question the relationship between events, and so on. One text, for example, quotes Washington, Jefferson, and John Adams on the question of foreign alliances and then asks, "What did John Adams assume that the international situation would be after the American Revolution? What did Washington's attitude toward the French alliance seem to be? How do you account for his attitude?" Finally, it asks, "Should a nation adopt a policy toward alliances and cling to it consistently, or should it vary its policies toward other countries as circumstances change?" In these books, history is clearly not a list of agreed-upon facts or a sermon on politics but a babble of voices and a welter of events which must be ordered by the historian.

* * *

Today, texts are written backward or inside out, as it were, beginning with public demand and ending with the historian. This system gives the publishers a certain security, since their books cannot be too far out of the mainstream. But, having minimized one kind of risk, they have created another, of a different order. By casting away scholarly claims to authority, they have set themselves adrift on the uncertain seas of public opinion. The voyage can be uncomfortable at times. It is difficult when opinions are divided or are changing rapidly, and it is just as difficult when, as happens quite frequently, people do not really know what they want to hear. For the past ten years, the publishers have suffered from both of these conditions.

Randall (student)

RAISING THE MINIMUM, RAISING CONCERN

In this research paper, Randall argues against an increase in the minimum wage. As you read the paper, try to outline the major points of his argument. What is his most compelling reason for maintaining the status quo? What alternatives does he offer?

Helping the poor to overcome their situation has become a growing concern in America. As a nation, we have looked for programs and policies to improve their status and this has led to federal legislation such as the proposed Kennedy-Hawkins bill. If passed, Kennedy-Hawkins would raise the minimum wage from the present level of $3.35 to 4.65 an hour over three years and increase the wage automatically to 60 percent of the average hourly wage thereafter ("Anti-Darwinism"). The intentions of this bill are entirely positive; however, Kennedy-Hawkins or any other legislation of the same nature would accomplish the opposite for the people it was designed for—it would increase unemployment and hurt the country's economic situation.

Giving a worker more money appears to improve his or her financial situation, but the converse actually happens. The worker very often receives more than just a money wage. In addition to hourly compensation, many employees receive extra benefits such as health insurance, company discounts, and flexible schedules (Lee and McKenzie 55). As hourly costs rise, employers cut their total costs by reducing or eliminating benefit packages, leaving the employee no better off than before the wage increase. Workers whose compensation consisted solely of the minimum wage might find themselves unemployed because the first jobs cut are those of the least value. Rarely in history has management been laid off before labor, and the first workers to go are also the youngest. Teenagers make up one-third of the minimum-wage work force (Campbell 105). As cuts are made, the jobs they hold will be eliminated first. Without these jobs, America's young lack the opportunity to develop the job skills that would allow them to move out of minimum-wage positions.

The country as a whole would also suffer a negative impact due to the increase in unemployment. The businesses would be forced to cut jobs due to the minimum wage hike. Robert B. McKenzie, a professor of economics at Clemson University, estimates that 1.9 million jobs would vanish in the eight-year period following the wage hike ("Job Loss" 105). Areas of low unemployment could absorb the increase because they already pay wages above the federal minimum to attract people to job openings (Ormiston). However, in areas with high unemployment, like the oil producing states of Texas, Oklahoma, and Louisiana, the effect would be extremely damaging. It could possibly send their local economies from recession into depression.

Another way the country would suffer economically stems from a ripple effect created by the minimum wage elevation. When the wage floor rises, the people above it demand a pay increase too (Campbell). The reason is, of course, that they feel they must be separated from workers traditionally paid less. The rise throughout the pay scale cannot be absorbed by benefit cuts or layoffs. Businesses would be forced to increase the prices they charge for their goods and services. This effect spread throughout the nation has the potential to start an upswing in the rate of inflation. That type of dollar devaluation would be felt within the country and in our overseas buying power as the dollar slips down in value against foreign currency, placing the overall economic health of America In jeopardy.

Legislation such as Kennedy-Hawkins has good intentions, but the negative aspects prevent it from being a feasible solution to the low wage earner's problem. The Congress might instead explore options such as increasing the earned-income tax credit or redirecting funds to more and better job training programs. Raising the minimum wage is not the answer.

Works Cited

"Anti-Darwinism." The Economist 10 Jan. 1988: 24-25.
Campbell, Jeffrey. "Don't Raise the Minimum Wage." Fortune 31 Aug. 1987:103-104.
"Job Loss from Wage Hike." Nation's Business Sept. 1987:103.
Lee, Dwight R., and Richard B. McKenzie. "Minimum Wage: A Wenker Case Both for and Against." Challenge Sept./Oct. 1987: 55-56.
Ormiston, Kathy Ann. "States Know Best What Labor's Worth." The Wall Street Journal 10 May 1988: 34.

Desmond Tutu

NOBEL PRIZE ACCEPTANCE SPEECH

Desmond Tutu (1931-   ), Archbishop of the Anglican Church in South Africa, was awarded the Nobel Peace Prize in 1984 for his efforts as a middleman and peace maker between the diverse organizations struggling for freedom for blacks and the apartheid government in South Africa. In this speech, while making many lighthearted comments, he also outlines his philosophy of the way religion should relate to politics. As you read, consider how your own religious beliefs shape your political ideals.

Your majesty, members of the Royal Family, Mr. Chairman, Ladies and Gentlemen:

Many thousands of people round the world have been thrilled with the award of the Nobel Peace Prize for 1984 to Desmond Mpilo Tutu. I was told of a delegation of American churchpeople who were visiting Russia. On hearing the news they and their Russian hosts celebrated the Nobel Peace Prize Winner.

There has been a tremendous volume of greetings from heads of state, world leaders of the Christian church and other faiths as well as from so-called ordinary people—notable exceptions being the Soviet and South African governments.

The prize has given fresh hope to many in the world that has sometimes had a pall of despondency cast over it by the experience of suffering, disease, poverty, famine, hunger, oppression, injustice, evil and war—a pall that has made many wonder whether God cared, whether He was omnipotent, whether He was loving and compassionate. The world is in such desperate straits, in such a horrible mess that it all provides almost conclusive proof that a good and powerful and loving God such as Christians and people of other faiths say they believe in could not exist, or if He did He really could not be a God who cared much about the fate of His creatures or the world they happened to inhabit which seemed to be so hostile to their aspirations to be fully human.

I once went to a friend's house in England.

There I found a charming book of cartoons entitled *My God*. One showed God with appeals and supplications bombarding Him from people below and He saying, "I wish I could say, 'Don't call me, I'll call you.'" And another declared "Create in 6 days and have eternity to regret it."

My favourite shows God somewhat disconsolate and saying, "Oh dear, I think I have lost my copy of the divine plan." Looking at the state of the world you would be forgiven for wondering if He ever had one and whether He had not really botched things up.

New hope has sprung in the breast of many as a result of this prize—the mother watching her child starve in a Bantustan homeland resettlement camp, or one whose flimsy plastic covering was demolished by the authorities in the K.T.C. squatter camp in Cape Town; the man emasculated by the Pass Laws as he lived for 11 months in a single sex hostel; the student receiving an inferior education; the activist languishing in a consulate or a solitary confinement cell, being tortured because he thought he was human and wanted that God-given right recognised; the exile longing to kiss the soil of her much loved motherland, the political prisoner watching the days of a life sentence go by like the drip of a faulty tap, imprisoned because he knew he was created by God not to have his human dignity or pride trodden underfoot.

A new hope has been kindled in the breast of the millions who are voiceless, oppressed, dispossessed, tortured by the powerful tyrants; lacking elementary human rights in Latin America, in South East Asia, the Far East, in many parts of Africa and behind the Iron Curtain, who have their noses rubbed in the dust. How wonderful, how appropriate that this award is made today— December 10, Human Rights Day. It says more eloquently than anything else that this is God's world and He is in charge. That our cause is a just cause; that we will attain human rights in South Africa and everywhere in the world. We shall be free in South Africa and everywhere in the world.

I want to thank the Nobel Committee, I want to thank the Churches in Norway and everywhere for their support, their love and their prayers.

On behalf of all these for whom you have given new hope, a new cause for joy, I want to accept this award in a wholly representative capacity.

I accept this prestigious award on behalf of my family, on behalf of the South African Council of Churches, on behalf of all in my motherland, on behalf of those committed to the cause of justice, peace, and reconciliation everywhere.

If God be for us who can be against us?

Frederick Douglass

A PLEA FOR FREE SPEECH IN BOSTON

Frederick Douglass (1817-1895), an orator and journalist, escaped from slavery at age 21 and dedicated his life to abolishing it. He made this speech in 1860 a few days after a gathering of abolitionists was broken up by a prominent group of Boston citizens. Notice how his strong sense of morality and justice pervades the speech, and how he appeals to the very qualities that make Bostonians proud of their city.

Boston is a great city—and Music Hall has a fame almost as extensive as that of Boston. Nowhere more than here have the principles of human freedom been expounded. But for the circumstances already mentioned, it would seem almost presumption for me to say anything here about those principles. And yet, even here, in Boston, the moral atmosphere is dark and heavy. The principles of human liberty, even if correctly apprehended, find but limited support in this hour of trial. The world moves slowly, and Boston is much like the world. We thought the principle of free speech was an accomplished fact. Here, if nowhere else, we thought the right of the people to assemble and to express their opinion was secure. Dr. Channing had defended the right, Mr. Garrison had practically asserted the right, and Theodore Parker had maintained it with steadiness and fidelity to the last. But here we are to-day contending for what we thought was gained years ago. The mortifying and disgraceful fact stares us in the face, that though Faneuil Hall and Bunker Hill Monument stand, freedom of speech is struck down. No lengthy detail of facts is needed. They are already notorious; far more so than will be wished ten years hence.

The world knows that last Monday a meeting assembled to discuss the question: "How Shall Slavery Be Abolished?" The world also knows that the meeting was invaded, insulted, captured, by a mob of gentlemen, and thereafter broken up and dispersed by the order of the mayor, who refused to protect it, though called upon to do so. If this had been a mere outbreak of passion and prejudice among the baser sort, maddened by rum and hounded on by some wily politician to serve some immediate purpose—a mere exceptional affair—it might be allowed to rest with what has already been said. But the leaders of the mob were gentlemen. They were men who pride themselves upon their respect for law and order.

These gentlemen brought their respect for the law with them and proclaimed it loudly while in the very act of breaking the law. Theirs was the law of slavery. The law of free speech and the law for the protection of public meetings they trampled under foot, while they greatly magnified the law of slavery.

The scene was an instructive one. Men seldom see such a blending of the gentleman with the rowdy, as was shown on that occasion. It proved that human nature is very much the same, whether in tarpaulin or broadcloth. Nevertheless, when gentlemen approach us in the character of lawless and abandoned loafers,—assuming for the moment their manners and tempers,—they have themselves to blame if they are estimated below their quality.

No right was deemed by the fathers of the Government more sacred than the right of speech. It was in their eyes, as in the eyes of all thoughtful men, the great moral renovator of society and government. Daniel Webster called it a homebred right, a fireside privilege. Liberty is meaningless where the right to utter one's thoughts and opinions has ceased to exist. That, of all rights, is the dread of tyrants. It is the right which they first of all strike down. They know its power. Thrones, dominions, principalities, and powers, founded in injustice and wrong, are sure to tremble, if men are allowed to reason of righteousness, temperance, and of a judgement to come in their presence. Slavery cannot tolerate free speech. Five years of its exercise would banish the auction block and break every chain in the South. They will have none of it there, for they have the power. But shall it be so here? Even here in Boston, and among the friends of freedom, we hear two voices: one denouncing the mob that broke up our meeting on Monday as a base and cowardly outrage; and another, deprecating and regretting the holding of such a meeting, by such men, at such a time. We are told that the meeting was ill-timed, and the parties to it unwise.

Why, what is the matter with us? Are we going to palliate and excuse a palpable and flagrant outrage on the right of speech, by implying that only a particular description of persons should exercise that right? Are we, at such a time, when a great principle has been struck down, to quench the moral indignation which the deed excites, by casting reflections upon those on whose persons the outrage has been committed? After all the arguments for liberty to which Boston has listened for more than a quarter of a century, has she yet to learn that the time to assert a right is the time when the right itself is called in question, and that the men of all others to assert it are the men to whom the right has been denied?

It would be no vindication of the right of speech to prove that certain gentlemen of great distinction, eminent for their learning and ability, are allowed to freely express their opinions on all subjects—including the subject of slavery. Such a vindication would need, itself, to be vindicated. It would add insult to injury. Not even an old-fashioned abolition meeting could vindicate that right in Boston just now. There can be no right of speech where any man, however lifted up, or however humble, however young, or however old, is overawed by force, and compelled to suppress his honest sentiments.

Equally clear is the right to hear. To suppress free speech is a double wrong. It violates the rights of the hearer as well as those of the speaker. It is just as criminal to rob a man of his right to speak and hear as it would be to rob him of his money. I have no doubt that Boston will vindicate this right. But in order to do so, there must be no concessions to the enemy. When a man is allowed to speak because he is rich and powerful, it aggravates the crime of denying the right to the poor and humble.

The principle must rest upon its own proper basis. And until the right is accorded to the humblest as freely as to the most exalted citizen, the government of Boston is but an empty name, and its freedom a mockery. A man's right to speak does not depend upon where he was born or upon his color. The simple quality of manhood is the solid basis of the right—and there let it rest forever.

John F. Kennedy

INAUGURAL ADDRESS

John F. Kennedy (1917-1963) set forth a tall agenda as he began his short presidency in 1961. He had been a war hero, a bestselling historian, and a popular senator. Nonetheless, his margin of victory in the election had been one of the smallest in history, and he needed to begin his term of office by bringing popular sentiment to his side. He needed to allay fears from the right that he would not be tough enough in the middle of the cold war, and fears from the left that he wouldn't be aggressive enough in gaining civil rights for all. The result was a highly patriotic, highly allusive speech, which includes some lines which are still quoted today. As you read the speech, which is populated with many generalities, see if you can recall specific historic events Kennedy might be referring to.

We observe today not a victory of party but a celebration of freedom—symbolizing an end as well as a beginning—signifying renewal as well as change. For I have sworn before you and Almighty God the same solemn oath our forebears prescribed nearly a century and three quarters ago.

The world is very different now. For man holds in his mortal hands the power to abolish all forms of human poverty and all forms of human life. And yet the same revolutionary beliefs for which our forebears fought are still at issue around the globe—the belief that the rights of man come not from the generosity of the state but from the hand of God.

We dare not forget today that we are the heirs of that first revolution. Let the word go forth from this time and place, to friend and foe alike, that the torch has been passed to a new generation of Americans—born in this century, tempered by war, disciplined by a hard and bitter peace, proud of our ancient heritage—and unwilling to witness or permit the slow undoing of those human rights to which this nation has always been committed, and to which we are committed today at home and around the world.

Let every nation know, whether it wishes us well or ill, that we shall pay any price, bear any burden, meet any hardship, support any friend, oppose any foe, to assure the survival and the success of liberty.

This much we pledge—and more.

To those old allies whose cultural and spiritual origins we share, we pledge the loyalty of faithful friends. United, there is little we cannot do in a host of cooperative ventures. Divided, there is little we can do—for we dare not meet a powerful challenge at odds and split asunder.

To those new states whom we welcome to the ranks of the free, we pledge our word that one form of colonial control shall not have passed away merely to be replaced by a far more iron tyranny. We shall not always expect to find them supporting our view. But we shall always hope to find them strongly supporting their own freedom—and to remember that in the past, those who foolishly sought power by riding the back of the tiger ended up inside.

To those peoples in the huts and villages of half the globe struggling to break the bonds of mass misery, we pledge our best efforts to help them help themselves, for whatever period is required—not because the Communists may be doing it, not because we seek their votes, but because it is right. If a free society cannot help the many who are poor, it cannot save the few who are rich.

To our sister republics south of our border, we offer a special pledge—to convert our good words into good deeds—in a new alliance for progress—to assist free men and free governments in casting off the chains of poverty. But this peaceful revolution of

hope cannot become the prey of hostile powers. Let all our neighbors know that we shall join with them to oppose aggression or
subversion anywhere in the Americas. And let every other power
know that this hemisphere intends to remain the master of its
own house.

To that world assembly of sovereign states, the United Nations,
our last best hope in an age where the instruments of war have
far outpaced the instruments of peace, we renew our pledge of
support—to prevent it from becoming merely a forum for invec-
tive—to strengthen its shield of the new and the weak—and to
enlarge the area in which its writ may run.

Finally, to those nations who would make themselves our ad-
versary, we offer not a pledge but a request: that both sides begin
anew the quest for peace, before the dark powers of destruction
unleashed by science engulf all humanity in planned or accidental
self-destruction.

We dare not tempt them with weakness. For only when our
arms are sufficient beyond doubt can we be certain beyond doubt
that they will never be employed.

But neither can two great and powerful groups of nations take
comfort from our present course—both sides overburdened by the
cost of modern weapons, both rightly alarmed by the steady
spread of the deadly atom, yet both racing to alter that uncertain
balance of terror that stays the hand of mankind's final war.

So let us begin anew—remembering on both sides that civility is
not a sign of weakness, and sincerity is always subject to proof. Let
us never negotiate out of fear. But let us never fear to negotiate.

Let both sides explore what problems unite us instead of belabor-
ing those problems which divide us.

Let both sides, for the first time, formulate serious and precise
proposals for the inspection and control of arms—and bring the
absolute power to destroy other nations under the absolute control
of all nations.

Let both sides seek to invoke the wonders of science instead of its
terrors. Together let us explore the stars, conquer the deserts,
eradicate disease, tap the ocean depths, and encourage the arts
and commerce.

Let both sides unite to heed in all corners of the earth the command of Isaiah—to "undo the heavy burdens [and] let the oppressed go free."

And if a beachhead of cooperation may push back the jungle of
suspicion, let both sides join in creating a new endeavor, not a new

balance of power, but a new world of law, where the strong are just and the weak secure and the peace preserved.

All this will not be finished in the first one hundred days. Nor will it be finished in the first one thousand days, nor in the life of this administration, nor even perhaps in our lifetime on this planet. But let us begin.

In your hands, my fellow citizens, more than mine, will rest the final success or failure of our course. Since this country was founded, each generation of Americans has been summoned to give testimony to its national loyalty. The graves of young Americans who answered the call to service surround the globe.

Now the trumpet summons us again—not as a call to bear arms, though arms we need—not as a call to battle, though embattled we are—but as a call to bear the burden of a long twilight struggle, year in and year out, "rejoicing in hope, patient in tribulation"—a struggle against the common enemies of man: tyranny, poverty, disease, and war itself.

Can we forge against these enemies a grand and global alliance, North and South, East and West, that can assure a more fruitful life for all mankind? Will you join in that historic effort?

In the long history of the world, only a few generations have been granted the role of defending freedom in its hour of maximum danger. I do not shrink from this responsibility—I welcome it. I do not believe that any of us would exchange places with any other people or any other generation. The energy, the faith, the devotion which we bring to this endeavor will light our country and all who serve it—and the glow from that fire can truly light the world.

And so, my fellow Americans: ask not what your country can do for you—ask what you can do for your country.

My fellow citizens of the world: ask not what America will do for you, but what together we can do for the freedom of man.

Finally, whether you are citizens of America or citizens of the world, ask of us here the same high standards of strength and sacrifice which we ask of you. With a good conscience our only sure reward, with history the final judge of our deeds, let us go forth to lead the land we love, asking His blessing and His help, but knowing that here on earth God's work must truly be our own.

Adlai E. Stevenson

VETO OF THE "CAT BILL"

Adlai Stevenson was elected governor of Illinois in 1948, was the
Democratic candidate for president in 1952 and in 1956, and in 1961
was named Ambassador to the United Nations by President John F.
Kennedy. In spite of his great wit, Stevenson was called an "egg-head"
by his political opponents—particularly when he tried "to talk sense to
the American people." His candidacy had little appeal for a nation
which, so soon after four years of World War II, wanted to think little,
if at all.

For many years some of the more fun-loving members of the Illinois
legislative branch had submitted to new governors a bill, the purpose
of which was (on its face) to restrict the free-movement of cats in the
State of Illinois. In truth, its purpose was to force a gubernatorial veto.
In 1949, Adlai E. Stevenson obliged them with this message. The "Cat
Bill" has not reappeared in the Illinois General Assembly since then.

To the honorable, the members of the Senate of the 66th general
assembly:

I herewith return, without my approval, Senate bill 93 entitled,
"an act to provide protection to insectivorous birds by restraining
cats." This is the so-called "cat bill." I veto and withhold my approval from this bill for the following reasons:

It would impose fines on owners or keepers who permitted their
cats to run at large off their premises. It would permit any person
to capture, or call upon the police to pick up and imprison, cats at
large. It would permit the use of traps. The bill would have state-
wide application—on farms, in villages, and in metropolitan
centers.

This legislation has been introduced in the past several sessions
of the legislature, and it has, over the years, been the source of
much comment—not all of which has been in a serious vein. It
may be that the general assembly has now seen fit to refer it to one
who can view it with a fresh outlook. Whatever the reasons for
passage at this session, I cannot believe there is a widespread pub-

lic demand for this law or that it could, as a practical matter, be enforced.

Furthermore, I cannot agree that it should be the declared public policy of Illinois that a cat visiting a neighbor's yard or crossing the highway is a public nuisance. It is in the nature of cats to do a certain amount of unescorted roaming. Many live with their owners in apartments or other restricted premises, and I doubt if we want to make their every brief foray an opportunity for a small game hunt by zealous citizens—with traps or otherwise.

I am afraid this bill could only create discord, recrimination and enmity. Also consider the owner's dilemma: To escort a cat abroad on a leash is against the nature of the cat, and to permit it to venture forth for exercise unattended into a night of new dangers is against the nature of the owner. Moreover, cats perform useful service, particularly in rural areas, in combating rodents—work they necessarily perform alone and without regard for party lines.

We are all interested in protecting certain varieties of birds. That cats destroy some birds, I well know, but I believe this legislation would further but little the worthy cause to which its proponents give such unselfish effort.

The problem of cat versus bird is as old as time. If we attempt to resolve it by legislation, who knows but what we may be called upon to take sides as well in the age old problems of dog versus cat, bird versus bird, or even bird versus worm. In my opinion, the state of Illinois and its local governing bodies already have enough to do without trying to control feline delinquency.

For these reasons, and not because I love birds the less or cats the more, I veto and withhold my approval from Senate bill No. 93.

Eileen (student)

MANDATORY AIDS TESTING FOR JOB APPLICANTS

There is no need to shy away from controversial topics in research papers. Here, Eileen puts forth a very convincing case for banning AIDS testing of job applicants. Note that her case is consistently supported by research—she doesn't just make undocumented assertions. As you read her paper, think about how you would treat a fellow worker if you knew he had AIDS.

AIDS is a rapidly spreading disease that is reaching epidemic proportions. According to a brochure entitled *Facts About AIDS* put out by the Public Health Service, AIDS was first reported in the United States in 1981 *(Facts)*. *By* early 1987, an estimated 1.5 million Americans had been infected with the AIDS virus, more than 30,000 had developed AIDS, and 17,000 had died from it. Researchers are predicting that by 1991, these latter two figures will be ten times as high ("AIDS: What We Know Now" 143). An issue evolving from the AIDS problem is that of whether or not employers can require job applicants to take a blood test for AIDS before the employers will consider hiring them. Although many workers feel they have the right to refuse to work with an AIDS victim because they do not want to risk contracting the illness, and although an employer might not want to invest in a person whose condition ends in death, these tests should not be made mandatory. They will only lead to discrimination in both the workplace and with insurance, and they are an invasion of privacy.

Once an AIDS test for a job applicant has come back positive, discrimination is likely to start. Many employees feel they do not have to work with a person infected with AIDS because they risk contracting the disease. This shows ignorance because over and over the U.S. Public Health Service has assured the public that AIDS cannot be transmitted through casual contact ("AIDS: No

Need" 51). The only ways known to transmit the virus are through sexual contact, the sharing of needles for intravenous drugs, blood transfusions, and rarely, a mother's breast milk *(Facts)*. One cannot contract the AIDS virus from a toilet seat or from sharing someone's eating utensils. These concerned employees have no logical or medical evidence to support them, only emotional input.

An employer might also want to require AIDS testing so he'll know if he wants to invest in a person whom he expects always to be sick and to have a short life expectancy. But in the *Facts About AIDS* brochure, it is stated that it might be up to five years after a person is infected with the virus before he starts experiencing symptoms. So even though he may have several good years to live and work, the employer will probably label him an AIDS victim and not hire him. This is discrimination because a person's life should not end the moment he or she is diagnosed as having AIDS. As long as he can, he should be allowed to lead a normal life, including working for as long as he is able. Fortunately, according to the article, "Workplace AIDS," most authorities feel that people with AIDS are included in the laws that protect the handicapped from discrimination. So if they don't have any symptoms that interfere with their work ability, they cannot be fired ("Workplace AIDS" 30). In all fairness, this should apply to hiring as well.

Discrimination doesn't remain only in the workplace, though. If job applicants' test results are passed on to insurance companies, they sometimes discriminate also. Fortunately, as stated in a *U.S. News and World Report* article, "contract law forbids insurers from barring newly diagnosed AIDS patients from group health plans" ("AIDS: A Time of Testing" 58). Yet, according to another U.S. *News* article, a man in Colorado sent a copy of his negative AIDS test to his insurance company, and they still refused him "on the basis that the fact he got tested at all made him too great a risk" ("Mandatory Tests" 62). These companies are presently fighting bills that would keep them from refusing AIDS victims ("AIDS: A Time of Testing" 58).

Along with causing discrimination, the AIDS tests are invading persons' privacy. Employers, by testing job applicants for AIDS, are prying into their personal lives. Employers don't test prospective employees for other diseases that aren't contagious through casual contact such as cancer, syphillis, and cerebral palsy, and for that matter, for diseases that are more easily contagious, such as hepatitis and pneumonia, so why should AIDS be an exception?

Besides, once employers explore all aspects of applicants' health and discover positive AIDS tests, what's to stop employers from looking into causes and discriminating against the applicants, not necessarily because of AIDS, but perhaps because they are homosexual? That is quite a generalization, and perhaps most employers are more unbiased than this, but it is certainly possible that discrimination could become this out-of-hand.

Yes, the population of AIDS victims is rapidly growing, and it is frightening because everyone is afraid of contracting this dreadful illness. But if we refrain from the activities known to transmit AIDS, we have no need to worry, even in the workplace. AIDS victims— like everyone else—have the right to live normal lives, and as long as they are able to perform their job duties, they should not be discriminated against. So, until the medical community finds any evidence that AIDS can be transmitted through casual contact, I don't see any risk with an AIDS victim in the workplace. Therefore, mandatory blood tests to check for AIDS in job applicants are unnecessary.

Works Cited

"AIDS: No Need for Worry in the Workplace." *Newsweek* 25 Nov. 1985: 51.
"AIDS: What We Know Now." *McCall's* April 1987:143-44.
Facts About AIDS. U.S. Dept. of Health and Human Services, Spring 1986.
"Mandatory Tests for AIDS?" *U.S. News & World Report* 9 March 1987: 62.
"Workplace AIDS." *Nation's Business* Nov. 1986: 30.

Jonathan Swift

A MODEST PROPOSAL

Jonathan Swift (1667-1745), writer and poet, used his works as an opportunity to comment on the society he lived in. He is best known for his novel, *Gulliver's Travels*, but *A Modest Proposal* is perhaps his most effective social commentary. As you read, ask yourself if the problems the United States face today are similar to those Swift describes—and if the remedies proposed today are as "modest" as his own.

It is a melancholy object to those who walk through this great town or travel in the country, when they see the streets, the roads and cabin doors crowded with beggars of the female sex, followed by three, four, or six children, all in rags and importuning every passenger for an alms. These mothers, instead of being able to work for their honest livelihood, are forced to employ all their time in strolling to beg sustenance for their helpless infants; who as they grow up either turn thieves for want of work, or leave their dear native country to fight for the Pretender in Spain, or sell themselves to the Barbadoes.

I think it is agreed by all parties that this prodigious number of children in the arms, or on the backs, or at the heels of their mothers, and frequently of their fathers, is in the present deplorable state of the kingdom a very great additional grievance; and, therefore, whoever could find out a fair, cheap, and easy method of making these children sound and useful members of the Commonwealth, would deserve so well of the public as to have his statue set up for a preserver of the nation.

But my intention is very far from being confined to provide only for the children of professed beggars; it is of a much greater extent, and shall take in the whole number of infants at a certain age who are born of parents in effect as little able to support them as those who demand our charity in the streets.

As to my own part, having turned my thoughts for many years upon this important subject, and maturely weighed the several schemes of other projectors, I have always found them grossly mistaken in their computation. It is true a child, just dropped from its dam, may be supported by her milk for a solar year, with little other nourishment; at most not above the value of two shillings, which the mother may certainly get, or the value in scraps, by her lawful occupation of begging; and it is exactly at one year old that I propose to provide for them in such a manner as instead of being a charge upon their parents or the parish, or wanting food and raiment for the rest of their lives, they shall on the contrary contribute to the feeding, and partly to the clothing, of many thousands.

There is likewise another great advantage in my scheme, that it will prevent those voluntary abortions, and that horrid practice of women murdering their bastard children, alas! too frequent among us, sacrificing the poor innocent babes, I doubt, more to avoid the expense than the shame, which would move tears and pity in the most savage and inhuman breast.

The number of souls in Ireland being usually reckoned one million and a half, of these I calculate there may be about two hundred thousand couples whose wives are breeders; from which number I subtract thirty thousand couples who are able to maintain their own children (although I apprehend there cannot be so many, under the present distresses of the kingdom); but this being granted, there will remain an hundred and seventy thousand breeders. I again subtract fifty thousand for those women who miscarry, or whose children die by accident or disease within the year. There only remain an hundred and twenty thousand children of poor parents annually born. The question therefore is, how this number shall be reared and provided for? which, as I have already said, under the present situation of affairs, is utterly impossible by all the methods hitherto proposed. For we can neither employ them in handicraft or agriculture; we neither build houses (I mean in the country) nor cultivate land; they can very seldom pick up a livelihood by stealing, till they arrive at six years old, except where they are of towardly parts; although I confess they learn the rudiments much earlier; during which time they can, however, be properly looked upon only as probationers; as I have been informed by a principal gentleman in the county of Cavan, who protested to me that he never knew above one or two instances under the age of six, even in a part of the kingdom so renowned for the quickest proficiency in that art.

I am assured by our merchants, that a boy or a girl before twelve years old is no saleable commodity; and even when they come to this age they will not yield above three pounds or three pounds and half a crown at most on the Exchange; which cannot turn to account either to the parents or the kingdom, the charge of nutriment and rags having been at least four times that value.

I shall now therefore humbly propose my own thoughts, which I hope will not be liable to the least objection.

I have been assured by a very knowing American of my acquaintance in London, that a young healthy child well nursed is, at year old, a most delicious, nourishing, and wholesome food, whether stewed, roasted, baked, or boiled; and I make no doubt that it will equally serve in a fricassee or a ragout.

I do therefore humbly offer it to public consideration that of the hundred and twenty thousand children already computed, twenty thousand may be reserved for breed, whereof only one-fourth part to be males; which is more than we allow to sheep, black cattle, or swine; and my reason is, that these children are seldom the fruits of marriage, a circumstance not much regarded by our savages; therefore one male will be sufficient to serve four females. That the remaining hundred thousand may, at a year old, be offered in sale to the persons of quality and fortune through the kingdom; always advising the mother to let them suck plentifully in the last month, so as to render them plump and fat for a good table. A child will make two dishes at an entertainment for friends; and when the family dines alone, the fore or hind quarter will make a reasonable dish, and seasoned with a little pepper or salt will be very good boiled on the fourth day, especially in winter.

I have reckoned upon a medium that a child just born will weigh twelve pounds, and in a solar year, if tolerably nursed, will increase to twenty-eight pounds.

I grant this food will be somewhat dear, and therefore very proper for landlords, who, as they have already devoured most of the parents, seem to have the best title to the children.

Infant's flesh will be in season throughout the year, but more plentiful in March, and a little before and after: for we are told by a grave author, an eminent French physician, that fish being a prolific diet, there are more children born in Roman Catholic countries about nine months after Lent than at any other season; therefore reckoning a year after , Lent, the markets will be more glutted than usual, because the number of popish infants is at least three to one in this kingdom: and therefore it will have one other collateral advantage, by lessening the number of Papists among us.

I have already computed the charge of nursing a beggar's child (in which list I reckon all cottagers, laborers, and four-fifths of the farmers) to be about two shillings per annum, rags included; and I believe no gentleman would repine to give ten shillings for the carcass of a good fat child, which, as I have said, will make four dishes of excellent nutritive meat, when he has only some particular friend or his own family to dine with him. Thus the squire will learn to be a good landlord, and grow popular among his tenants; the mother will have eight shillings net profit, and be fit for work till she produces another child.

Those who are more thrifty (as I must confess the times require) may flay the carcass; the skin of which artificially dressed will make admirable gloves for ladies, and summer boots for fine gentlemen.

As to our city of Dublin, shambles may be appointed for this purpose in the most convenient parts of it, and butchers we may be assured will not be wanting: although I rather recommend buying the children alive, and dressing them hot from the knife as we do roasting pigs.

A very worthy person, a true lover of his country, and whose virtues I highly esteem, was lately pleased in discoursing on this matter to offer a refinement upon my scheme. He said that many gentlemen of this kingdom, having of late destroyed their deer, he conceived that the want of venison might be well supplied by the bodies of young lads and maidens, not exceeding fourteen years of age nor under twelve; so great a number of both sexes in every county being now ready to starve for want of work and service; and these to be disposed of by their parents, if alive, or otherwise by their nearest relations. But with due deference to so excellent a friend and so deserving a patriot, I cannot be altogether in his sentiments. For as to the males, my American acquaintance assured me from frequent experience that their flesh was generally tough and lean, like that of our schoolboys by continual exercise, and their taste disagreeable; and to fatten them would not answer the charge. Then as to the females, it would, I think, with humble submission be a loss to the public, because they soon would become breeders themselves: and besides, it is not improbable that some scrupulous people might be apt to censure such a practice (although indeed very unjustly) as a little bordering upon cruelty; which, I confess, has always been with me the strongest objection against any project, how well soever intended.

But in order to justify my friend, he confessed that this expedient was put into his head by the famous Salmanaazor? a native of the island Formosa, who came from thence to London above twenty years ago: and in conversation told my friend, that in his country when any young person happened to be put to death, the executioner sold the carcass to persons of quality as a prime dainty; and that in his time the body of a plump girl of fifteen, who was crucified for an attempt to poison the emperor, was sold to his imperial majesty's prime minister of state, and other great mandarins of the court, in joints from the gibbet, at four hundred crowns. Neither indeed can I deny, that if the same use were made of several plump young girls in this town, who without one single groat to their fortunes cannot stir abroad without a chair, and appear at the playhouse and assemblies in foreign fineries which they never will pay for, the kingdom would not be the worse.

Some persons of a desponding spirit are in great concern about that vast number of poor people, who are aged, diseased, or maimed, and I have been desired to employ my thoughts what cause may be taken to ease the nation of so grievous an encumbrance. But I am not in the least pain upon that matter, because it is very well known that they are every day dying and rotting by cold and famine, and filth and vermin, as fast as can be reasonably expected. And as to the young, labourers, they are now in as hopeful a condition: they cannot get work, and consequently pine away for want of nourishment, to a degree that if at any time they are accidentally hired to common labour, they have not strength to perform it; and thus the country and themselves are in a fair way of being soon delivered from the evils to come.

I have too long digressed, and therefore shall return to my subject. I think the advantages by the proposal which I have made are obvious and many, as well as of the highest importance.

For first, as I have already observed, it would greatly lessen the number of Papists, with whom we are yearly overrun, being the principal breeders of the nation as well as our most dangerous enemies; and who stay at home on purpose with a design to deliver the kingdom to the Pretender, hoping to take their advantage by the absence of so many good Protestants, who have chosen rather to leave their country than stay at home and pay tithes against their conscience to an idolatrous Episcopal curate.

Secondly, the poor tenants will have something valuable of their own, which by law may be made liable to distress and help to pay their landlord's rent, their corn and cattle being already seized, and money thing unknown.

Thirdly, whereas the maintenance of an hundred thousand children from two years old and upwards, cannot be computed at less than ten schillings apiece per annum, the nation's stock will be thereby increased fifty thousand pounds per annum, beside the profit of a new dish introduced to the tables of all gentlemen of fortune in the kingdom who have any refinement in taste. And the money will circulate among ourselves, the goods being entirely of our own growth and manufacture.

Fourthly, the constant breeders besides the gain of eight shillings sterling per annum by the sale of their children, will be rid of the charge of maintaining them after the first year.

Fifthly, this food would likewise bring great custom to taverns, where the vintners will certainly be so prudent as to procure the best receipts for dressing it to perfection, and consequently have their houses frequented by all the fine gentlemen, who justly value themselves upon their knowledge in good eating; and a skilful cook who understands how to oblige his guests, will contrive to make it as expensive as they please.

Sixthly, this would be a great inducement to marriage, which all wise nations have either encouraged by rewards or enforced by laws and penalties. It would increase the care and tenderness of mothers towards their children, when they were sure of a settlement for life to the poor babes, provided in some sort by the public, to their annual profit instead of expense. We should soon see an honest emulation among the married women, which of them could bring the fattest child to the market. Men would become as fond of their wives during the time of their pregnancy as they are now of their mares in foal, their cows in calf, their sows when they are ready to farrow; nor offer to beat or kick them (as is too frequent a practice) for fear of a miscarriage.

Many other advantages might be enumerated. For instance, the addition of some thousand carcasses in our exportation of barreled beef, the propagation of swine's flesh, and improvement in the art of making good bacon, so much wanted among us by the great destruction of pigs, too frequent at our tables, and which are no way comparable in taste or magnificence to a well-grown, fat, yearling child, which roasted whole will make a considerable figure at a Lord Mayor's feast or any other public entertainment. But this and many others I omit, being studious of brevity.

Supposing that one thousand families in this city would be constant customers for infant's flesh, besides others who might have it at merry meetings, particularly weddings and christenings, I compute that Dublin would take off annually about twenty thousand carcasses; and the rest of the kingdom (where probably they will be sold somewhat cheaper) the remaining eighty thousand.

I can think of no one objection that will possibly be raised against this proposal, unless it should be urged that the number of people will be thereby much lessened in the kingdom. This I freely own, and it was indeed one principal design in offering it to the world. I desire the reader will observe, that I calculate my remedy for this one individual kingdom of Ireland and for no other that ever was, is, or I think ever can be upon earth. Therefore let no man talk to me of other expedients: of taxing our absentees at five shillings a pound: of using neither clothes nor household furniture except what is of our own growth and manufacture: of utterly rejecting the materials and instruments that promote foreign luxury: of curing the expensiveness of pride, vanity, idleness, and gaming in our women: of introducing a vein of parsimony, prudence, and temperance: of learning to love our country, wherein we differ even from Laplanders and the inhabitants of Topinamboo: of quitting our animosities and factions, nor act any longer like the Jews, who were murdering one another at the very moment their city was taken: of being a little cautious not to sell our country and conscience for nothing: of teaching landlords to have at least one degree of mercy towards their tenants. Lastly, of putting a spirit of honesty, industry, and skill into our shopkeepers; who, if a resolution could now be taken to buy only our native goods, would immediately unite to cheat and exact upon us in the price, the measure, and the goodness, nor could ever yet be brought to make one fair proposal of just dealing, though often and earnestly invited to it.

Therefore, I repeat, let no man talk to me of these and the like expedients,till he has at least a glimpse of hope that there will ever be some hearty and sincere attempt to put them in practice.

But as to myself, having been wearied out for many years with offering vain, idle, visionary thoughts, and at length utterly despairing of success, I fortunately fell upon this proposal; which, as it is wholly new, so it has something solid and real, of no expense and little trouble, full in our own power, and whereby we can incur no danger in disobliging England. For this kind of commodity will not bear exportation, the flesh being of too tender a consistence to admit a long continuance in salt, although perhaps I could name a country which would be glad to eat up our whole nation without it.

After all, I am not so violently bent upon my own opinion as to reject any offer proposed by wise men, which shall be found equally innocent, cheap, easy, and effectual. But before something of that kind shall be advanced in contradiction to my scheme, and offering a better, I desire the author or authors will be pleased maturely to consider two points. First, as things now stand, how they will be able to find food and raiment for a hundred thousand useless mouths and backs? And secondly, there being a round million of creatures in human figure throughout this kingdom, whose whole subsistence put into a common stock would leave them in debt two millions of pounds sterling, adding those who are beggars by profession to the bulk of farmers, cottagers, and labourers, with the wives and children who are beggars in effect; I desire those politicians who dislike my overture, and may perhaps be so bold to attempt an answer, that they will first ask the parents of these mortals, whether they would not at this day think it a great happiness to have been sold for food at a year old in the manner I prescribe, and thereby have avoided such a perpetual scene of misfortunes as they have since gone through by the oppression of landlords, the impossibility of paying rent without money or trade, the want of common sustenance, with neither house nor clothes to cover them from the inclemencies of weather, and the most inevitable prospect of entailing the like or greater miseries upon their breed for ever.

I profess, in the sincerity of my heart, that I have not the least personal interest in endeavouring to promote this necessary work, having no other motive than the public good of my country, by advancing our trade, providing for infants, relieving the poor, and giving some pleasure to the rich. I have no children by which I can propose to get a single penny; the youngest being nine years old, and my wife past child-bearing.

Carl (Student)

PLEASE EXTINGUISH ALL SMOKING MATERIAL NOW

Since Carl wrote his paper, smoking has been banned on all domestic flights of less than six hours. Separate smoking sections are still allowed on many international flights and domestic flights of over six hours. As you read the paper, see which points are mitigated by the new information, and which points still have merit. Should smoking be banned on longer flights as well?

Straining to see my way clear, I emerged from the jet, my contact lenses dry and coated with a smoky film, my throat and nose irritated, not to mention the smell that would cling and follow me the rest of the day, just because the people seated around me decided to light up. Fortunately, I don't have asthma, allergies, or heart disease. Nevertheless, passive smoke endangers even my health. Although some people contend that smoking has become a right that does not present health or safety hazards to others, because of the confined space of an aircraft cabin where ventilation and air quality become a major concern, smoking should be eliminated from commercial aircraft. The trend in society away from smoking justifying nonsmoker's rights, new studies showing the harmful effects of passive smoke, and the safety and air quality issues inherent in air travel warrant a smoking ban.

First, the issue of rights inevitably arises in the smoking controversy. Smokers claim possession of an individual right to smoke whereas nonsmokers contend they are entitled to breathe fresh air. Lee S. Glass, a doctor and lawyer, while questioning whether a person can even claim smoking as his/her right, states that people "ought not be able to smoke in an airplane, when to do so may leave an asthmatic 10 rows away gasping for breath" (18). Common courtesy to others should always prevail. A right is not guaranteed when it proves harmful to others. Additionally, rules and regulations in general are intended to benefit the most people in society. Thus, smoking in public, airplanes included, becomes a matter of the rights of an individual versus the rights of the majority. The trend in society today moves away from smoking as the norm toward nonsmokers as the emerging majority. According to William U. Chandler, senior researcher at Worldwatch Institute in Washington, D.C., the United States has experienced a drop of more than a third in the percentage of males who smoke (57).

The time has arrived to recognize nonsmokers as the prevailing interest. Because of the confining quarters of an aircraft, with most passengers seated together in an open cabin, nonsmokers have no means of escape from the drifting and circulating smoke. Thus, outdated regulations favoring smoking on aircraft, fast becoming a habit of the past, should be eliminated and new ordinances established to protect the rising interests of nonsmokers.

Besides protecting interests of the majority, recent studies have exposed health hazards associated with passive smoke. Joseph Califano, former Secretary of Health, Education and Welfare, places the toll of Americans who die yearly of complications attributed to secondary smoke at 5,000. He cites involuntary smoking as contributing to lung cancer, pneumonia, asthma, bronchitis, and heart disease ("Restrict Smoking" 65). Keep in mind that these are *non*smokers dying as a result of smoke generated by others. In his article urging the banishment of tobacco, Chandler stresses that "Sidestream smoke—which wafts from a smoker's cigarette to an involuntary smoker—puts into the surrounding air fifty times the amount of carcinogens inhaled by the user." Accordingly, he states that passive smokers face a risk of succumbing to lung cancer three times higher than if the exposure was avoided (56, 60). Eliot Marshall, in an issue of *Science,* reported the findings of the National Research Council appointed to study the issue. They found young children brought up in smoking environments are highly susceptible to respiratory problems, nonsmoking adults married to smokers are more prone to lung cancer, and many nonsmokers suffer severe eye, nose, and throat irritation as a result of passive smoke (1066). These alarming discoveries and statistics illustrate the harm inflicted on innocent people. These are people who have chosen not to smoke, whether out of pride and respect for their health, simple distaste for the habit, or realization of the inherent risks. Yet to see these same adults and children, however careful they have been in this respect, suffering and dying from the effects of smoke created by others illustrates the need for action in this matter. When seated in an airplane, then, should it be so difficult to consider the health and well-being of those around you? Most domestic commercial flights reach their destinations within an hour or two, some with layovers to provide a break. Smokers, while in flight, could make use of commercially available alternatives such as smokeless cigarettes or nicotine gum to tide them over. As more facts arise about the risks of secondary smoke, clearly measures should be taken to eliminate smoke from airplanes, where close personal contact cannot be avoided.

Additionally, airplanes themselves harbor exclusive safety and air quality problems not found in other public places, making a smoking ban essential. First, at the top of safety concerns, in the event of fire caused by a careless smoker, there clearly exists no escape from a cruising aircraft. Also, an article by Pepper Leeper cites conclusions drawn from a study done by the National Research Council committee on federal standards in air travel as mandated by Congress. With ventilation and air quality their primary concern, the committee released information that new aircrafts recirculate as much as half of the stale cabin air for greater general efficiency of the plane. Most of the ventilation systems are set to provide the minimum airflow rate allowable, before any tobacco smoke or contaminants are introduced into the pressurized compartments. Thus, the committee believes that smoking causes a drop of air quality in planes below federal standards (30). According to Thomas C. Chalmers, chairperson of the National Research Council committee and president emeritus of Mount Sinai Medical Center in New York, present filters in the ventilation system do not dispel those pollutants resulting from cigarette smoking, so those gases remain free in the cabins for a long period (5B).

Not only does the smoke recirculate, but it causes mechanical problems as well. Speaking to a maintenance supervisor of an airline, Lee S. Glass found that smoke accumulates in the metal tubing of the ventilation system, not only inhibiting circulation through the network, but requiring money to clean and restore the system (18). These statements indicate that because of the design, pressurization, and ventilation requirements of airplanes, no solution now exists to safely rid the smoke and ash from the cabin air. The only acceptable answer is a complete ban on the source of the pollution, tobacco smoke.

In response, the opponents of a smoking ban present various "resolutions" to the problem, none of which satisfy the core issue. While current seating may seem adequate, separate seating sections for smokers do not improve air quality for nonsmokers, but instead aggravate the condition. The research committee declares that separating smokers into one section concentrates the smoke so that it becomes too intense for the ventilation system, and cloudy air results. However, dispersing smokers among nonsmokers to lessen concentrations would meet overwhelming opposition from the public (Leeper 31). Other suggestions considered by the committee according to Chalmers included erecting physical barriers or air curtains that would interfere with safety standards and escape routes, redesigning cabin layouts that prove too costly, and increasing the flow of outside air into the aircraft that would rob the jet engines of their power (5B). Clearly, a feasible solution does not presently exist to warrant safe smoking aboard airplanes. The general nature of airplanes themselves, where balance and stability dictate design, limited and restricted public quarters exist, requirements for a pressurized and sealed com-

partment arise, and safety and air quality become critical, does
not allow support for the threat that smoking aboard clearly
imposes.

In ending, hustle and bustle along with a general lack of concern characterizes today's society. The days have vanished when
people on the streets greeted one another with a smile and a
"hello" and when people actively acquainted themselves with
neighbors and other citizens. Presently, society consists of corporate executives, industrialists, capitalists, merchants, wage earners, and ordinary people so wrapped up in their own problems
that a general disregard pervades. The nearest airport measures
the essence of this hubbub, where everyone seems to be jockeying
for some crucial position. With airports working to their limits to
meet the demand, meeting safety and health criteria becomes an
intricate but vital endeavor. In this respect, smoking has no merit
aboard airplanes. Until the time that enough people realize on
their own the value of respect and consideration for others and
show genuine interest, regulations will have to intervene. For
these reasons, smoking should be banned on airplanes.

Works Cited

Chalmers, Thomas C. "Ban All Smoking on Planes." *Denver Post*
5 Sept. 1986: 5B.
Chandler, William U. "Banishing Tobacco." *Transaction Social
Science and Modern Society* May/June 1986: 56-64.
Glass, Lee S. "Fly the Smoke-Free Skies." *Newsweek* 16 April
1984: 18.
Leeper, Pepper. "Cleaning Up the Air in Commercial Airlines."
The Air Conditioning, Heating and Refrigeration News 13
October 1986: *30-31*.
Marshall, Eliot. "Involuntary Smokers Face Health Risks."
Science 28 Nov. 1986: 1066-67.
"Restrict Smoking in Public Places?" *U.S. News & World Report*.

Mark Twain

RUNNING FOR PRESIDENT

This essay contains enough of Twain's typical wry wit and dry humor to make up for *Two Views of the Mississippi* (see the introduction
to that selection in chapter 2). When Twain expressed his opinions
about politicians, it was generally to denigrate the species. In this
work, he does the same—but he's the politician. As you read, ask
yourself if anything has really changed about politicians since this
piece was originally published in 1879.

I have pretty much made up my mind to run for President.
What the country wants is a candidate who cannot be injured by
investigation of his past history, so that the enemies of the party
will be unable to rake up anything against him that nobody ever
heard of before. If you know the worst about a candidate, to begin
with, every attempt to spring things on him will be checkmated.
Now I am going to enter the field with an open record. I am going
to own up in advance to all the wickedness I have done, and if any
Congressional committee is disposed to prowl around my biography in the hope of discovering any dark and deadly deed that I
have secreted, why—let it prowl.

In the first place, I admit that I treed a rheumatic grandfather
of mine in the winter of 1850. He was old and inexpert in climbing
trees, but with the heartless brutality that is characteristic of me I
ran him out of the front door in his nightshirt at the point of a
shotgun, and caused him to bowl up a maple tree, where he remained all night, while I emptied shot into his legs. I will do it
again if I ever have another grandfather. I am as inhuman now
as I was in 1850. I candidly acknowledge that I ran away at the
battle of Gettysburg. My friends have tried to smooth over this
fact by asserting that I did so for the purpose of imitating
Washington, who went into the woods at Valley Forge for the
purpose of saying his prayers. It was a miserable subterfuge. I
struck out in a straight line for the Tropic of Cancer because I was
scared. I wanted my country saved, but I preferred to have some-

body else save it. I entertain that preference yet. If the bubble reputation can be obtained only at the cannon's mouth, I am willing to go there for it provided the cannon is empty. If it is loaded my immortal and inflexible purpose is to get over the fence and go home. My invariable practice in war has been to bring out of every fight two-thirds more men than when I went in. This seems to me Napoleonic in its grandeur.

My financial views are of the most decided character, but they are not likely, perhaps, to increase my popularity with the advocates of inflation. I do not insist upon the special supremacy of rag money or hard money. The great fundamental principle of my life is to take any kind I can get.

The rumor that I buried a dead aunt under my grapevine was correct. The vine needed fertilizing, my aunt had to be buried, and I dedicated her to this high purpose. Does that unfit me for the Presidency? The Constitution of this country does not say so. No other citizen was ever considered unworthy of this office because he enriched his grapevines with his dead relatives. Why should I be selected as the first victim of an absurd prejudice?

I admit also that I am not a friend of the poor man. I regard the poor man, in his present condition, as so much wasted raw material. Cut up and properly canned, he might be made useful to fatten the natives of the cannibal islands and to improve our export trade in that region. I shall recommend legislation upon the subject in my first message. My campaign cry will be: "Desiccate the poor workingman; stuff him into sausages."

These are about the worst parts of my record. On them I come before the country. If my country don't want me, I will go back again. But I recommend myself as a safe man—a man who starts from the basis of total depravity and proposes to be fiendish to the last.

Chapter 6:
Science Through the Centuries

Aristotle

THE PARTS OF ANIMALS

Aristotle (384-322 B.C.), an ancient Greek philosopher, scientist, and critic, was a student of Plato before establishing his own school and producing many important works. His influence in Europe extended for centuries past his own time, reaching a peak during the Medieval and Renaissance periods (roughly the 11th century through the 16th), but continuing through to the present. Here he expresses some principles of scientific inquiry that remain relevant even today. As you read the selection, consider how the Greek approach toward science differs from the way in which we approach it today.

Every systematic science, the humblest and the noblest alike, seems to admit of two distinct kinds of proficiency; one of which may be properly called scientific knowledge of the subject, while the other is a kind of educational acquaintance with it. For an educated man should be able to form a fair off-hand judgement as to the goodness or badness of the method used by a professor in his exposition. To be educated is in fact to be able to do this; and even the man of universal education we deem to be such in virtue of his having this ability. It will, however, of course, be understood that we only ascribe universal education to one who in his own individual person is thus critical in all or nearly all branches of knowledge, and not to one who has a like ability merely in some special subject. For it is possible for a man to have this competence in some one branch of knowledge without having it in all.

It is plain then that, as in other sciences, so in that which inquires into nature, there must be certain canons, by reference to which a hearer shall be able to criticize the method of a professed exposition, quite independently of the question whether the statements made be true or false. Ought we, for instance (to give an illustration of what I mean), to begin by discussing each separate species—man, lion, ox, and the like—taking each kind in hand independently of the rest, or ought we rather to deal first with the attributes which they have in common in virtue of some common element of their nature, and proceed from this as a basis for the consideration of them separately? For genera that are quite distinct yet oftentimes present many identical phenomena, sleep, for instance, respiration, growth, decay, death, and other similar affections and conditions, which may be passed over for the present, as we are not yet prepared to treat of them with clearness and precision. Now it is plain that if we deal with each species independently of the rest, we shall frequently be obliged to repeat the same statements over and over again; for horse and dog and man present, each and all, every one of the phenomena just enumerated. A discussion therefore of the attributes of each such species separately would necessarily involve frequent repetitions as to characters, themselves identical but recurring in animals specifically distinct. (Very possibly also there may be other characters which, though they present specific differences, yet come under one and the same category. For instance, flying, swimming, walking, creeping, are plainly specifically distinct, but yet are all forms of animal progression.) We must, then, have some clear understanding as to the manner in which our investigation is to be conducted; whether, I mean, we are first to deal with the common or generic characters, and afterwards to take into consideration special peculiarities; or whether we are to start straight off with the ultimate species. For as yet no definite rule has been laid down in this matter. So also there is a like uncertainty as to another point now to be mentioned. Ought the writer who deals with the works of nature to follow the plan adopted by the mathematicians in their astronomical demonstrations, and after considering the phenomena presented by animals, and their several parts, proceed subsequently to treat of the causes and the reason why; or ought he to follow some other method? And when these questions are answered, there yet remains another. The causes concerned in the generation of the works of nature are, as we see, more than one. There is the final cause and there is the motor cause. Now we must decide which of these two causes comes first, which second. Plainly, however, that cause is the first which we call the final one. For this is the Reason, and the Reason forms the starting-point, alike in the works of art and in works of nature. For consider how the physician or how the builder sets about his work. He starts by forming for himself a definite picture, in the one case perceptible to mind, in the other to sense, of his end—the physician of health, the builder of a house—and this he holds forward as the reason and explanation of each subsequent step that he takes, and of his action in this or that way as the case may be. Now in the works of nature: the good end and the final cause is still more dominant than in works of art such as these, nor is necessity a factor with the same significance in them all; though almost all writers, while they try to refer their origin to this cause, do so without distinguishing the various senses in which the term necessity is used. For there is absolute necessity, manifested in eternal phenomena; and there is hypothetical necessity, manifested in everything that is generated by nature as in everything that is produced by art, be it a house or what it may. For if a house or other such final object is to be realized, it is necessary that such and such material shall exist; and it is necessary that first this and then that shall be produced, and first this and then that set in motion, and so on in continuous succession, until the end and final result is reached, for the sake of which each prior thing is produced and exists. As with these productions of art, so also is it with the productions of nature. The mode of necessity, however, and the mode of ratiocination are different in natural science from what they are in the theoretical sciences; of which we have spoken elsewhere. For in the latter the starting-point is that which is; in the former that which is to be. For it is that which is yet to be— health, let us say, or a man—that, owing to its being of such and such characters, necessitates the pre-existence or previous production of this and that antecedent; and not this or that antecedent which, because it exists or has been generated, makes it necessary that health or a man is in, or shall come into, existence. Nor is it possible to trace back the series of necessary antecedents to a starting-point, of which you can say that, existing itself from eternity, it has determined their existence as its consequent. These however, again, are matters that have been dealt with in another treatise. There too it was stated in what cases absolute and hypothetical necessity exist; in what cases also the proposition expressing hypothetical necessity is simply convertible, and what cause it is that determines this convertibility.

Another matter which must not be passed over without consideration is, whether the proper subject of our exposition is that with which the ancient writers concerned themselves, namely, what is the process of formation of each animal; or whether it is not rather, what are the characters of a given creature when formed. For there is no small difference between these two views. The best course appears to be that we should follow the method already mentioned, and begin with the phenomena presented by each group of animals, and, when this is done, proceed afterwards to state the causes of those phenomena, and to deal with their evolution. For elsewhere, as for instance in house building, this is the true sequence. The plan of the house, or the house, has this and that form; and because it has this and that form, therefore is its construction carried out in this or that manner. For the process of evolution is for the sake of the thing finally evolved, and not this for the sake of the process. Empedocles, then, was in error when he said that many of the characters presented by animals were merely the results of incidental occurrences during their development; for instance, that the backbone was divided as it is into vertebrae, because it happened to be broken owing to the contorted position of the foetus in the womb. In so saying he overlooked the fact that propagation implies a creative seed endowed with certain formative properties. Secondly, he neglected another fact, namely, that the parent animal pre-exists, not only in idea, but actually in time. For man is generated from man; and thus it is the possession of certain characters by the parent that determines the development of like characters in the child. The same statement holds good also for the operations of art, and even for those which are apparently by chance. For the same result as is produced by art may occur by chance. Chance, for instance, may bring about the restoration of health. The products of art, however, require the pre-existence of an efficient cause homogeneous with themselves, such as the statuary's art, which must necessarily precede the statue; for this cannot possibly be produced by chance. Art indeed consists in the conception of the result to be produced before its realization in the material. As with chance, so with fortune; for this also produces the same result as art, and by the same process.

The fittest mode, then, of treatment is to say, a man has such and such parts, because the conception of a man includes their presence, and because they are necessary conditions of his existence, or, if we cannot quite say this, which would be best of all, then the next thing to it, namely, that it is either quite impossible for him to exist without them, or, at any rate, that it is better for him that they should be there; and their existence involves the existence of other antecedents. Thus we should say, because man is an animal with such and such characters, therefore is the process of his development necessarily such as it is; and therefore is it accomplished in such and such an order, this Part being formed first, that next, and so on in succession; and after a like fashion should we explain the evolution of all other works of nature.

Francis Bacon

NOVUM ORGANUM

Francis Bacon (1561-1626) was both a philosopher and a statesman, but he will always be known best as an essayist. Many of his essays describe scientific and philosophic investigations Bacon conducted as part of his long-term plan to reorganize the systems of thought and the means of obtaining power over nature that prevailed in his day. At the age of thirty-one, Bacon wrote in a letter to his uncle "I have taken all knowledge as my province." In spite of his great plans, the philosopher died with only the first two parts of his planned six-part system completed.

In the sixth rank of prerogative instances we will place similar or proportionate instances, which we are also wont to call physical parallels, or resemblances. They are such as exhibit the resemblances and connection of things, not in minor forms (as the constitutive do), but at once in the concrete. They are therefore, as it were, the first and lowest steps toward the union of nature; nor do they immediately establish any axiom, but merely indicate and observe a certain relation of bodies to each other. But although they be not of much assistance in discovering forms, yet they are of great advantage in disclosing the frame of parts of the universe, upon whose members they practise a species of anatomy, and thence occasionally lead us gently on to sublime and noble axioms, especially such as relate to the construction of the world, rather than to simple natures and forms.

As an example, take the following similar instances: a mirror and the eye; the formation of the ear, and places which return an echo. From such similarity, besides observing the resemblance (which is useful for many purposes), it is easy to collect and form this axiom. That the organs of the senses, and bodies which produce reflections to the senses, are of a similar nature. Again, the understanding once informed of this, rises easily to a higher and nobler axiom; namely, that the only distinction between sensitive and inanimate bodies, in those points in which they agree and sympathize, is this; in the former, animal spirit is added to the arrangement of the body, in the latter it is wanting. So that there might be as many senses in animals as there are points of agreement with inanimate bodies, if the animated body were perforated, so as to allow the spirit to have access to the limb properly disposed for action, as a fit organ. And, on the other hand, there are, without doubt, as many motions in an inanimate as there are senses in the animated body, though the animal spirit be absent. There must, however, be many more motions in inanimate bodies than senses in the animated, from the small number of organs of sense. A very plain example of this is afforded by pains. For, as animals are liable to many kinds and various descriptions of pains (such as those of burning, of intense cold, of pricking, squeezing, stretching, and the like), so is it most certain, that the same circumstances, as far as motion is concerned, happen to inanimate bodies, such as wood or stone when burnt, frozen, pricked, cut, bent, bruised, and the like; although there be no sensation, owing to the absence of animal spirit.

Again, wonderful as it may appear, the roots and branches of trees are similar instances. For every vegetable swells and throws out its constituent parts towards the circumference, both upwards and downwards. And there is no difference between the roots and branches, except that the root is buried in the earth, and the branches are exposed to the air and sun. For if one take a young and vigorous shoot, and bend it down to a small portion of loose earth, although it be not fixed to the ground, yet will it immediately produce a root, and not a branch. And, vice versa, if earth be placed above, and so forced down with a stone or any hard substance, as to confine the plant and prevent its branching upwards, it will throw out branches into the air downwards.

The gum of trees, and most rock gems, are similar instances; for both of them are exudations and filtered juices, derived in the former instance from trees, in the latter from stones; the brightness and clearness of both arising from a delicate and accurate filtering. For nearly the same reason, the hair of animals is less beautiful and vivid in its color than the plumage of most birds, because the juices are less delicately filtered through the skin than through the quills.

The scrotum of males and matrix of females are also similar instances; so that the noble formation which constitutes the difference of the sexes appears to differ only as to the one being internal and the other external; a greater degree of heat causing the genitals to protrude in the male, whilst the heat of the female being too weak to effect this, they are retained internally.

The fins of fishes and the feet of quadrupeds, or the feet and wings of birds, are similar instances; to which Aristotle adds the four folds in the motion of serpents; so that in the formation of the universe, the motion of animals appears to be chiefly effected by four joints or bendings.

The teeth of land animals, and the beaks of birds, are similar instances, whence it is clear, that in all perfect animals there is a determination of some hard substance towards the mouth.

Again, the resemblance and conformity of man to an inverted plant is not absurd. For the head is the root of the nerves and animal faculties, and the seminal parts are the lowest, not including the extremities of the legs and arms. But in the plant, the root (which resembles the head) is regularly placed in the lowest, and the seeds in the highest part.

Lastly, we must particularly recommend and suggest, that man's present industry in the investigation and compilation of natural history be entirely changed, and directed to the reverse of the present system. For it has hitherto been active and curious in noting the variety of things, and explaining the accurate differences of animals, vegetables, and minerals, most of which are the mere sport of nature, rather than of any real utility as concerns the sciences. Pursuits of this nature are certainly agreeable, and sometimes of practical advantage, but contribute little or nothing to the thorough investigation of nature. Our labor must therefore be directed towards inquiring into and observing resemblances and analogies, both in the whole and its parts, for they unite nature, and lay the foundation of the sciences.

Here, however, a severe and rigorous caution must be observed, that we only consider as similar and proportionate instances, those which (as we first observed) point out physical resemblances; that is, real and substantial resemblances, deeply founded in nature, and not casual and superficial, much less superstitious or curious; such as those which are constantly put forward by the writers on natural magic (the most idle of men, and who are scarcely fit to be named in connection with such serious matters as we not treat of), who, with much vanity and folly, describe, and sometimes too, invent, unmeaning resemblances and sympathies.

But leaving such to themselves, similar instances are not to be neglected, in the greater portions of the world's conformation; such as Africa and the Peruvian continent, which reaches to the Straits of Magellan; both of which possess a similar isthmus and similar capes, a circumstance not to be attributed to mere accident.

Again, the New and Old World are both of them broad and expanded towards the north, and narrow and pointed towards the south.

Again, we have very remarkable similar instances in the intense cold, towards the middle regions (as it is termed) of the air, and the violent fires which are often found to burst from subterraneous spots, the similarity consisting in both being ends and extremes; the extreme of the nature of cold, for instance, is towards the boundary of heaven, and that of the nature of heat towards the centre of the earth, by a similar species of opposition or rejection of the contrary nature.

Lastly, in the axioms of the sciences, there is a similarity of instances worthy of observation. Thus the rhetorical trope which is called surprise, is similar to that of music termed the declining of a cadence. Again, the mathematical postulate that things which are equal to the same are equal to one another, is similar to the form of the syllogism in logic, which unites things agreeing in the middle term. Lastly, a certain degree of sagacity, in collecting and searching for physical points of similarity, is very useful in many respects.

Galileo Galilei

LETTER TO THE GRAND DUCHESS CHRISTINA

Galileo Galilei (1564-1642) was a scientist who made important discoveries in the fields of physics and astronomy. His most controversial "discovery" was actually a confirmation of Nicolaus Copernicus' earlier theory, which said that the sun rather than the earth was the center of the universe. In this letter, written in 1610, Galileo defends his observation, which was condemned because it apparently contradicted the Bible. He was eventually forced to recant his theory, and lived the last nine years of his life under house arrest. As you read, observe how Galileo uses evidence to form scientific fact, and how his facility with biblical interpretation makes his argument even stronger.

Some years ago, as Your Serene Highness well knows, I discovered in the heavens many things that had not been seen before our own age. The novelty of these things, as well as some consequences which followed from them in contradiction to the physical notions commonly held among academic philosophers, stirred up against me no small number of professors—as if I had placed these things in the sky with my own hands in order to upset nature and overturn the sciences. They seemed to forget that the increase of known truths stimulates the investigation, establishment, and growth of the arts; not their diminution or destruction.

Showing a greater fondness for their own opinions than for truth, they sought to deny and disprove the new things which, if they had cared to look for themselves, their own senses would have demonstrated to them. To this end they hurled various charges and published numerous writings filled with vain arguments, and they made the grave mistake of sprinkling these with passages taken from places in the Bible which they had failed to understand properly, and which were ill suited to their purposes.

These men would perhaps not have fallen into such error had they but paid attention to a most useful doctrine of St. Augustine's, relative to our making positive statements about things which are obscure and hard to understand by means of reason alone. Speaking of a certain physical conclusion about the heavenly bodies, he wrote: "Now keeping always our respect for moderation in grave piety, we ought not to believe anything inadvisedly on a dubious point, lest in favor to our error we conceive a prejudice against something that truth hereafter may reveal to be not contrary in any way to the sacred books of either the Old or the New Testament."

Well, the passage of time has revealed to everyone the truths that I previously set forth; and, together with the truth of the facts, there has come to light the great difference in attitude between those who simply and dispassionately refused to admit the discoveries to be true, and those who combined with their incredulity some reckless passion of their own. Men who were well grounded in astronomical and physical science were persuaded as soon as they received my first message. There were others who denied them or remained in doubt only because of their novel and unexpected character, and because they had not yet had the opportunity to see for themselves. These men have by degrees come to be satisfied. But some, besides allegiance to their original error, possess I know not what fanciful interest in remaining hostile not so much toward the things in question as toward their discoverer. No longer being able to deny them, these men now take refuge in obstinate silence, but being more than ever exasperated by that which has pacified and quieted other men, they divert their thoughts to other fancies and seek new ways to damage me.

I should pay no more attention to them than to those who previously contradicted me—at whom I always laugh, being assured of the eventual outcome—were it not that in their new calumnies and persecutions I perceive that they do not stop at proving themselves more learned than I am (a claim which I scarcely contest), but go so far as to cast against me imputations of crimes which must be, and are, more abhorrent to me than death itself. I cannot remain satisfied merely to know that the injustice of this is recognized by those who are acquainted with these men and with me, as perhaps it is not known to others.

Persisting in their original resolve to destroy me and everything mine by any means they can think of, these men are aware of my views in astronomy and philosophy. They know that as to the arrangement of the parts of the universe, I hold the sun to be situated motionless in the center of the revolution of the celestial orbs while the earth rotates on its axis and revolves about the sun.

They know also that I support this position not only by refuting the arguments of Ptolemy and Aristotle, but by producing many counterarguments; in particular, some which relate to physical effects whose causes can perhaps be assigned in no other way. In addition there are astronomical arguments derived from many things in my new celestial discoveries that plainly confute the Ptolemaic system while admirably agreeing with and confirming the contrary hypothesis. Possibly because they are disturbed by the known truth of other propositions of mine which differ from those commonly held, and therefore mistrusting their defense so long as they confine themselves to the field of philosophy, these men have resolved to fabricate a shield for their fallacies out of the mantle of pretended religion and the authority of the Bible. These they apply, with little judgment, to the refutation of arguments that they do not understand and have not even listened to.

First they have endeavored to spread the opinion that such propositions in general are contrary to the Bible and are consequently damnable and heretical. They know that it is human nature to take up causes whereby a man may oppress his neighbor, no matter how unjustly, rather than those from which a man may receive some just encouragement. Hence they have had no trouble in finding men who would preach the damnability and heresy of the new doctrine from their very pulpits with unwonted confidence, thus doing impious and inconsiderate injury not only to that doctrine and its followers but to all mathematics and mathematicians in general. Next, becoming bolder, and hoping (though vainly) that this seed which first took root in their hypocritical minds would send out branches and ascend to heaven, they began scattering rumors among the people that before long this doctrine would be condemned by the supreme authority. They know, too, that official condemnation would not only suppress the two propositions which I have mentioned, but would render damnable all other astronomical and physical statements and observations that have any necessary relation or connection with these.

In order to facilitate their designs, they seek so far as possible (at least among the common people) to make this opinion seem new and to belong to me alone. They pretend not to know that its author, or rather its restorer and confirmer, was Nicolaus Copernicus; and that he was not only a Catholic, but a priest and a canon. He was in fact so esteemed by the church that when the Lateran Council under Leo X took up the correction of the church calendar, Copernicus was called to Rome from the most remote parts of Germany to undertake its reform. At that time the calendar was defective because the true measures of the year and the lunar month were not exactly known. The Bishop of Culm, then superintendent of this matter, assigned Copernicus to seek more light and greater certainty concerning the celestial motions by means of constant study and labor. With Herculean toil he set his admirable mind to this task, and he made such great progress in this science and brought our knowledge of the heavenly motions to such precision that he became celebrated as an astronomer. Since that time not only has the calendar been regulated by his teachings, but tables of all the motions of the planets have been calculated as well.

Having reduced his system into six books, he published these at the instance of the Cardinal of Capua and the Bishop of Culm. And since he has assumed his laborious enterprise by order of the supreme pontiff, he dedicated this book *On the Celestial Revolutions* to Pope Paul III. When printed, the book was accepted by the holy Church, and it has been read and studied by everyone without the faintest hint of any objection ever being conceived against its doctrines. Yet now that manifest experiences and necessary proofs have shown them to be well grounded, persons exist who would strip the author of his reward without so much as looking at his book, and add the shame of having him pronounced a heretic. All this they would do merely to satisfy their personal displeasure conceived without any cause against another man, who has no interest in Copernicus beyond approving his teachings.

Now as to the false aspersions which they so unjustly seek to cast upon me, I have thought it necessary to justify myself in the eyes of all men, whose judgment in matters of religion and of reputation I must hold in great esteem. I shall therefore discourse of the particulars which these men produce to make this opinion detested and to have it condemned not merely as false but as heretical. To this end they make a shield of their hypocritical zeal for religion. They go about invoking the Bible, which they would have minister to their deceitful purposes. Contrary to the sense of the Bible and the intention of the holy Fathers, if I am not mistaken, they would extend such authorities until even in purely physical matters—where faith is not involved—they would have us altogether abandon reason and the evidence of our senses in favor of some biblical passage, though under the surface meaning of its words this passage may contain a different sense.

I hope to show that I proceed with much greater piety than they do, when I argue not against condemning this book, but against condemning it in the way they suggest—that is, without understanding it, weighing it, or so much as reading it. For Copernicus never discusses matters of religion or faith, nor does he use arguments that depend in any way upon the authority of sacred writings which he might have interpreted erroneously. He stands always upon physical conclusions pertaining to the celestial motions, and deals with them by astronomical and geometrical demonstrations, founded primarily upon sense experiences and very exact observations. He did not ignore the Bible, but he knew very well that if his doctrine were proved, then it could not contradict the Scriptures when they were rightly understood. And thus at the end of his letter of dedication, addressing the pope, he said:

"If there should chance to be any exegetes ignorant of mathematics who pretend to skill in that discipline, and dare to condemn and censure this hypothesis of mine upon the authority of some scriptural passage twisted to their purpose, I value them not, but disdain their unconsidered judgment. For it is known that Lactantius—a poor mathematician though in other respects a worthy author—writes very childishly about the shape of the earth when he scoffs at those who affirm it to be a globe. Hence it should not seem strange to the ingenious if people of that sort should in turn deride me. But mathematics is written for mathematicians, by whom, if I am not deceived, these labors of mine will be recognized as contributing something to their domain, as also to that of the Church over which Your Holiness now reigns."

Such are the people who labor to persuade us that an author like Copernicus may be condemned without being read, and who produce various authorities from the Bible, from theologians, and from Church Councils to make us believe that this is not only lawful but commendable. Since I hold these to be of supreme authority, I consider it rank temerity for anyone to contradict them—when employed according to the usage of the holy Church. Yet I do not believe it is wrong to speak out when there is reason to suspect that other men wish, for some personal motive, to produce and employ such authorities for purposes quite different from the sacred intention of the holy Church.

Therefore I declare (and my sincerity will make itself manifest) not only that I mean to submit myself freely and renounce any errors into which I may fall in this discourse through ignorance of matters pertaining to religion, but that I do not desire in these matters to engage in disputes with anyone, even on points that are disputable. My goal is this alone; that if, among errors that may abound in these considerations of a subject remote from my profession, there is anything that may be serviceable to the holy Church in making a decision concerning the Copernican system, it may be taken and utilized as seems best to the superiors. And if not, let my book be torn and burnt, as I neither intend nor pretend to gain from it any fruit that is not pious and Catholic. And though many of the things I shall reprove have been heard by my own ears, I shall freely grant to those who have spoken them that they never said them, if that is what they wish, and I shall confess myself to have been mistaken. Hence let whatever I reply be addressed not to them, but to whoever may have held such opinions.

The reason produced for condemning the opinion that the earth moves and the sun stands still is that in many places in the Bible one may read that the sun moves and the earth stands still. Since the Bible cannot err, it follows as a necessary consequence that anyone takes an erroneous and heretical position who maintains that the sun is inherently motionless and the earth movable.

With regard to this argument, I think in the first place that it is very pious to say and prudent to affirm that the holy Bible can never speak untruth—whenever its true meaning is understood. But I believe nobody will deny that it is often very abstruse, and may say things which are quite different from what its bare words signify. Hence in expounding the Bible if one were always to confine oneself to the unadorned grammatical meaning, one might fall into error. Not only contradictions and propositions far from true might thus be made to appear in the Bible, but even grave heresies and follies. Thus it would be necessary to assign to God feet, hands, and eyes, as well as corporeal and human affections, such as anger, repentance, hatred, and sometimes even the forgetting of things past and ignorance of those to come. These propositions uttered by the Holy Ghost were set down in that manner by the sacred scribes in order to accommodate them to the capacities of the common people, who are rude and unlearned. For the sake of those who deserve to be separated from the herd, it is necessary that wise expositors should produce the true senses of such passages, together with the special reasons for which they were set down in these words. This doctrine is so widespread and so definite with all theologians that it would be superfluous to adduce evidence for it.

Hence I think that I may reasonably conclude that whenever the Bible has occasion to speak of any physical conclusion (especially those which are very abstruse and hard to understand), the rule has been observed of avoiding confusion in the minds of the common people which would render them contumacious toward the higher mysteries. Now the Bible, merely to condescend to popular capacity, has not hesitated to obscure some very important pronouncements, attributing to God himself some qualities extremely remote from (and even contrary to) His essence. Who, then, would positively declare that this principle has been set aside, and the Bible has confined itself rigorously to the bare and restricted sense of its words, when speaking but casually of the earth, of water, of the sun, or of any other created thing? Especially in view of the fact that these things in no way concern the primary purpose of the sacred writings, which is the service of God and the salvation of souls—matters infinitely beyond the comprehension of the common people.

This being granted, I think that in discussions of physical problems we ought to begin not from the authority of scriptural passages, but from sense-experiences and necessary demonstrations; for the holy Bible and the phenomena of nature proceed alike from the divine Word, the former as the dictate of the Holy Ghost and the latter as the observant executrix of God's commands. It is necessary for the Bible, in order to be accommodated to the understanding of every man, to speak many things which appear to differ from the absolute truth so far as the bare meaning of the words is concerned. But Nature, on the other hand, is inexorable and immutable; she never transgresses the laws imposed upon her, or cares a whit whether her abstruse reasons and methods of operation are understandable to men. For that reason it appears that nothing physical which sense-experience sets before our eyes, or which necessary demonstrations prove to us, ought to be called in question (much less condemned) upon the testimony of biblical passages which may have some different meaning beneath their words. For the Bible is not chained in every expression to conditions as strict as those which govern all physical effects; nor is God any less excellently revealed in Nature's actions than in the sacred statements of the Bible. Perhaps this is what Tertullian meant by these words:

"We conclude that God is known first through Nature, and then again, more particularly, by doctrine; by Nature in His Works, and by doctrine in His revealed word."

From this I do not mean to infer that we need not have an extraordinary esteem for the passages of holy Scripture. On the contrary, having arrived at any certainties in physics, we ought to utilize these as the most appropriate aids in the true exposition of the Bible and in the investigation of those meanings which are necessarily contained therein, for these must be concordant with demonstrated truths. I should judge that the authority of the Bible was designed to persuade men of those articles and propositions which, surpassing all human reasoning, could not be made credible by science, or by any other means than through the very mouth of the Holy Spirit.

Yet even in those propositions which are not matters of faith, this authority ought to be preferred over that of all human writings which are supported only by bare assertions or probable arguments, and not set forth in a demonstrative way. This I hold to be necessary and proper to the same extent that divine wisdom surpasses all human judgment and conjecture.

But I do not feel obliged to believe that that same God who has endowed us with senses, reason, and intellect has intended to forgo their use and by some other means to give us knowledge which we can attain by them. He would not require us to deny sense and reason in physical matters which are set before our eyes and minds by direct experience or necessary demonstrations. This must be especially true in those sciences of which but the faintest trace (and that consisting of conclusions) is to be found in the Bible. Of astronomy, for instance, so little is found that none of the planets except Venus are so much as mentioned, and this only once or twice under the name of "Lucifer." If the sacred scribes had had any intention of teaching people certain arrangements and motions of the heavenly bodies, or had they wished us to derive such knowledge from the Bible, then in my opinion they would not have spoken of these matters so sparingly in comparison with the infinite number of admirable conclusions which are demonstrated in that science. Far from pretending to teach us the constitution and motions of the heavens and the stars, with their shapes, magnitudes, and distances, the authors of the Bible intentionally forbore to speak of these things, though all were quite well known to them. Such is the opinion of the holiest and most learned Fathers, and in St. Augustine we find the following words:

"It is likewise commonly asked what we may believe about the form and shape of the heavens according to the Scriptures, for many contend much about these matters. But with superior prudence our authors have forborne to speak of this, as in no way furthering the student with respect to a blessed life—and, more important still, as taking up much of that time which should be spent in holy exercises. What is it to me whether heaven, like a sphere, surrounds the earth on all sides as a mass balanced in the center of the universe, or whether like a dish it merely covers and overcasts the earth? Belief in Scripture is urged rather for the reason we have often mentioned; that is, in order that no one, through ignorance of divine passages, finding anything in our Bibles or hearing anything cited from them of such a nature as may seem to oppose manifest conclusions, should be induced to suspect their truth when they teach, relate, and deliver more profitable matters. Hence let it be said briefly, touching the form of heaven, that our authors knew the truth but the Holy Spirit did not desire that men should learn things that are useful to no one for salvation."

The same disregard of these sacred authors toward beliefs about the phenomena of the celestial bodies is repeated to us by St. Augustine in his next chapter. On the question whether we are to believe that the heaven moves or stands still, he writes thus:

"Some of the brethren raise a question concerning the motion of heaven, whether it is fixed or moved. If it is moved, they say, how is it a firmament? If it stands still, how do these stars which are held fixed in it go round from east to west, the more northerly performing shorter circuits near the pole, so that heaven (if there is another pole unknown to us) may seem to revolve upon some axis, or (if there is no other pole) may be thought to move as a discus? To these men I reply that it would require many subtle and profound reasonings to find out which of these things is actually so; but to undertake this and discuss it is consistent neither with my leisure nor with the duty of those whom I desire to instruct in essential matters more directly conducing to their salvation and to the benefit of the holy Church."

From these things it follows as a necessary consequence that, since the Holy Ghost did not intend to teach us whether heaven moves or stands still, whether its shape is spherical or like a discus or extended in a plane, nor whether the earth is located at its center or off to one side, then so much the less was it intended to settle for us any other conclusion of the same kind. And the motion or rest of the earth and the sun is so closely linked with the things just named, that without a determination of the one, neither side can be taken in the other matters. Now if the Holy Spirit has purposely neglected to teach us propositions of this sort as irrelevant to the highest goal (that is, to our salvation), how can anyone affirm that it is obligatory to take sides on them, and that one belief is required by faith, while the other side is erroneous? Can an opinion be heretical and yet have no concern with the salvation of souls? Can the Holy Ghost be asserted not to have intended teaching us something that does concern our salvation? I would say here something that was heard from an ecclesiastic of the most eminent degree: "That the intention of the Holy Ghost is to teach us how one goes to heaven, not how heaven goes."

But let us again consider the degree to which necessary demonstrations and sense experiences ought to be respected in physical conclusions, and the authority they have enjoyed at the hands of holy and learned theologians. From among a hundred attestations I have selected the following:

"We must also take heed, in handling the doctrine of Moses, that we altogether avoid saying positively and confidently anything which contradicts manifest experiences and the reasoning of philosophy or the other sciences. For since every truth is in agreement with all other truth, the truth of Holy Writ cannot be contrary to the solid reasons and experiences of human knowledge."

And in St. Augustine we read: "If anyone shall set the authority of Holy Writ against clear and manifest reason, he who does this knows not what he has undertaken; for he opposes to the truth not the meaning of the Bible, which is beyond his comprehension, but rather his own interpretation; not what is in the Bible, but what he has found in himself and imagines to be there."

This granted, and it being true that two truths cannot contradict one another, it is the function of wise expositors to seek out the true senses of scriptural texts. These will unquestionably accord with the physical conclusions which manifest sense and necessary demonstrations have previously made certain to us. Now the Bible, as has been remarked, admits in many places expositions that are remote from the signification of the words for reasons we have already given. Moreover, we are unable to affirm that all interpreters of the Bible speak by divine inspiration, for if that were so there would exist no differences between them about the sense of a given passage. Hence I should think it would be the part of prudence not to permit anyone to usurp scriptural texts and force them in some way to maintain any physical conclusion to be true, when at some future time the senses and demonstrative or necessary reasons may show the contrary. Who indeed will set bounds to human ingenuity? Who will assert that everything in the universe capable of being perceived is already discovered and known? Let us rather confess quite truly that "Those truths which we know are very few in comparison with those which we do not know."

We have it from the very mouth of the Holy Ghost that God delivered up the world to disputations, *so that man cannot find out the work that God hath done from the beginning even to the end.* In my opinion no one, in contradiction to that dictum, should close the road to free philosophizing about mundane and physical things, as if everything had already been discovered and revealed with certainty. Nor should it be considered rash not to be satisfied with those opinions which have become common. No one should be scorned in physical disputes for not holding to the opinions which happen to please other people best, especially concerning problems which have been debated among the greatest philosophers for thousands of years. One of these is the stability of the sun and mobility of the earth, a doctrine believed by Pythagoras and all his followers, by Heracleides of Pontus (who was one of them), by Philolaus the teacher of Plato, and by Plato himself according to Aristotle. Plutarch writes in his *Life of Numa* that Plato, when he had grown old, said it was most absurd to believe otherwise. The same doctrine was held by Aristarchus of Samos, as Archimedes tells us; by Seleucus the mathematician, by Nicetas the philosopher (on the testimony of Cicero), and by many others. Finally this opinion has been amplified and confirmed with many observations and demonstrations by Nicolaus Copernicus.

Benjamin Franklin

THE KITE

Benjamin Franklin (1706-1790), inventor, writer, and statesman, was a participant in the formation of both the United States and the American identity. He helped write the Declaration of Independence, generated many useful inventions, tinkered with scientific experiments more in the manner of a hobbyist than that of a true scientist. This casual attitude toward science is evident here, in the recounting of his most famous experiment—using a kite to show that lightning is the same as electricity. The importance of his discovery—particularly in its application in lightning rods, is belied by his glib prose style.

To Peter Collinson

Philadelphia, October 19, 1752

Sir,

As frequent mention is made in public papers from Europe of the success of the Philadelphia experiment for drawing the electric fire from clouds by means of pointed rods of iron erected on high buildings, etc, it may be agreeable to the curious to be informed that the same experiment has succeeded in Philadelphia, though made in a different and more easy manner, which is as follows:

Make a small cross of two light strips of cedar, the arms so long as to reach to the four corners of a large thin silk handkerchief when extended; tie the corners of the handkerchief to the extremities of the cross, so you have the body of a kite, which, being properly accommodated with a tail, loop, and string, will rise in the air, like those made of paper, but this, being of silk, is fitter to bear the wet and wind of a thunder-gust without tearing. To the top of the upright stick of the cross is to be fixed a very sharp-pointed wire, rising a foot or more above the wood. To the end of the twine, next the hand, is to be tied a silk ribbon, and where the silk and twine join, a key may be fastened. This kite is to be raised when a thunder-gust appears to be coming on, and the person who holds the string must stand within a door or window or under some cover, so that the silk ribbon may not be wet; and care must be taken that the twine does not touch the frame of the door or window. As soon as any of the thunderclouds come over the kite, the pointed wire will draw the electric fire from them, and the kite, with all the twine, will be electrified, and the loose filaments of the twine will stand out every way, and be attracted by an approaching finger. And when the rain has wet the kite and twine, so that it can conduct the electric fire freely, you will find it stream out plentifully from the key on the approach of your knuckle. At this key the phial may be charged; and from electric fire thus obtained, spirits may be kindled, and all the other electric experiments be performed, which are usually done by the help of a rubbed glass globe or tube, and thereby the sameness of the electric matter with that of lightning completely demonstrated.

B Franklin

Charles Darwin

THE DESCENT OF MAN

When botanist Charles Darwin (1809-1882) published his book *The Origin of Species* in 1859, he had no reason to suspect that it would have the enormous impact that it did; after all, the most important aspects of his theory of natural selection had been published more than a year before. Though Darwin himself never felt the theory had any implications outside the field of biology, everyone from economists to dictators had their own interpretation and application of "survival of the fittest." Nonetheless, the theory's most important applications today are in the area of science, and an important part of his theory as it relates to humans is reprinted here.

We have now seen that man is variable in body and mind; and that the variations are induced, either directly or indirectly, by the same general causes, and obey the same general laws, as with the lower animals. Man has spread widely over the face of the earth, and must have been exposed, during his incessant migration, to the most diversified conditions. The inhabitants of Tierra del Fuego, the Cape of Good Hope, and Tasmania in the one hemisphere, and of the Arctic regions in the other, must have passed through many climates, and changed their habits many times, before they reached their present homes. The early progenitors of man must also have tended, like all other animals, to have increased beyond their means of subsistence; they must, therefore, occasionally have been exposed to a struggle for existence, and consequently to the rigid law of natural selection. Beneficial variations of all kinds will thus, either occasionally or habitually, have been preserved and injurious ones eliminated. I do not refer to strongly-marked deviations of structure, which occur only at long intervals of time, but to mere individual differences. We know, for instance, that the muscles of our hands and feet, which determine our powers of movement, are liable, like those of the lower animals, to incessant variability. If then the progenitors of man inhabiting any district, especially one undergoing some change in its conditions, were divided into two equal bodies, the one half which included all the individuals best adapted by their powers of movement for gaining subsistence, or for defending themselves, would on an average survive in greater numbers, and procreate more offspring than the other and less well endowed half.

Man in the rudest state in which he now exists is the most dominant animal that has ever appeared on this earth. He has spread more widely than any other highly organised form: and all others have yielded before him. He manifestly owes this immense superiority to his intellectual faculties, to his social habits, which lead him to aid and defend his fellows, and to his corporeal structure. The supreme importance of these characters has been proved by the final arbitrament of the battle for life. Through his powers of intellect, articulate language has been evolved; and on this his wonderful advancement has mainly depended. As Mr. Chauncey Wright remarks: "a psychological analysis of the faculty of language shews, that even the smallest proficiency in it might require more brain power than the greatest proficiency in any other direction." He has invented and is able to use various weapons, tools, traps, &c. with which he defends himself, kills or catches prey, and otherwise obtains food. He has made rafts or canoes for fishing or crossing over to neighbouring fertile islands. He has discovered the art of making fire, by which hard and stringy roots can be rendered digestible, and poisonous roots or herbs innocuous. This discovery of fire, probably the greatest ever made by man, excepting language, dates from before the dawn of history. These several inventions, by which man in the rudest state has become so pre-eminent, are the direct results of the development of his powers of observation, memory, curiosity, imagination, and reason. . . .

In regard to bodily size or strength, we do not know whether man is descended from some small species, like the chimpanzee, or from one as powerful as the gorilla; and, therefore, we cannot say whether man has become larger and stronger, or smaller and weaker, than his ancestors. We should, however, bear in mind that an animal possessing great size, strength, and ferocity, and which, like the gorilla, could defend itself from all enemies, would not perhaps have become social: and this would most effectually have checked the acquirement of the higher mental qualities, such as sympathy and the love of his fellows. Hence it might have been an immense advantage to man to have sprung from some comparatively weak creature. MAKING HYPOTHESES

The small strength and speed of man, his want of natural weapons, &c., are more than counterbalanced, firstly, by his intellectual powers, through which he has formed for himself weapons, tools, &c., though still remaining in a barbarous state, and, secondly, by his social qualities which lead him to give and receive aid from his fellow-men. No country in the world abounds in a greater degree with dangerous beasts than Southern Africa; no country presents more fearful physical hardships than the Arctic regions; yet one of the puniest of races, that of the Bushmen, maintains itself in Southern Africa, as do the dwarfed Esquimaux in the Arctic regions. The ancestors of man were, no doubt, inferior in intellect, and probably in social disposition, to the lowest existing savages; but it is quite conceivable that they might have existed, or even flourished, if they had advanced in intellect, whilst gradually losing their brute-like powers, such as that of climbing trees, &c. But these ancestors would not have been exposed to any special danger, even if far more helpless and defenceless than any existing savages, had they inhabited some warm continent or large island, such as Australia, New Guinea, or Borneo, which is now the home of the orang. And natural selection arising from the competition of tribe with tribe, in some such large area as one of these, together with the inherited effects of habit, would, under favourable conditions, have sufficed to raise man to his present high position in the organic scale.

Thomas Henry Huxley

THE METHOD OF SCIENTIFIC INVESTIGATION

The achievements of Thomas H. Huxley (1825-1895) as a scientific investigator, as a teacher, and a lecturer were many, but probably the greatest contribution he made to his own and future generations of scientists and to humankind as a whole was his ability to make clear to the public the results and the significance of the work of other scientists. He could, and did, take abstract terms and ideas and make them comprehensible to the ordinary reader—as in this essay, which spells out precisely the principles of induction and deduction.

The method of scientific investigation is nothing but the expression of the necessary mode of working of the human mind. It is simply the mode at which all phenomena are reasoned about, rendered precise and exact. There is no more difference, but there is just the same kind of difference, between the mental operations of a man of science and those of an ordinary person, as there is between the operations and methods of a baker or of a butcher weighing out his goods in common scales, and the operations of a chemist in performing a difficult and complex analysis by means of his balance and finely graduated weights. It is not that the action of the scales in the one case, and the balance in the other, differ in the principles of their construction of manner of working; but the beam of one is set on an infinitely finer axis than the other, and of course turns by the addition of a much smaller weight.

You will understand this better, perhaps, if I give you some familiar example. You have all heard it repeated, I dare say, that men of science work by means of Induction and Deduction, and that by the help of these operations, they, in a sort of sense, wring from Nature certain other things, which are called Natural Laws, and Causes, and that out of these, by some cunning skill of their own, they build up Hypotheses and Theories. And it is imagined by many, that the operations of the common mind can be by no means compared with these processes, and that they have to be acquired by a sort of special apprenticeship to the craft. To hear all these large words, you would think that the mind of a man of science must be constituted differently from that of his fellow-men; but if you will not be frightened by terms, you will discover that you are quite wrong, and that all these terrible apparatus are being used by yourselves every day and every hour of your lives.

There is a well-known incident in one of Moliere's plays, where the author makes the hero express unbounded delight on being told that he had been talking prose during the whole of his life. In the same way, I trust that you will take comfort, and be delighted with yourselves, on the discovery that you have been acting on the principles of inductive and deductive philosophy during the same period. Probably there is not one here who has not in the course of the day had occasion to set in motion a complex train of reasoning, of the very same kind, though differing of course in degree, as that which a scientific man goes through in tracing the causes of natural phenomena.

A very trivial circumstance will serve to exemplify this. Suppose you go into a fruiterer's shop, wanting an apple—you take up one, and, on biting it, you find it sour; you look at it, and see that it is hard and green. You take up another one, and that too is hard, green, and sour. The shopman offers you a third; but, before biting it you examine it, and find that it is hard and green, and you immediately say that you will not have it, as it must be sour, like those that you have already tried.

Nothing can be more simple than that, you think; but if you will take the trouble to analyze and trace out into its logical elements what has been done by the mind, you will be greatly surprised. In the first place, you have performed the operation of Induction. You found that, in two experiences, hardness and greenness in apples went together with sourness. It was so in the first case, and it was confirmed by the second. True, it is a very small basis, but still it is enough to make an induction from; you generalize the facts, and you expected to find sourness in apples where you get hardness and greenness. You found upon that a general law, that all hard and green apples are sour; and that, so far as it goes, is a perfect induction. Well, having got your natural law in this way, when you are offered another apple which you find is hard and green, you say, "All hard and green apples are sour; this apple is hard and green, therefore this apple is sour." That train of reasoning is what logicians call a syllogism, and has all its various parts and terms—its major premise, its minor premise, and its

conclusion. And, by the help of further reasoning, which, if drawn
out, would have to be exhibited in two or three other syllogisms,
you arrive at your final determination, "I will not have that apple." So that, you see, you have in the first place, established a law
by Induction, and upon that you have founded a Deduction, and
reasoned out the special conclusion of the particular case. Well
now, suppose, having got your law, that at some time afterward,
you are discussing the qualities of apples with a friend: you will
say to him, "It is a very curious thing—but I find that all hard and
green apples are sour!" Your friend says to you, "But how do you
know that?" You at once reply, "Oh, because I have tried them
over and over again, and have always found them to be so." Well,
if we were talking science instead of common sense, we should
call that an Experimental Verification. And, if still opposed, you go
further, and say, "I have heard from the people in Somersetshire
and Devonshire, where a large number of apples are grown, that
they have observed the same things. It is also found to be the case
in Normandy, and in North America. In short, I find it to be the
universal experience of mankind wherever attention has been directed to the subject." Whereupon, your friend, unless he is a very
unreasonable man, agrees with you, and is convinced that you are
quite right in the conclusion you have drawn. He believes,
although perhaps he does not know he believes it, that the more
extensive verifications are—that the more frequently experiments have been made, and results of the same kind arrived at—
that the more varied the conditions under which the same results
are attained, the more certain is the ultimate conclusion, and he
disputes the question no further. He sees that the experiment has
been tried under all sorts of conditions, as to time, place, and people, with the same result; and he says with you, therefore, that the
law you have laid down must be a good one, and he must believe it.

In science we do the same thing—the philosopher exercises
precisely the same faculties, though in a much more delicate
manner. In scientific inquiry it becomes a matter of duty to expose
a supposed law to every possible kind of verification, and to take
care, moreover, that this is done intentionally, and not left to a
mere accident, as in the case of the apples. And in science, as in
common life, our confidence in a law is in exact proportion to the
absence of variation in the result of our experimental verifications. For instance, if you let go your grasp of an article you may
have in your hand, it will immediately fall to the ground. That is a
very common verification of one of the best established laws of

Nature—that of gravitation. The method by which men of science establish the existence of that law is exactly the same as that by which we have established the trivial proposition about the sourness of hard and green apples. But we believe it in such an extensive, thorough, and unhesitating manner because the universal experience of mankind verifies it, and we can verify it ourselves at any time; and that is the strongest possible foundation on which any natural law can rest.

So much, then, by way of proof that the method of establishing laws in science is exactly the same as that pursued in common life.

Denise (student)

CHARCOAL AND BLUEING

> What is your attitude toward Science? Do you find it utterly repulsive or does it fascinate you? As you read Denise's essay, consider whether the humanities and science are mutually exclusive—does one have to hate one to love the other? A perusal of Matthew Arnold's *Literature and Science* might help you come up with an answer.

I am an unabashed humanist; the lure of Science has never attracted me. I realize that this is an ignorant thing to say, because there are so many different branches of science that they may as well be different disciplines altogether, but I'm not interested in any of them. Biology? Little squiggly things. Chemistry? Making test tubes explode. Physics? Making test tubes implode. And geology? A pile of rocks.

My mother thinks I'm foolish to reject Science as a whole, but I can only barely tolerate it. Where does this intolerance come from? In elementary school, I enjoyed doing things like making crystals grow out of charcoal and blueing, burning holes in dry leaves with a magnifying glass, and dipping strips of litmus paper into every fish tank and water glass in the schoolroom, but that was when I was little. As I got older, things changed.

The first thing that changed was having to write about what you did in Science, and the second was having to read about it. I never understood why you would have to write about "How I Made Crystals Grow from Charcoal and Blueing" when the teacher had either just told you how or handed you a dittoed sheet that said "How to Make Crystals Grow from Charcoal and Blueing." What's the point? As far as reading about science, forget it. You can read science textbooks forever and never get clue one about what they're trying to say: "The cingulate gyrus engirdles the corpus callosum"—yeah, right.

Now, let me make it clear that I started out as a child, a blank slate like everyone else, wide-eyed with wonder and open to each and every new experience, and so forth. I was happy—giddy, delirious—to be able to make crystals grow from charcoal and blueing—and I would do it over and over. I loved making crystals! I would even make crystals from water, supersaturated with sugar: candy as Science! Please! So when it came time, I approached my required elective Science courses in middle school bravely and with no fear. I even chose "interesting" ones: genetics, oceanography, biology. My best friend was taking those courses too. Her presence should have made things more enjoyable, more interesting, fun even! Charcoal and Blueing, all over again! We learned how to diagram the colors of pea-blossoms. We learned how the plates of the earth moved together to form mountains, apart to form valleys, and side by side to make earthquakes. And we learned mitosis and meiosis, cell growth by division and multiplication, how babies are made, why grass is green. Fine. Good. These credits were required and we made the best of them. But it wasn't because of reading about Science, it was despite it. It was *despite* books like *Biology Today* and *Genetics Now* and *Here We Go with Oceanography* that I remember anything. These so-called tools for learning turned out to be blunt instruments with which I literally pounded myself on the head, first in frustration, then thinking dazedly that maybe by pounding I could force the words onto my brain, as the sperm fertilizes the egg! But as with true fertilization, in which most sperm die on their way to the fulfillment of their biological purpose, so most seeds of knowledge died out before they reached the necessary part of my brain, and lay strewn about until they were reabsorbed into my bloodstream and disposed of as bodily waste.

I don't even want to talk about high school, but I will. In eleventh grade, in order to to bring to life the process of DNA replication, my chemistry teachers had the entire school participate in "The Dance of the Polypeptides." We zipped and unzipped the zipper of life and went about the room in incomprehensible but regulated patterns, joining three letter sequences one to the other. I still can't remember which is a sugar and which is a protein and whether you start with your left foot or your right. I stumbled through the entire dance and I still haven't any clue.

Here I am, my toes crushed, my mother calling me a fool. My bright crystal-making beginnings have been thwarted and my forehead has been blunted by textbooks. I realize I am in danger of succumbing to the myth that humanists cannot "do" Science because of some innate brain lack. (All scientists, however, seem to be able to conquer Humanities if they want to.) I am rapidly becoming one of those for whom scientists become high priests and make all the decisions about societal uses about Science. All I want is to create one perfect blue irregular trichite, one more time, and not have to write about it. Is that too much for a humanist to ask?

Alexander Petrunkevitch

THE SPIDER AND THE WASP

Alexander Petrunkevitch (1875-1964) was an expert on spiders and a translator from his native Russian into English. As you read his essay, observe how Petrunkevitch uses comparisons to human intelligence and instinct to make the behavior of animals more relevant to us.

In the feeding and safeguarding of their progeny insects and spiders exhibit some interesting analogies to reasoning and some crass examples of blind instinct. The case I propose to describe here is that of the tarantula spiders and their archenemy, the digger wasps of the genus *Pepsis*. It is a classic example of what looks like intelligence pitted against instinct—a strange situation in which the victim, though fully able to defend itself, submits unwittingly to its destruction.

Most tarantulas live in the tropics, but several species occur in the temperate zone and a few are common in the southern U.S. Some varieties are large and have powerful fangs with which they can inflict a deep wound. These formidable-looking spiders do not, however, attack man; you can hold one in your hand, if you are gentle, without being bitten. Their bite is dangerous only to insects and small mammals such as mice; for man it is no worse than a hornet's sting.

Tarantulas customarily live in deep cylindrical burrows, from which they emerge at dusk and into which they retire at dawn. Mature males wander about after dark in search of females and occasionally stray into houses. After mating, the male dies in a few weeks, but a female lives much longer and can mate several years in succession. In a Paris museum is a tropical specimen which is said to have been living in captivity for 25 years.

A fertilized female tarantula lays from 200 to 400 eggs at a time; thus it is possible for a single tarantula to produce several thousand young. She takes no care of them beyond weaving a cocoon of silk to enclose the eggs. After they hatch, the young walk away, find convenient places in which to dig their burrows and spend the rest of their lives in solitude. The eyesight of tarantulas is poor, being limited to a sensing of change in the intensity of light and to the perception of moving objects. They apparently have little or no sense of hearing, for a hungry tarantula will pay no attention to a loudly chirping cricket placed in its cage unless the insect happens to touch one of its legs.

But all spiders, and especially hairy ones, have an extremely delicate sense of touch. Laboratory experiments prove that tarantulas can distinguish three types of touch: pressure against the body wall, stroking of the body hair, and riffling of certain very fine hairs on the legs called trichobothria. Pressure against the body, by the finger or the end of a pencil, causes the tarantula to move off slowly for a short distance. The touch excites no defensive response unless the approach is from above where the spider can see the motion, in which case it rises on its hind legs, lifts its front legs, opens its fangs and holds this threatening posture as long as the object continues to move.

The entire body of a tarantula, especially its legs, is thickly clothed with hair. Some of it is short and wooly, some long and stiff. Touching this body hair produces one of two distinct reactions. When the spider is hungry, it responds with an immediate and swift attack. At the touch of a cricket's antennae the tarantula seizes the insect so swiftly that a motion picture taken at the rate of 64 frames per second shows only the result and not the process of capture. But when the spider is not hungry, the stimulation of its hairs merely causes it to shake the touched limb. An insect can walk under its hairy belly unharmed.

The trichobothria, very fine hairs growing from disklike membranes on the legs, are sensitive only to air movement. A light breeze makes them vibrate slowly, without disturbing the common hair. When one blows gently on the trichobothria, the tarantula reacts with a quick jerk of its four front legs. If the front and hind legs are stimulated at the same time, the spider makes a sudden jump. This reaction is quite independent of the state of its appetite.

These three tactile responses—to pressure on the body wall, to moving of the common hair, and to flexing of the trichobothria— are so different from one another that there is no possibility of confusing them. They serve the tarantula adequately for most of its needs and enable it to avoid most annoyances and dangers. But they fail the spider completely when it meets its deadly enemy, the digger wasp *Pepsis*.

These solitary wasps are beautiful and formidable creatures. Most species are either a deep shiny blue all over, or deep blue with rusty wings. The largest have a wing span of about 4 inches. They live on nectar. When excited, they give off a pungent odor— a warning that they are ready to attack. The sting is much worse than that of a bee or common wasp, and the pain and swelling last longer. In the adult stage the wasp lives only a few months. The female produces but a few eggs, one at a time at intervals of two or three days. For each egg the mother must provide one adult tarantula, alive but paralyzed. The mother wasp attaches the egg to the paralyzed spider's abdomen. Upon hatching from the egg, the larva is many hundreds of times smaller than its living but helpless victim. It eats no other food and drinks no water. By the time it has finished its single Gargantuan meal and become ready for wasphood, nothing remains of the tarantula but its indigestible chitinous skeleton.

The mother wasp goes tarantula-hunting when the egg in her ovary is almost ready to be laid. Flying low over the ground late on a sunny afternoon, the wasp looks for its victim or for the mouth of a tarantula burrow, a round hole edged by a bit of silk. The sex of the spider makes no difference, but the mother is highly discriminating as to species. Each species of *Pepsis* requires a certain species of tarantula, and the wasp will not attack the wrong species. In a cage with a tarantula which is not its normal prey, the wasp avoids the spider and is usually killed by it in the night.

Yet when a wasp finds the correct species, it is the other way about. To identify the species the wasp apparently must explore the spider with her antennae. The tarantula shows an amazing tolerance to this exploration. The wasp crawls under it and walks over it without evoking any hostile response. The molestation is so great and so persistent that the tarantula often rises on all eight legs, as if it were on stilts. It may stand this way for several minutes. Meanwhile the wasp, having satisfied itself that the victim is of the right species, moves off a few inches to dig the spider's grave. Working vigorously with legs and jaws, it excavates a hole 8 to 10 inches deep with a diameter slightly larger than the spider's girth. Now and again the wasp pops out of the hole to make sure that the spider is still there.

When the grave is finished, the wasp returns to the tarantula to complete her ghastly enterprise. First she feels it all over once more with her antennae. Then her behavior becomes more aggressive. She bends her abdomen, protruding her sting, and searches for the soft membrane at the point where the spider's legs join its body—the only spot where she can penetrate the horny skeleton. From time to time, as the exasperated spider slowly shifts ground, the wasp turns on her back and slides along with the aid of her wings, trying to get under the tarantula for a shot at the vital spot. During all this maneuvering, which can last for several minutes, the tarantula makes no move to save itself. Finally the wasp corners it against some obstruction and grasps one of its legs in her powerful jaws. Now at last the harassed spider tries a desperate but vain defense. The two contestants roll over and over on the ground. It is a terrifying sight and the outcome is always the same. The wasp finally manages to thrust her sting into the soft spot and holds it there for a few seconds while she pumps in the poison. Almost immediately the tarantula falls paralyzed on its back. Its legs stop twitching; its heart stops beating. Yet it is not dead, as is shown by the fact that if taken from the wasp it can be restored to some sensitivity by being kept in a moist chamber for several months.

After paralyzing the tarantula, the wasp cleans herself by dragging her body along the ground and rubbing her feet, sucks a drop of blood oozing from the wound in the spider's abdomen, then grabs a leg of the flabby, helpless animal in her jaws and drags it down to the bottom of the grave. She stays there for many minutes, sometimes for several hours, and what she does all that time in the dark we do not know. Eventually she lays her egg and attaches it to the side of the spider's abdomen with a sticky secretion. Then she emerges, fills the grave with soil carried bit by bit in her jaws, and finally tramples the ground all around to hide any trace of the grave from prowlers. Then she flies away, leaving her descendant safely started in life.

In all this the behavior of the wasp evidently is qualitatively different from that of the spider. The wasp acts like an intelligent animal. This is not to say that instinct plays no part or that she reasons as man does. But her actions are to the point; they are not automatic and can be modified to fit the situation. We do not know for certain how she identifies the tarantula—probably it is by some olfactory or chemo-tactile sense—but she does it purposefully and does not blindly tackle a wrong species.

On the other hand, the tarantula's behavior shows only confusion. Evidently the wasp's pawing gives it no pleasure, for it tries to move away. That the wasp is not simulating sexual stimulation is certain because male and female tarantulas react in the same way to its advances. That the spider is not anesthetized by some odorless secretion is easily shown by blowing lightly at the tarantula and making it jump suddenly. What, then, makes the tarantula behave as stupidly as it does?

No clear, simple answer is available. Possibly the stimulation by the wasp's antennae is masked by a heavier pressure on the spider's body, so that it reacts as when prodded by a pencil. But the explanation may be much more complex. Initiative in attack is not in the nature of tarantulas; most species fight only when cornered so that escape is impossible. Their inherited patterns of behavior apparently prompt them to avoid problems rather than attack them. For example, spiders always weave their webs in three dimensions, and when a spider finds that there is insufficient space to attach certain threads in the third dimension, it leaves the place and seeks another, instead of finishing the web in a single plane. This urge to escape seems to arise under all circumstances, in all phases of life, and to take the place of reasoning. For a spider to change the pattern of its web is as impossible as for an inexperienced man to build a bridge across a chasm obstructing his way.

In a way the instinctive urge to escape is not only easier but often more efficient than reasoning. The tarantula does exactly what is most efficient in all cases except in an encounter with a ruthless and determined attacker dependent for the existence of her own species on killing as many tarantulas as she can lay eggs.

Perhaps in this case the spider follows its usual pattern of trying to escape, instead of seizing and killing the wasp, because it is not aware of its danger. In any case, the survival of the tarantula species as a whole is protected by the fact that the spider is much more fertile than the wasp.

Heather (student)

· **THE CITY CELL**

Heather uses the analogy of a city to explain the structure of a cell. Analogy is a useful way to explain concepts which are completely new to an audience. However, care must be taken not to extend the analogy too far. An analogy which is illuminating at one level may be confusing or misleading at another. As you read Heather's essay, see if you can use the city metaphor to help remember difficult terms like "Golgi complex."

Every cell in your body functions like a small city, each producing special goods, but not all the goods necessary for a productive city, making it dependent on other cities. Every cell can satisfy its needs but not the needs of the entire body. A wall surrounds the city, and the cell has its own wall—the plasma membrane. Inside the cell exist different factories or organelles to produce different products or provide different services. Organelles in the cytoplasm resemble factories located along roads in the city, enabling easy transportation and communication. Although the size of the city overwhelms the size of the cell, the complexity and organization of both resemble each other.

The plasma membrane or wall of the cell composes the outermost portion of the cell. It keeps all the other portions of the cell inside the wall. Unlike the wall of the city, composed of wood and concrete, the plasma membrane contains proteins and lipids, two chemical compounds. The lipids form an outer and inner wall and the proteins solidify the wall from the space in between the two lipid layers. This organization of the wall is called the fluid mosaic model. The plasma membrane also possesses the property called selective permeability. The plasma membrane allows things to enter and exit the cell like gates in a city wall. Some particles can fit through the gate and require no energy to move. Other particles are too large or try to enter when everything else is leaving (this is called opposing the concentration gradient). For these particles, entering the city is like climbing the wall, and energy must be supplied for the particles to enter the cell. Entering the cell without the use of energy is called passive transport, while those particles requiring energy move by active transport. Along with allowing particles to enter and exit the cell, the plasma membrane can make contact with other cells and receive nutrients, hormones and other chemicals from other cells like importing materials for a city. The plasma membrane provides both protection and regulation for the cell like a wall does for the city.

The city must have a basic layout and the cytoplasm fulfills this function in the cell. The cytoplasm contains the organelles. Most of the chemical reactions in the cell take place in the cytoplasm. The cytoplasm also receives substances from outside of the cell and converts them into viable energy sources for the cell. Also functioning as the receiving site, the cytoplasm packages materials and transports them to other parts of the cell. The cytoplasm has many functions including transport, synthesis, packaging and receiving. In the middle of the city lies the headquarters; in the cell this place is occupied by the nucleus. The nucleus acts like the administration of a very dominant government. The nucleus regulates what, how fast, and how much will be produced by the organelles in the cell. Also included inside the administration building are plans for the next cities which are identical to the existing city. In the cell the plans are called genetic information contained in thread-like chromatin strands composed of DNA. These chromatin threads will later condense and become chromosomes which more easily divide and get placed into new cells. The nuclear membrane surrounds the nucleus and functions like the plasma membrane surrounding the cell. The nucleus is the headquarters for the cell and controls all the processes of the cell including plans for future cells.

Another organelle, ribosomes, composed mostly of ribose nucleic acid, acts like a factory. This factory produces proteins, a basic component of several larger substances—mostly enzymes or antigens for the body. The cell contains many protein factories. Those located in the cytoplasm are called free ribosomes. The free ribosomes produce proteins for use in the cell. Other ribosomes, attached ribosomes, produce proteins for use outside the cell like a factory that exports its goods. Ribosomes are like factories that produce parts for assembly in another factory which may be inside or outside of the city.

Factories like ribosomes must have some way to transport their products; in the cell this need is fulfilled by the endoplasmic reticulum. When the endoplasmic reticulum transports material it acts like a highway system. In the cell the highway system consists of a series of membranes acting like roads. The endoplasmic reticulum transports the proteins produced by the ribosomes, among other materials, throughout the cytoplasm. If ribosomes are directly attached to the endoplasmic reticulum, it is considered rough; without ribosomes attached, the endoplasmic reticulum is considered smooth. Both types help transport materials and absorb materials from the cytoplasm. The roads created by the endoplasmic reticulum can lead many places including storage areas for the cell, the nuclear membrane which allows contact with the nucleus, and the Golgi complex where packaging of materials occurs.

The Golgi complex is another factory or organelle in the cell. The Golgi complex acts like a packaging and export company. It has three major products to package and export for use outside the cell. The proteins transported to the Golgi complex by the endoplasmic reticulum are packaged in sack-like structures. Several proteins are placed in each sack and then pinched off from the Golgi complex and sent out of the cell through the plasma membrane like a truck released from the warehouse and sent across the country. The Golgi complex also takes lipids produced by the smooth endoplasmic reticulum and packages them in the same way the proteins are packaged for use outside of the cell. Finally the Golgi complex can produce some carbohydrates and package them. The Golgi complex operates as a packaging and export factory for proteins, lipids and carbohydrates.

Energy for all the factories in the cell is produced by the power plant of the cell—the mitochondria. The mitochondria has two membranes, an outer one which is just like an outer wall for the plant and an inner membrane which has many folds and acts like a furnace. Chemical reactions take place in the folds of the inner membrane and release adenosine triphosphate, the main energy source for the cell. The mitochondria is the only power plant in the cell and produces all the energy used by the cell. The last organelle is the lysosome which acts like a garbage collector, picking up and eliminating everything used and discarded by the other organelles and nucleus. The lysosome forms from the secreted protein granules produced by the Golgi complex but not released from the cell. They are high-powered enzymes that destroy sick cells, parts of cells, and wastes in the cell. The lysosome travels through the cytoplasm and can eliminate things as does a garbage collector in the city.

Each cell operates independently from other cells, but they all have contact among themselves, just as cities are independent but trade and communicate with each other. Inside the city wall or plasma membrane many factories or organelles function to keep the city-cell running. But unlike a city, a cell is much more highly ordered and, for its size, is so complex that it can carry out all the functions of the body.

Stephen Jay Gould

SEX, DRUGS, DISASTERS, AND THE EXTINCTION OF DINOSAURS

Stephen Jay Gould (1941-   ), a professor of zoology at Harvard University, often writes about scientific ideas to a non-scientific audience. In this essay, he shows how good science is done by comparing two ineffective and one effective theory about the extinction of dinosaurs. As you read, notice how Gould makes a difficult subject clear by giving plenty of examples and relating it to ideas we all understand.

Science, in its most fundamental definition, is a fruitful mode of inquiry, not a list of enticing conclusions. The conclusions are the consequence, not the essence.

My greatest unhappiness with most popular presentations of science concerns their failure to separate fascinating claims from the methods that scientists use to establish the facts of nature. Journalists, and the public, thrive on controversial and stunning statements. But science is, basically, a way of knowing—in P. B. Medawar's apt words, "the art of the soluble." If the growing corps of popular science writers would focus on *how* scientists develop and defend those fascinating claims, they would make their greatest possible contribution to public understanding. Consider three ideas, proposed in perfect seriousness to explain that greatest of all titillating puzzles—the extinction of dinosaurs. Since these three notions invoke the primally fascinating themes of our culture—sex, drugs, and violence—they surely reside in the category of fascinating claims. I want to show why two of them rank as silly speculation, while the other represents science at its grandest and most useful. Science works with testable proposals. If, after much compilation and scrutiny of data, new information continues to affirm a hypothesis, we may accept it provisionally and gain confidence as further evidence mounts. We can never be completely sure that a hypothesis is right, though we may be able to show with confidence that it is wrong. The best scientific hypotheses are also generous and expansive: they suggest extensions and implications that enlighten related, and even far distant, subjects. Simply consider how the idea of evolution has influenced virtually every intellectual field.

Useless speculation, on the other hand, is restrictive. It generates no testable hypothesis, and offers no way to obtain potentially refuting evidence. Please note that I am not speaking of truth or falsity. The speculation may well be true; still, if it provides, in principle, no material for affirmation or rejection, we can make nothing of it. It must simply stand forever as an intriguing idea. Useless speculation turns in on itself and leads nowhere; good science, containing both seeds for its potential refutation and implications for more and different testable knowledge, reaches out. But, enough preaching. Let's move on to dinosaurs, and the three proposals for their extinction.

1. Sex: Testes function only in a narrow range of temperature (those of mammals hang externally in a scrotal sac because internal body temperatures are too high for their proper function). A worldwide rise in temperature at the close of the Cretaceous period caused the testes of dinosaurs to stop functioning and led to their extinction by sterilization of males.

2. Drugs: Angiosperms (flowering plants) first evolved toward the end of the dinosaurs' reign. Many of these plants contain psychoactive agents, avoided by mammals today as a result of their bitter taste. Dinosaurs had neither means to taste the bitterness nor livers effective enough to detoxify the substances. They died of massive overdoses.

3. Disasters: A large comet or asteroid struck the earth some 65 million years ago, lofting a cloud of dust into the sky and blocking sunlight, thereby suppressing photosynthesis and so drastically lowering world temperatures that dinosaurs and hosts of other creatures became extinct.

Before analyzing these three tantalizing statements, we must establish a basic ground rule often violated in proposals for the dinosaurs' demise. *There is no separate problem of the extinction of dinosaurs.* Too often we divorce specific events from their wider contexts and systems of cause and effect. The fundamental fact of dinosaur extinction is its synchrony with the demise of so many other groups across a wide range of habitats, from terrestrial to marine.

The history of life has been punctuated by brief episodes of mass extinction. A recent analysis by University of Chicago paleontologists Jack Sepkoski and Dave Raup, based on the best and most exhaustive tabulation of data ever assembled, shows clearly that five episodes of mass dying stand well above the "background" extinctions of normal times (when we consider all mass extinctions, large and small, they seem to fall in a regular 26-million-year cycle). The Cretaceous debacle, occurring 65 million years ago and separating the Mesozoic and Cenozoic eras of our geological time scale, ranks prominently among the five. Nearly all the marine plankton (single-celled floating creatures) died with geological suddenness; among marine invertebrates, nearly 15 percent of all families perished, including many previously dominant groups, especially the ammonites (relatives of squids in coiled shells). On land, the dinosaurs disappeared after more than 100 million years of unchallenged domination.

In this context, speculations limited to dinosaurs alone ignore the larger phenomenon. We need a coordinated explanation for a system of events that includes the extinction of dinosaurs as one component. Thus it makes little sense, though it may fuel our desire to view mammals as inevitable inheritors of the earth, to guess that dinosaurs died because small mammals ate their eggs (a perennial favorite among untestable speculations). It seems most unlikely that some disaster peculiar to dinosaurs befell these massive beasts—and that the debacle happened to strike just when one of history's five great dyings had enveloped the earth for completely different reasons.

The testicular theory, an old favorite from the 1940s, had its root in an interesting and thoroughly respectable study of temperature tolerances in the American alligator, published in the staid *Bulletin of The American Museum of Natural History* in 1946 by three experts on living and fossil reptiles—E. H. Colbert, my own first teacher in paleontology; R. B. Cowles; and C. M. Bogert.

The first sentence of their summary reveals a purpose beyond alligators: "This report describes an attempt to infer the reactions of extinct reptiles, especially the dinosaurs, to high temperatures as based upon reactions observed in the modern alligator." They studied, by rectal thermometry, the body temperatures of alligators under changing conditions of heating and cooling. (Well, let's face it, you wouldn't want to try sticking a thermometer under alligator's tongue.) The predictions under test go way back to an old theory first stated by Galileo in the 1630s—the unequal scaling of surfaces and volumes. As an animal, or any object, grows (provided its shape doesn't change), surface areas must increase more slowly than volumes—since surfaces get larger as length squared, while volumes increase much more rapidly, as length cubed. Therefore, small animals have high ratios of surface to volume, while large animals cover themselves with relatively little surface.

Among cold-blooded animals lacking any physiological mechanism for keeping their temperatures constant, small creatures have a hell of a time keeping warm—because they lose so much heat through their relatively large surfaces. On the other hand, large animals, with their relatively small surfaces, may lose heat so slowly that, once warm, they may maintain effectively constant temperatures against ordinary fluctuations of climate. (In fact, the resolution of the "hot-blooded dinosaur" controversy that burned so brightly a few years back may simply be that, while large dinosaurs possessed no physiological mechanism for constant temperature, and were not therefore warm-blooded in the technical sense, their large size and relatively small surface area kept them warm.)

Colbert, Cowles, and Bogert compared the warming rates of small and large alligators. As predicted, the small fellows heated up (and cooled down) more quickly. When exposed to a warm sun, a tiny 50-gram (1.76-ounce) alligator heated up one degree Celsius every minute and a half, while a large alligator, 260 times bigger at 13,000 grams (28.7 pounds), took seven and a half minutes to gain a degree. Extrapolating up to an adult 10-ton di-nosaur, they concluded that a one-degree rise in body tempera-ture would take eighty-six hours. If large animals absorb heat so slowly (through their relatively small surfaces), they will also be unable to shed any excess heat gained when temperatures rise above a favorable level.

The authors then guessed that large dinosaurs lived at or near their optimum temperatures; Cowles suggested that a rise in global temperatures just before the Cretaceous extinction caused the dinosaurs to heat up beyond their optimal tolerance—and, being so large, they couldn't shed the unwanted heat. (In a most unusual statement within a scientific paper, Colbert and Bogert then explicitly disavowed this speculative extension of their em-pirical work on alligators.) Cowles conceded that this excess heat probably wasn't enough to kill or even to enervate the great beasts, but since testes often function only within a narrow range of temperature, he proposed that this global rise might have ster-ilized all the males, causing extinction by natural contraception.

The overdose theory has recently been supported by UCLA psy-chiatrist Ronald K. Siegel. Siegel has gathered, he claims, more than 2,000 records of animals who, when given access, administer various drugs to themselves—from a mere swig of alcohol to massive doses of the big H. Elephants will swill the equivalent of twenty beers at a time, but do not like alcohol in concentrations greater than 7 percent. In a silly bit of anthropocentric specu-lation, Siegel states that "elephants drink, perhaps, to forget. . . the anxiety produced by shrinking rangeland and the competition for food."

Since fertile imaginations can apply almost any hot idea to the extinction of dinosaurs, Siegel found a way. Flowering plants did not evolve until late in the dinosaurs' reign. These plants also pro-duced an array of aromatic, amino acid-based alkaloids—the major group of psychoactive agents. Most mammals are "smart" enough to avoid these potential poisons. The alkaloids simply don't taste good (they are bitter); in any case, we mammals have livers happily supplied with the capacity to detoxify them. But, Siegel speculates, perhaps dinosaurs could neither taste the bitterness nor detoxify the substances once ingested. He recently told mem-bers of the American Psychological Association: "I'm not sug-gesting that all dinosaurs OD'd on plant drugs, but it certainly was a factor." He also argued that death by overdose may help explain why so many dinosaur fossils are found in contorted positions. (Do not go gentle into that good night.)

Extraterrestrial catastrophes have long pedigrees in the popular literature of extinction, but the subject exploded again in 1979, after a long lull, when the father-son, physicist-geologist team of Luis and Walter Alvarez proposed that an asteroid, some 10 km in diameter, struck the earth 65 million years ago (comets, rather than asteroids, have since gained favor. Good science is self-corrective).

The force of such a collision would be immense, greater by far than the megatonnage of all the world's nuclear weapons. In trying to reconstruct a scenario that would explain the simultaneous dying of dinosaurs on land and so many creatures in the sea, the Alvarezes proposed that a gigantic dust cloud, generated by particles blown aloft in the impact, would so darken the earth that photosynthesis would cease and temperatures drop precipitously. (Rage, rage against the dying of the light.) The single-celled photosynthetic oceanic plankton, with life cycles measured in weeks, would perish outright, but land plants might survive through the dormancy of their seeds (land plants were not much affected by the Cretaceous extinction, and any adequate theory must account for the curious pattern of differential survival). Dinosaurs would die by starvation and freezing; small, warm-blooded mammals, with more modest requirements for food and better regulation of body temperature, would squeak through. "Let the bastards freeze in the dark," as bumper stickers of our chauvinistic neighbors in sunbelt states proclaimed several years ago during the Northeast's winter oil crisis.

All three theories, testicular malfunction, psychoactive overdosing, and asteroidal zapping, grab our attention mightily. As pure phenomenology, they rank about equally high on any hit parade of primal fascination. Yet one represents expansive science, the others restrictive and untestable speculation. The proper criterion lies in evidence and methodology; we must probe behind the superficial fascination of particular claims.

How could we possibly decide whether the hypothesis of testicular frying is right or wrong? We would have to know things that the fossil record cannot provide. What temperatures were optimal for dinosaurs? Could they avoid the absorption of excess heat by staying in the shade, or in caves? At what temperatures did their testicles cease to function? Were late Cretaceous climates ever warm enough to drive the internal temperatures of dinosaurs close to this ceiling? Testicles simply don't fossilize, and how could we infer their temperature tolerances even if they did? In short, Cowles's hypothesis is only an intriguing speculation leading nowhere. The most damning statement against it appeared right in the conclusion of Colbert, Cowles, and Bogert's paper, when they admitted: "It is difficult to advance any definite arguments against this hypothesis." My statement may seem paradoxical—isn't a hypothesis really good if you can't devise any arguments against it? Quite the contrary. It is simply untestable and unusable.

Siegel's overdosing has even less going for it. At least Cowles extrapolated his conclusion from some good data on alligators. And he didn't completely violate the primary guideline of siting dinosaur extinction in the context of a general mass dying—for rise in temperature could be the root cause of a general catastrophe, zapping dinosaurs by testicular malfunction and different groups for other reasons. But Siegel's speculation cannot touch the extinction of ammonites or oceanic plankton (diatoms make their own food with good sweet sunlight; they don't OD on the chemicals of terrestrial plants). It is simply a gratuitous, attention-grabbing guess. It cannot be tested, for how can we know what dinosaurs tasted and what their livers could do? Livers don't fossilize any better than testicles.

The hypothesis doesn't even make any sense in its own context. Angiosperms were in full flower ten million years before dinosaurs went the way of all flesh. Why did it take so long? As for the pains of a chemical death recorded in contortions of fossils, I regret to say (or rather I'm pleased to note for the dinosaurs' sake) that Siegel's knowledge of geology must be a bit deficient: muscles contract after death and geological strata rise and fall with motions of the earth's crust after burial—more than enough reason to distort a fossil's pristine appearance.

The impact story, on the other hand, has a sound basis in evidence. It can be tested, extended, refined and, if wrong, disproved. The Alvarezes did not just construct an arresting guess for public consumption. They proposed their hypothesis after laborious geochemical studies with Frank Asaro and Helen Michael had revealed a massive increase of iridium in rocks deposited right at the time of extinction. Iridium, a rare metal of the platinum group, is virtually absent from indigenous rocks of the earth's crust; most of our iridium arrives on extraterrestrial objects that strike the earth.

The Alvarez hypothesis bore immediate fruit. Based originally
on evidence from two European localities, it led geochemists
throughout the world to examine other sediments of the same
age. They found abnormally high amounts of iridium everywhere—from continental rocks of the western United States to
deep sea cores from the South Atlantic. Cowles proposed his testicular hypothesis in the mid-1940s. Where has it gone since
then? Absolutely nowhere, because scientists can do nothing with
it. The hypothesis must stand as a curious appendage to a solid
study of alligators. Siegel's overdose scenario will also win a few
press notices and fade into oblivion. The Alvarezes' asteroid falls
into a different category altogether, and much of the popular
commentary has missed this essential distinction by focusing on
the impact and its attendant results, and forgetting what really
matters to a scientist—the iridium. If you talk just about asteroids,
dust, and darkness, you tell stories no better and no more enter-
taining than fried testicles or terminal trips. It is the iridium—the
source of testable evidence—that counts and forges the crucial
distinction between speculation and science.

The proof, to twist a phrase,—lies in the doing. Cowles's hypothesis has generated nothing in thirty-five years. Since its proposal in 1979, the Alvarez hypothesis has spawned hundreds of
studies, a major conference, and attendant publications. Geologists
are fired up. They are looking for iridium at all other extinction
boundaries. Every week exposes a new wrinkle in the scientific
press. Further evidence that the Cretaceous iridium represents
extraterrestrial impact and not indigenous volcanism continues
to accumulate. As I revise this essay in November 1984 (this
paragraph will be out of date when the book is published), new
data include chemical "signatures" of other isotopes indicating
unearthly provenance, glass spherules of a size and sort produced
by impact and not by volcanic eruptions, and high-pressure varieties of silica formed (so far as we know) only under the
tremendous shock of impact.

My point is simply this: Whatever the eventual outcome (I suspect it will be positive), the Alvarez hypothesis is exciting, fruitful
science because it generates tests, provides us with things to do,
and expands outward. We are having fun, battling back and forth,
moving toward a resolution, and extending the hypothesis beyond
its original scope.

As just one example of the unexpected, distant cross-fertilization
that good science engenders, the Alvarez hypothesis made a ma-

jor contribution to a theme that has riveted public attention in the past few months—so-called nuclear winter. In a speech delivered in April 1982, Luis Alvarez calculated the energy that a ten-kilometer asteroid would release on impact. He compared such an explosion with a full nuclear exchange and implied that all-out atomic war might unleash similar consequences.

This theme of impact leading to massive dust clouds and falling temperatures formed an important input to the decision of Carl Sagan and a group of colleagues to model the climatic consequences of nuclear holocaust. Full nuclear exchange would probably generate the same kind of dust cloud and darkening that may have wiped out the dinosaurs. Temperatures would drop precipitously and agriculture might become impossible. Avoidance of nuclear war is fundamentally an ethical and political imperative, but we must know the factual consequences to make firm judgments. I am heartened by a final link across disciplines and deep concerns—another criterion, by the way, of science at its best: A recognition of the very phenomenon that made our evolution possible by exterminating the previously dominant dinosaurs and clearing a way for the evolution of large mammals, including us, might actually help to save us from joining those magnificent beasts in contorted poses among the strata of the earth.

Lewis Thomas

CETI

Lewis Thomas (1913-   ) is a medical doctor who in the last two decades has turned to writing about scientific topics of popular interest. A majestic style and grace makes his writing immediately appealing to people who wouldn't ordinarily read about science. As you read, notice how seamlessly he shifts from extraterrestrial observation to humanistic achievement, as if the two pursuits were always discussed in the same breath. In the end, he makes the point that studies of the heavens can and should be taken to be of the profoundest human importance.

Tau Ceti is a relatively nearby star that sufficiently resembles our sun to make its solar system a plausible candidate for the existence of life. We are, it appears, ready to begin getting in touch with Ceti, and with any other interested celestial body in more remote places, out to the edge. CETI is also, by intention, the acronym of the First International Conference on Communication with Extraterrestrial Intelligence, held in 1972 in Soviet Armenia under the joint sponsorship of the National Academy of Sciences of the United States and the Soviet Academy, which involved eminent physicists and astronomers from various countries, most of whom are convinced that the odds for the existence of life elsewhere are very high, with a reasonable probability that there are civilizations, one place or another, with technologic mastery matching or exceeding ours.

On this assumption, the conferees thought it likely that radioastronomy would be the generally accepted mode of interstellar communication, on grounds of speed and economy. They made a formal recommendation that we organize an international cooperative program, with new and immense radio telescopes, to probe the reaches of deep space for electromagnetic signals making sense. Eventually, we would plan to send out messages on our own and receive answers, but at the outset it seems more practical to begin by catching snatches of conversation between others.

So, the highest of all our complex technologies in the hardest of our sciences will soon be engaged, full scale, in what is essentially biologic research—and with some aspects of social science, at that.

The earth has become, just in the last decade, too small a place. We have the feeling of being confined—shut in; it is something like outgrowing a small town in a small county. The views of the dark, pocked surface of Mars, still lifeless to judge from the latest photographs, do not seem to have extended our reach; instead, they bring closer, too close, another unsatisfactory feature of our local environment. The blue noonday sky, cloudless, has lost its old look of immensity. The word is out that the sky is not limitless; it is finite. It is, in truth, only a kind of local roof, a membrane under which we live, luminous but confusingly refractile when suffused with sunlight; we can sense its concave surface a few miles over our heads. We know that it is tough and thick enough so that when hard objects strike it from the outside they burst into flames. The color photographs of the earth are more amazing than anything outside: we live inside a blue chamber, a bubble of air blown by ourselves. The other sky beyond, absolutely black and appalling, is wide-open country, irresistible for exploration.

Here we go, then. An extraterrestrial embryologist, having a close look at us from time to time, would probably conclude that the morphogenesis of the earth is coming along well, with the beginnings of a nervous system and fair-sized ganglions in the form of cities, and now with specialized, dish-shaped sensory organs, miles across, ready to receive stimuli. He may well wonder, however, how we will go about responding. We are evolving into the situation of a Skinner pigeon in a Skinner box, peering about in all directions, trying to make connections, probing.

When the first word comes in from outer space, finally, we will probably be used to the idea. We can already provide a quite good explanation for the origin of life, here or elsewhere. Given a moist planet with methane, formaldehyde, ammonia, and some usable minerals, all of which abound, exposed to lightning or ultraviolet irradiation at the right temperature, life might start off almost anywhere. The tricky, unsolved thing is how to get the polymers to arrange in membranes and invent replication. The rest is clear going. If they follow our protocol, it will be anaerobic life at first, then photosynthesis and the first exhalation of oxygen, then respiring life and the great burst of variation, then speciation, and, finally, some kind of consciousness. It is easy, in the telling.

I suspect that when we have recovered from the first easy acceptance of signs of life from elsewhere, and finished nodding at each other, and finished smiling, we will be in shock. We have had it our way, relatively speaking, being unique all these years, and it will be hard to deal with the thought that the whole, infinitely huge, spinning, clocklike apparatus around us is itself animate, and can sprout life whenever the conditions are right. We will respond, beyond doubt, by making connections after the fashion of established life, floating out our filaments, extending pili, but we will end up feeling smaller than ever, as small as a single cell, with a quite new sense of continuity. It will take some getting used to.

The immediate problem, however, is a much more practical, down-to-earth matter, and must be giving insomnia to the CETI participants. Let us assume that there is, indeed, sentient life in one or another part of remote space, and that we will be successful in getting in touch with it. What on earth are we going to talk about? If, as seems likely, it is a hundred or more light years away, there are going to be some very long pauses. The barest amenities, on which we rely for opening conversations—Hello, are you there?, from us, followed by Yes, hello, from them—will take two hundred years at least. By the time we have our party we may have forgotten what we had in mind.

We could begin by gambling on the rightness of our technology and just send out news of ourselves, like a mimeographed Christmas letter, but we would have to choose our items carefully, with durability of meaning in mind. Whatever information we provide must still make sense to us two centuries later, and must still seem important, or the conversation will be an embarrassment to all concerned. In two hundred years it is, as we have found, easy to lose the thread.

Perhaps the safest thing to do at the outset, if technology permits, is to send music. This language may be the best we have for explaining what we are like to others in space, with least ambiguity. I would vote for Bach, all of Bach, streamed out into space, over and over again. We would be bragging, of course, but it is surely excusable for us to put the best possible face on at the beginning of such an acquaintance. We can tell the harder truths later. And, to do ourselves justice, music would give a fairer picture of what we are really like than some of the other things we might be sending, like *Time,* say, or a history of the U.N. or Presidential speeches. We could send out our science, of course, but just think of the wincing at this end when the polite comments arrive two hundred years from now. Whatever we offer as today's items of liveliest interest are bound to be out of date and irrelevant, maybe even ridiculous. I think we should stick to music.

Perhaps, if the technology can be adapted to it, we should send some paintings. Nothing would better describe what this place is like, to an outsider, than the Cezanne demonstrations that an apple is really part fruit, part earth.

What kinds of questions should we ask? The choices will be hard, and everyone will want his special question first. What are your smallest particles? Did you think yourselves unique? Do you have colds? Have you anything quicker than light? Do you always tell the truth? Do you cry? There is no end to the list.

Perhaps we should wait a while, until we are sure we know what we want to know, before we get down to detailed questions. After all, the main question will be the opener: Hello, are you there? If the reply should turn out to be Yes, hello, we might want to stop there and think about that, for quite a long time.

Chapter 7:
Worth Fighting for?

Thucydides

PERICLES' FUNERAL ORATION

Thucydides the historian lived from 460-400 B.C. Most of what we know of him (he was an unsuccessful general and a wealthy landowner) comes from his own *History of the Peloponnesian War*. The war itself took place from 431-404 B.C. We know from his own admission and historical evidence that Thucydides' recounting of Pericles' Funeral Oration was probably something between a partially honest reconstruction and a complete fabrication. Nonetheless, Thucydides felt this was justified, since he made the speakers say "what was called for" at the time. Perhaps the best way to think of speeches in Thucydides' history is as analyses of historical events, rather than a word-for-word record of what was said. The funeral oration was delivered in 429 B.C. after Sparta had invaded Athenian territory for the first time. Pericles' stirring words were spoken (or written by Thucydides) to remind the Athenians of what was unique about their nation—what made it worth fighting for. (Athens eventually lost the war.) As you read the speech, ask yourself which characteristics of ancient Athens we would consider admirable today. Which would be worthy of scorn?

In the same winter the Athenians, following their annual custom, gave a public funeral for those who had been the first to die in
the war. These funerals are held in the following way: two days
before the ceremony the bones of the fallen are brought and put in
a tent which has been erected, and people make whatever offerings they wish to their own dead. Then there is a funeral procession in which coffins of cypress wood are carried on wagons.
There is one coffin for each tribe, which contains the bones of
members of that tribe. One empty bier is decorated and carried in
the procession: this is for the missing, whose bodies could not be recovered. Everyone who wishes to, both citizens and foreigners, can
join in the procession, and the women who are related to the dead
are there to make their laments at the tomb. The bones are laid in
the public burial place, which is in the most beautiful quarter outside the city walls. Here the Athenians always bury those who
have fallen in war. The only exception is those who died at
Marathon, who, because their achievement was considered absolutely outstanding, were buried on the battlefield itself.

When the bones have been laid in the earth, a man chosen by
the city for his intellectual gifts and for his general reputation
makes an appropriate speech in praise of the dead, and after the
speech all depart. This is the procedure at these burials, and all
through the war, when the time came to do so, the Athenians followed this ancient custom. Now, at the burial of those who were
the first to fall in the war Pericles, the son of Xanthippus, was
chosen to make the speech. When the moment arrived, he came
forward from the tomb and, standing on a high platform, so that
he might be heard by as many people as possible in the crowd, he
spoke as follows:

'Many of those who have spoken here in the past have praised
the institution of this speech at the close of our ceremony. It
seemed to them a mark of honour to our soldiers who have fallen
in a war that a speech should be made over them. I do not agree.
These men have shown themselves valiant in action, and it would
be enough, I think, for their glories to be proclaimed in action, as
you have just seen it done at this funeral organized by the state.
Our belief in the courage and manliness of so many should not be
hazarded on the goodness or badness of one man's speech. Then it
is not easy to speak with a proper sense of balance, when a man's
listeners find it difficult to believe in the truth of what one is saying. The man who knows the facts and loves the dead may well
think that an oration tells less than what he knows and what he

would like to hear: others who do not know so much may feel
envy for the dead, and think the orator over-praises them, when
he speaks of exploits that are beyond their own capacities. Praise
of other people is tolerable only up to a certain point, the point
where one still believes that one could do oneself some of the things
one is hearing about. Once you get beyond this point, you will find
people becoming jealous and incredulous. However, the fact is that
this institution was set up and approved by our forefathers and it
is my duty to follow the tradition and do my best to meet the
wishes and the expectations of every one of you.

'I shall begin by speaking about our ancestors, since it is only
right and proper on such an occasion to pay them the honour of
recalling what they did. In this land of ours there have always
been the same people living from generation to generation up till
now, and they, by their courage and their virtues, have handed it
on to us, a free country. They certainly deserve our praise. Even
more so do our fathers deserve it. For to the inheritance they had
received they added all the empire we have now, and it was not
without blood and toil that they handed it down to us of the present
generation. And then we ourselves, assembled here today, who are
mostly in the prime of life, have, in most directions, added to the
power of our empire and have organized our State in such a way
that it is perfectly well able to look after itself both in peace and in
war.

'I have no wish to make a long speech on subjects familiar to
you all: so I shall say nothing about the warlike deeds by which we
acquired our power or the battles in which we or our fathers gal-
lantly resisted our enemies, Greek or foreign. What I want to do is,
in the first place, to discuss the spirit in which we faced our trials
and also our constitution and the way of life which has made us
great. After that I shall speak in praise of the dead, believing that
this kind of speech is not inappropriate to the present occasion,
and that this whole assembly, of citizens and foreigners, may listen to it with advantage.

'Let me say that our system of government does not copy the
institutions of our neighbours. It is more the case of our being a
model to others than of our imitating anyone else. Our constitution is called a democracy because power is in the hands not of a
minority but of the whole people. When it is a question of settling
private disputes, everyone is equal before the law; when it is a
question of putting one person before another in positions of public
responsibility, what counts is not membership of a particular

class, but the actual ability which the man possesses. No one, so long he has it in him to be of service to the state, is kept in political obscurity because of poverty. And, just as our political life is free and open, so is our day-to-day life in our relations with each other. We do not get into a state with our next-door neighbour if he enjoys himself in his own way, nor do we give him the kind of black looks which, though they do no real harm, still do hurt people's feelings. We are free and tolerant in our private lives; but in public affairs we keep to the law. This is because it commands our deep respect.

'We give our obedience to those whom we put in positions of authority, and we obey the laws themselves, especially those which are for the protection of the oppressed, and those unwritten laws which it is an acknowledged shame to break.

'And here is another point. When our work is over, we are in a position to enjoy all kinds of recreation for our spirits. There are various kinds of contests and sacrifices throughout the year; in our own homes we find a beauty and a good taste which delight us every day and which drive away our cares. Then the greatness of our city brings it about that all the good things from all over the world flow in to us, so that it just seems natural to enjoy foreign goods as our own local products.

'Then there is a great difference between us and our opponents in our attitude towards military security. Here are some examples: Our city is open to the world, and we have no periodical deportations in order to prevent people observing or finding out secrets which might be of military advantage to the enemy. This is because we rely, not on secret weapons, but on our own real courage and loyalty. There is a difference, too, in our educational systems. The Spartans from their earliest boyhood, are submitted to the most laborious training in courage; we pass our lives without all these restrictions, and yet are just as ready to face the same dangers as they are. Here is a proof of this: when the Spartans invade our land. they do not come by themselves, but bring all their allies with them: whereas we, when we launch an attack abroad, do the job by ourselves, and, though fighting on foreign soil do not often fail to defeat opponents who are fighting for their own hearths and homes. As a matter of fact none of our enemies has ever yet been confronted with our total strength, because we have to divide our attention between our navy and the many missions on which our troops are sent on land. Yet, if our enemies engage a detachment of our forces and defeat it, they give themselves credit for having thrown back our entire army; or, if they lose, they claim that they were beaten by us in full strength. There are certain advantages, I think, in our way of meeting danger voluntarily, with an easy mind, instead of with a laborious training, with natural rather than with state-induced courage. We do not have to spend our time practising to meet sufferings which are still in the future; and when they are actually upon us we show ourselves just as brave as these others who are always in strict training. This is one point in which, I think our city deserves to be admired. There are also others:

'Our love of what is beautiful does not lead to extravagance; our love of the things of the mind does not make us soft. We regard wealth as something to be properly used, rather than as something to boast about. As for poverty, no one need be ashamed to admit it: the real shame is in not taking practical measures to escape from it. Here each individual is interested not only in his own affairs but in the affairs of the state as well; even those who are mostly occupied with their own business are extremely well-informed on general politics—this is a peculiarity of ours: we do not say that a man who takes no interest in politics is a man who minds his own business, we say that he has no business here at all. We Athenians, in our own persons, take our decisions on policy or submit them to proper discussions: for we do not think that there is an incompatibility between words and deeds; the worst thing is to rush into action before the consequences have been properly debated. And this is another point where we differ from other people. We are capable at the same time of taking risks and of estimating them beforehand. Others are brave out of ignorance; and, when they stop to think, they begin to fear. But the man who can most truly be accounted brave is he who best knows the meaning of what is sweet in life and of what is terrible, and then goes out undeterred to meet what is to come.

'Again, in questions of general good feeling there is a great contrast between us and most other people. We make friends by doing good to others, not by receiving good from them. This makes our friendship all the more reliable, since we want to keep alive the gratitude of those who are in our debt by showing continued goodwill to them: whereas the feelings of one who owes us something lack the same enthusiasm, since he knows that, when he repays our kindness, it will be more like paying back a debt than giving some thing spontaneously. We are unique in this. When we do kindnesses to others, we do not do them out of any calculations of profit or loss: we do them without afterthought, relying on our free liberality. Taking everything together, then, I declare that our city is an education to Greece, and I declare that in my opinion each single one of our citizens, in all the manifold aspects of life, is able to show himself the rightful lord and owner of his own person, and do this, moreover, with exceptional grace and exceptional versatility. And to show that this is no empty boasting for the present occasion, but real tangible fact, you have only to consider the power which our city possesses and which has been won by those very qualities which I have mentioned. Athens, alone of the states we know, comes to her testing time in a greatness that surpasses what was imagined of her. In her case, and in her case alone, no invading enemy is ashamed at being defeated, and no subject can complain of being governed by people unfit for their responsibilities. Mighty indeed are the marks and monuments of our empire which we have left. Future ages will wonder at us, as the present age wonders at us now. We do not need the praises of a Homer, or of anyone else whose words may delight us for the moment, but whose estimation of facts will fall short of what is really true. For our adventurous spirit has forced an entry into every sea and into every land; and everywhere we have left behind us everlasting memorials of good done to our friends or suffering inflicted on our enemies.

'This, then, is the kind of city for which these men, who could not bear the thought of losing her, nobly fought and nobly died. It is only natural that every one of us who survive them should be willing to undergo hardships in her service. And it was for this reason that I have spoken at such length about our city, because I wanted to make it clear that for us there is more at stake than there is for others who lack our advantages; also I wanted my words of praise for the dead to be set in the bright light of evidence. And now the most important of these words has been spoken. I have sung the praises of our city; but it was the courage and gallantry of these men, and of people like them, which made her splendid. Nor would you find it true in the case of many of the Greeks, as it is true of them, that no words can do more than justice to their deeds.

'To me it seems that the consummation which has overtaken these men shows us the meaning of manliness in its first revelation and in its final proof. Some of them, no doubt, had their faults; but what we ought to remember first is the gallant conduct against the enemy in defence of their native land. They have blotted out evil with good, and done more service to the commonwealth than they ever did harm in their private lives. No one of these men weakened because he wanted to go on enjoying his wealth; no one put off the awful day in the hope that he might live to escape his poverty and grow rich. More to be desired than such things, they chose to check the enemy's pride. This, to them, was a risk most glorious, and they accepted it, willing to strike down the enemy and relinquish everything else. As for success or failure, they left that in the doubtful hands of Hope, and when the reality of battle was before their faces, they put their trust in their own selves. In the fighting they thought it more honourable to stand their ground and suffer death than to give in to save their lives. So they fled from the reproaches of men, abiding with life and limb the brunt of battle; and in a small moment of time, the climax of their lives, a culmination of glory, not of fear, were swept away from us.

'So and such they were, these men—worthy of their city. We who remain behind may hope to be spared their fate, but must resolve to keep the same daring spirit against the foe. It is not simply a question of estimating the advantages in theory. I could tell you a long story (and you know it as well as I do) about what is to be gained by beating the enemy back. What I would prefer is that you should fix your eyes every day on the greatness of Athens as she really is, and should fall in love with her. When you realize her greatness, then reflect that what made her great was men with a spirit of adventure, men who knew their duty, men who were ashamed to fall below a certain standard. If they ever failed in an enterprise, they made up their minds that at any rate the city should not find their courage lacking to her, and they gave to her the best contribution that they could. They gave her their lives, to her and to all of us, and for their own selves they won praises that never grow old, the most splendid of sepulchres—not the sepulchre in which their bodies are laid, but where their glory remains eternal in men's minds, always there on the right occasion to stir others to speech or to action. For famous men have the whole earth as their memorial: it is not only the inscriptions on their graves in their own country that mark them out; no, in foreign lands also, not in any visible form but in people's hearts, their memory abides and grows. It is for you to try to be like them. Make up your minds that happiness depends on being free and freedom depends on being courageous. Let there be no relaxation in the face of the perils of the war. The people who have most excuse for despising death are not the wretched and unfortunate, who have no hope of doing well for themselves, but those who run the risk of a complete reversal in their lives, and who would feel the difference most intensely, if things went wrong for them. Any intelligent would find a humiliation caused by his own slackness more painful to bear than death, when death comes to him unperceived, in battle, and in the confidence of his patriotism.

'For these reasons I shall not commiserate with those parents of the dead, who are present here. Instead I shall try to comfort them. They are well aware that they have grown up in a world where there are many changes and chances. But this is good fortune—for men to end their lives with honour, as these have done, and for you honourably to lament them: their life was set to a measure where death and happiness went hand in hand. I know that it is difficult to convince you of this. When you see other people happy you will often be reminded of what used to make you happy too. One does not feel sad at not having some good thing which is outside one's experience: real grief is felt at the loss of something which one is used to. All the same, those of you who are of the right age must bear up and take comfort in the thought of having more children. In your own homes these new children will prevent you from brooding over those who are no more, and they will be a help to the city, too, both in filling the empty places, and in assuring her security. For it is impossible for a man to put forward fair and honest views about our affairs if he has not, like everyone else, children whose lives may be at stake. As for those of you who are now too old to have children, I would ask you to count as gain the greater part of your life, in which you have been happy, and remember that what remains is not long, and let your hearts be lifted up at the thought of the fair fame of the dead. One's sense of honour is the only thing that does not grow old, and the last pleasure, when one is worn out with age, is not, as the poet said, making money, but having the respect of one's fellow men.

'As for those of you who are sons or brothers of the dead, I can see a hard struggle in front of you. Everyone always speaks well of the dead and, even if you rise to the greatest heights of heroism, it will be a hard thing for you to get the reputation of having come near, let alone equalled, their standard. When one is alive, one is always liable to the jealousy of one's competitors, but when one is out of the way, the honour one receives is sincere and unchallenged.

'Perhaps I should say a word or two on the duties of women to those among you who are now widowed. I can say all I have to say in a short word of advice. Your great glory is not to be inferior to what God has made you, and the greatest glory of a woman is to be least talked about by men, whether they are praising you or criticizing you. I have now, as the law demanded, said what I had to say. For the time being our offerings to the dead have been made, and for the future their children will be supported at the public expense by the city, until they come of age. This is the crown and prize which she offers, both to the dead and to their children, for the ordeals which they have faced. Where the rewards of valour are the greatest, there you will find also the best and bravest spirits among the people. And now, when you have mourned for your dear ones, you must depart.'

Abraham Lincoln

THE GETTYSBURG ADDRESS

President Abraham Lincoln (1809-1865) gave this speech in 1863 after the most crucial Union victory of the Civil War. If the Confederate army had won at Gettysburg, it would have had the potential to deal severe damage to the North, if not win the war outright. Fittingly, then, it was here that Lincoln gave his most memorable speech. As you read, see if you can identify phrases that Lincoln borrows from other famous speeches and documents.

Four score and seven years ago our fathers brought forth on this continent, a new nation, conceived in Liberty, and dedicated to the proposition that all men are created equal.

Now we are engaged in a great civil war, testing whether that nation, or any nation so conceived and so dedicated, can long endure. We are met on a great battle-field of that war. We have come to dedicate a portion of that field, as a final resting place for those who here gave their lives that that nation might live. It is altogether fitting and proper that we should do this.

But, in a larger sense, we can not dedicate—we can not consecrate—we can not hallow—this ground. The brave men, living and dead, who struggled here, have consecrated it, far above our poor power to add or detract. The world will little note, nor long remember what we say here, but it can never forget what they did here. It is for us the living, rather, to be dedicated here to the unfinished work which they who fought here have thus far so nobly advanced. It is rather for us to be here dedicated to the great task remaining before us—that from these honored dead we take increased devotion to that cause for which they gave the last full measure of devotion—that we here highly resolve that these dead shall not have died in vain—that this nation, under God, shall have a new birth of freedom—and that government of the people, by the people, for the people, shall not perish from the earth.

Phil (student)

PERICLES AND LINCOLN

Phil here uses the devices of synthesis and comparison to make an enlightening point about the similarities between The Gettysburg Address and Pericles' Funeral Oration.

Pericles, in his Funeral Oration, addresses a war torn nation, Athens. Abraham Lincoln, in his speech at Gettysburg, addresses a war torn nation, the United States during the civil war. Over 2000 miles and over 2000 years separate these men. Each speech is a product of its own culture and of its own time. Yet, in the end, the speeches are strikingly similar.

Civil War America and ancient Greece are, of course, not identical. There are differences between these two cultures which are evident in the speech. The conception of death is an example. For the Greeks, a death certainly is a sad event. Pericles talks of the "real grief" of parents. Yet, one can see in many places that the Greeks think differently about death from Lincoln's audience. Pericles follows the above statement with one that may seem cold to modern men. He tells the parents of the dead "to take comfort in the thought of having more children." The sadness about death in the Gettysburg address is absent. At Gettysburg, the challenge for the living is to see that the dead "shall not have died in vain." Lincoln's words are ponderous and somber: "we cannot dedicate—consecrate—we cannot hallow—this ground." The Greeks, on the other hand, have to be warned not to grow tired of all this talk about the great deeds of the dead men. Pericles says "Praise of other people is tolerable only up to a certain point, the point where one still believes that one could do oneself some of the things one is hearing about."

The remarkable thing, however, about these speeches is how they underline the similarities between Greeks and Americans. Pericles and Lincoln, both men who knew their audiences well, can say almost identical things. They appeal to their audiences' sense of nostalgia. Both speeches look backwards. Pericles says: "I shall begin by speaking about our ancestors. . ." Lincoln says: "Four score and seven years ago. . ."

Both men can appeal to the glories of their nation to stir their audience to action. Pericles, after summarizing the glories of Athens, says: "What I would prefer is that you should fix your eyes every day on the greatness of Athens as she really is, and should fall in love with her." Lincoln speaks of the glories of the United States, saying it was "conceived in liberty." Democracy, as it was for Pericles and the Greeks, is also the crowning glory of the United States. Lincoln speaks of "government of the people, by the people, for the people. . ."

Both men resort to similar rhetorical tricks. Lincoln plays down the importance of what he is saying. He says: "The world will little note, nor long remember, what we say here, but it can never forget what they did here." Pericles, too, seems to say that speeches are a waste of time: "These men have shown themselves valiant in action, and it would be enough, I think, for their glories to be proclaimed in action. . ."

The climax of both speeches deals with dying for one's country. Though their conceptions of death are different, both men extol the glory of dying in battle. Lincoln spoke of the world never forgetting the soldiers of Gettysburg. The living must be "dedicated. . .to the unfinished work which they who fought here have thus far so nobly advanced." Pericles says of the Athenian dead: "their glory remains eternal in men's minds, always there on the right occasion to stir others to speech or to action."

Both Lincoln and Pericles were professional politicians. Both knew the electorate well. These two great leaders, at similar occasions, give very similar orations. Not only must the leaders have been similar, but their audiences must have been as well. It may be too much to say that over time men are essentially the same. However, if these speeches are any indication, ancient Greece and 19th century America have a lot in common.

Thomas Jefferson and others

THE DECLARATION OF INDEPENDENCE

Thomas Jefferson (1743-1826), architect, inventor, philosopher, statesman, and third President of the United States, composed the final draft of the Declaration of Independence by himself, working from a draft prepared by a committee of the Continental Congress. As you read, consider the effect of the list of complaints against the King. Does any of the complaints, taken individually, merit such a drastic action—seceding from the nation and starting a war?

IN CONGRESS, JULY 4, 1776
THE UNANIMOUS DECLARATION OF THE
THIRTEEN UNITED STATES OF AMERICA

When in the Course of human events it becomes necessary for one people to dissolve the political bands which have connected them with another, and to assume among the powers of the earth, the separate and equal station to which the Laws of Nature and of Nature's God entitle them, a decent respect to the opinions of mankind requires that they should declare the causes which impel them to the separation.

We hold these truths to be self-evident, that all men are created equal, that they are endowed by their Creator with certain unalienable Rights, that among these are Life, Liberty and the pursuit of Happiness. That to secure these rights, Governments are instituted among Men, deriving their just powers from the consent of the governed. That whenever any Form of Government becomes destructive of these ends, it is the Right of the People to alter or to abolish it, and to institute new Government, laying its foundation on such principles and organizing its powers in such form, as to them shall seem most likely to affect their Safety and Happiness. Prudence, indeed, will dictate that Governments long established should not be changed for light and transient causes; and accordingly all experience hath shewn that mankind are more disposed to suffer, while evils are sufferable, than to right themselves by abolishing the forms to which they are accustomed. But when a long train of abuses and usurpations, pursuing invariably the same Object evinces a design to reduce them under absolute Despotism, it is their right, it is their duty, to throw off such Government, and to provide new Guards for their future security. Such has been the patient sufferance of these Colonies; and such is now the necessity which constrains them to alter their former Systems of Government. The history of the present King of Great Britain is a history of repeated injuries and usurpations, all having in direct object the establishment of an absolute Tyranny over these States. To prove this, let Facts be submitted to a candid world.

He has refused his Assent to Laws, the most wholesome and necessary for the public good.

He has forbidden his Government to pass laws of immediate and pressing importance, unless suspended in their operation till his Assent should be obtained; and when so suspended, he has utterly neglected to attend to them.

He has refused to pass other Laws for the accommodation of large districts of people, unless those people would relinquish the right of Representation in the Legislature, a right inestimable to them and formidable to tyrants only.

He has called together legislative bodies at places unusual, uncomfortable, and distant from the depository of their Public Records, for the sole purpose of fatiguing them into compliance with his measures.

He has dissolved Representative Houses repeatedly, for opposing with manly firmness his invasions on the rights of the people.

He has refused for a long time, after such dissolutions, to cause others to be elected; whereby the Legislative Powers, incapable of Annihilation, have returned to the People at large for their exercise; the State remaining in the mean time exposed to all the dangers of invasion from without, and convulsions within.

He has endeavored to prevent the population of these States; for that purpose obstructing the Laws for Naturalization of Foreigners; refusing to pass others to encourage their migration hither, and raising the conditions of new Appropriations of Lands.

He has obstructed the Administration of Justice, by refusing his Assent to Laws for establishing Judiciary Powers.

He has made Judges dependent on his Will alone, for the tenure of their offices, and the amount and payment of their salaries.

He has erected a multitude of New Offices, and sent hither swarms of Officers to harass our people, and eat out their substance.

He has kept among us, in times of peace, Standing Armies without the Consent of our legislatures.

He has affected to render the Military independent of and superior to the Civil Power.

He has combined with others to subject us to a jurisdiction foreign to our constitution, and unacknowledged by our laws; giving his Assent to their Acts of pretended Legislation:

For quartering large bodies of armed troops among us:

For protecting them, by a mock Trial, from punishment for any Murders which they should commit on the Inhabitants of these States:

For cutting off our Trade with all parts of the world:

For imposing Taxes on us without our Consent:

For depriving us in many cases, of the benefits of Trial by Jury;

For transporting us beyond Seas to be tried for pretended offenses:

For abolishing the free System of English Laws in a neighboring Province, establishing therein an Arbitrary government, and enlarging its Boundaries so as to render it at once an example and fit instrument for introducing the same absolute rule into these Colonies:

For taking away our Charters, abolishing our most valuable Laws and altering fundamentally the Forms of our Governments:

For suspending our own Legislatures, and declaring themselves invested with power to legislate for us in all cases whatsoever.

He has abdicated Government here, by declaring us out of his Protection and waging War against us.

He has plundered our seas, ravaged our Coasts, burnt our towns, and destroyed the lives of our people.

He is at this time transporting large Armies of foreign Mercenaries to complete the works of death, desolation and tyranny, already begun with circumstances of Cruelty & Perfidy scarcely paralleled in the most barbarous ages, and totally unworthy the Head of a civilized nation.

He has constrained our fellow Citizens taken Captive on the high Seas to bear Arms against their Country, to become the executioners of their friends and Brethren, or to fall themselves by their Hands.

He has excited domestic insurrections amongst us, and has endeavored to bring on the inhabitants of our frontiers, the merciless Indian Savages, whose known rule of warfare, is an undistinguished destruction of all ages, sexes, and conditions.

In every stage of these Oppressions We have Petitioned for Redress in the most humble terms: Our repeated Petitions have been answered only by repeated injury. A Prince, whose character is thus marked by every act which may define a Tyrant, is unfit to be the ruler of a free people.

Nor have We been wanting in attention to our British brethren. We have warned them from time to time of attempts by their legislature to extend an unwarrantable jurisdiction over us. We have reminded them of the circumstances of our emigration and settlement here. We have appealed to their native justice and magnanimity, and we have conjured them by the ties of our common kindred to disavow these usurpations, which would inevitably interrupt our connections and correspondence. They too have been deaf to the voice of justice and of consanguinity. We must, therefore, acquiesce in the necessity, which denounces our Separation, and hold them, as we hold the rest of mankind, Enemies in War, in Peace Friends.

We, THEREFORE the Representatives of the UNITED STATES OF AMERICA, in General Congress, Assembled, appealing to the Supreme Judge of the world for the rectitude of our intentions, do, in the Name, and by Authority of the good People of these Colonies, solemnly publish and declare, That these United Colonies are, and of Right ought to be FREE AND INDEPENDENT STATES; that they are Absolved from all Allegiance to the British Crown, and that all political connection between them and the State of Great Britain, is and ought to be totally dissolved; and that as Free and Independent States, they have full Power to levy War, conclude Peace, contract Alliances, establish Commerce, and to do all other Acts and Things which Independent States may of right do. And for the support of this Declaration, with a firm reliance on the protection of Divine Providence, we mutually pledge to each other our Lives, our Fortunes, and our sacred Honor.

Franklin Delano Roosevelt

WAR MESSAGE TO CONGRESS

President Franklin Roosevelt (1882-1945) won the election of 1940 on a platform of staying out of the war, but at the end of 1941, when Japan attacked Pearl Harbor, there seemed to be no choice but to get involved. Minutes after he gave this speech, congress voted to declare war on Japan. Three days later, war was declared on Germany and Italy. The case for war against Japan was certainly strong, but were we fighting Germany simply because we were fighting Japan? As you read this speech, ask yourself what it was, precisely, that meant the United States had to go to war.

Yesterday, December 7, 1941—a date which will live infamy— the United States of America was suddenly and deliberately attacked by naval and air forces of the Empire of Japan.

The United States was at peace with that nation and, at the solicitation of Japan, was still in conversation with its Government and its Emperor looking toward the maintenance of peace in the Pacific. Indeed, one hour after Japanese air squadrons had commenced bombing in the American Island of Oahu, the Japanese Ambassador to the United States and his colleague delivered to our Secretary of State a formal reply to a recent American message. And while this reply stated that it seemed useless to continue the existing diplomatic negotiations, it contained no threat or hint of war or of armed attack.

It will be recorded that the distance of Hawaii from Japan makes it obvious that the attack was deliberately planned many days or even weeks ago. During the intervening time the Japanese Government has deliberately sought to deceive the United States by false statements and expressions of hope for continued peace.

The attack yesterday on the Hawaiian Islands has caused severe damage to American naval and military forces. I regret to tell you that very many American lives have been lost. In addition

American ships have been reported torpedoed on the high seas between San Francisco and Honolulu.

Yesterday the Japanese Government also launched an attack against Malaya.

Last night Japanese forces attacked Hong Kong.

Last night Japanese forces attacked Guam.

Last night Japanese forces attacked the Philippine Islands.

Last night the Japanese attacked Wake Island.

And this morning the Japanese attacked Midway Island.

Japan has, therefore, undertaken a surprise offensive extending throughout the Pacific area. The facts of yesterday and today speak for themselves. The people of the United States have already formed their opinions and well understand the implications to the very life and safety of our nation.

As Commander-in-Chief of the Army and Navy I have directed that all measures be taken for our defense.

But always will our whole nation remember the character of the onslaught against us.

No matter how long it may take us to overcome this premeditated invasion the American people in their righteous might will win through to absolute victory.

I believe that I interpret the will of the Congress and of the people when I assert that we will not only defend ourselves to the uttermost but will make it very certain that this form of treachery shall never again endanger us.

Hostilities exist. There is no blinking at the fact that our people, our territory and our interests are in grave danger.

With confidence in our armed forces—with the unbounding determination of our people—we will gain the inevitable triumph—so help us God.

I ask that the Congress declare that since the unprovoked and dastardly attack by Japan on Sunday, December seventh 1941, a state of war has existed between the United States and the Japanese Empire.

Karl Marx and Friedrich Engels

THE COMMUNIST MANIFESTO

Karl Marx (1818-1883) and Friedrich Engels (1820-1895) worked together in 1848 to publish this manifesto of the Communist Party. It is
a summary of Marx's work to that date. Marx was adamant that capitalism be destroyed by any means necessary—a sentiment that caused
him to be an exile for much of his life. The first successful communist
revolution, in Russia, didn't occur until after Marx's death.
Nonetheless, the Manifesto remains a powerful exposition and call to
arms. As you read, try to put yourself in the position of an exploited
proletarian of the mid-19th century, and ask yourself if this document
would have been convincing to you then. Would you have been too concerned with providing your own sustenance to fight?

A spectre is haunting Europe—the spectre of Communism. All
the Powers of old Europe have entered into a holy alliance to ex-
orcise this spectre: Pope and Czar, Metternich and Guizot,
French Radicals and German police-spies.

Where is the party in opposition that has not been decried as
Communistic by its opponents in power? Where the Opposition
that has not hurled back the branding reproach of Communism,
against the more advanced opposition parties, as well as against
its reactionary adversaries?

Two things result from this fact.

I. Communism is already acknowledged by all European
Powers to be itself a Power.

II. It is high time that Communists should openly, in the face of
the whole world, publish their views, their aims, their tendencies,
and meet this nursery tale of the Spectre of Communism with a
Manifesto of the party itself.

To this end, Communists of various nationalities have assembled in London, and sketched the following Manifesto, to be published in the English, French, German, Italian, Flemish and
Danish languages.

I. BOURGEOIS AND PROLETARIANS

The history of all hitherto existing society is the history of class struggles.

Freeman and slave, patrician and plebeian, lord and serf, guild-master and journeyman, in a word, oppressor and oppressed, stood in constant opposition to one another, carried on an uninterrupted, now hidden, now open fight, a fight that each time ended, either in a revolutionary re-constitution of society at large, or in the common ruin of the contending classes.

In the earlier epochs of history, we find almost everywhere a complicated arrangement of society into various orders, a manifold gradation of social rank. In ancient Rome we have patricians, knights, plebeians, slaves; in the Middle Ages, feudal lords, vassals, guild-masters, journeymen, apprentices, serfs; in almost all of these classes, again, subordinate gradations.

The modern bourgeois society that has sprouted from the ruins of feudal society has not done away with class antagonisms. It has but established new classes, new conditions of oppression, new forms of struggle in place of the old ones.

Our epoch, the epoch of the bourgeoisie, possesses, however, this distinctive feature: it has simplified the class antagonisms: Society as a whole is more and more splitting up into two great hostile camps, into two great classes directly facing each other: Bourgeoisie and Proletariat.

From the serfs of the Middle Ages sprang the chartered burghers of the earliest towns. From these burgesses the first elements of the bourgeoisie were developed.

The discovery of America, the rounding of the Cape, opened up fresh ground for the rising bourgeoisie. The East-Indian and Chinese markets, the colonisation of America, trade with the colonies, the increase in the means of exchange and in commodities generally, gave to commerce, to navigation, to industry, an impulse never before known, and thereby, to the revolutionary element in the tottering feudal society, a rapid development.

The feudal system of industry, under which industrial production was monopolised by closed guilds, now no longer sufficed for the growing wants of the new markets. The manufacturing system took its place. The guild-masters were pushed on one side by the manufacturing middle class; division of labour between the different corporate guilds vanished in the face of division of labour in each single workshop.

Meantime the markets kept ever growing, the demand ever rising. Even manufacture no longer sufficed. Thereupon, steam and machinery revolutionised industrial production. The place of manufacture was taken by the giant, Modern Industry, the place of the industrial middle class, by industrial millionaires, the leaders of whole industrial armies, the modern bourgeois. Modern industry has established the world-market, for which the discovery of America paved the way. This market has given an immense development to commerce, to navigation, to communication by land. This development has, in its turn, reacted on the extension of industry; and in proportion as industry, commerce, navigation, railways extended, in the same proportion the bourgeoisie developed, increased its capital, and pushed into the background every class handed down from the Middle Ages.

We see, therefore, how the modern bourgeoisie is itself the product of a long course of development, of a series of revolutions in the modes of production and of exchange.

Each step in the development of the bourgeoisie was accompanied by a corresponding political advance of that class. An oppressed class under the sway of the feudal nobility, an armed and self-governing association in the mediaeval commune; here independent urban republic (as in Italy and Germany), there taxable "third estate" of the monarchy (as in France), afterwards, in the period of manufacture proper, serving either the semi-feudal or the absolute monarchy as a counterpoise against the nobility, and, in fact, corner-stone of the great monarchies in general, the bourgeoisie has at last, since the establishment of Modern Industry and of the world-market, conquered for itself, in the modern representative State, exclusive sway. The executive of the modern State is but a committee for managing the common affairs of the whole bourgeoisie.

The bourgeoisie, historically, has played a most revolutionary part.

The bourgeoisie, wherever it has got the upper hand, has put an end to all feudal, patriarchal, idyllic relations. It has pitilessly torn asunder the motley feudal ties that bound man to his "natural superiors," and has left remaining no other nexus between man and man than naked self-interest, than callous "cash payment." It has drowned the most heavenly ecstasies of religious fervour, of chivalrous enthusiasm, of philistine sentimentalism, in the icy water of egotistical calculation. It has resolved personal worth into exchange value, and in place of the numberless indefeasible

chartered freedoms, has set up that single, unconscionable freedom—Free Trade. In one word, for exploitation, veiled by religious and political illusions, it has substituted naked, shameless,
direct, brutal exploitation.

The bourgeoisie has stripped of its halo every occupation hitherto honoured and looked up to with reverent awe. It has converted the physician, the lawyer, the priest, the poet, the man of
science, into its paid wage labourers.

The bourgeoisie has torn away from the family its sentimental
veil, and has reduced the family relation to a mere money relation.

The bourgeoisie has disclosed how it came to pass that the brutal
display of vigour in the Middle Ages, which Reactionists so much
admire, found its fitting complement in the most slothful indo-
lence. It has been the first to show what man's activity can bring
about. It has accomplished wonders far surpassing Egyptian
pyramids, Roman aqueducts, and Gothic cathedrals; it has conducted expeditions that put in the shade all former Exoduses of
nations and crusades.

The bourgeoisie cannot exist without constantly revolutionising
the instruments of production, and thereby the relations of production, and with them the whole relations of society.
Conservation of the old modes of production in unaltered form,
was, on the contrary, the first condition of existence for all earlier
industrial classes. Constant revolutionising of production, uninterrupted disturbance of all social conditions, everlasting uncertainty and agitation distinguish the bourgeois epoch from all earlier ones. All fixed, fast-frozen relations, with their train of ancient
and venerable prejudices and opinions, are swept away, all new-
formed ones become antiquated before they can ossify. All that is
solid melts into air, all that is holy is profaned, and man is at last
compelled to face with sober senses, his real conditions of life, and
his relations with his kind.

The need of a constantly expanding market for its products
chases the bourgeoisie over the whole surface of the globe. It must
nestle everywhere, settle everywhere, establish connexions
everywhere.

The bourgeoisie has through its exploitation of the world-market given a cosmopolitan character to production and consumption in every country. To the great chagrin of Reactionists, it has
drawn from under the feet of industry the national ground on
which it stood. All old-established national industries have been

destroyed or are daily being destroyed. They are dislodged by new industries, whose introduction becomes a life and death question for all civilised nations, by industries that no longer work up indigenous raw material, but raw material drawn from the remotest zones; industries whose products are consumed, not only at home, but in every quarter of the globe. In place of the old wants, satisfied by the productions of the country, we find new wants, requiring for their satisfaction the products of distant lands and climes. In place of the old local and national seclusion and self-sufficiency, we have intercourse in every direction, universal inter-dependence of nations. And as in material, so also in intellectual production. The intellectual creations of individual nations become common property. National one-sidedness and narrow-mindedness become more and more impossible, and from the numerous national and local literatures, there arises a world literature.

The bourgeoisie, by the rapid improvement of all instruments of production, by the immensely facilitated means of communication, draws all, even the most barbarian, nations into civilisation. The cheap prices of its commodities are the heavy artillery with which it batters down all Chinese walls, with which it forces the barbarians' intensely obstinate hatred of foreigners to capitulate. It compels all nations, on pain of extinction, to adopt the bourgeois mode of production; it compels them to introduce what it calls civilisation into their midst, i.e., to become bourgeois themselves. In one word, it creates a world after its own image.

The bourgeoisie has subjected the country to the rule of the towns. It has created enormous cities, has greatly increased the urban population as compared with the rural, and has thus rescued a considerable part of the population from the idiocy of rural life. Just as it has made the country dependent on the towns, so it has made barbarian and semi-barbarian countries dependent on the civilised ones, nations and peasants on nations of bourgeois, the East on the West.

The bourgeoisie keeps more and more doing away with the scattered state of the population, of the means of production, and of property. It has agglomerated population, centralised means of production, and has concentrated property in a few hands. The necessary consequence of this was political centralisation. Independent, or but loosely connected provinces, with separate interests, laws, governments and systems of taxation, became lumped together into one nation, with one government, one code of laws, one national class-interest, one frontier and one customs-tariff. The bourgeoisie, during its rule of scarce one hundred years, has created more massive and more colossal productive forces than have all preceding generations together. Subjection of Nature's forces to man, machinery, application of chemistry to industry and agriculture, steam-navigation, railways, electric telegraphs, clearing of whole continents for cultivation, canalisation of rivers, whole populations conjured out of the ground—what earlier century had even a presentiment that such productive forces slumbered in the lap of social labour?

We see then: the means of production and of exchange, on whose foundation the bourgeoisie built itself up, were generated in feudal society. At a certain stage in the development of these means of production and of exchange, the conditions under which feudal society produced and exchanged, the feudal organisation of agriculture and manufacturing industry, in one word, the feudal relations of property became no longer compatible with the already developed productive forces; they became so many fetters. They had to be burst asunder; they were burst asunder.

Into their place stepped free competition, accompanied by a social and political constitution adapted to it, and by the economical and political sway of the bourgeois class.

A similar movement is going on before our own eyes. Modern bourgeois society with its relations of production, of exchange and of property, a society that has conjured up such gigantic means of production and of exchange, is like the sorcerer, who is no longer able to control the powers of the nether world whom he has called up by his spells. For many a decade past the history of industry and commerce is but the history of the revolt of modern productive forces against modern conditions of production, against the property relations that are the conditions for the existence of the bourgeoisie and of its rule. It is enough to mention the commercial crises that by their periodical return put on its trial, each time more threateningly, the existence of the entire bourgeois society. In these crises a great part not only of the existing products, but also of the previously created productive forces, are periodically destroyed. In these crises there breaks out an epidemic that, in all earlier epochs, would have seemed an absurdity—the epidemic of over-production. Society suddenly finds itself put back into a state of momentary barbarism; it appears as if a famine, a universal war of devastation had cut off the supply of every means of subsistence; industry and commerce seem to be destroyed; and why?

Because there is too much civilisation, too much means of subsistence, too much industry, too much commerce. The productive forces at the disposal of society no longer tend to further the development of the conditions of bourgeois property; on the contrary, they have become too powerful for these conditions, by which they are fettered, and so soon as they overcome these fetters, they bring disorder into the whole of bourgeois society, endanger the existence of bourgeois property. The conditions of bourgeois society are too narrow to comprise the wealth created by them. And how does the bourgeoisie get over these crises? On the one hand by enforced destruction of a mass of productive forces; on the other, by the conquest of new markets, and by the more thorough exploitation of the old ones. That is to say, by paving the way for more extensive and more destructive crises, and by diminishing the means whereby crises are prevented.

The weapons with which the bourgeoisie felled feudalism to the ground are now turned against the bourgeoisie itself.

But not only has the bourgeoisie forged the weapons that bring death to itself; it has also called into existence the men who are to wield those weapons—the modern working class—the proletarians.

In proportion as the bourgeoisie, *i.e.,* capital, is developed, in the same proportion is the proletariat, the modern working class, developed—a class of labourers, who live only so long as they find work, and who find work only so long as their labour increases capital. These labourers, who must sell themselves piece-meal, are a commodity, like every other article of commerce, and are consequently exposed to all the vicissitudes of competition, to all the fluctuations of the market. STEADY JOB & STEADY PAY

Owing to the extensive use of machinery and to division of labour, the work of the proletarians has lost all individual character, and consequently, all charm for the workman. He becomes an appendage of the machine, and it is only the most simple, most monotonous, and most easily acquired knack, that is required of him. Hence, the cost of production of a workman is restricted, almost entirely, to the means of subsistence that he requires for his maintenance, and for the propagation of his race. But the price of a commodity, and therefore also of labour, is equal to its cost of production. In proportion, therefore, as the repulsiveness of the work increases, the wage decreases. Nay more, in proportion as the use of machinery and division of labour increases, in the same proportion the burden of toil also increases, whether by prolonga-

PEOPLE RELATE TO THIS BECAUSE AT THIS POINT THAT'S ALL THEY ARE

tion of the working hours, by increase of the work exacted in a given time or by increased speed of the machinery, etc.

Modern industry has converted the little workshop of the patriarchal master into the great factory of the industrial capitalist. Masses of labourers, crowded into the factory, are organised like soldiers. As privates of the industrial army they are placed under the command of a perfect hierarchy of officers and sergeants. Not only are they slaves of the bourgeois class, and of the bourgeois State; they are daily and hourly enslaved by the machine, by the over-looker, and, above all, by the individual bourgeois manufacturer himself. The more openly this despotism proclaims gain to be its end and aim, the more petty, the more hateful and the more embittering it is. CAPITALISM IS UNDESIRABLE

The less the skill and exertion of strength implied in manual labour, in other words, the more modern industry becomes developed, the more is the labour of men superseded by that of women. Differences of age and sex have no longer any distinctive social validity for the working class. All are instruments of labour, more or less expensive to use, according to their age and sex.

No sooner is the exploitation of the labourer by the manufacturer, so far, at an end, that he receives his wages in cash, than he is set upon by the other portions of the bourgeoisie, the landlord, the shopkeeper, the pawnbroker, etc.

The lower strata of the middle class—the small tradespeople, shopkeepers, and retired tradesmen generally, the handicraftsmen and peasants—all these sink gradually into the proletariat, partly because their diminutive capital does not suffice for the scale on which Modern Industry is carried on, and is swamped in the competition with the large capitalists, partly because their specialised skill is rendered worthless by new methods of production. Thus the proletariat is recruited from all classes of the population. PEOPLE RELATE → DRAWS IN OLD PEOPLE, PEASANTS, CRAFTSMAN

The proletariat goes through various stages of development. With its birth begins its struggle with the bourgeoisie. At first the contest is carried on by individual labourers, then by the workpeople of a factory, then by the operatives of one trade, in one locality, against the individual bourgeois who directly exploits them. They direct their attacks not against the bourgeois conditions of production, but against the instruments of production themselves; they destroy imported wares that compete with their labour, they smash to pieces machinery, they set factories ablaze, they seek to restore by force the vanished status of the workman of the Middle Ages.

At this stage the labourers still form an incoherent mass scattered over the whole country, and broken up by their mutual competition. If anywhere they unite to form more compact bodies, this is not yet the consequence of their own active union, but of the union of the bourgeoisie, which class, in order to attain its own political ends, is compelled to set the whole proletariat in motion, and is moreover yet, for a time, able to do so. At this stage, therefore, the proletarians do not fight their enemies, but the enemies of their enemies, the remnants of absolute monarchy, the landowners, the non-industrial bourgeois, the petty bourgeoisie. Thus the whole historical movement is concentrated in the hands of the bourgeoisie; every victory so obtained is a victory for the bourgeoisie.

But with the development of industry the proletariat not only increases in number; it becomes concentrated in greater masses, its strength grows, and it feels that strength more. The various interests and conditions of life within the ranks of the proletariat are more and more equalised, in proportion as machinery obliterates all distinctions of labour, and nearly everywhere reduces wages to the same low level. The growing competition among the bourgeois, and the resulting commercial crises, make the wages of the workers ever more fluctuating. The unceasing improvement of machinery, ever more rapidly developing, makes their livelihood more and more precarious; the collisions between individual workmen and individual bourgeois take more and more the character of collisions between two classes. Thereupon the workers begin to form combinations (Trades Unions) against the bourgeois; they club together in order to keep up the rate of wages; they found permanent associations in order to make provision beforehand for these occasional revolts. Here and there the contest breaks out into riots.

Now and then the workers are victorious, but only for a time. The real fruit of their battles lies, not in the immediate result, but in the ever-expanding union of the workers. This union is helped on by the improved means of communication that are created by modern industry and that place the workers of different localities in contact with one another. It was just this contact that was needed to centralise the numerous local struggles, all of the same character, into one national struggle between classes. But every class struggle is a political struggle. And that union, to attain which the burghers of the Middle Ages, with their miserable highways, required centuries, the modern proletarians, thanks to railways, achieve in a few years.

This organisation of the proletarians into a class, and consequently into a political party, is continually being upset again by the competition between the workers themselves. But it ever rises up again, stronger, firmer, mightier. It compels legislative recognition of particular interests of the workers, by taking advantage of the divisions among the bourgeoisie itself. Thus the ten-hours' bill in England was carried.

Altogether collisions between the classes of the old society further, in many ways, the course of development of the proletariat. The bourgeoisie finds itself involved in a constant battle. At first with the aristocracy; later on, with those portions of the bourgeoisie itself, whose interests have become antagonistic to the progress of industry; at all times, with the bourgeoisie of foreign countries. In all these battles it sees itself compelled to appeal to the proletariat, to ask for its help, and thus, to drag it into the political arena. The bourgeoisie itself, therefore, supplies the proletariat with its own elements of political and general education, in other words, it furnishes the proletariat with weapons for fighting the bourgeoisie.

Further, as we have already seen, entire sections of the ruling classes are, by the advance of industry, precipitated into the proletariat, or are at least threatened in their conditions of existence. These also supply the proletariat with fresh elements of enlightenment and progress.

Finally, in times when the class struggle nears the decisive hour, the process of dissolution going on within the ruling class, in fact within the whole range of society, assumes such a violent, glaring character, that a small section of the ruling class cuts itself adrift, and joins the revolutionary class, the class that holds the future in its hands. Just as, therefore, at an earlier period, a section of the nobility went over to the bourgeoisie, so now a portion of the bourgeoisie goes over to the proletariat, and in particular, a portion of the bourgeois ideologists, who have raised themselves to the level of comprehending theoretically the historical movement as a whole.

Of all the classes that stand face to face with the bourgeoisie today, the proletariat alone is a really revolutionary class. The other classes decay and finally disappear in the face of Modern Industry; the proletariat is its special and essential product.

The lower middle class, the small manufacturer, the shop-keeper, the artisan, the peasant, all these fight against the bourgeoisie, to save from extinction their existence as fractions of the middle class. They are therefore not revolutionary, but conservative. Nay more, they are reactionary, for they try to roll back the wheel of history. If by chance they are revolutionary, they are so only in view of their impending transfer into the proletariat, they thus defend not their present, but their future interests, they desert their own standpoint to place themselves at that of the proletariat.

The "dangerous class," the social scum, that passively rotting mass thrown off by the lowest layers of old society, may, here and there, be swept into the movement by a proletarian revolution; its conditions of life, however, prepare it far more for the part of a bribed tool of reactionary intrigue.

In the conditions of the proletariat, those of old society at large are already virtually swamped. The proletarian is without property; his relation to his wife and children has no longer anything in common with the bourgeois family-relations; modern industrial labour, modern subjection to capital, the same in England as in France, in America as in Germany, has stripped him of every trace of national character. Law, morality, religion, are to him so many bourgeois prejudices, behind which lurk in ambush just as many bourgeois interests.

All the preceding classes that got the upper hand, sought to fortify their already acquired status by subjecting society at large to their conditions of appropriation. The proletarians cannot become masters of the productive forces of society, except by abolishing their own previous mode of appropriation, and thereby also every other previous mode of appropriation. They have nothing of their own to secure and to fortify; their mission is to destroy all previous securities for, and insurances of, individual property.

All previous historical movements were movements of minorities, or in the interests of minorities. The proletarian movement is the self-conscious, independent movement of the immense majority, in the interests of the immense majority. The proletariat, the lowest stratum of our present society, cannot stir, cannot raise itself up, without the whole superincumbent strata of official society being sprung into the air.

Though not in substance, yet in form, the struggle of the proletariat with the bourgeoisie is at first a national struggle. The proletariat of each country must, of course, first of all settle matters with its own bourgeoisie.

In depicting the most general phases of the development of the proletariat, we traced the more or less veiled civil war, raging within existing society, up to the point where that war breaks out into open revolution, and where the violent overthrow of the bourgeoisie lays the foundation for the sway of the proletariat.

Hitherto, every form of society has been based, as we have already seen, on the antagonism of oppressing and oppressed classes. But in order to oppress a class, certain conditions must be assured to it under which it can, at least, continue its slavish existence. The serf, in the period of serfdom, raised himself to membership in the commune, just as the petty bourgeois, under the yoke of feudal absolutism, managed to develop into a bourgeois. The modern labourer, on the contrary, instead of rising with the progress of industry, sinks deeper and deeper below the conditions of existence of his own class. He becomes a pauper, and pauperism develops more rapidly than population and wealth. And here it becomes evident, that the bourgeoisie is unfit any longer to be the ruling class in society, and to impose its conditions of existence upon society as an over-riding law. It is unfit to rule because it is incompetent to assure an existence to its slave within his slavery, because it cannot help letting him sink into such a state, that it has to feed him, instead of being fed by him. Society can no longer live under this bourgeoisie, in other words, its existence is no longer compatible with society.

The essential condition for the existence, and for the sway of the bourgeois class, is the formation and augmentation of capital; the condition for capital is wage-labour. Wage-labour rests exclusively on competition between the labourers. The advance of industry, whose involuntary promoter is the bourgeoisie, replaces the isolation of the labourers, due to competition, by their revolutionary combination, due to association. The development of Modern Industry, therefore, cuts from under its feet the very foundation on which the bourgeoisie produces and appropriates products. What the bourgeoisie, therefore, produces, above all, is its own grave-diggers. Its fall and the victory of the proletariat are equally inevitable.

In the beginning of part II, not included here, Marx and Engels discuss the following measures which the Communist party wishes to enact, primary among them the abolition of private property.

These measures will of course be different in different countries. Nevertheless in the most advanced countries, the following will be pretty generally applicable.

1. Abolition of property in land and application of all rents of land to public purposes.

2. A heavy progressive or graduated income tax.

3. Abolition of all right of inheritance.

4. Confiscation of the property of all emigrants and rebels.

5. Centralisation of credit in the hands of the State, by means of a national bank with State capital and an exclusive monopoly.

6. Centralisation of the means of communication and transport in the hands of the State.

7. Extension of factories and instruments of production owned by the State; the bringing into cultivation of waste-lands, and the improvement of the soil generally in accordance with a common plan.

8. Equal liability of all to labour. Establishment of industrial armies, especially for agriculture.

9. Combination of agriculture with manufacturing industries; gradual abolition of the distinction between town and country, by a more equable distribution of the population over the country.

10. Free education for all children in public schools. Abolition of children's factory labour in its present form. Combination of education with industrial production, &c., &c.

When, in the course of development, class distinctions have disappeared, and all production has been concentrated in the hands of a vast association of the whole nation, the public power will lose its political character. Political power, properly so called, is merely the organised power of one class for oppressing another. If the proletariat during its contest with the bourgeoisie is compelled, by the force of circumstances, to organise itself as a class, if, by means of a revolution, it makes itself the ruling class, and, as such, sweeps away by force the old conditions of production, then it will, along with these conditions, have swept away the conditions for the existence of class antagonisms and of classes generally, and will thereby have abolished its own supremacy as a class.

In place of the old bourgeois society, with its classes and class antagonisms, we shall have an association, in which the free development of each is the condition for the free development of all.

In section III, not included here, Marx and Engels dismiss other socialist movements because they all do not incorporate the type of change that Marx and Engels favor.

IV. POSITION OF THE COMMUNISTS IN RELATION TO THE VARIOUS EXISTING OPPOSITION PARTIES

Section II has made clear the relations of the Communists to the existing working-class parties, such as the Chartists in England and the Agrarian Reformers in America.

The Communists fight for the attainment of the immediate aims, for the enforcement of the momentary interests of the working class; but in the movement of the present, they also represent and take care of the future of that movement. In France the Communists ally themselves with the Social-Democrats, against the conservative and radical bourgeoisie, reserving, however, the right to take up a critical position in regard to phrases and illusions traditionally handed down from the great Revolution.

In Switzerland they support the Radicals, without losing sight of the fact that this party consists of antagonistic elements, partly of Democratic Socialists, in the French sense, partly of radical bourgeois.

In Poland they support the party that insists on an agrarian revolution as the prime condition for national emancipation, that party which fomented the insurrection of Cracow in 1846.

In Germany they fight with the bourgeoisie whenever it acts in a revolutionary way, against the absolute monarchy, the feudal squirearchy, and the petty bourgeoisie.

But they never cease, for a single instant, to instil into the working class the clearest possible recognition of the hostile antagonism between bourgeoisie and proletariat, in order that the German workers may straightway use, as so many weapons against the bourgeoisie, the social and political conditions that the bourgeoisie must necessarily introduce along with its supremacy, and in order that, after the fall of the reactionary classes in Germany, the fight against the bourgeoisie itself may immediately begin.

The Communists turn their attention chiefly to Germany, because that country is on the eve of a bourgeois revolution that is bound to be carried out under more advanced conditions of European civilisation, and with a much more developed proletariat, than that of England was in the seventeenth, and of France in the eighteenth century, and because the bourgeois revolution in Germany will be but the prelude to an immediately following proletarian revolution.

In short, the Communists everywhere support every revolutionary movement against the existing social and political order of things.

In all these movements they bring to the front, as the leading question in each, the property question, no matter what its degree of development at the time.

Finally, they labour everywhere for the union and agreement of the democratic parties of all countries.

The Communists disdain to conceal their views and aims. They openly declare that their ends can be attained only by the forcible overthrow of all existing social conditions. Let the ruling classes tremble at a Communistic revolution. The proletarians have nothing to lose but their chains. They have a world to win.

WORKING MEN OF ALL COUNTRIES, UNITE!

Martin Luther King, Jr.

LETTER FROM BIRMINGHAM JAIL*

Martin Luther King, Jr. (1929-1968), minister, orator, and civil rights leader, was inspired by Thoreau and Gandhi to use non-violent civil disobedience as a means to gain equality for blacks. This letter, composed while in prison for just such a protest, is perhaps the definitive, and certainly the most stirring statement of his non-violent philosophy. As you read this letter, ask yourself if King's philosophy of non-violence would have been effective in other situations addressed

---

* This response to a published statement by eight fellow clergymen from Alabama (Bishop C.C.J Carpenter, Bishop Joseph A. Durick, Rabbi Milton L. Grafman, Bishop Paul Hardin, Bishop Holan B. Harmon, the Reverend George M. Murray, the Reverend Edward V. Ramage, and the Reverend Earl Stallings) was composed under somewhat constricting circumstances. Begun on the margins of the newspaper in which the statement appeared while I was in jail, the letter was continued on scraps of writing paper supplied by a friendly Negro trusty, and concluded on a pad my attorneys were eventually permitted to leave me. Although the text remains in substance unaltered, I have indulged in the author's prerogative of polishing it for publication.

in this chapter. Why was it so effective in the black civil rights movement?

MY DEAR FELLOW CLERGYMEN:

While confined here in the Birmingham city jail, I came across your recent statement calling my present activities "unwise and untimely." Seldom do I pause to answer criticism of my work and ideas. If I sought to answer all the criticisms that cross my desk, my secretaries would have little time for anything other than such correspondence in the course of the day, and I would have no time for constructive work. But since I feel that you are men of genuine good will and that your criticisms are sincerely set forth, I want to try to answer your statement in what I hope will be patient and reasonable terms.

I think I should indicate why I am here in Birmingham, since you have been influenced by the view which argues against "outsiders coming in." I have the honor of serving as president of the Southern Christian Leadership Conference, an organization operating in every southern state, with headquarters in Atlanta, Georgia. We have some eighty-five affiliated organizations across the South, and one of them is the Alabama Christian Movement for Human Rights. Frequently we share staff, educational, and financial resources with our affiliates. Several months ago the affiliate here in Birmingham asked us to be on call to engage in a nonviolent direct-action program if such were deemed necessary. We readily consented, and when the hour came we lived up to our promise. So I, along with several members of my staff, am here because I was invited here. I am here because I have organizational ties here.

But more basically, I am in Birmingham because injustice is here. Just as the prophets of the eighth century B.C. left their villages and carried their "thus saith the Lord" far beyond the boundaries of their home towns, and just as the Apostle Paul left his village of Tarsus and carried the gospel of Jesus Christ to the far corners of the Greco-Roman world, so am I compelled to carry the gospel of freedom beyond my own home town. Like Paul, I must constantly respond to the Macedonian call for aid.

Moreover, I am cognizant of the interrelatedness of all communities and states. I cannot sit idly by in Atlanta and not be concerned about what happens in Birmingham. Injustice anywhere is a threat to justice everywhere. We are caught in an inescapable network of mutuality, tied in a single garment of destiny.

Whatever affects one directly, affects all indirectly. Never again can we afford to live with the narrow, provincial "outside agitator" idea. Anyone who lives inside the United States can never be considered an outsider anywhere within its bounds.

You deplore the demonstrations taking place in Birmingham. But your statement, I am sorry to say, fails to express a similar concern for the conditions that brought about the demonstrations. I am sure that none of you would want to rest content with the superficial kind of social analysis that deals merely with effects and does not grapple with underlying causes. It is unfortunate that demonstrations are taking place in Birmingham, but it is even more unfortunate that the city's white power structure left the Negro community with no alternative.

In any nonviolent campaign there are four basic steps: collection of the facts to determine whether injustices exist; negotiation; self-purification; and direct action. We have gone through all these steps in Birmingham. There can be no gainsaying the fact that racial injustice engulfs this community. Birmingham is probably the most thoroughly segregated city in the United States. Its ugly record of brutality is widely known. Negroes have experienced grossly unjust treatment in the courts. There have been more unsolved bombings of Negro homes and churches in Birmingham than in any other city in the nation. These are the hard, brutal facts of the case. On the basis of these conditions, Negro leaders sought to negotiate with the city fathers. But the latter consistently refused to engage in good-faith negotiation.

Then, last September, came the opportunity to talk with leaders of Birmingham's economic community. In the course of the negotiations, certain promises were made by the merchants—for example, to remove the stores' humiliating racial signs. On the basis of these promises, the Reverend Fred Shuttlesworth and the leaders of the Alabama Christian Movement for Human Rights agreed to a moratorium on all demonstrations. As the weeks and months went by, we realized that we were the victims of a broken promise. A few signs, briefly removed, returned; the others remained.

As in so many past experiences, our hopes had been blasted, and the shadow of deep disappointment settled upon us. We had no alternative except to prepare for direct action, whereby we would present our very bodies as a means of laying our case before the conscience of the local and the national community. Mindful of the difficulties involved, we decided to undertake a process of self-purification. We began a series of workshops on nonviolence, and we repeatedly asked ourselves: "Are you able to accept blows without retaliating?" "Are you able to endure the ordeal of jail?" We decided to schedule our direct-action program for the Easter season, realizing that except for Christmas, this is the main shopping period of the year. Knowing that a strong economic-withdrawal program would be the by-product of direct action, we felt that this would be the best time to bring pressure to bear on the merchants for the needed change.

Then it occurred to us that Birmingham's mayoral election was coming up in March, and we speedily decided to postpone action until after election day. When we discovered that the Commissioner of Public Safety, Eugene "Bull" Connor, had piled up enough votes to be in the run-off, we decided again to postpone action until the day after the runoff so that the demonstrations could not be used to cloud the issues. Like many others, we wanted to see Mr. Connor defeated, and to this end we endured postponement after postponement. Having aided in this community need, we felt that our direct-action program could be delayed no longer.

You may well ask, "Why direct action? Why sit-ins, marches, and so forth? Isn't negotiation a better path?" You are quite right in calling for negotiation. Indeed, this is the very purpose of direct action. Nonviolent direct action seeks to create such a crisis and foster such a tension that a community which has constantly refused to negotiate is forced to confront the issue. It seeks so to dramatize the issue that it can no longer be ignored. My citing the creation of tension as part of the work of the nonviolent-resister may sound rather shocking. But I must confess that I am not afraid of the word "tension." I have earnestly opposed violent tension, but there is a type of constructive, nonviolent tension which is necessary for growth. Just as Socrates felt that it was necessary to create a tension in the mind so that individuals could rise from the bondage of myths and half-truths to the unfettered realm of creative analysis and objective appraisal, so must we see the need for nonviolent gadflies to create the kind of tension in society that will help men rise from the dark depths of prejudice and racism to the majestic heights of understanding and brotherhood.

The purpose of our direct-action program is to create a situation so crisis-packed that it will inevitably open the door to negotiation. I therefore concur with you in your call for negotiation. Too long has our beloved Southland been bogged down in a tragic effort to live in monologue rather than dialogue.

One of the basic points in your statement is that the action that I and my associates have taken in Birmingham is untimely. Some have asked: "Why didn't you give the new city administration time to act?" The only answer that I can give to this query is that the new Birmingham administration must be prodded about as much as the outgoing one, before it will act. We are sadly mistaken if we feel that the election of Albert Boutwell as mayor will bring the millennium to Birmingham. While Mr. Boutwell is a much more gentle person than Mr. Connor, they are both segregationists, dedicated to maintenance of the status quo. I have hoped that Mr. Boutwell will be reasonable enough to see the futility of massive resistance to desegregation. But he will not see this without pressure from devotees of civil rights. My friends, I must say to you that we have not made a single gain in civil rights without determined legal and nonviolent pressure. Lamentably, it is an historical fact that privileged groups seldom give up their privileges voluntarily. Individuals may see the moral light and voluntarily give up their unjust posture; but, as Reinhold Niebuhr has reminded us, groups tend to be more immoral than individuals.

We know through painful experience that freedom is never voluntarily given by the oppressor; it must be demanded by the oppressed. Frankly, I have yet to engage in a direct-action campaign that was "well timed" in the view of those who have not suffered unduly from the disease of segregation. For years now I have heard the word "Wait!" It rings in the ear of every Negro with piercing familiarity. This "Wait" has almost always meant "Never." We must come to see, with one of our distinguished jurists, that "justice too long delayed is justice denied."

We have waited for more than 340 years for our constitutional and God-given rights. The nations of Asia and Africa are moving with jetlike speed toward gaining political independence, but we still creep at horse-and-buggy pace toward gaining a cup of coffee at a lunch counter. Perhaps it is easy for those who have never felt the stinging darts of segregation to say, "Wait." But when you have seen vicious mobs lynch your mothers and fathers at will and drown your sisters and brothers at whim; when you have seen hate-filled policemen curse, kick, and even kill your black brothers and sisters; when you see the vast majority of your twenty million Negro brothers smothering in an airtight cage of poverty in the midst of an affluent society; when you suddenly find your tongue twisted and your speech stammering as you seek to explain to your six-year-old daughter why she can't go to the public amusement park that has just been advertised on television, and see tears welling up in her eyes when she is told that Funtown is closed to colored children, and see ominous clouds of inferiority beginning to form in her little mental sky, and see her beginning to distort her personality by developing an unconscious bitterness toward white people; when you have to concoct an answer for a five-year-old son who is asking, "Daddy, why do white people treat colored people so mean?"; when you take a cross-country drive and find it necessary to sleep night after night in the uncomfortable corners of your automobile because no motel will accept you; when you are humiliated day in and day out by nagging signs "white" and "colored"; when your first name becomes "nigger," your middle name becomes "boy" (however old you are) and your last name becomes "John," and your wife and mother are never given the respected title "Mrs."; when you are harried by day and haunted by night by the fact that you are a Negro, living constantly at tiptoe stance, never quite knowing what to expect next, and are plagued with inner fears and outer resentments; when you are forever fighting a degenerating sense of "nobodiness"—then you will understand why we find it difficult to wait. There comes a time when the cup of endurance runs over, and men are no longer willing to be plunged into the abyss of despair. I hope, sirs, you can understand our legitimate and unavoidable impatience.

You express a great deal of anxiety over our willingness to break laws. This is certainly a legitimate concern. Since we so diligently urge people to obey the Supreme Court's decision of 1954 outlawing segregation in the public schools, at first glance it may seem rather paradoxical for us consciously to break laws. One may well ask: "How can you advocate breaking some laws and obeying others?" The answer lies in the fact that there are two types of laws: just and unjust. I would be the first to advocate obeying just laws. One has not only a legal but a moral responsibility to obey just laws. Conversely, one has a moral responsibility to disobey unjust laws. I would agree with St. Augustine that "an unjust law is no law at all."

Now, what is the difference between the two? How does one determine whether a law is just or unjust? A just law is a man-made code that squares with the moral law or the law of God. An unjust law is a code this is out of harmony with the moral law. To put it in the terms of St. Thomas Aquinas: An unjust law is a human law that is not rooted in eternal law and natural law. Any law that uplifts human personality is just. Any law that degrades human personality is unjust. All segregation statutes are unjust because segregation distorts the soul and damages the personality. It gives the segregator a false sense of superiority and the segregated a false sense of inferiority. Segregation, to use the terminology of the Jewish philosopher Martin Buber, substitutes an "I-it" relationship for an "I-thou" relationship and ends up relegating persons to the status of things. Hence segregation is not only politically, economically, and sociologically unsound, it is morally wrong and sinful. Paul Tillich has said that sin is separation. Is not segregation an existential expression of man's tragic separation, his awful estrangement, his terrible sinfulness? Thus it is that I can urge men to obey the 1954 decision of the Supreme Court, for it is morally right; and I can urge them to disobey segregation ordinances, for they are morally wrong.

Let us consider a more concrete example of just and unjust laws. An unjust law is a code that a numerical or power majority group compels a minority group to obey but does not make binding on itself. This is difference made legal. By the same token, a just law is a code that a majority compels a minority to follow and that it is willing to follow itself. This is sameness made legal.

Let me give another explanation. A law is unjust if it is inflicted on a minority that, as a result of being denied the right to vote, had no part in enacting or devising the law. Who can say that the legislature of Alabama which set up that state's segregation laws was democratically elected? Throughout Alabama all sorts of devious methods are used to prevent Negroes from becoming registered voters, and there are some counties in which, even though Negroes constitute a majority of the population, not a single Negro is registered. Can any law enacted under such circumstances be considered democratically structured?

Sometimes a law is just on its face and unjust in its application. For instance, I have been arrested on a charge of parading without a permit. Now, there is nothing wrong in having an ordinance which requires a permit for a parade. But such an ordinance becomes unjust when it is used to maintain segregation and to deny citizens the First-Amendment privilege of peaceful assembly and protest.

I hope you are able to see the distinction I am trying to point out. In no sense do I advocate evading or defying the law, as would the rabid segregationist. That would lead to anarchy. One who breaks an unjust law must do so openly, lovingly, and with a willingness to accept the penalty. I submit that an individual who breaks a law that conscience tells him is unjust, and who willingly accepts the penalty of imprisonment in order to arouse the conscience of the community over its injustice, is in reality expressing the highest respect for law.

Of course, there is nothing new about this kind of civil disobedience. It was evidenced sublimely in the refusal of Shadrach, Meshach, and Abednego to obey the laws of Nebuchadnezzar, on the ground that a higher moral law was at stake. It was practiced superbly by the early Christians, who were willing to face hungry lions and the excruciating pain of chopping blocks rather than submit to certain unjust laws of the Roman Empire. To a degree, academic freedom is a reality today because Socrates practiced civil disobedience. In our own nation, the Boston Tea Party represented a massive act of civil disobedience.

We should never forget that everything Adolf Hitler did in Germany was "legal" and everything the Hungarian freedom fighters did in Hungary was "illegal." It was "illegal" to aid and comfort a Jew in Hitler's Germany. Even so, I am sure that, had I lived in Germany at the time, I would have aided and comforted my Jewish brothers. If today I lived in a Communist country where certain principles dear to the Christian faith are suppressed, I would openly advocate disobeying that country's anti-religious laws.

I must make two honest confessions to you, my Christian and Jewish brothers. First, I must confess that over the past few years I have been gravely disappointed with the white moderate. I have almost reached the regrettable conclusion that the Negro's great stumbling block in his stride toward freedom is not the White Citizen's Counciler or the Ku Klux Klanner, but the white moderate, who is more devoted to "order" than to justice; who prefers a negative peace which is the absence of tension to a positive peace which is the presence of justice, who constantly says, "I agree with you in the goal you seek, but I cannot agree with your methods of direct action"; who paternalistically believes he can set the timetable for another man's freedom; who lives by a mythical concept of time and who constantly advises the Negro to wait for a "more convenient season." Shallow understanding from people of good will is more frustrating than absolute misunderstanding from people of ill will. Lukewarm acceptance is much more bewildering than outright rejection.

I had hoped that the white moderate would understand that law and order exist for the purpose of establishing justice and that when they fail in this purpose they become the dangerously structured dams that block the flow of social progress. I had hoped that the white moderate would understand that the present tension in the South is a necessary phase of the transition from an obnoxious negative peace, in which the Negro passively accepted his unjust plight, to a substantive and positive peace, in which all men will respect the dignity and worth of human personality. Actually, we who engage in nonviolent direct action are not the creators of tension. We merely bring to the surface the hidden tension that is already alive. We bring it out in the open, where it can be seen and dealt with. Like a boil that can never be cured so long as it is covered up but must be opened with all its ugliness to the natural medicines of air and light, injustice must be exposed, with all the tension its exposure creates, to the light of human conscience and the air of national opinion, before it can be cured.

In your statement you assert that our actions, even though peaceful, must be condemned because they precipitate violence. But is this a logical assertion? Isn't this like condemning a robbed man because his possession of money precipitated the evil act of robbery? Isn't this like condemning Socrates because his unswerving commitment to truth and his philosophical inquiries precipitated the act by the misguided populace in which they made him drink hemlock? Isn't this like condemning Jesus because his unique God-consciousness and never-ceasing devotion to God's will precipitated the evil act of crucifixion? We must come to see that, as the federal courts have consistently affirmed, it is wrong to urge an individual to cease his efforts to gain his basic constitutional rights because the quest may precipitate violence. Society must protect the robbed and punish the robber.

I had also hoped that the white moderate would reject the myth concerning time in relation to the struggle for freedom. I have just received a letter from a white brother in Texas. He writes: "All Christians know that the colored people will receive equal rights eventually, but it is possible that you are in too great a religious hurry. It has taken Christianity almost two thousand years to accomplish what it has. The teachings of Christ take time to come to earth." Such an attitude stems from a tragic misconception of time, from the strangely irrational notion that there is something in the very flow of time that will inevitably cure all ills. Actually, time itself is neutral; it can be used either destructively or constructively. More and more I feel that the people of ill will have used time much more effectively than have the people of good will. We will have to repent in this generation not merely for the hateful words and actions of the bad people, but for the appalling silence of the good people. Human progress never rolls in on wheels of inevitability; it comes through the tireless efforts of men willing to be co-workers with God, and without this hard work, time itself becomes an ally of the forces of social stagnation. We must use time creatively, in the knowledge that the time is always ripe to do right. Now is the time to make real the promise of democracy and transform our pending national elegy into a creative psalm of brotherhood. Now is the time to lift our national policy from the quicksand of racial injustice to the solid rock of human dignity.

You speak of our activity in Birmingham as extreme. At first I was rather disappointed that fellow clergymen would see my nonviolent efforts as those of an extremist. I began thinking about the fact that I stand in the middle of two opposing forces in the Negro community. One is a force of complacency, made up in part of Negroes who, as a result of long years of oppression, are so drained of self-respect and a sense of "somebodiness" that they have adjusted to segregation; and in part of a few middle-class Negroes who, because of a degree of academic and economic security and because in some ways they profit by segregation, have become insensitive to the problems of the masses. The other force is one of bitterness and hatred, and it comes perilously close to advocating violence. It is expressed in the various black nationalist groups that are springing up across the nation, the largest and best-known being Elijah Muhammad's Muslim movement. Nourished by the Negro's frustration over the continued existence of racial discrimination, this movement is made up of people who have lost faith in America, who have absolutely repudiated Christianity, and who have concluded that the white man is an incorrigible "devil."

I have tried to stand between these two forces, saying that we need emulate neither the "do-nothingism" of the complacent nor the hatred and despair of the black nationalist. For there is the more excellent way of love and nonviolent protest. I am grateful to

God that, through the influence of the Negro church, the way of nonviolence became an integral part of our struggle.

If this philosophy had not emerged, by now many streets of the South would, I am convinced, be flowing with blood. And I am further convinced that if our white brothers dismiss as "rabblerousers" and "outside agitators" those of use who employ nonviolent direct action, and if they refuse to support our non-violent efforts, millions of Negroes will, out of frustration and de-spair, seek solace and security in black-nationalist ideologies—a development that would inevitably lead to a frightening racial nightmare.

Oppressed people cannot remain oppressed forever. The yearning for freedom eventually manifests itself, and that is what has happened to the American Negro. Something within has re-minded him of his birthright of freedom, and something without has reminded him that it can be gained. Consciously or uncon-sciously, he has been caught up by the Zeitgeist, and with his black brothers of Africa and his brown and yellow brothers of Asia, South America, and the Caribbean, the United States Negro is moving with a sense of great urgency toward the promised land of racial justice. If one recognizes this vital urge that has engulfed the Negro community, one should readily understand why public demonstrations are taking place. The Negro has many pent-up resentments and latent frustrations, and he must release them. So let him march; let him make prayer pilgrimages to the city hall; let him go on freedom rides—and try to understand why he must do so. If his repressed emotions are not released in nonviolent ways, they will seek expression through violence; this is not a threat but a fact of history. So I have not said to my people, "Get rid of your discontent." Rather, I have tried to say that this nor-mal and healthy discontent can be channeled into the creative outlet of nonviolent direct action. And now this approach is being termed extremist.

But though I was initially disappointed at being categorized as an extremist, as I continued to think about the matter I gradually gained a measure of satisfaction from the label. Was not Jesus an extremist for love: "Love your enemies, bless them that curse you, do good to them that hate you, and pray for them which despite-fully use you, and persecute you." Was not Amos an extremist for justice: "Let justice roll down like waters and righteousness like an ever-flowing stream." Was not Paul an extremist for the Christian gospel: "I bear in my body the marks of the Lord Jesus."

Was not Martin Luther an extremist: "Here I stand; I cannot do otherwise, so help me God." And John Bunyan: "I will stay in jail to the end of my days before I make a butchery of my conscience." And Abraham Lincoln: "This nation cannot survive half slave and half free." And Thomas Jefferson: "We hold these truths to be self-evident, that all men are created equal...." So the question is not whether we will be extremists, but what kind of extremists we will be. Will we be extremists for hate or for love? Will we be extremists for the preservation of injustice or for the extension of justice? In that dramatic scene on Calvary's hill three men were crucified. We must never forget that all three were crucified for the same crime—the crime of extremism. Two were extremists for immorality, and thus fell below their environment. The other, Jesus Christ, was an extremist for love, truth, and goodness, and thereby rose above his environment. Perhaps the South, the nation, and the world are in dire need of creative extremists.

I had hoped that the white moderate would see this need. Perhaps I was too optimistic; perhaps I expected too much. I suppose I should have realized that few members of the oppressor race can understand the deep groans and passionate yearnings of the oppressed race, and still fewer have the vision to see that injustice must be rooted out by strong, persistent, and determined action. I am thankful, however, that some of our white brothers in the South have grasped the meaning of this social revolution and committed themselves to it. They are still all too few in quantity, but they are big in quality. Some—such as Ralph McGill, Lillian Smith, Harry Golden, James McBridge Dabbs, Ann Braden, and Sarah Patton Boyle—have written about our struggle in eloquent and prophetic terms. Others have marched with us down nameless streets of the South. They have languished in filthy, roach-infested jails, suffering the abuse and brutality of policemen who view them as "dirty nigger-lovers." Unlike so many of their moderate brothers and sisters, they have recognized the urgency of the moment and sensed the need for powerful "action" antidotes to combat the disease of segregation.

Let me take note of my other major disappointment. I have been so greatly disappointed with the white church and its leadership. Of course, there are some notable exceptions. I am not unmindful of the fact that each of you has taken some significant stands on this issue. I commend you, Reverend Stallings, for your Christian stand on this past Sunday, in welcoming Negroes to your worship service on a nonsegregated basis. I commend the

Catholic leaders of this state for integrating Spring Hill College
several years ago.

But despite these notable exceptions, I must honestly reiterate
that I have been disappointed with the church. I do not say this as
one of those negative critics who can always find something
wrong with the church. I say this as a minister of the gospel, who
loves the church; who was nurtured in its bosom; who has been
sustained by its spiritual blessings and who will remain true to it
as long as the cord of life shall lengthen.

When I was suddenly catapulted into the leadership of the bus
protest in Montgomery, Alabama, a few years ago, I felt we would
be supported by the white church. I felt that the white ministers,
priests, and rabbis of the South would be among our strongest allies. Instead, some have been outright opponents, refusing to understand the freedom movement and misrepresenting its leaders;
all too many others have been more cautious than courageous
and have remained silent behind the anesthetizing security of
stained glass windows.

In spite of my shattered dreams, I came to Birmingham with
the hope that the white religious leadership of this community
would see the justice of our cause and, with deep moral concern,
would serve as the channel through which our just grievances
could reach the power structure. I had hoped that each of you
would understand. But again I have been disappointed.

I have heard numerous southern religious leaders admonish
their worshipers to comply with a desegregation decision because
it is the law, but I have longed to hear white ministers declare:
"Follow this decree because integration is morally right and because the Negro is your brother." In the midst of blatant injustices
inflicted upon the Negro, I have watched white churchmen stand
on the sideline and mouth pious irrelevancies and sanctimonious
trivialities. In the midst of a mighty struggle to rid our nation of
racial and economic injustice, I have heard many ministers say:
"Those are social issues, with which the gospel has no real concern." And I have watched many churches commit themselves to
a completely otherworldly religion which makes a strange, un-
Biblical distinction between body and soul, between the sacred and
the secular.

I have traveled the length and breadth of Alabama, Mississippi,
and all the other southern states. On sweltering summer days and
crisp autumn mornings I have looked at the South's beautiful
churches with their lofty spires pointing heavenward. I have be-

held the impressive outlines of her massive religious-education buildings. Over and over I have found myself asking: "What kind of people worship here? Who is their God? Where were their voices when the lips of Governor Barnett dripped with words of interposition and nullification? Where were they when Governor Wallace gave a clarion call for defiance and hatred? Where were their voices of support when bruised and weary Negro men and women decided to rise from the dark dungeons of complacency to the bright hills of creative protest?"

Yes, these questions are still in my mind. In deep disappointment I have wept over the laxity of the church. But be assured that my tears have been tears of love. There can be no deep disappointment where there is not deep love. Yes, I love the church. How could I do otherwise? I am in the rather unique position of being the son, the grandson, and the great-grandson of preachers. Yes, I see the church as the body of Christ. But, oh! How we have blemished and scarred that body through social neglect and through fear of being nonconformists.

There was a time when the church was very powerful—in the time when the early Christians rejoiced at being deemed worthy to suffer for what they believed. In those days the church was not merely a thermometer that recorded the ideas and principles of popular opinion; it was a thermostat that transformed the mores of society. Whenever the early Christians entered a town, the people in power became disturbed and immediately sought to convict the Christians for being "disturbers of the peace" and "outside agitators." But the Christians pressed on, in the conviction that they were "a colony of heaven," called to obey God rather than man. Small in number, they were big in commitment. They were too God-intoxicated to be "astronomically intimidated." By their effort and example they brought an end to such ancient evils as infanticide and gladiatorial contests.

Things are different now. So often the contemporary church is a weak, ineffectual voice with an uncertain sound. So often it is an archdefender of the status quo. Far from being disturbed by the presence of the church, the power structure of the average community is consoled by the church's silent—and often even vocal—sanction of things as they are.

But the judgment of God is upon the church as never before. If today's church does not recapture the sacrificial spirit of the early church, it will lose its authenticity, forfeit the loyalty of millions, and be dismissed as an irrelevant social club with no meaning for

the twentieth century. Every day I meet young people whose disappointment with the church has turned into outright disgust.

Perhaps I have once again been too optimistic. Is organized religion too inextricably bound to the status quo to save our nation
and the world? Perhaps I must turn my faith to the inner spiritual church, the church within the church, as the true *ekklesia*
and the hope of the world. But again I am thankful to God that
some noble souls from the ranks of organized religion have broken loose from the paralyzing chains of conformity and joined us
as active partners in the struggle for freedom. They have left their
secure congregations and walked the streets of Albany, Georgia,
with us. They have gone down the highways of the South on tor-
tuous rides for freedom. Yes, they have gone to jail with us. Some
have been dismissed from their churches, have lost the support of
their bishops and fellow ministers. But they have acted in the faith
that right defeated is stronger than evil triumphant. Their witness has been the spiritual salt that has preserved the true
meaning of the gospel in these troubled times. They have carved a
tunnel of hope through the dark mountain of disappointment.

I hope the church as a whole will meet the challenge of this decisive hour. But even if the church does not come to the aid of justice, I have no despair about the future. I have no fear about the
outcome of our struggle in Birmingham, even if our motives are
at present misunderstood. We will reach the goal of freedom in
Birmingham and all over the nation, because the goal of America
is freedom. Abused and scorned though we may be, our destiny is
tied up with America's destiny. Before the pilgrims landed at
Plymouth, we were here. Before the pen of Jefferson etched the
majestic words of the Declaration of Independence across the
pages of history, we were here. For more than two centuries our
forebears labored in this country without wages; they made cotton
king; they built the homes of their masters while suffering gross
injustice and shameful humiliation—and yet out of a bottomless
vitality they continued to thrive and develop. If the inexpressible
cruelties of slavery could not stop us, the opposition we now face
will surely fail. We will win our freedom because the sacred heritage of our nation and the eternal will of God are embodied in our
echoing demands.

Before closing I feel impelled to mention one other point in your
statement that has troubled me profoundly. You warmly commended the Birmingham police force for keeping "order" and
"preventing violence." I doubt that you would have so warmly

commended the police force if you had seen its dogs sinking their teeth into unarmed, nonviolent Negroes. I doubt that you would so quickly commend the policemen if you were to observe their ugly and inhumane treatment of Negroes here in the city jail; if you were to watch them push and curse old Negro women and young Negro girls; if you were to see them slap and kick old Negro men and young boys; if you were to observe them, as they did on two occasions, refuse to give us food because we wanted to sing our grace together. I cannot join you in your praise of the Birmingham police department.

It is true that the police have exercised a degree of discipline in handling the demonstrators. In this sense they have conducted themselves rather "nonviolently" in public. But for what purpose? To preserve the evil system of segregation. Over the past few years I have consistently preached that nonviolence demands that the means we use must be as pure as the ends we seek. I have tried to make clear that it is wrong to use immoral means to attain moral ends. But now I must affirm that it is just as wrong, or perhaps even more so, to use moral means to preserve immoral ends. Perhaps Mr. Connor and his policemen have been rather nonviolent in public, as was Chief Pritchett in Albany, Georgia, but they have used the moral means of nonviolence to maintain the immoral end of racial injustice. As T. S. Eliot has said, "The last temptation is the greatest treason: To do the right deed for the wrong reason."

I wish you had commended the Negro sit-inners and demonstrators of Birmingham for their sublime courage, their willingness to suffer, and their amazing discipline in the midst of great provocation. One day the South will recognize its real heroes. They will be the James Merediths, with the noble sense of purpose that enables them to face jeering and hostile mobs, and with the agonizing loneliness that characterizes the life of the pioneer. They will be old, oppressed, battered Negro women, symbolized in a seventy-two-year-old woman in Montgomery, Alabama, who rose up with a sense of dignity and with her people decided not to ride segregated buses, and who responded with ungrammatical profundity to one who inquired about her weariness: "My feets is tired, but my soul is at rest." They will be the young high school and college students, the young ministers of the gospel and a host of their elders, courageously and nonviolently sitting in at lunch counters and willingly going to jail for conscience' sake. One day the South will know that when these disinherited children of God sat down at lunch counters, they were in reality standing up for what is best in the American dream and for the most sacred values in our Judaeo-Christian heritage, thereby bringing our nation back to those great wells of democracy which were dug deep by the founding fathers in their formulation of the Constitution and the Declaration of Independence.

Never before have I written so long a letter. I'm afraid it is much too long to take your precious time. I can assure you that it would have been much shorter if I had been writing from a comfortable desk, but what else can one do when he is alone in a narrow jail cell, other than write long letters, think long thoughts, and pray long prayers?

If I have said anything in this letter that overstates the truth and indicates an unreasonable impatience, I beg you to forgive me. If I have said anything that understates the truth and indicates my having a patience that allows me to settle for anything less than brotherhood, I beg God to forgive me.

I hope this letter finds you strong in the faith. I also hope that circumstances will soon make it possible for me to meet each of you, not as an integrationist or a civil-rights leader but as a fellow clergyman and a Christian brother. Let us all hope that the dark clouds of racial prejudice will soon pass away and the deep fog of misunderstanding will be lifted from our fear-drenched communities, and in some not too distant tomorrow the radiant stars of love and brotherhood will shine over our great nation with all their scintillating beauty.

Yours for the cause of Peace and Brotherhood,
MARTIN LUTHER KING, JR.

Catherine (student)

KING'S WAY WITH WORDS

In this response to King's *Letter*, Catherine shows how King's words can have such a powerful impact on the reader

In Martin Luther King, Jr.'s own note on the writing of the "Letter from Birmingham Jail," he says that it was begun in secret, on smuggled scraps of paper at first, then on a notepad he was eventually permitted. "Although the text remains in substance unaltered," he wrote, "I have indulged the author's prerogative of polishing it for publication." Yet the letter reads like spoken words, with some of the natural diction of speech, combined with the power and righteous force of a sermon. King's skill as a preacher is highlighted in the "Letter," as is his talent as a letter-writer.

That particular talent is for some people hard to come by. A good letter-writer may have a large point to make, or a small tale to relate, but both kinds of things are expressed in a clear, relaxed manner. Although what King was writing is powerful, both in subject matter and tone, he easily visualizes his audience and is able to address them as though he were speaking to them in person. It is this semblance of real speech that distinguishes a good, readable letter from one that is too formal to struggle through.

King's rhetoric is so powerful at times that his stated subject matter—his controversial personal involvement in Birmingham racial politics and consequent jailing—sometimes disappears under waves of great truth that splash across and wash away his detractors' criticisms. He is accused of being an outside agitator, and therefore impolitic in his participation; he replies "Injustice anywhere is a threat to justice everywhere." He echoes the poetic "No man is an island" when he declares that "Whatever affects one directly, affects all indirectly." It is difficult to disagree, difficult not to nod and say "Amen." The force of his rhetoric, combined with the truth of his vision and the personal yet speechlike style of his address bring weight and persuasion to his argument.

King suggests that he and his stated audience of eight clergy may already be on the same side. He and they share the same goal: desegregation of Alabama's—and the nation's—institutions, specifically at this time, Birmingham's economic community. When he writes, he assumes that all people of good will share this goal. Starting with this assumption of agreement allows him to draw his audience in, believing that they are already with him, or, if they aren't, they should be. He assumes they are united, and uses his words to gently but powerfully instill that belief in them.

It is difficult to say anything new—or anything at all—about the subject matter of King's "Letter." As you read it, it is difficult to resist agreeing with the truth and beauty of what he had to say on the subject of growing up in Black America, hated by White America. You feel as if he is writing, speaking, directly to your heart. Next to his works, it is King's way with words we will remember him for. As the results in America today confirm, the two make a powerful combination.

Chapter 8:
Coming of Age

Zora Neale Hurston

I GET BORN

Zora Neale Hurston (1901-1961), a novelist and journalist, wrote autobiographical works, novels, and plays incorporating her knowledge of black folklore. In this selection, her wit and glib style come through as she recounts the events of her very early childhood. As you read, recall what you have been told about your own birth. Do you retain any of your early-childhood characteristics today?

This is all hear-say. Maybe some of the details of my birth as told me might be a little inaccurate, but it is pretty well established that I really did get born.

The saying goes like this. My mother's time had come and my father was not there. Being a carpenter, successful enough to have other helpers on some jobs, he was away often on building business, as well as preaching. It seems that my father was away from home for months this time. I have never been told why. But I did hear that he threatened to cut his throat when he got the news. It seems that one daughter was all that he figured he could stand. My sister, Sarah, was his favorite child, but that one girl was enough. Plenty more sons, but no more girl babies to wear out shoes and bring in nothing. I don't think he ever got over the trick he felt that I played on him by getting born a girl, and while he was off from home at that. A little of my sugar used to sweeten his coffee right now. That is a Negro way of saying his patience was short with me. Let me change a few words with him—and I am of the word changing kind—and he was ready to change ends. Still and all, I looked more like him than any child in the house. Of course, by the time I got born, it was too late to make any suggestions, so the old man had to put up with me. He was nice about it in a way. He didn't tie me in a sack and drop me in the lake, as he probably felt like doing.

People were digging sweet potatoes, and then it was hog-killing time. Not at our house, but it was going on in general over the country like, being January and a bit cool. Most people were either butchering for themselves, or off helping other folks do their butchering, which was almost just as good. It is a gay time. A big pot of hasslits cooking with plenty of seasoning, lean slabs of fresh-killed pork frying for the helpers to refresh themselves after the work is done. Over and above being neighborly and giving aid, there is the food, the drinks and the fun of getting together.

So there was no grown folks dose around when Mama's water broke. She sent one of the smaller children to fetch Aunt Judy, the mid-wife, but she was gone to Woodbridge, a mile and a half away, to eat at a hog-killing. The child was told to go over there and tell Aunt Judy to come. But nature, being indifferent to human arrangements, was impatient. My mother had to make it alone. She was too weak after I rushed out to do anything for herself, so she just was lying there, sick in the body, and worried in mind, wondering what would become of her, as well as me. She was so weak, she couldn't even reach down to where I was. She had one consolation. She knew I wasn't dead, because I was crying strong.

Help came from where she never would have thought to look for it. A white man of many acres and things, who knew the family well, had butchered the day before. Knowing that Papa was not at home, and that consequently there would be no fresh meat in our house, he decided to drive the five miles and bring a half of a shoat, sweet potatoes, and other garden stuff along. He was there a few minutes after I was born. Seeing the front door standing open, he came on in, and hollered, "Hello, there! Call your dogs!"

That is the regular way to call in the country because nearly everybody who has anything to watch has biting dogs.

Nobody answered, but he claimed later that he heard me spreading my lungs all over Orange County, so he shoved the door open and bolted on into the house.

He followed the noise and then he saw how things were, and, being the kind of a man he was, he took out his Barlow Knife and cut the navel cord, then he did the best he could about other things. When the mid-wife, locally known as a granny, arrived about an hour later, there was a fire in the stove and plenty of hot water on. I had been sponged off in some sort of a way, and Mama was holding me in her arms.

As soon as the old woman got there, the white man unloaded what he had brought, and drove off cussing about some blankety-blank people never being where you could put your hands on them when they were needed. He got no thanks from Aunt Judy. She grumbled for years about it. She complained that the cord had not been cut just right, and the bellyband had not been put on tight enough. She was mighty scared I was going to have a weak back, and that I would have trouble holding my water until I reached puberty. I did.

The next day or so a Mrs. Neale, a friend of Mama's, came in and reminded her that she had promised to let her name the baby in case it was a girl. She had picked up a name somewhere which she thought was very pretty. Perhaps she had read it somewhere, or somebody back in those woods was smoking Turkish cigarettes. So I became Zora Neale Hurston.

There is nothing to make you like other human beings so much as doing things for them. Therefore, the man who grannied me was back next day to see how I was coming along. Maybe it was a pride in his own handiwork, and his resourcefulness in a pinch, that made him want to see it through. He remarked that I was a God-damned fine baby, fat and plenty of lung-power. As time went on, he came infrequently, but somehow kept a pinch of interest in my welfare. It seemed that I was spying noble, growing like a gourd vine, and yelling bass like a gator. He was the kind of man that had no use for puny things, so I was all to the good with him. He thought my mother was justified in keeping me.

But nine months rolled around, and I just would not get on with the walking business. I was strong, crawling well, but showed no inclination to use my feet. I might remark in passing, that I still don't like to walk. Then I was over a year old, but still I would not walk. They made allowances for my weight, but yet, that was no real reason for my not trying.

They tell me that an old sow-hog taught me how to walk. That is, she didn't instruct me in detail, but she convinced me that I really ought to try. It was like this. My mother was going to have collard greens for dinner, so she took the dishpan and went down to the spring to wash the greens. She left me sitting on the floor, and gave me a hunk of cornbread to keep me quiet. Everything was going along all right, until the sow with her litter of pigs in convoy came abreast of the door. She must have smelled the cornbread I was messing with and scattering crumbs about the floor. So, she came right on in, and began to nuzzle around.

My mother heard my screams and came running. Her heart must have stood still when she saw the sow in there, because hogs have been known to eat human flesh.

But I was not taking this thing sitting down. I had been placed by a chair, and when my mother got inside the door, I had pulled myself up by that chair and was getting around it right smart.

As for the sow, poor misunderstood lady, she had no interest in me except my bread. I lost that in scrambling to my feet and she was eating it. She had much less intention of eating Mama's baby, than Mama had of eating hers. With no more suggestions from the sow or anybody else, it seems that I just took to walking and kept the thing a-going. The strangest thing about it was that once I found the use of my feet, they took to wandering. I always wanted to go. I would wander off in the woods all alone, following some inside urge to go places. This alarmed my mother a great deal. She used to say that she believed a woman who was an enemy of hers had sprinkled "travel dust" around the doorstep the day I was born. That was the only explanation she could find. I don't know why it never occurred to her to connect my tendency with my father, who didn't have a thing on his mind but this town and the next one. That should have given her a sort of hint. Some children are just bound to take after their fathers in spite of women's prayers.

Annie Dillard

From AN AMERICAN CHILDHOOD

Annie Dillard (1945-   ), a poet, critic, and writer, lived an ordinary childhood in Pittsburgh before moving to quick success as a writer. She is now an editor for *Harper's* magazine and continues to write poetry and books. As you read this excerpt. ask yourself why Dillard counts *getting caught* throwing snowballs as one of the happiest experiences of her life.

Some boys taught me to play football. This was fine sport. You thought up a new strategy for every play and whispered it to the others. You went out for a pass, fooling everyone. Best, you got to throw yourself mightily at someone's running legs. Either you brought him down or you hit the ground flat out on your chin, with your arms empty before you. It was all or nothing. If you hesitated in fear, you would miss and get hurt: you would take a hard fall while the kid got away, or you would get kicked in the face while the kid got away. But if you flung yourself wholeheartedly at the back of his knees—if you gathered and joined body and soul and pointed them diving fearlessly—then you likely wouldn't get hurt, and you'd stop the ball. Your fate, and your team's score, depended on your concentration and courage. Nothing girls did could compare with it. Boys welcomed me at baseball, too, for I had, through enthusiastic practice, what was weirdly known as a boy's arm. In winter, in the snow, there was neither baseball nor football, so the boys and I threw snowballs at passing cars. I got in trouble throwing snowballs, and have seldom been happier since.

On one weekday morning after Christmas, six inches of new snow had just fallen. We were standing up to our boot tops in snow on a front yard on trafficked Reynolds Street, waiting for cars. The cars traveled Reynolds Street slowly and evenly; they were targets all but wrapped in red ribbons, cream puffs. We couldn't miss. I was seven; the boys were eight, nine, and ten. The oldest

two Fahey boys were there—Mikey and Peter—polite blond boys
who lived near me on Lloyd Street, and who already had four
brothers and sisters. My parents approved Mikey and Peter
Fahey. Chickie McBride was there, a tough kid, and Billy Paul
and Mackie Kean too, from across Reynolds, where the boys grew
up dark and furious, grew up skinny, knowing, and skilled. We
had all drifted from our houses that morning looking for action,
and had found it here on Reynolds Street.

It was cloudy but cold. The cars' tires laid behind them on the
snowy street a complex trail of beige chunks like crenellated castle walls. I had stepped on some earlier; they squeaked. We could
have wished for more traffic. When a car came, we all popped it
one. In the intervals between cars we reverted to the natural
solitude of children.

I started making an iceball—a perfect iceball, from perfectly
white snow, perfectly spherical, and squeezed perfectly translu-
cent so no snow remained all the way through. (The Fahey boys
and I considered it unfair actually to throw an iceball at somebody, but it had been known to happen.) I had just embarked on
the iceball project when we heard tire chains come clanking from
afar. A black Buick was moving toward us down the street. We all
spread out, banged together some regular snowballs, took aim,
and, when the Buick drew nigh, fired.

A soft snowball hit the driver's windshield right before the
driver's face. It made a smashed star with a hump in the middle.

Often, of course, we hit our target, but this time, the only time in
all of life, the car pulled over and stopped. Its wide black door
opened; a man got out of it, running. He didn't even close the car
door.

He ran after us, and we ran away from him, up the snowy
Reynolds sidewalk. At the corner, I looked back; incredibly, he was
still after us. He was in city clothes: a suit and tie, street shoes. Any
normal adult would have quit, having sprung us into flight and
made his point. This man was gaining on us. He was a thin man,
all action. All of a sudden, we were running for our lives.

Wordless, we split up. We were on our turf; we could lose ourselves in the neighborhood backyards, everyone for himself. I
paused and considered. Everyone had vanished except Mikey
Fahey, who was just rounding the corner of a yellow brick house.
Poor Mikey, I trailed him. The driver of the Buick sensibly picked
the two of us to follow. The man apparently had all day. He chased
Mikey and me around the yellow house and up a backyard path

we knew by heart: under a low tree, up a bank, through a hedge, down some snowy steps, and across the grocery store's delivery driveway. We smashed through a gap in another hedge, entered a scruffy backyard and ran around its back porch and tight between houses to Edgerton Avenue; we ran across Edgerton to an alley and up our own sliding woodpile to the Halls' front yard; he kept coming. We ran up Lloyd Street and wound through mazy backyards toward the steep hilltop at Willard and Lang.

He chased us silently, block after block. He chased us silently over picket fences, through thorny hedges, between houses, around garbage cans, and across streets. Every time I glanced back, choking for breath, I expected he would have quit. He must have been as breathless as we were. His jacket strained over his body. It was an immense discovery, pounding into my hot head with every sliding, joyous step, that this ordinary adult evidently knew what I thought only children who trained at football knew: that you have to fling yourself at what you're doing, you have to point yourself, forget yourself, aim, dive. Ꙅ𝟷𝗎𝒶ᴛꓲᴑ𝗇ꟼ ꙇ𝗇 ꞁꙆᖷꓱ

Mikey and I had nowhere to go, in our own neighborhood or out of it, but away from this man who was chasing us. He impelled us forward; we compelled him to follow our route. The air was cold; every breath tore my throat. We kept running, block after block; we kept improvising, backyard after backyard, running a frantic course and choosing it simultaneously, failing always to find small places or hard places to slow him down, and discovering always, exhilarated, dismayed, that only bare speed could save us—for he would never give up, this man—and we were losing speed. He chased us through the backyard labyrinths of ten blocks before he caught us by our jackets. He caught us and we all stopped.

We three stood staggering, half blinded, coughing, in an obscure hilltop backyard: a man in his twenties, a boy, a girl. He had released our jackets, our pursuer, our captor, our hero: he knew we weren't going anywhere. We all played by the rules. Mikey and I unzipped our jackets. I pulled off my sopping mittens. Our tracks multiplied in the backyard's new snow. We had been breaking new snow all morning. We didn't look at each other. I was cherishing my excitement. The man's lower pants legs were wet; his cuffs were full of snow, and there was a prow of snow beneath them on his shoes and socks. Some trees bordered the little flat backyard, some messy winter trees. There was no one around: a clearing in a grove, and we the only players.

It was a long time before he could speak. I had some difficulty at first recalling why we were there. My lips felt swollen; I couldn't see out of the sides of my eyes; I kept coughing.

"You stupid kids," he began perfunctorily.

We listened perfunctorily indeed, if we listened at all, for the chewing out was redundant, a mere formality, and beside the point. The point was that he had chased us passionately without giving up, and so he had caught us. Now he came down to earth. I wanted the glory to last forever.

But how could the glory have lasted forever? We could have run through every backyard in North America until we got to Panama. But when he trapped us at the lip of the Panama Canal, what precisely could he have done to prolong the drama of the chase and cap its glory? I brooded about this for the next few years. He could only have fried Mikey Fahey and me in boiling oil, say, or dismembered us piecemeal, or staked us to anthills. None of which I really wanted, and none of which any adult was likely to do, even in the spirit of fun. He could only chew us out there in the Panamanian jungle, after months or years of exalting pursuit. He could only begin, "You stupid kids," and continue in his ordinary Pittsburgh accent with his normal righteous anger and the usual common sense.

If in that snowy backyard the driver of the black Buick had cut off our heads, Mikey's and mine, I would have died happy, for nothing has required so much of me since as being chased all over Pittsburgh in the middle of winter—running terrified, exhausted—by this sainted, skinny, furious redheaded man who wished to have a word with us. I don't know how he found his way back to his car.

Pearl Klein (student)

S.S. KRESGE'S & CO.

As you read Pearl's essay, compare it to Annie Dillard's *An American Childhood*. What is similar about the two tales? What is different? Do they make the same point?

When I was little, the best store—the best place—in the world was S.S. Kresge's & Co.in Market Square Shopping Plaza. No other store had the variety of good, cheap stuff that I craved and could afford with my allowance, and for a while my Aunt Adaire worked at the lunch counter there and had to wear a hairnet. Outside in front sat two coin-operated horses, a big one and a little one, and once when I was there with my dad he took a picture of me on top of the big, rearing one.

I must have bought every kind of candy they sold, and every kind of paper doll, at least once. Something about the gumballs they sold make them crunchier on the outside, sweeter and stickier and gummier than gumballs you got anyplace else. The wonderful smell seemed to come from everywhere and nowhere at once, and smelled nothing like anything you'd find out-of-doors.

One day when I was about eight years old, I was there waiting for my mom to come over from the boring old bank. Mostly because I had spent my allowance already, and because Aunt Adaire wasn't working that day, I was hanging out in the clothing section. Kresge's took itself very seriously, offering a wide variety of clothing for the whole family; there was even a saleslady to help you pick stuff out and try it on. Looking back, I see Kresge's as being a lot like Woolworth's, full of cheap plastic junk, but when I was little all I wanted was cheap plastic junk, and Kresge's was a place of mystery to me. One of the mysteries was a sign on a metal stand at the end of the baby clothes aisle. It was red print on a white background and it said "Please ring bell for service." I knew that "please" was phony, just like the phony smile the saleslady gave my mom that disappeared when it was just me. I seemed to be alone among the baby dresses, and I seemed completely, safely out of sight. I reached over, tapped the ringer with the exact center of my palm, and ran.

And ran. And I should have made it, but the saleslady was mean, and quick, and prepared. She cut me off just before the door, grabbed my upper arm, and squeezed. She was the meanest, scariest, boredest woman I had ever seen; I had given her the gift of excitement, and she reveled in it.

I couldn't speak. I got one of those painful nervous feelings in my face, and I know I, mistakenly, smiled. She looked into my face and her eyes breathed into my eyes.

Meaner than mean, she choked it out: "Don't you *ever* come back to this store again!"

I showed her, and I showed Kresge's, the best place in the world:
I never did.

Richard Rodriguez

ARIA

Richard Rodriguez (1944-   ), a writer and teacher, here discusses
the issue of bilingual education from the perspective of his own experience growing up in a bilingual setting. The excerpt shows the value
of personal experience in demonstrating a point. As you read, compare Rodriguez's experience of learning English in school to your
own, whether English was your first or a second language. Do you
agree with Rodriguez about how it should be taught?

Supporters of bilingual education today imply that students like
me miss a great deal by not being taught in their family's language. What they seem not to recognize is that, as a socially disadvantaged child, I considered Spanish to be a private language.
What I needed to learn in school was that I had the right—and
the obligation—to speak the public language of *los gringos*. The
odd truth is that my first-grade classmates could have become
bilingual, in the conventional sense of that word, more easily than
I. Had they been taught (as upper-middle-class children are often
taught early) a second language like Spanish or French, they
could have regarded it simply as that: another public language. In
my case such bilingualism could not have been so quickly
achieved. What I did not believe was that I could speak a single
public language.

Without question, it would have pleased me to hear my teachers
address me in Spanish when I entered the classroom. I would
have felt much less afraid. I would have trusted them and responded with ease. But I would have delayed—for how long post-
poned?—having to learn the language of public society. I would
have evaded—and for how long could I have afforded to delay?—
learning the great lesson of school, that I had a public identity.

Fortunately, my teachers were unsentimental about their responsibility. What they understood was that I needed to speak a

public language. So their voices would search me out, asking me questions. Each time I'd hear them, I'd look up in surprise to see a nun's face frowning at me. I'd mumble, not really meaning to answer. The nun would persist, "Richard, stand up. Don't look at the floor. Speak up. Speak to the entire class, not just to me!" But I couldn't believe that the English language was mine to use. (In part, I did not want to believe it.) I continued to mumble. I resisted the teacher's demands. (Did I somehow suspect that once I learned public language my pleasing family life would be changed?) Silent, waiting for the bell to sound, I remained dazed, diffident, afraid. Because I wrongly imagined that English was intrinsically a public language and Spanish an intrinsically private one, I easily noted the difference between classroom language and the language of home. At school, words were directed to a general audience of listeners. ("Boys and girls.") Words were meaningfully ordered. And the point was not self-expression alone but to make oneself understood by many others. The teacher quizzed: "Boys and girls, why do we use that word in this sentence? Could we think of a better word to use there? Would the sentence change its meaning if the words were differently arranged? And wasn't there a better way of saying much the same thing?" (I couldn't say. I wouldn't try to say.)

Three months. Five. Half a year passed. Unsmiling, ever watchful, my teachers noted my silence. They began to connect my behavior with the difficult progress my older sister and brother were making. Until one Saturday morning three nuns arrived at the house to talk to our parents. Stiffly, they sat on the blue living room sofa. From the doorway of another room, spying the visitors, I noted the incongruity—the clash of two worlds, the faces and voices of school intruding upon the familiar setting of home. I overheard one voice gently wondering, "Do your children speak only Spanish at home, Mrs. Rodriguez?" While another voice added, "That Richard especially seems so timid and shy."

That Rich-heard!

With great tact the visitors continued, "Is it possible for you and your husband to encourage your children to practice their English when they are home?" Of course, my parents complied. What would they not do for their children's well-being? And how could they have questioned the Church's authority which those women represented? In an instant, they agreed to give up the language (the sounds) that had revealed and accentuated our family's closeness. The moment after the visitors left, the change was

observed. "*Ahora*, speak to us *en inglés*," my father and mother
united to tell us. At first, it seemed a kind of game. After dinner
each night, the family gathered to practice "our" English. (It was
still then *inglés*, a language foreign to us, so we felt drawn as
strangers to it.) Laughing, we would try to define words we could
not pronounce. We played with strange English sounds, often
overanglicizing our pronunciations. And we filled the smiling
gaps of our sentences with familiar Spanish sounds. But that was
cheating, somebody shouted. Everyone laughed. In school, meanwhile, like my brother and sister, I was required to attend a daily
tutoring session. I needed a full year of special attention. I also
needed my teachers to keep my attention from straying in class
by calling out, *Rich-heard*— their English voices slowly prying
loose my ties to my other name, its three notes, *Ri-car-do*. Most of
all I needed to hear my mother and father speak to me in a moment of seriousness in broken—suddenly heartbreaking—
English. The scene was inevitable: One Saturday morning I entered the kitchen where my parents were talking in Spanish. I did
not realize that they were talking in Spanish however until, at the
moment they saw me, I heard their voices change to speak
English. Those *gringo* sounds they uttered startled me. Pushed
me away. In that moment of trivial misunderstanding and profound insight, I felt my throat twisted by unsounded grief. I
turned quickly and left the room. But I had no place to escape to
with Spanish. (The spell was broken.) My brother and sisters
were speaking English in another part of the house.

Again and again in the days following, increasingly angry, I was
obliged to hear my mother and father: "Speak to us *en inglés*."
(Speak.) Only then did I determine to learn classroom English.
Weeks after, it happened: One day in school I raised my hand to
volunteer an answer. I spoke out in a loud voice. And I did not
think it remarkable when the entire class understood. That day, I
moved very far from the disadvantaged child I had been only days
earlier. The belief, that calming assurance that I belonged in public, had at last taken hold.

Shortly after, I stopped hearing the high and loud sounds of *los
gringos*. A more and more confident speaker of English, I didn't
trouble to listen to how strangers sounded, speaking to me. And
there simply were too many English-speaking people in my day
for me to hear American accents anymore. Conversations quickened. Listening to persons who sounded eccentrically pitched
voices, I usually noted their sounds for an initial few seconds be-

fore I concentrated on what they were saying. Conversations became content-full. Transparent. Hearing someone's tone of voice—angry or questioning or sarcastic or happy or sad—I didn't distinguish it from the words it expressed. Sound and word were thus tightly wedded. At the end of a day, I was often bemused, always relieved, to realize how "silent," though crowded with words, my day in public had been. (This public silence measured and quickened the change in my life.)

At last, seven years old, I came to believe what had been technically true since my birth: I was an American citizen.

But the special feeling of closeness at home was diminished by then. Gone was the desperate, urgent, intense feeling of being at home; rare was the experience of feeling myself individualized by family intimates. We remained a loving family, but one greatly changed. No longer so close; no longer bound tight by the pleasing and troubling knowledge of our public separateness. Neither my older brother nor sister rushed home after school anymore. Nor did I. When I arrived home there would often be neighborhood kids in the house. Or the house would be empty of sounds.

Following the dramatic Americanization of their children, even my parents grew more publicly confident. Especially my mother. She learned the names of all the people on our block. And she decided we needed to have a telephone installed in the house. My father continued to use the word *gringo*. But it was no longer charged with the old bitterness or distrust. (Stripped of any emotional content, the word simply became a name for those Americans not of Hispanic descent.) Hearing him, sometimes, I wasn't sure if he was pronouncing the Spanish word *gringo* or saying gringo in English.

Matching the silence I started hearing in public was a new quiet at home. The family's quiet was partly due to the fact that, as we children learned more and more English, we shared fewer and fewer words with our parents. Sentences needed to be spoken slowly when a child addressed his mother or father. (Often the parent wouldn't understand.) The child would need to repeat himself. (Still the parent misunderstood.) The young voice, frustrated, would end up saying, "Never mind"—the subject was closed. Dinners would be noisy with the clinking of knives and forks against dishes. My mother would smile softly between her remarks; my father at the other end of the table would chew and chew at his food, while he stared over the heads of his children.

My *mother*! My *father*! After English became my primary language, I no longer knew what words to use in addressing my parents. The old Spanish words (those tender accents of sound) I had used earlier—*mamá* and *papá*—I couldn't use anymore. They would have been too painful reminders of how much had changed in my life. On the other hand, the words I heard neighborhood kids call the;r parents seemed equally unsatisfactory. *Mother and Father; Ma, Papa, Pa, Dad, Pop* (how I hated the all American sound of that last word especially)—all these terms I felt were unsuitable, not really terms of address for my parents. As a result, I never used them at home. Whenever I'd speak to my parents, I would try to get their attention with eye contact alone, In public conversations, I'd refer to "my parents" or "my mother and father."

My mother and father, for their part, responded differently, as their children spoke to them less. She grew restless, seemed troubled and anxious at the scarcity of words exchanged in the house. It was she who would question me about my day when I came home from school. She smiled at small talk. She pried at the edges of my sentences to get me to say something more. (What?) She'd join conversations she overhead, but her intrusions often stopped her children's talking. By contrast, my father seemed reconciled to the new quiet. Though his English improved somewhat, he retired into silence. At dinner he spoke very little. One night his children and even his wife helplessly giggled at his garbled English pronunciation of the Catholic Grace before Meals. Thereafter he made his wife recite the prayer at the start of each meal, even on formal occasions, when there were guests in the house. Hers became the public voice of the family. On official business, it was she, not my father, one would usually hear on the phone or in stores, talking to strangers. His children grew so accustomed to his silence that, years later, they would speak routinely of his shyness. (My mother would often try to explain: Both his parents died when he was eight. He was raised by an uncle who treated him like little more than a menial servant. He was never encouraged to speak. He grew up alone. A man of few words.) But my father was not shy, I realized, when I'd watch him speaking Spanish with relatives. Using Spanish, he was quickly effusive. Especially when talking with other men, his voice would spark, flicker, flare alive with sounds. In Spanish, he expressed ideas and feelings he rarely revealed in English. With firm Spanish sounds, he conveyed confidence and authority English would never allow him.

The silence at home, however, was finally more than a literal silence. Fewer words passed between parent and child, but more profound was the silence that resulted from my inattention to sounds. At about the time I no longer bothered to listen with care to the sounds of English in public, I grew careless about listening to the sounds family members made when they spoke. Most of the time I heard someone speaking at home and didn't distinguish his sounds from the words people uttered in public. I didn't even pay much attention to my parents' accented and ungrammatical speech. At least not at home. Only when I was with them in public would I grow alert to their accents. Though, even then, their sounds caused me less and less concern. For I was increasingly confident of my own public identity.

I would have been happier about my public success had I not sometimes recalled what it had been like earlier, when my family had conveyed its intimacy through a set of conveniently private sounds. Sometimes in public, hearing a stranger, I'd hark back to my past. A Mexican farmworker approached me downtown to ask directions to somewhere, "*¿Hijito. . . ?*" he said. And his voice summoned deep longing. Another time, standing beside my mother in the visiting room of a Carmelite convent, before the dense screen which rendered the nuns shadowy figures, I heard several Spanish-speaking nuns—their busy, singsong overlapping voices—assure us that yes, yes, we were remembered, all our family was remembered in their prayers. (Their voices echoed faraway family sounds.) Another day, a dark-faced old woman— her hand light on my shoulder—steadied herself against me as she boarded a bus. She murmured something I couldn't quite comprehend. Her Spanish voice came near, like the face of a never-before-seen relative in the instant before I was kissed. Her voice, like so many of the Spanish voices I'd hear in public, recalled the golden age of my youth. Hearing Spanish then, I continued to be a careful, if sad, listener to sounds. Hearing a Spanish-speaking family walking behind me, I turned to look. I smiled for an instant, before my glance found the Hispanic-looking faces of strangers in the crowd going by.

Today I hear bilingual educators say that children lose a degree of "individuality" by becoming assimilated into public society. (Bilingual schooling was popularized in the seventies, that decade when middle-class ethnics began to resist the process of assimilation—the American melting pot.) But the bilingualists simplistically scorn the value and necessity of assimilation. They do not seem to realize that there are two ways a person is individualized. So they do not realize that while one suffers a diminished sense of *private* individuality by becoming assimilated into public society, such assimilation makes possible the achievement of *public* individuality.

The bilingualists insist that a student should be reminded of his difference from others in mass society, his heritage. But they equate mere separateness with individuality. The fact is that only in private—with intimates—is separateness from the crowd a prerequisite for individuality. (An intimate draws me apart, tells me that I am unique, unlike all others.) In public, by contrast, full individuality is achieved, paradoxically, by those who are able to consider themselves members of the crowd. Thus it happened for me: Only when I was able to think of myself as an American, no longer an alien in *gringo* society, could I seek the rights and opportunities necessary for full public individuality. The social and political advantages I enjoy as a man result from the day that I came to believe that my name, indeed, is *Rich-heard Road-ree-guess*. It is true that my public society today is often impersonal. (My public society is usually mass society). Yet despite the anonymity of the crowd and despite the fact that the individuality I achieve in public is often tenuous—because it depends on my being one in a crowd—I celebrate the day I acquired my new name. Those middle-class ethnics who scorn assimilation seem to me filled with decadent self-pity, obsessed by the burden of public life. Dangerously, they romanticize public separateness and they trivialize the dilemma of the socially disadvantaged.

My awkward childhood does not prove the necessity of bilingual education. My story discloses instead an essential myth of childhood—inevitable pain. If I rehearse here the changes in my private life after my Americanization, it is finally to emphasize the public gain. The loss implies the gain: The house I returned to each afternoon was quiet. Intimate sounds no longer rushed to the door to greet me. There were other noises inside. The telephone rang. Neighborhood kids ran past the door of the bedroom where I was reading my schoolbooks—covered with shopping-bag paper. Once I learned public language, it would never again be easy for me to hear intimate family voices. More and more of my day was spent hearing words. But that may only be a way of saying that the day I raised my hand in class and spoke loudly to an entire roomful of faces, my childhood started to end.

Russell Baker

from GROWING UP

Russell Baker (1925-   ) is a journalist whose ideas were shaped as
he grew up in a poor family during the Great Depression. In this excerpt from his autobiography, he recounts the shame of "going on relief" and contrasts it with joy of Christmas. As you read the selection,
think about whether society's ideas about people "on relief" or welfare
have changed in sixty years since his story took place.

[My] paper route earned me three dollars a week, sometimes
four, and my mother, in addition to her commissions on magazine
sales, also had her monthly check coming from Uncle Willie, but
we'd been in Baltimore a year before I knew how desperate things
were for her. One Saturday morning she told me she'd need Doris
and me to go with her to pick up some food. I had a small wagon
she'd bought me to make it easier to move the Sunday papers, and
she said I'd better bring it along. The three of us set off eastward,
passing the grocery stores we usually shopped at, and kept walking until we came to Fremont Avenue, a grim street of dilapi-
dation and poverty in the heart of the West Baltimore black belt.

"This is where we go," she said when we reached the corner of
Fremont and Fayette Street. It looked like a grocery, with big
plate-glass windows and people lugging out cardboard cartons
and bulging bags, but it wasn't. I knew very well what it was. "Are
we going on relief?" I asked her.

"Don't ask questions about things you don't know anything
about," she said. "Bring that wagon inside."

I did, and watched with a mixture of shame and greed while
men filled it with food. None of it was food I liked. There were
huge cans of grapefruit juice, big paper sacks of cornmeal, cello-
phane bags of rice and prunes. It was hard to believe all this was
ours for no money at all, even though none of it was very appe-
tizing. My wonder at this free bounty quickly changed to embarrassment as we headed home with it. Being on relief was a

shameful thing. People who accepted the government's handouts were scorned by everyone I knew as idle no-accounts without enough self-respect to pay their own way in the world. I'd often heard my mother say the same thing of families in the neighborhood suspected of being on relief. These, I'd been taught to believe, were people beyond hope. Now we were as low as they were.

Pulling the wagon back toward Lombard Street, with Doris following behind to keep the edible proof of our disgrace from falling off, I knew my mother was far worse off than I'd suspected. She'd never have accepted such shame otherwise. I studied her as she walked along beside me, head high as always, not a bit bowed in disgrace, moving at her usual quick, hurry-up pace. If she'd given up on life, she didn't show it, but on the other hand she was unhappy about something. I dared to mention the dreaded words only once on that trip home.

"Are we on relief now, Mom?"

"Let me worry about that," she said.

What worried me most as we neared home was the possibility we'd be seen with the incriminating food by somebody we knew. There was no mistaking government-surplus food. The grapefruit juice cans, the prunes and rice, the cornmeal—all were ostentatiously unlabeled, thus advertising themselves as "government handouts." Everybody in the neighborhood could read them easily enough, and our humiliation would be gossiped through every parlor by sundown. I had an inspiration.

"It's hot pulling this wagon," I said. "I'm going to take my sweater off."

It wasn't hot, it was on the cool side, but after removing the sweater I laid it across the groceries in the wagon. It wasn't a very effective cover, but my mother was suddenly affected by the heat too.

"It is warm, isn't it, Buddy?" she said. Removing her topcoat, she draped it over the groceries, providing total concealment. "You want to take your coat off, Doris?" asked my mother.

"I'm not hot, I'm chilly," Doris said.

It didn't matter. My mother's coat was enough to get us home without being exposed as three of life's failures. From then on I assumed we were paupers. For this reason I was often astonished when my mother did me some deed of generosity, as when she bought me my first Sunday suit with long pants. The changeover from knickers to long pants was the ritual recognition that a boy had reached adolescence, or "the awkward age," as everybody

called it. The "teenager," like the atomic bomb, was still unin-
vented, and there were few concessions to adolescence, but the
change to long pants was a ritual of recognition. There was no
ceremony about it. You were taken downtown one day and your
escort—my mother in my case—casually said to the suit salesman, "Let's see what you've got in long pants." For me the ritual
was performed in the glossy, mirrored splendor of Bond's clothing
store on Liberty Street. She had taken me for a Sunday suit and,
having decided I looked too gawky in knickers, said, "Let's see
what you've got in long pants." My physique at this time was described by relatives and friends with such irritating words as
"beanpole," "skinny," and "all bones." My mother, seeing me
through eyes that loved, chose to call me "a tall man."

The suit salesman displayed a dazzling assortment of garments.
Suit designers made no concessions to youth; suits for boys were
just like suits for men, only smaller. My mother expressed a preference for something with the double-breasted cut. "A tall man
looks good in a double-breasted suit," she said.

The salesman agreed. Gary Cooper, he said, looked especially
good in double-breasted suits. He produced one. I tried it on. It was
a hard fabric, built to endure. The color was green, not the green
of new grass in spring, but the green of copper patina on old stat-
ues. The green was relieved by thin, light gray stripes, as though
the designer had started to create cloth for a bunco artist, then
changed his mind and decided to appeal to bankers.

"Well, I just don't know," my mother said.

Her taste in clothes was sound rather than flamboyant, but I
considered the suit smashing, and would have nothing else. The
price was $20, which was expensive even though it came with two
pairs of pants, and upon hearing it I said, "We can't afford it."

"That's what you think, mister," she said to me. "It's worth a
little money to have the man of the house look like a gentleman."
In conference with the salesman, it was agreed that she would
pay three dollars down and three dollars a month until the cost
was amortized. On my attenuated physique, this magnificent,
striped, green, double-breasted suit hung like window drapes on a
scarecrow. My mother could imagine Gary Cooper's shoulders
gradually filling out the jacket, but she insisted that Bond's do
something about the voluminous excesses of the pants, which in
the seat area could have accommodated both me and a watermelon. The salesman assured her that Bond's famous tailors
would adjust the trousers without difficulty. They did so. When fi-

nally I had the suit home and put it on for its first trip to church, so much fabric had been removed from the seat that the two hip pockets were located with seams kissing right over my spine.

My mother was dazzled. With visions of a budding Gary Cooper under her wing, she said, "Now you look like somebody I can be proud of," and off to church we went.

She was a magician at stretching a dollar. That December, with Christmas approaching, she was out at work and Doris was in the kitchen when I barged into her bedroom one afternoon in search of a safety pin. Since her bedroom opened onto a community hall-way, she kept the door locked, but needing the pin, I took the key from its hiding place, unlocked the door, and stepped in. Standing against the wall was a big, black bicycle with balloon tires. I rec-ognized it instantly. It was the same second hand bike I'd been admiring in a Baltimore Street shop window I'd even asked about the price. It was horrendous. Something like $15. Somehow my mother had scraped together enough for a dow payment and meant to surprise me with the bicycle on Christmas morning.

I was overwhelmed by the discovery that she had squandered such money on me and sickened by the knowledge that, bursting into her room like this, I had robbed her of the pleasure of seeing me astonished and delighted on Christmas day. I hadn't wanted to know her lovely secret; still, stumbling upon it like this made me feel as though I'd struck a blow against her happiness. I backed out, put the key back in its hiding place, and brooded pri-vately.

I resolved that between now and Christmas I must do nothing, absolutely nothing, to reveal the slightest hint of my terrible knowledge. I must avoid the least word, the faintest intonation, the weakest gesture that might reveal my possession of her secret. Nothing must deny her the happiness of seeing me stunned with amazement on Christmas day.

In the privacy of my bedroom I began composing and testing exclamations of delight: "Wow!" "A bike with balloon tires! I don't believe it!" "I'm the luckiest boy alive!" And so on. They all owed a lot to movies in which boys like Mickey Rooney had seen their wildest dreams come true, and I realized that, with my lack of acting talent, all of them were going to sound false at the critical moment when I wanted to cry out my love spontaneously from the heart. Maybe it would be better to say nothing but appear to be shocked into such deep pleasure that speech had escaped me. I wasn't sure, though. I'd seen speechless gratitude in the movies too, and it never really worked until the actors managed to cry a few quiet tears. I doubted I could cry on cue, so I began thinking about other expressions of speechless amazement. In front of a hand-held mirror in my bedroom I tried the whole range of expressions: mouth agape and eyes wide; hands slapped firmly against both cheeks to keep the jaw from falling off; ear-to-ear grin with all teeth fully exposed while hugging the torso with both arms. These and more I practiced for several days without acquiring confidence in any of them. I decided to wait until Christmas morning and see if anything came naturally.

Christmas was the one occasion on which my mother surrendered to unabashed sentimentality. A week beforehand she always concocted homemade root beer, sealed it in canning jars, and stored it in the bathroom for the yeast to ferment. Now and then, sitting in the adjoining kitchen, we heard a loud thump from the bathroom and knew one of the jars had exploded, but she always made enough to allow for breakage. She took girlish delight in keeping her brightly wrapped gifts hidden in closets. Christmas Eve she spent in frenzies of baking—cakes, pies, gingerbread cookies cut and decorated to look like miniature brown pine trees and Santa Clauses. In the afternoon she took Doris and me to the street corner where trees were piled high and searched through them until she found one that satisfied our taste for fullness and symmetry. It was my job and Doris's to set the tree up in the parlor and weight it with ornaments, lights, and silver icicles, while she prepared Christmas Eve dinner. This was a ritual meal at which the centerpiece was always oysters. She disliked oysters but always ate them on Christmas Eve. Oysters were the centerpiece of the traditional Christmas Eve supper she remembered from her girlhood in Virginia. By serving them she perpetuated the customs of Papa's household.

She did not place her gifts under the tree that night until Doris and I had gone to bed. We were far beyond believing in Santa Claus, but she insisted on preserving the forms of the childhood myth that these were presents from some divine philanthropist. She planned all year for this annual orgy of spending and girded for it by putting small deposits month after month into her Christmas Club account at the bank.

That Christmas morning she roused us early, "to see what Santa Claus brought," she said with just the right tone of irony to indicate we were all old enough to know who Santa Claus was. I came out of my bedroom with my presents for her and Doris, and

Doris came with hers. My mother's had been placed under the tree during the night. There were a few small glittering packages, a big doll for Doris, but no bicycle. I must have looked disappointed.

"It looks like Santa Claus didn't do too well by you this year, Buddy," she said, as I opened packages. A shirt. A necktie. I said something halfhearted like, "It's the thought that counts," but what I felt was bitter disappointment. I supposed she'd found the bike intolerably expensive and sent it back.

"Wait a minute!" she cried, snapping her fingers. "There's something in my bedroom I forgot all about."

She beckoned to Doris, the two of them went out, and a moment later came back wheeling between them the big black two-wheeler with balloon tires. I didn't have to fake my delight, after all. The three of us—Doris, my mother, and I—were people bred to repress the emotional expressions of love, but I did something that startled both my mother and me. I threw my arms around her spontaneously and kissed her.

"All right now, don't carry on about it. It's only a bicycle," she said.

Still, I knew that she was as happy as I was to see her so happy.

Mark Gerrard (student)

BOZO REVISITED

Mark's story could be that of any child—finding out about Santa Claus, the Easter Bunny, or Superman. In his case, it happened to be Bozo. What makes his story so effective is precisely that it *is* something we have all experienced in one way or another. As you read, notice how Mark builds anticipation in the same way a child does when looking forward to an exciting event.

I do not remember very much of Kenny Weinguard. The memory I have of him is hazy, and the face my mind connects with the name could very well be wrong. However, I do remember his birthdays. Mrs. Weinguard, Kenny's mother, was a fierce, talkative and overbearing woman who was sickeningly attached to her son. The birthday parties she threw for his were the envy of the entire neighborhood.

My memory of her is quite vivid. She was an artist and fancied herself to be the Auntie Mame type. She wore long colorful gowns with baubles, beads and bangles of every shape and color imaginable hanging everywhere. I was very frightened of her, thinking she was some sort of Gypsy sorceress. I always had the feeling she never liked me much. But her "events," as she liked to call them, were above reproach. For Kenny's fifth birthday she rented a movie theater and showed us "The Man Who Would Be King." For Kenny's sixth birthday she took us to a Cubs game. But on Kenny's seventh birthday she outdid even herself; she managed to get hold of a birthday party's worth of tickets to the taping of Bozo's Circus. This was quite a feat at the time. The waiting list for tickets was just under seven years. I have visions of her recovering in the maternity ward dictating a letter for tickets.

When I received my invitation, though I knew it was sent only as a favor to my mother, I was thrilled. I was an avid Bozo watcher, and I knew every aspect of the show. I thought of Bozo, Cookie and Mr. Ned as my own personal friends. The circus acts amazed me. I was enraptured by the cartoons. The most exciting thought, however, was the chance to be chosen out of the studio audience to play the Bozo Bucket game. Even at the young age of seven I was a television addict. My sister and I spent endless hours pretending to do our own television shows. The thought of being a TV star, even for just a moment, fulfilled my every fantasy.

After what seemed to be years of waiting, the big day finally arrived. I bounded out of bed that morning and rushed to my mother. I was astounded to find her still in bed sleeping. I rushed and woke her up, imploring her to wake up and get me ready. She informed me, in that "I wish I never had a child" voice that parents take in the early hours of the morning, that it was six thirty, and as the show was not until two in the afternoon, I should leave her alone and find something else to occupy my time. I was heartbroken at this rebuke. How could my own mother be so unconcerned on this, the most important day of my life? After what seemed to be another decade, my mother took my best clothes and got me dressed. She drove me over to the Weinguard's house and dropped me off.

As I walked to the door a strange sense of foreboding overtook me. I looked at the gradually darkening sky and realized a big storm was on its way. I ran to the door and rang the bell. Mrs.

Weinguard opened it. The door creaked ominously. I felt like I was in the middle of a *Munsters* episode. I tried to shake thoughts of disaster out of my mind, but they persisted even as Mrs. Weinguard herded us out of the house and into her station wagon.

The ride to the studio was a nightmare. The rain by the middle of the car ride became so heavy that it was impossible to see out any of the windows. I was terrified. The car was crowded with eight other screaming seven-year-olds. I was hot in my rain gear but too cramped to manage to get out of it. Mrs. Weinguard led us in a round of "Row, Row, Row Your Boat" as she maneuvered the car blindly at death-defying speeds. I was never so happy in my life as when we finally arrived and I again put my young feet on solid ground.

We ran for cover in the main entrance of the WGN building. Before I had time to dry, I was standing in the Bozo studio. My original feeling of excitement crept back, and the horrors of the car ride faded into the background. We were ushered up to the top row of a set of bleachers, and the usher made a point of sitting Kenny on the aisle. I was squeezed between Kenny and his mother. I looked around and was astounded at how small the studio looked. What appeared to be a huge circus tent at home was actually the size of a small gymnasium. I mentioned this to Mrs. Weinguard. She looked down at me, straightened my tie, and told me I didn't know how to dress myself.

Then the music started and my heart jumped. Mr. Ned, the ringmaster, appeared. He greeted us, and excitedly told us to turn our heads to the center ring to watch some performing poodles. I eagerly turned my head and saw nothing. The music in the background came to a halt. An announcement was made that the poodles had been pre-recorded and that if we wished to see them we could look at the monitors. I searched for a monitor. The closest one was so far away I could see and hear nothing. After five minutes the poodles stopped and commercials appeared on the distant monitor. During this break, another announcement was made. We were told that Bozo was sick and would not be performing. A gasp went through the audience. I was devastated. Before I could gather my thoughts the show resumed. Mr. Ned announced a clown act. This time it was live. I was so angry that the clowns didn't strike me to be the least bit funny. After the clown act had come to a conclusion, Cookie, one of the clowns, introduced a cartoon. The cartoon, like the poodles, was pre-recorded. I could hardly contain myself. I looked around, bewildered, and noticed the audience felt the same as I did. My anger gradually turned to self-pity. I resigned myself to the fact that Bozo was all a great hoax.

Eventually the Bozo Bucket Game, the climax of the show, arrived. The magic arrows began flashing across the distant TV monitor. My self-pity vanished as I intently watched the screen. Would I be the one picked? Would I have the chance to be seen by millions of people across the world? Would I win all those fabulous prizes? I watched as the magic arrows landed. I gasped as they landed on me. I jumped up. I was screaming and carrying on. My thoughts began to move in slow motion. I could imagine my mother sitting at home, beaming with parental pride, watching as her son became a television superstar. I started to move sideways, only to see Kenny half way down the bleachers already. Mrs. Weinguard turned to me, smiled, and informed me that the arrows had landed on Kenny because it was his birthday. I stopped dead in my tracks. I sat down completely dumbfounded. They had sat Kenny down at the aisle because he was chosen beforehand. The magic arrows were a fraud. Bozo's circus was a fraud. I watched silently as Kenny loused up the game.

The ride home seemed like an eternity. I told Mrs. Weinguard that I was sick and didn't wish to go back to her house for the party portion of the "event." Mrs. Weinguard pleasantly agreed. When I got home, I ran upstairs and collapsed crying in my mother's arms. I was too incoherent to tell her what had happened. She assumed I had gotten into a fight with someone. I felt oddly comforted by my mother's inappropriate comforting words. At the very least my mother was not pre-recorded.

Anne Frank

DIARY

Anne Frank (1929-1945) was a young girl in Amsterdam who went into hiding with her family during World War II to avoid the horrors of the Holocaust. Her diary ("kitty") is her personal record of their hiding—a hiding which ended in her own internment and death. It was published by her family after the war, and was adopted by children

and adults around the world as the honest, innocent story of an average girl trapped in extraordinary circumstances. In this excerpt, she
recounts the changes she has gone through since her family went into
hiding.

Tuesday, 7 March, 1944

Dear Kitty,

If I think now of my life in 1942, it all seems so unreal. It was
quite a different Anne who enjoyed that heavenly existence from
the Anne who has grown wise within these walls. Yes, it was a
heavenly life. Boy friends at every turn, about twenty friends and
acquaintances of my own age, the darling of nearly all the
teachers, spoiled from top to toe by Mummy and Daddy, lots of
sweets, enough pocket money, what more could one want? You
will certainly wonder by what means I got around all these people.
Peter s word "attractiveness" is not altogether true. All the teachers were entertained by my cute answers, my amusing remarks,
my smiling face, and my questioning looks. That is all I was—a
terrible flirt, coquettish and amusing. I had one or two advantages, which kept me rather in favor. I was industrious, honest,
and frank. I would never have dreamed of cribbing from anyone
else [I would never have refused anyone who wanted to crib from
me]. I shared my sweets generously, and I wasn't conceited.

Wouldn't I have become rather forward with so much admiration? It was a good thing that in the midst of, at the height of, all
this gaiety, I suddenly had to face reality and it took me at least a
year to get used to the fact that there was no more admiration
forthcoming.

How did I appear at school? The one who thought of new jokes
and pranks, always "king of the castle," never in a bad mood,
never a crybaby. No wonder everyone liked to cycle with me, and
I got their attentions.

Now I look back at that Anne as an amusing, but very superficial girl, who has nothing to do with the Anne of today. Peter said
quite rightly about me: "If ever I saw you, you were always surrounded by two or more boys and a whole troupe of girls. You
were always laughing and always the center of everything!"

What is left of this girl? Oh, don't worry, I haven't forgotten how
to laugh or to answer back readily. I'm just as good, if not better, at
criticizing people, and I can still flirt if. . . I wish. That's not it
though, I'd like that sort of life again for an evening, a few days, or
even a week; the life which seems so carefree and gay. But at the

end of that week, I should be dead beat and would be only too thankful to listen to anyone who began to talk about something sensible.

I don't want followers, but friends, admirers who fall not for a flattering smile but for what one does and for one's character. I know quite well that the circle around me would be much smaller. But what does that matter, as long as one still keeps a few sincere friends? Yet I wasn't entirely happy in 1942 in spite of everything; I often felt deserted, but because I was on the go the whole day long, I didn't think about it and enjoyed myself as much as I could. Consciously or unconsciously, I tried to drive away the emptiness I felt with jokes and pranks. Now I think seriously about life and what I have to do. One period of my life is over forever. The carefree schooldays are gone, never to return. I don't even long for them any more; I have outgrown them, I can't just only enjoy myself as my serious side is always there.

I look upon my life up till the New Year, as it were, through a powerful magnifying glass. The sunny life at home, then coming here in 1942, the sudden change, the quarrels, the bickerings, I couldn't understand it, I was taken by surprise, and the only way I could keep up some bearing was by being impertinent.

The first half of 1943: my fits of crying, the loneliness, how I slowly began to see all my faults and shortcomings, which are so great and which seemed much greater then. During the day I deliberately talked about anything and everything that was farthest from my thoughts, tried to draw Pim to me; but couldn't. Alone I had to face the difficult task of changing myself, to stop the everlasting reproaches, which were so oppressive and which reduced me to such terrible despondency.

Things improved slightly in the second half of the year, I became a young woman and was treated more like a grownup. I started to think, and write stories, and came to the conclusion that the others no longer had the right to throw me about like an india-rubber ball. I wanted to change in accordance with my own desires. But one thing that struck me even more was when I realized that even Daddy would never become my confidant over everything. I didn't want to trust anyone but myself any more. At the beginning of the New Year: the second great change, my dream.... And with it I discovered my longing, not for a girl friend, but for a boy friend. I also discovered my inward happiness and my defensive armor of superficiality and gaiety. In due time I quieted down and discovered my boundless desire for all that is beautiful and good.

And in the evening, when I lie in bed and end my prayers with the words, "I thank you, God, for all that is good and dear and beautiful," I am filled with joy. Then I think about "the good" of going into hiding, of my health and with my whole being of the "dearness" of Peter, of that which is still embryonic and impressionable and which we neither of us dare to name or touch, of that which will come sometime; love, the future, happiness and of "the beauty" which exists in the world; the world, nature, beauty and all, all that is exquisite and fine.

I don't think then of all the misery, but of the beauty that still remains. This is one of the things that Mummy and I are so entirely different about. Her counsel when one feels melancholy is: "Think of all the misery in the world and be thankful that you are not sharing in it!" My advice is: "Go outside, to the fields, enjoy nature and the sunshine, go out and try to recapture happiness in yourself and in God. Think of all the beauty that's still left in and around you and be happy!"

I don't see how Mummy's idea can be right, because then how are you supposed to behave if you go through the misery yourself? Then you are lost. On the contrary, I've found that there is always some beauty left—in nature, sunshine, freedom, in yourself; these can all help you. Look at these things, then you find yourself again, and God, and then you regain your balance.

And whoever is happy will make others happy too. He who has courage and faith will never perish in misery!

Yours, Anne

Woody Allen

MY SPEECH TO GRADUATES

Woody Allen (1935-   ), a writer, actor, and film director, started as a writer for television shows like *The Tonight Show*, but soon became an independent talent, gaining great fame by writing, directing, and acting in his own movies. Today, he continues to live in New York City, and continues to produce films. In this essay, he comments on the enormous expectations put on college graduates by making light of the terrific problems they face. As you read this selection, consider whether you ever felt you could help solve any of the problems Allen brings up. Do you still feel that way?

More than any other time in history, mankind faces a crossroads. One path leads to despair and utter hopelessness. The other, to total extinction. Let us pray we have the wisdom to choose correctly. I speak, by the way, not with any sense of futility, but with a panicky conviction of the absolute meaninglessness of existence which could easily be misinterpreted as pessimism. It is not. It is merely a healthy concern for the predicament of modern man. (Modern man is here defined as any person born after Nietzsche's edict that "God is dead," but before the hit recording "I Wanna Hold Your Hand.") This "predicament" can be stated one of two ways, though certain linguistic philosophers prefer to reduce it to a mathematical equation where it can be easily solved and even carried around in the wallet.

Put in its simplest form, the problem is: How is it possible to find meaning in a finite world given my waist and shirt size? This is a very difficult question when we realize that science has failed us. True, it has conquered many diseases, broken the genetic code, and even placed human beings on the moon, and yet when a man of eighty is left in a room with two eighteen-year-old cocktail waitresses nothing happens. Because the real problems never change. After all, can the human soul be glimpsed through a microscope? Maybe—but you'd definitely need one of those very good ones with two eyepieces. We know that the most advanced computer in the world does not have a brain as sophisticated as that of an ant. True, we could say that of many of our relatives but we only have to put up with them at weddings or special occasions. Science is something we depend on all the time. If I develop a pain in the chest I must take an X-ray. But what if the radiation from the X-ray causes me deeper problems? Before I know it, I'm going in for surgery. Naturally, while they're giving me oxygen an intern decides to light up a cigarette. The next thing you know I'm rocketing over the World Trade Center in bed clothes. Is this science? True, science has taught us how to pasteurize cheese. And true, this can be fun in mixed company—but what of the H-bomb? Have you ever seen what happens when one of those things falls off a desk accidentally? And where is science when one ponders the eternal riddles? How did the cosmos originate? How long

has it been around? Did matter begin with an explosion or by the
word of God? And if by the latter, could He not have begun it just
two weeks earlier to take advantage of some of the warmer
weather? Exactly what do we mean when we say, man is mortal?
Obviously it's not a compliment.

Religion too has unfortunately let us down. Miguel de
Unamuno writes blithely of the "eternal persistence of consciousness," but this is no easy feat. Particularly when reading
Thackeray. I often think how comforting life must have been for
early man—because he believed in a powerful, benevolent
Creator who looked after all things. Imagine his disappointment
when he saw his wife putting on weight. Contemporary man, of
course, has no such peace of mind. He finds himself in the midst of
a crisis of faith. He is what we fashionably call "alienated." He has
seen the ravages of war, he has known natural catastrophes, he
has been to singles bars. My good friend Jacques Monod spoke
often of the randomness of the cosmos. He believed everything in
existence occurred by pure chance with the possible exception of
his breakfast, which he felt certain was made by his housekeeper.
Naturally belief in a divine intelligence inspires tranquillity. But
this does not free us from our human responsibilities. Am I my
brother's keeper? Yes. Interestingly, in my case I share that honor
with the Prospect Park Zoo. Feeling godless then, what we have
done is made technology God. And yet can technology really be the
answer when a brand new Buick, driven by my close associate,
Nat Zipsky, winds up in the window of Chicken Delight causing
hundreds of customers to scatter? My toaster has never once
worked properly in four years. I follow the instructions and push
two slices of bread down in the slots and seconds later they rifle
upward. Once they broke the nose of a woman I loved very dearly.
Are we counting on nuts and bolts and electricity to solve our
problems? Yes, the telephone is a good thing—and the refrig-
erator—and the air conditioner. But not every air conditioner.
Not my sister Henny's, for instance. Hers makes a loud noise and
still doesn't cool. When the man comes over to fix it, it gets worse.
Either that or he tells her she needs a new one. When she com-
plains, he says not to bother him. This man is truly alienated. Not
only is he alienated but he can't stop smiling.

The trouble is, our leaders have not adequately prepared us for a
mechanized society. Unfortunately our politicians are either incompetent or corrupt. Sometimes both on the same day. The
Government is unresponsive to the needs of the little man. Under

five-seven, it is impossible to get your Congressman on the phone. I am not denying that democracy is still the finest form of government. In a democracy at least, civil liberties are upheld. No citizen can be wantonly tortured, imprisoned, or made to sit through certain Broadway shows. And yet this is a far cry from what goes on in the Soviet Union. Under their form of totalitarianism, a person merely caught whistling is sentenced to thirty years in a labor camp. If, after fifteen years, he still will not stop whistling, they shoot him. Along with this brutal fascism we find its handmaiden, terrorism. At no other time in history has man been so afraid to cut into his veal chop for fear that it will explode. Violence breeds more violence and it is predicted that by 1990 kidnapping will be the dominant mode of social interaction. Overpopulation will exacerbate problems to the breaking point. Figures tell us there are already more people on earth than we need to move even the heaviest piano. If we do not call a halt to breeding, by the year 2000 there will be no room to serve dinner unless one is willing to set the table on the heads of strangers. Then they must not move for an hour while we eat. Of course energy will be in short supply and each car owner will be allowed only enough gasoline to back up a few inches.

Instead of facing these challenges we turn instead to distractions like drugs and sex. We live in far too permissive a society. Never before has pornography been this rampant. And those films are lit so badly! We are a people who lack defined goals. We have never learned to love. We lack leaders and coherent programs. We have no spiritual center. We are adrift alone in the cosmos wreaking monstrous violence on one another out of frustration and pain. Fortunately, we have not lost our sense of proportion. Summing up, it is clear the future holds great opportunities. It also holds pitfalls. The trick will be to avoid the pitfalls, seize the opportunities, and get back home by six o'clock.

E. B. White

ONCE MORE TO THE LAKE

In this selection, White examines the contrast between his recol-
lection of a lake he had visited as a child and his experience of visiting
it as an adult. The result is a cutting statement on our own mortality.
And as always, White saves the best for last. As you read, look for evidence of the similarities between the lake as White describes it and as
he remembers it. Notice the change in tone when he describes the differences.

One summer, along about 1904, my father rented a camp on a
lake in Maine and took us all there for the month of August. We
all got ringworm from some kittens and had to rub Pond's
Extract on our arms and legs night and morning, and my father
rolled over in a canoe with all his clothes on; but outside of that the
vacation was a success and from then on none of us ever thought
there was any place in the world like that lake in Maine. We returned summer after summer—always on August 1st for one
month. I have since become a salt-water man, but sometimes in
summer there are days when the restlessness of the tides and the
fearful cold of the sea water and the incessant wind that blows
across the afternoon and into the evening make me wish for the
placidity of a lake in the woods. A few weeks ago this feeling got so
strong I bought myself a couple of bass hooks and a spinner and
returned to the lake where we used to go, for a week's fishing and
to revisit old haunts.

I took along my son, who had never had any fresh water up his
nose and who had seen lily pads only from train windows. On the
journey over to the lake I began to wonder what it would be like. I
wondered how time would have marred this unique, this holy
spot— the coves and streams, the hills that the sun set behind, the
camps and the paths behind the camps. I was sure that the tarred
road would have found it out and I wondered in what other ways
it would be desolated. It is strange how much you can remember
about places like that once you allow your mind to return into the

grooves that lead back. You remember one thing, and that suddenly reminds you of another thing. I guess I remembered clearest of all the early mornings, when the lake was cool and motionless, remembered how the bedroom smelled of the lumber it was made of and of the wet woods whose scent entered through the screen. The partitions in the camp were thin and did not extend clear to the top of the rooms, and as I was always the first up I would dress softly so as not to wake the others, and sneak out into the sweet outdoors and start out in the canoe, keeping close along the shore in the long shadows of the pines. I remembered being very careful never to rub my paddle against the gunwale for fear of disturbing the stillness of the cathedral.

The lake had never been what you would call a wild lake. There were cottages sprinkled around the shores, and it was in farming country although the shores of the lake were quite heavily wooded. Some of the cottages were owned by nearby farmers, and you would live at the shore and eat your meals at the farmhouse. That's what our family did. But although it wasn't wild, it was a fairly large and undisturbed lake and there were places in it which, to a child at least, seemed infinitely remote and primeval.

I was right about the tar: it led to within half a mile of the shore. But when I got back there, with my boy, and we settled into a camp near a farmhouse and into the kind of summertime I had known, I could tell that it was going to be pretty much the same as it had been before—I knew it, lying in bed the first morning, smelling the bedroom, and hearing the boy sneak quietly out and go off along the shore in a boat. I began to sustain the illusion that he was I, and therefore, by simple transposition, that I was my father. This sensation persisted, kept cropping up all the time we were there. It was not an entirely new feeling, but in this setting it grew much stronger. I seemed to be living a dual existence. I would be in the middle of some simple act, I would be picking up a bait box or laying down a table fork, or I would be saying something, and suddenly it would be not I but my father who was saying the words or making the gesture. It gave me a creepy sensation.

We went fishing the first morning. I felt the same damp moss covering the worms in the bait can, and saw the dragonfly alight on the tip of my rod as it hovered a few inches from the surface of the water. It was the arrival of this fly that convinced me beyond any doubt that everything was as it always had been, that the years were a mirage and there had been no years. The small waves were the same, chucking the rowboat under the chin as we fished at anchor, and the boat was the same boat, the same color green and the ribs broken in the same places, and under the floorboards the same fresh-water leavings and debris—the dead hellgrammite, the wisps of moss, the rusty discarded fishhook, the dried blood from yesterday's catch. We stared silently at the tips of our rods, at the dragonflies that came and went. I lowered the tip of mine into the water, tentatively, pensively dislodging the fly, which darted two feet away, poised, darted two feet back, and came to rest again a little farther up the rod. There had been no years between the ducking of this dragonfly and the other one— the one that was part of memory. I looked at the boy, who was silently watching his fly, and it was my hands that held his rod, my eyes watching. I felt dizzy and didn't know which rod I was at the end of.

We caught two bass, hauling them in briskly as though they were mackerel, pulling them over the side of the boat in a businesslike manner without any landing net, and stunning them with a blow on the back of the head. When we got back for a swim before lunch, the lake was exactly where we had left it, the same number of inches from the dock, and there was only the merest suggestion of a breeze. This seemed an utterly enchanted sea, this lake you could leave to its own devices for a few hours and come back to, and find that it had not stirred, this constant and trustworthy body of water. In the shallows, the dark, water-soaked sticks and twigs, smooth and old, were undulating in clusters on the bottom against the clean ribbed sand, and the track of the mussel was plain. A school of minnows swam by, each minnow with its small individual shadow, doubling the attendance, so clear and sharp in the sunlight. Some of the other campers were in swimming, along the shore, one of them with a cake of soap, and the water felt thin and clear and unsubstantial. Over the years there had been this person with the cake of soap, this cultist, and here he was. There had been no years.

Up to the farmhouse to dinner through the teeming, dusty field, the road under our sneakers was only a two-track road. The middle track was missing, the one with the marks of the hooves and splotches of dried, flaky manure. There had always been three tracks to choose from in choosing which track to walk in; now the choice was narrowed down to two. For a moment I missed terribly the middle alternative. But the way led past the tennis court, and something about the way it lay there in the sun reassured me; the tape had loosened along the backline, the alleys were green with plantains and other weeds, and the net I installed in June and removed in September sagged in the dry noon, and the whole place steamed with midday heat and hunger and emptiness. There was a choice of pie for dessert, and one was blueberry and one was apple, and the waitresses were the same country girls, there having been no passage of time, only the illusion of it as in a dropped curtain—the waitresses were still fifteen; their hair had been washed, that was the only difference—they had been to the movies and seen the pretty girls with the clean hair.

Summertime, oh summertime, pattern of life indelible, the fadeproof lake, the woods unshatterable, the pasture with the sweetfern and the juniper forever and ever, summer without end; this was the background, and the life along the shore was the design, the cottages with their innocent and tranquil design, their tiny docks with the flagpole and the American flag floating against the white clouds in the blue sky, the little paths over the roots of the trees leading from camp to camp and the paths leading back to the outhouses and the can of lime for sprinkling, and at the souvenir counters at the store the miniature birch-bark canoes and the post cards that showed things looking a little better than they looked. This was the American family at play, escaping the city heat, wondering whether the newcomers in the camp at the head of the cove were "common" or "nice," wondering whether it was true that the people who drove up for Sunday dinner at the farmhouse were turned away because there wasn't enough chicken.

It seemed to me, as I kept remembering all this, that those times and those summers had been infinitely precious and worth saving. There had been jollity and peace and goodness. The arriving (at the beginning of August) had been so big a business in itself, at the railway station the farm wagon drawn up, the first smell of the pine-laden air, the first glimpse of the smiling farmer, and the great importance of the trunks and your father's enormous authority in such matters, and the feel of the wagon under you for the long ten-mile haul, and at the top of the last long hill catching the first view of the lake after eleven months of not seeing this cherished body of water. The shouts and cries of the other campers when they saw you, and the trunks to be unpacked, to give up their rich burden. (Arriving was less exciting nowadays, when you sneaked up in your car and parked it under a tree near the

camp and took out the bags and in five minutes it was all over, no
fuss, no loud wonderful fuss about trunks.)

Peace and goodness and jollity. The only thing that was wrong
now, really, was the sound of the place, an unfamiliar nervous
sound of the outboard motors. This was the note that jarred, the
one thing that would sometimes break the illusion and set the
years moving. In those other summertimes all motors were in-
board; and when they were at a little distance, the noise they made
was a sedative, an ingredient of summer sleep. They were one-
cylinder and two-cylinder engines, and some were make-and-
break and some were jump-spark, but they all made a sleepy
sound across the lake. The one-lungers throbbed and fluttered,
and the twin-cylinder ones purred and purred and that was a
quiet sound too. But now the campers all had outboards. In the
daytime, in the hot mornings, these motors made a petulant, irri-
table sound; at night, in the still evening when the afterglow lit the
water, they whined about one's ears like mosquitoes. My boy loved
our rented outboard, and his great desire was to achieve single-
handed mastery over it, and authority, and he soon learned the
trick of choking it a little but not too much, and the adjustment of
the needle valve. Watching him I would remember the things you
could do with the old one-cylinder engine with the heavy flywheel,
how you could have it eating out of your hand if you got really
close to it spiritually. Motor boats in those days didn't have
clutches, and you would make a landing by shutting off the motor
at the proper time and coasting in with a dead rudder. But there
was a way of reversing them, if you learned the trick, by cutting
the switch and putting it on again exactly on the final dying revolution of the flywheel, so that it would kick back against com-
pression and begin reversing. Approaching a dock in a strong following breeze, it was difficult to slow up sufficiently by the ordinary coasting method, and if a boy felt he had complete mastery
over his motor, he was tempted to keep it running beyond its time
and then reverse it a few feet from the dock. It took a cool nerve,
because if you threw the switch a twentieth of a second too soon
you could catch the flywheel when it still had speed enough to go
up past center, and the boat would leap ahead, charging bull-
fashion at the dock.

We had a good week at the camp. The bass were biting well and
the sun shone endlessly, day after day. We would be tired at night
and lie down in the accumulated heat of the little bedrooms after
the long hot day and the breeze would stir almost imperceptibly

outside and the smell of the swamp drift in through the rusty
screens. Sleep would come easily and in the morning the red
squirrel would be on the roof, tapping out his gay routine. I kept
remembering everything, lying in bed in the mornings—the
small steamboat that had a long rounded stern like the lip of a
Ubangi, and how quietly she ran on the moonlight sails, when the
older boys played their mandolins and the girls sang and we ate
doughnuts dipped in sugar, and how sweet the music was on the
water in the shining light, and what it had felt like to think about
girls then. After breakfast we would go up to the store and the
things were in the same place—the minnows in a bottle, the plugs
and spinners disarranged and pawed over by the youngsters from
the boys' camp, the fig newtons and the Beeman's gum. Outside,
the road was tarred and cars stood in front of the store. Inside, all
was just as it had always been, except there was more Coca-Cola
and not so much Moxie and root beer and birch beer and
sarsaparilla. We would walk out with a bottle of pop apiece and
sometimes the pop would backfire up our noses and hurt. We ex-
plored the streams, quietly, where the turtles slid off the sunny
logs and dug their way into the soft bottom; and we lay on the
town wharf and fed worms to the tame bass. Everywhere we
went I had trouble making out which was I, the one walking at
my side, the one walking in my pants.

One afternoon while we were there at that lake a thunderstorm
came up. It was like the revival of an old melodrama that I had
seen long ago with childish awe. The second-act climax of the
drama of the electrical disturbance over a lake in America had
not changed in any important respect. This was the big scene, still
the big scene. The whole thing was so familiar, the first feeling of
oppression and heat and a general air around camp of not wanting to go very far away. In midafternoon (it was all the same) a
curious darkening of the sky, and a lull in everything that had
made life tick; and then the way the boats suddenly swung the
other way at their moorings with the coming of a breeze out of the
new quarter, and the premonitory rumble. Then the kettle drum,
then the snare, then the bass drum and cymbals, then crackling
light against the dark, and the gods grinning and licking their
chops in the hills. Afterward the calm, the rain steadily rustling in
the calm lake, the return of light and hope and spirits, and the
campers running out in joy and relief to go swimming in the rain,
their bright cries perpetuating the deathless joke about how they
were getting simply drenched, and the children screaming with

delight at the new sensation of bathing in the rain, and the joke about getting drenched linking the generations in a strong inde- structible chain. And the comedian who waded in carrying an umbrella.

When the others went swimming my son said he was going in too. He pulled his dripping trunks from the line where they had hung all through the shower, and wrung them out. Languidly, and with no thought of going in, I watched him, his hard little body, skinny and bare, saw him wince slightly as he pulled up around his vitals the small, soggy, icy garment. As he buckled the swollen belt suddenly my groin felt the chill of death.

Janet (Student)

ONCE MORE TO THE POOL

Janet's essay follows the pattern of White's, but since her reflection comes at a younger age, the conclusion is different. As you read, see how Janet uses different rhetorical patterns to further distinguish her essay from White's.

From the time I could swim until I was nine years old, I spent every summer underwater. All summer long, from the moment the municipal pool opened, my family and I would be there for a full day of fun in the concrete, three different-sized pools, glo- riously sticky snack foods at breaks for grown-up swims, and home again to sweat underneath a fan and the Indiana moon.

When we first arrived, if the pool was just opening, the dressing room would be almost dry, with the only light a murky grey nat- ural light that leaked through transomlike windows near the ceiling. You were required to take a shower before entering the pool, but getting your hair wet counted. The shower didn't have knobs for the water, just a space-age round button, the size of a baby's fist, which we'd punch as hard as we could; when the but- ton came back out, automatically, the water would stop and the sentence was up.

The next two steps that impeded our progress to the pool were the footbath and the basket. Early in the day, like during the summer when I took swim lessons at eight-thirty in the morning, the footbath would be almost empty, just a little trickle of water covering a rubber mat. By the time we left, it would be ankle-deep, or knee-deep for tots. The water would be either freezing and fresh or warmly overused, and if I hadn't been in a hurry, I might have enjoyed the massage of the rubber mat. But all I could think of was getting to the pool.

The last step was to exchange a clothing basket for a pin with a number on it. Nothing was locked up but I knew everything would be safe in the locker room, full of sullen teenagers hiding behind a dutch door and a sign that said "Authorized Personnel Only." I felt sorry for those people, trapped without visitors, but they seemed to enjoy their authority, or at least, their authorization. They gave you a numbered metal tag attached to a safety pin, you pinned it to your bathing suit, and you were off!

Not so fast, kids! No running on the concrete! No roughhousing by the pool! First, we put our towels down. Then we took off our rubber thongs. We had to make sure Mom could see us. Only accompanied children allowed in the medium pool—come on, Mom!

I couldn't dive without noseplugs and I never liked the breathing they taught for the crawlstroke, so most of the time I did somersaults or handstands, swam in endless rotation with my friend Jessica: between her legs, she between mine, or sat on the steps that gradually got deeper in gradually colder water. Sometimes I would rescue ladybugs from drowning or being sucked into the mysterious water-cleaning system, but they were all so dumb they just went right back in. On my toughest days I'd plow down the waterslide face forward on my belly, screaming all the way.

Other days I preferred the calm warmth of the tot pool to more visceral thrills, and I'd daydream while water bubbled out of the center of this shallow fountain, sometimes getting bumped into by a floating toddler. But the best times I ever had were in the medium pool. We were allowed to take inflatable toys in this pool, and until it popped, we had a yellow dolphin that would dive and leap as you tried to gain a seat on its slippery back. Sometimes we'd be there when the clouds coated the sky but before lightning cleared and closed the pool. It would just be me and my brother and sister in our chlorinated blue heaven, riding a yellow dolphin, waiting until the last alarm.

My underwater years ended abruptly when my family moved from sunny Indiana to moist Seattle, land of the indoor pool. Pools were serious places there, with divided lanes, rectangles with ladders but no stairs, no slides, no lost ladybugs. Pools without fences or wading depths, no clouds above and no room for a dolphin or a dreamer. I left the water within the walls and, unable to adapt to graceful, boring laps, have rarely returned.

ACKNOWLEDGEMENTS

ALLEN: "My Speech to Graduates" from *Side Effects*. Copyright © 1980 by Woody Allen. Reprinted by permission of Random House, Inc.

ALEXANDER: "Fashions in Funerals" from *Talking Woman* by Shana Alexander, pp. 120-121. Copyright © 1986 by Shana Alexander. Reprinted by permission.

ANGELOU: "Graduation" from *I Know Why the Caged Bird Sings* by Maya Angelou. Copyright © 1969 by Maya Angelou. Reprinted by permission of Random House, Inc.

ARISTOTLE: "De Partibus Anamalium" translated by William Ogle in *Aristotle*, Richard McKeon, Ed., reprinted by permission of the University of Chicago Press.

ATWOOD: "Pornography," by Margaret Atwood. Copyright © 1983 by Margaret Atwood. Reprinted by permission of Margaret Atwood.

BAKER: from *Growing Up* by Russell Baker. Copyright © 1982 by Russell Baker. Used with permission of Congdon & Weed, Chicago.

DIDION: "On Keeping a Notebook" from *Slouching Towards Bethlehem* by Joan Didion. Copyright © 1966, 1968 by Joan Didion. Reprinted by permission of Farrar, Straus, and Giroux, Inc.

DILLARD: "An American Childhood" from *An American Childhood* by Annie Dillard. Copyright © 1987 by Annie Dillard. Reprinted by permission of HarperCollins Publishers.

FITZGERALD: "Rewriting American History" from *America Revised* by Frances FitzGerald. Copyright © 1979 by Frances FitzGerald. First appeared in *The New Yorker*. By permission of Little, Brown and Company.

FRANK: from *The Diary of Anne Frank: The Critical Edition*. Copyright © 1986 by Rijksinstituut voor Oorlogsdocumentatie, Amsterdam/the Netherlands, for preface, introduction, commentary, notes. Copyright© 1947 by Uitgeverij Contact, Amsterdam/the Netherlands, for *Het Achterhuis*. Copyright © 1967 by Doubleday & Company, Inc. Copyright © 1986 by Anne Frank-Fonds Basle/Cosmopress SA, Geneva/Switzerland for all photos and facsimiles unless otherwise stated. Copyright © 1952 by Otto Frank. English translation Copyright © 1989 by Doubleday and by Penguin Books Ltd. Used by permission of Doubleday, a division of Bantam Doubleday Dell Publishing Group, Inc.

GALILEO: "Letter to the Grand Duchess Christina," from *Discoveries and Opinions of Galileo* by Galileo Galilei. Copyright © 1957 by Stillman Drake. Used by permission of Doubleday, a division of Bantam Doubleday Dell Publishing Group, Inc.

GOULD: "Sex, Drugs, Disasters, and the Extinction of Dinosaurs," from *The Flamingo's Smile, Reflections in Natural History*, by Stephen Jay Gould. Reprinted by permission of W. W. Norton & Co, Inc. Copyright © 1985 by Stephen Jay Gould.

HURSTON: "I Get Born" from *Dust Tracks on a Road* by Zora Neale Hurston. Copyright© 1942 by Zora Neale Hurston. Copyright renewed 1970 by John C. Hurston. Reprinted by permission of HarperCollins Publishers.

KING: "Letter from Birmingham Jail" from *Why Can't We Wait* by Martin Luther King, Jr. Copyright © 1963, 1964 by Martin Luther King, Jr. Reprinted by permission of HarperCollins Publishers.

KONNER: "Kick off your Heels," *The New York Times* (Magazine), 31 January 1988. Copyright © 1988 by the New York Times Company. Reprinted by permission

LAWRENCE: "Pornography" from *Pornography and Obscenity* by D. H. Lawrence. Copyright © 1930 by Alfred A. Knopf, Inc. Reprinted by the permission of the publisher.